Constructions in Use

Alexander auf der Straße

d|u|p

Hana Filip, Peter Indefrey, Laura Kallmeyer,
Sebastian Löbner, Gerhard Schurz & Robert D. Van Valin, Jr.
(eds.)

Dissertations in Language and Cognition

4

Alexander auf der Straße

2017

Constructions in Use

d|u|p

**Bibliografische Information
der Deutschen Nationalbibliothek**
Die Deutsche Nationalbibliothek verzeichnet diese
Publikation in der Deutschen Nationalbiblio-
grafie; detaillierte bibliografische Daten sind im
Internet über http://dnb.dnb.de abrufbar.

D 61

© düsseldorf university press, Düsseldorf 2017
http://www.dupress.de
Einbandgestaltung: Doris Gerland, Christian Horn, Albert Ortmann
Satz: Alexander auf der Straße, LaTeX
Herstellung: docupoint GmbH, Barleben

Gesetzt aus der Linux Libertine und der Linux Biolinum
ISBN 978-3-95758-033-7

Dedicated to the Atlantean Kodex

Beneath the fragile crust of this modern age of reason
A darker world lies waiting, primordial and pure
Hidden in the shades from ratio's great pondering
To rise when the stars are right

Acknowledgements

In bringing this thesis into its final shape I benefited from many people's help. First of all, there is my supervisor, Gottfried Vosgerau, who initially came up to me with the idea of exploring the philosophical implications of the rise of construction grammar. He supported me and my project literally in every possible respect. He was always available whenever I asked for advice or when there was need to discuss details of my arguments.

Several people read individual chapters of the thesis and thereby helped me improving the manuscript. Insa Lawler, being a linguist by training, provided the most thorough critique of my main theses in the 'empirical' part of the book. I did my best to respond to at least some of her concerns, though countering all her objections would have meant writing a complete new thesis. The more 'theoretical' aspects of the book profited from criticism from Ramiro Glauer, Mark Pinder, Michael Pleyer, and Louise Röska-Hardy. Thank you all for your help! Also, thanks to everyone with whom I was able to discuss various of my ideas at conferences and workshops, and to those who otherwise helped me in polishing details of this book. In particular, I would like to thank Jörg Bücker, Stefan Hartmann, Ole Hjortland, Wolfgang Imo, and Alexander Ziem.

I am most grateful to Markus Kohm, creator of the LaTeX document class KOMA-SCRIPT, who is probably the most generous person I ever had the privilege to meet. Nick Quaintmere wiped out all linguistic errors from the entire manuscript. Friedhelm Sowa, düsseldorf university press's mastermind, supervised the layout process. Thank you so much!

I would like to express my gratitude to the editors of *Dissertations in Language and Cognition* for their support and the possibility to publish my work as part of their series.

It's a pity that I discovered Daniel Gutzmann's work only just after having finished my thesis. In a way, he defends exactly the opposite position of what I propose in this book. My hope is that—even though my criticism of truth-conditional semantics isn't tailored to his specific framework (2015)—my stance on his theory will shine through at several points of the book.

Most important for the completion of this thesis was the constant encouragement and support by my family, especially my wonderful wife. I can't thank you enough.

Last but not least: many thanks to my team mates for many philosophical discussions in areas of semantics and—mostly—beyond: Nicolas Lindner, Max Seeger, Tim Seuchter, Patrice Soom, Alex Tillas, and Arne Weber.

Contents

1 Introduction — 13
   1.1 Structure of the Book 15
   1.2 Terminological Preliminaries 17

I Meaning — 19

2 Meaning: Primary, Pragmatic, and Others — 21
   2.1 Meaning Statements are Descriptions 22
       2.1.1 What is Meaning and What is It Good For? 24
       2.1.2 Meaning Liberalism 30
       2.1.3 Primary Meaning and Compositionality 46
   2.2 Constructionist Approaches to Semantics 53
       2.2.1 Construction Grammar: From Cognitive Semantics to Philosophy 54
       2.2.2 The Tomasellian Programme 64
       2.2.3 Multimodality 69
       2.2.4 Compositionality Applied to Multimodality 73
       2.2.5 Constructionist Primary Meaning: The Case of Malapropisms 82
       2.2.6 Constructionist Language Acquisition 87

3 Usage-based Theories of Meaning — 93
   3.1 Use 94
       3.1.1 U Equals A(x) 94
       3.1.2 The Private Language Argument 99
       3.1.3 Acceptance in Usage-based Theories 102

	3.2	Understanding	108
		3.2.1 Understanding and Knowing the Meaning	108
		3.2.2 Horwich on Understanding	110
		3.2.3 Understanding and Knowledge Covary	113
	3.3	Explicating the Claim	114
		3.3.1 Core Use Properties	114
		3.3.2 Linguistic-Philosophical Terminology	120
4	**Truth-conditional Theories of Meaning**		**127**
	4.1	Donald Davidson et al.	128
		4.1.1 Introduction to the Framework	129
		4.1.2 Understanding Sentences	130
		4.1.3 Truth-Conditional Semantics	136
	4.2	Truth-Conditional Semantics at Work	146
		4.2.1 Linking Novelty and Compositionality	147
		4.2.2 Truth-conditional Semantics Does the Trick	152
		4.2.3 Novelty and Usage-Based Theories of Meaning	159

II Disposition 171

5	**Theories of Truth & Meaning**		**173**
	5.1	Literal/Non-Literal Interface	175
		5.1.1 Intuitive Propositional Content	177
		5.1.2 Functions of Primary Meaning	180
		5.1.3 Novelty Only Via Recursion	194
	5.2	Cooperative Contexts	198
		5.2.1 Playing Unfair	198
		5.2.2 Good and Bad Reasons for Primary Meanings	201
		5.2.3 A Very Brief Overview of Compositionality	203
		5.2.4 Sentence Comprehension & CxG	206
6	**Dispositional Analyses**		**217**
	6.1	The Role of the Refined Notion of Primary Meaning	218
		6.1.1 Again, The Case of Malapropisms	218
		6.1.2 Primary Meaning in the Current Framework	225

	6.2	Meanings Are Dispositional Analyses	228
		6.2.1 From Descriptions to Dispositions	229
		6.2.2 More On Dispositions	253

III Method   259

7 Semantic-Methodological Concerns   261
    7.1 Background Assumptions 261
        7.1.1 A Liberal Stance On Contrary Explanations 262
        7.1.2 Meaning & Concept 267
        7.1.3 Compatibility of Acquisition Theories and Theories of Meaning 272
    7.2 Methodological Commitments 277
        7.2.1 Unity of Science 277
        7.2.2 Basic Meaningful Entities 289

8 On Phenomena and Tokenings   293
    8.1 The Big Picture 293
    8.2 Use, Token, Constitution 296
        8.2.1 Meaning Shifts 302
        8.2.2 Appropriate Descriptions 303
        8.2.3 Specifying Context, Tokening, and Meaning Constitution 306
    8.3 Constitution Base 307

9 Conclusion   313

Bibliography   337

1 Introduction

Language is a complex system that consists of atomic units called morphemes. These units can be combined in the form of structured entities called sentences. There are two main sorts of words: singular terms and predicates. While the former refer to individual objects, the latter refer to sets thereof. Words *mean* something by virtue of referring. Sentences mean something by virtue of expressing truths and falsehoods.

Something along these lines is the orthodox view in formal semantics and the mainstream opinion conveyed in contemporary philosophy of language textbooks. The main thesis of this book is that this view is essentially wrong-headed. The opposite view to the above approach is usage-based semantics. This book explains why current strands in empirical research undermine formal semantic theories.

Classifications always imply simplifications. I take it that one quite plausible divide in the area of *philosophical* approaches to meaning is along the lines of 'truth-conditional vs usage-based'. In the following chapters, I shall therefore present the current debate in philosophy guided by this distinction. Truth-conditional semantics is the orthodox view in philosophy in two distinct respects. There are many *explicit* adherents of this research tradition, most notably Emma Borg, Ernest Lepore, and Kirk Ludwig.[1] But then there are even more people who are *implicitly* committed to this view or related views. Although it is hard to *prove* this point, usage-based semantics is probably the minority view in current philosophy of language. The currently by far most influential usage-based philosopher is Paul Horwich. Much of this book is inspired by his 1998 book *Meaning*.

The main thesis of the present book is that current *empirical* research in linguistics clearly suggests that philosophical semantics should be pur-

---

[1] Among the historically most influential scholars in that area are people like Gottlob Frege, Richard Montague, and Bertrand Russell.

1 Introduction

sued on a usage-based basis.² In the empirical disciplines, the research paradigm of construction grammar has gained more and more popularity recently—especially in the area of language acquisition, language evolution, and grammar theory.³ The idea of construction grammar is that all different kinds of linguistic information can be represented in a common format: constructions. That is, from words to complex phrases to syntactic structures, everything might be a construction, where a construction is, roughly speaking, a pairing of form and meaning. Up to now, there has been no satisfying account that could serve as a philosophical underpinning of construction grammar. This is the main reason for the existence of this book.

Construction grammar has quite a few features that are highly relevant from a philosophical perspective. The most important ones are: (i) construction grammar suggests that there is no clear-cut divide between semantics and pragmatics; (ii) furthermore, it suggests that semantics can't be pursued formally; (iii) it suggests that a theory of meaning should be part of a theory of communication, and not the other way around; (iv) it suggests that pragmatics is by far more relevant for the study of semantics than the reverse.

Construction grammar is a movement in which a variety of disciplines are involved, among them semantics, developmental psychology, conversational analysis, anthropology, and psycholinguistics. The general tendencies that I just cited apply universally to all strands of 'construction grammar', although, to be sure, many different theories sail under this flag. There is not *just one* construction grammar but many different theories that go by this name. Still, for most philosophical concerns these differences are irrelevant. More importantly, the unifying characteristic as regards philosophy is that they are all incompatible with the mainstream view, i.e. with truth-conditional semantics.

---

² I shall lay out in detail in 2.2.1 why certain developments in linguistics can impose restrictions on what a corresponding philosophical theory should look like.

³ Which, to be sure, is far from saying that construction grammar is universally accepted in these areas, or even accepted by the majority of linguists. The only thing I am saying here is that there is a significant increase in popularity of the constructionist paradigm in linguistics; and that this is a fact philosophy of language should respond to.

Accordingly, this book explains why—in view of the evidence provided by theorists working within a constructionist research framework—truth-conditional semantics is flawed in that most varieties of construction grammar clearly work on the assumption that their relevant semantics are usage-based. It also explains why established usage-based approaches to meaning à la Horwich are incapable of providing the philosophical underpinning of construction grammar. Last but not least, this book provides an alternative theory framework that is capable of providing such an underpinning in the required sense.

1.1 Structure of the Book

This book has three parts. The first part, 'Meaning', is an extended review of the state of the art. Chapter 2 gives a general overview of some of the most important theories of meaning on the market. This chapter serves as a backdrop for the whole discussion. I shall show in this chapter that the notion 'meaning' can serve all sorts of different purposes. Moreover, my main aim here is to demonstrate that (philosophical) semantics is best off if it begins by observing *actual practice* in the empirical disciplines, and by 'incorporating' their *actual results*. The following two chapters provide overviews of usage-based approaches to meaning and of truth-conditional semantics. Both chapters include critical remarks. In the chapter on usage-based theories, these remarks concern Horwich's identification of 'use properties' with 'acceptance properties', which I will explain in due course. This strategy of identifying 'use properties' with something else, namely acceptance, has some undesirable consequences. The most important one is that the restriction to acceptance properties implies accompanying restrictions in the classes of words that are covered by the semantic theory; i.e. that such a theory is, in effect, limited to descriptions of words that contribute truth-evaluable content. In the chapter on truth-conditional semantics, the focus lies on Davidson's 'psychological' argument that the learnability of natural languages suggests that semantic knowledge is based on the knowledge of recursively defined rules. These rules, which operate on word meaning, are supposed to explain why languages are learnable in the first place. I show that the crucial deficit of this argument is that research in lan-

1 Introduction

guage acquisition indicates that just the opposite is true: during language learning, hearers understand syntactically 'complex' expressions without parsing their underlying structure.

I present my own view in part two and three. The second part, 'Disposition', consists of chapters 5 and 6, the first of which directly links to the critical discussion of Davidson. My main point here is that two distinct issues often get mixed up in the literature.[4] One is the phenomenon that people seem to understand sentences that they have not encountered before. The other issue is compositionality. I argue that keeping both issues apart helps seeing what is going on in language acquisition. Chapter 6 is highly relevant for the rest of the book. There, I defend the view that one should clearly distinguish between the metaphysical basis of meaning[5] and adequate semantic descriptions that try to 'capture' this basis. Many serious counterarguments against usage-based semantics can be disarmed by showing that the notion of 'meaning' that they apply oscillates between these two readings. I argue that the most appropriate semantic descriptions are dispositional analyses.

The third part of the book is entitled 'Method' and contains my methodological convictions that shine through at several points throughout the book. Chapter 7 contains important background assumptions, most notably my arguments for why philosophical theories of meaning should strive at compatibility with relevant theories of language acquisition. Constructionist theories of language acquisition are usage-based, which lends further support to the idea that philosophical semantics should be pursued usage-based as well. Chapter 8, then, is an argument to the effect that tokens (as opposed to types) play a central role in any usage-based theory

---

[4] The least I would defend here is that many people, even if they do not literally conflate the two notions, they still tend to think that it goes without saying that compositionality is the only reasonable option you could possibly think of for explaining learnability of natural languages. And that suggestion, I think, comes too soon.

[5] When it comes to semantic theories in philosophy, we are typically dealing with theories devoted to the 'reductionist programme', i.e. theories that try to answer the question: by virtue of which *underlying*—more basic—properties do natural language expressions have the *semantic* properties that they de facto have? In this sense, theories of this sort try to 'reduce' higher-order properties (the semantic ones) to some lower-order properties in a systematic way. So when I talk about 'metaphysical basis', I typically mean these lower-order properties that serve as one's reduction base.

of meaning. Thus, in this chapter my focus lies in explaining why this is, in effect, a virtue of usage-based theories, and how token-based theory frameworks can cope with the most relevant counter-objections. In particular, I explain why token-based theories of meaning are well-designed to handle meaning shifts, i.e. long-term developments of word semantics. Chapter 9 concludes my discussion and gives a short summary.

1.2 Terminological Preliminaries

Given that this book is primarily dealing with language, it seems reasonable to state the applicable terminological and notational conventions at the very beginning. Throughout the book, I use double quotation marks ("apple") whenever I mention a word or phrase. I use single quotation marks ('apple') for basically four purposes: (i) quotations in the text that are not indented; (ii) mixed quotations in which a phrase is mentioned and used at the same time; (iii) figurative use of particular words or phrases; (iv) paraphrases of meaning ("apple" means 'apple'). I did not align the use of my quotation marks in quotes with my own system, in particular I left single quotation marks that indicate metalanguage in American English untouched. Note, though, that this deviates from the standard applied in the rest of this book. I use quasi-quotation ($\ulcorner apple \urcorner$) where appropriate. I use SMALL CAPS to denote concepts; in contrast to capital letters (APPLE), which were only employed in the discussion of Horwich's so-called capitalisation convention, which I will explain later on. Italics are solely used for emphasis. Here and there I indicate talk of propositions by use of angle brackets ("<apples are green>" abbreviates "(the proposition) that apples are green").

For sake of simplicity, I talk about the meaning of *words* most of the time (rather than sentences, phrases, morphemes, syntactic structures, and so on). Generally, most considerations apply to words and sentences alike.[6]

---

[6] For the simple reason that I do not mean to discuss the semantics of specific expressions, be they words or sentences or whatever, but rather the philosophy behind specific theory frameworks. In this respect, I am concerned with whether there is evidence in linguistics or psychology, for example, that may support or, alternatively, undermine a particular approach. But I am not particularly interested in whether that evidence is established on the basis of a discussion of words, or on the basis of a discussion of sentences.

1 Introduction

I tend to use the terms "semantics" and "theory of meaning" interchangeably. The term "sentence" usually denotes sentence types, whereas I reserve the term "type of sentence" for types of sentence (declaratives, interrogatives, imperatives, etc.). The term "use theory" exclusively denotes Horwich's theory of meaning; all other usage-based theories of meaning (both in philosophy and in linguistics) are called "usage-based theories". For most parts of the book, I use "context of utterance" only to denote Kaplanian contexts comprising speaker, place, and time. In contrast, I use the phrase "conversational context" as a neutral term for contexts of utterance that may also include contextual features beyond these three variables: e.g. cotext[7], common ground, world knowledge, and so forth.

---

[7] The cotext of an expression is its immediate linguistic surrounding (Catford 1965). For a given word, for instance, the corresponding sentence in which that word is embedded belongs to its cotext.

Part I

Meaning

2 Meaning: Primary, Pragmatic, and Others

This chapter serves two purposes: firstly, it introduces the idea that meaning statements—i.e. statements of the form "*x* means *y*"—can be conceived as descriptions. Descriptions that are such that, relative to a given background theory, they illuminate the role a specific word plays in a particular language. The discussion of this idea is an excellent backdrop against which I can give an overview of established theories of meaning. The basic idea of this overview is not to argue for a particular position, but rather to get to grips with the massive *variety* of possible approaches in the field of semantics. Secondly, it gives a rough overview on construction grammar (CxG, henceforth). In particular, I will introduce those aspects of CxG that are especially relevant to *philosophical* theories of meaning (rather than for semantics per se). That is to say, my main emphasis here lies on (i) showing that CxG fosters the decline of a sharp boundary between semantics and pragmatics and on (ii) showing how CxG fits with modern theories of language acquisition. These two points are particularly relevant as they lend support to a broadly usage-based approach to meaning, despite the prevailing success of formal theories in philosophical semantics.

Accordingly, the chapter is divided into two sections. In the first section (2.1), I will be dealing with meaning statements in general. Besides giving an overview of semantic theories, in this section I propose to take a liberal stance toward meaning statements; a topic that I take up again in the third part of this book. Also, I give a first overview on compositionality, because compositionality will become quite important in later chapters in the discussion of truth-conditional semantics. In the second section (2.2), I give an overview on CxG. In this section, I also briefly introduce the notion of multimodality, as compositionality is an aspect of language that CxG seems particularly well suited to cope with.

2.1 Meaning Statements are Descriptions

All sorts of theories get labelled 'theories of meaning' or 'semantic theory'. The purpose of this section is to give an overview on how varied the field of semantics actually is. By doing this, I propose to conceive of all semantic statements—statements of the form "x means y"—as descriptions. More precisely, I shall argue that semantic statements describe that particular set of knowledge concerning a particular linguistic item that a competent natural-language user associates with this item. This indeed quite general characterisation of "meaning" will serve as something like an 'outer boundary', if you like. That is to say, all actual semantic statements are, in fact, descriptions.[1] But something else must be added to a proper characterisation of "meaning" in order to sort out *inappropriate* descriptions. Framing such an 'inner boundary', then, will be the task of later chapters.

---

[1] Prima facie, this seems to be in stark contrast to what people like Lewis think semantics does actually (Lewis 1970, e.g. p. 18). Although I would tend to think that there is a fundamental difference between treating 'meanings' as entities and treating them as something else, I would argue that the claim that all *semantic statements* are descriptions is well justified, despite that difference. The reason is that—see 6.2—I distinguish between semantic descriptions and their respective justifications. In that sense, even Lewis, who thinks that 'genuinely semantic relations [...are] relations between symbols and the world of non-symbols' and that semantics (in his sense of the term) is a 'description of possible languages or grammars as abstract semantic systems whereby symbols are associated with aspects of the world' (1970, 19), effectively offers some sort of description when it comes to semantic statements. No matter *what* semantic statements describe (use, reference relations, or something else) and no matter *how* they do it (specifically for individual terms, or rather generically for types of terms), they all, at least, *describe* what 'meaning' is, from their perspective. For Lewis, the meanings of names can generically described thus:

> [A] meaning for a name is something that determines what thing, if any, the name names in various possible states of affair, at various times, and so on. [...A]n appropriate intension for a name is any function from indices to things [...]. (1970, 23)

Accordingly, in line with that view, what I call 'constitutive basis' further below is not use, but rather a certain symbol–world relation. And that is what legitimises a certain semantic statement, or not. Be that as it may, the differences between different semantics concern only their justificatory bases, not their way of describing relationships between certain linguistic units (e.g. words) and some other things (e.g. things).

2.1 Meaning Statements are Descriptions

In line with established practice in linguistics and philosophy, I need to note right at the beginning that in the following I will presuppose the fundamental distinction between literal and non-literal meaning. Thus, for a large part of this book, I will presuppose that there is *some* theoretically relevant difference between, say, "There is no milk in the fridge" meaning 'that there is no milk in the fridge' and 'that there is no more milk *to drink* available in the fridge'. Although, eventually, one of the main aims of this book is to show that this strict distinction is unjustified, it makes sense to take it for granted in the following overview. Because, firstly, it is a common assumption in all relevant semantic theories anyway; accordingly, presenting an overview in line with the distinction seems required. And, secondly, literal meaning is theoretically relevant in several respects (e.g. in explaining metaphors); so there is independent reason to equip the theory framework that I will present in the course of this book with a theoretic notion that is capable of explaining non-literality.

As just indicated, one major position to be defended in the chapters below is that it is not entirely unproblematic to assume that semantics should be dealing solely with literal meaning, i.e. context-free, formally specifiable meaning. Rather, semantics should be viewed as an enterprise that involves far more elements from (traditional) pragmatics than usually assumed. This view is motivated mainly by some recent developments in linguistics, in particular in grammar theory (CxG) and language evolution (Tomasello's programme)[2]. Both will be explained at length later on. The notion "literal meaning" has quite a few cognates in the literature, among them "lexical", "stable", "first", "semantic", "invariant", and "conventional". The conceptual differences between these notions, if any, are not relevant for my present purposes though. Just to avoid confusion, I will stick to "primary meaning" in the following. In a first step, I will present the way pragmatic meaning is typically conceived in the literature, i.e. in terms of reference relations. In a second step, I propose a refined definition of the

---

[2] One of the readers of this chapter reminded me of the fact that this paradigm is not entirely uncontroversial. Yes, but what is? Moreover, what, I take it, is relatively uncontroversial is that within the last decade, Tomasello's approach to language acquisition gained significant popularity within the relevant scientific community. This should be enough of a starting point for a philosophical theory that is supposed to correspond to the developments taking place in the empirical disciplines.

term that fits better with my demands. For reasons that will emerge later, I will dub the counterpart "pragmatic meaning" (instead of "non-literal" or "derived").

Primary meaning as a theoretical notion is essentially needed to account for a variety of important, systematic linguistic effects such as irony, slip of the tongue, etc. In this chapter, I will argue for a liberal stance on meaning in general. Note that the qualification "literal" (or its equivalent) is often omitted in the literature in otherwise unambiguous contexts, which is to say that the following remarks apply primarily to 'meaning statements' that deal specifically with *primary* meaning in my sense of the term. Yet, since my plan is to omit ordinary primary meaning altogether (by proposing a new definition of the term that is capable of fulfilling the task of accounting for effects such as irony, slip of the tongue, etc.), it seems natural to take one step at a time. I begin with a general overview on meaning statements; after this I then turn to issues that are particularly relevant for primary meaning.

2.1.1 What is Meaning and What is It Good For?

For the task at hand, I understand "meaning" provisionally as follows (further qualifications in due course): the meaning of a word is a description of what competent language users typically associate with this word, i.e. a description of how they understand the term in question. This definition only serves the purpose of motivating a great deal of examples and will be specified later on. Prototypical examples of meaning statements are lexicon entries. Lexicon entries *reformulate* or *paraphrase*, in more common terms, what a competent speaker associates with a given word. The meaning of a sentence, then, would be a description of what competent language users typically associate with this sentence, a description that is often systematically dependent on (primary) meanings of sub-sentential parts and syntactic structure.[3]

---

[3] See also the sections on compositionality (2.1.3 and 5.2.3).

2.1 Meaning Statements are Descriptions

I shall first clarify this definition step by step. What is a description? A description is any paraphrase of a given word (or sentence)[4] that helps illuminating how a competent speaker understands this word. 'Understanding a term', in turn, means implicitly knowing how to use this term (Horwich 1998, 16–18). Descriptions are paraphrases of a given word by any person or institution that enjoys authority concerning the relevant language: for instance, lexicons, linguists, native speakers, etc. Here is an example: "church service", for example, means 'a formalized period of communal worship'[5]. Now assume the following: Mary asks Peter: "Peter, what is a church service?" Peter replies: "A church service is a formalised period of communal worship." Assume further that Mary *understands* "formalised", "period", "communal", and "worship", and the relevant syntactic structure (copula sentence).[6] In the terminology that I adopt here, this amounts to saying that she implicitly knows how to use the terms (i.e. how to apply them and how they are actually used by other members of her linguistic community). Relative to these assumptions, Mary understands "church service" after having heard Peter's instructions. His description was illuminating—as, in fact, any other description would have been that would have had the same effect in Mary. In general, a description of the meaning of a given term is *correct* if it enables an otherwise competent speaker to know how this term is used in the respective language community. Conversely, if the latter is already known (which is the more interesting case in linguistics), a given description is correct if, and only if, it accords with this prior knowledge. In this way, meaning statements, varied as they are in practice, are all alike in that their adequacy necessarily hinges on whether they accord with prior knowledge concerning use.

---

[4] For sake of brevity, I omit reference to sentences in the following. In many cases it will be clear in which way explanations for words can be applied, mutatis mutandis, to sentences. Whenever there are potential ambiguities, I will explicitly mention them.

[5] Entry 'Church service', Wikipedia, http://en.wikipedia.org/wiki/Church_service, accessed on: 28/02/2013.

[6] Please note that the line of argument that follows takes Paul Horwich's notion of 'understanding' for granted, including his justification. This notion is controversial. In particular, people question Horwich's view on implicit knowledge (Fodor & Lepore 2002, ch. 3, pp. 43–62). Thus, my argument hinges on the success of Horwich's.

2 Meaning: Primary, Pragmatic, and Others

All this, to be sure, is about knowing-how.[7] In line with Horwich's approach, I assume that when Mary learns how to use "church service", she is not (necessarily) in a position to declare what this knowledge is. She is not (necessarily) able to tell in which situations "church service" would be applicable, for instance. Rather, her knowledge, if any, consists in her ability to apply "church service" in a way that is sufficiently similar to the way other competent speakers of English would use it. Nothing over and above this ability is required in order to be justified in ascribing understanding to Mary. In other words, learning the meaning of "church service" is, in important respects, more like learning to ski (knowing-how) than learning that green is a colour (knowing-that). This is even more important when it comes to syntactic knowledge, which is typically not available to language users in such a way that they could actually declare what their (syntactic) knowledge consists in.

So far I have talked rather naïvely about someone's knowing *how to apply a given term*. Even if we agree that this kind of knowledge is implicit, there is still a certain degree of controversy regarding how to narrow it down any further. Following Wittgenstein's terminology, knowledge concerning the use of a term is often conceived of in terms of the relevant *rules* that supposedly 'guide' one's use. Again, the nature and status of rules is highly controversial.[8] I bracket this issue here (and elaborate further in 3.1.2). Let me just stress that the implicit knowledge that constitutes a subject S's understanding of a word "w" is just that kind of knowledge that manifests itself in specific, systematic, behavioural patterns of S towards occurrences of "w".

I propose to conceive of the notion of a 'description' in a liberal manner. I said that descriptions *paraphrase* how a given term is used. A paraphrase, however, can only be illuminating relative to a given system. The most obvious such system is natural languages. For example, the paraphrase "a formalised period of communal worship" is illuminating relative to the system of English. Apparently, there are also many statements that can legitimately be considered proper meaning statements but which are only

---

[7] For issues surrounding this notion, cf. Jung & Newen (2010) and Stanley & Williamson (2001).

[8] See, e.g., the references in Biletzki & Matar (2014, section 3.5).

2.1 Meaning Statements are Descriptions

informative or illuminating relative to some other system. What makes a meaning statement illuminating (relative to a specific system) is sometimes only remotely similar to what makes natural language paraphrases illuminating.

To see this, consider grammar theory, for instance. A grammar theory such as head-driven phrase structure grammar (HPSG) consists of meaning statements, among other things. Yet, the fundamental purpose of a grammar theory is to distinguish grammatical from ungrammatical sentences. That is to say, its purpose is to determine, for any complex string of symbols, whether a specific string in a given language is grammatical relative to the formation rules provided by the theory.[9] The 'meaning statements' in HPSG are, arguably, the semantic aspects of (HPSG) lexicon entries. It seems reasonable to suppose that these representations are a kind of *paraphrase*, because they illuminate how words are used (or are thought to be used) relative to the system of HPSG. For example, they illustrate what semantic aspect a single word contributes to the meaning of a complex expression. Hence, there is reason to define "meaning" in such a way that it is capable of covering formalisms such as HPSG. Relative to their respective systems, the representations of at least certain grammar formalisms paraphrase the meaning of a given term.

Another quite illustrative example of what a 'paraphrase' might look like is translation. Consider the two terms "breakfast" (an English word) and "Frühstück" (a German word). Both, let us suppose, mean the same. In other words, there are structural similarities between how "breakfast" is used in English, relative to the rest of English, and how "Frühstück" is used in German, relative to the rest of German. Teaching an English-speaking

---

[9] At least, this is what is done in *HPSG*. Other grammar theories might be different in this respect. HPSG is a lexicon-based grammar, i.e. a grammar that 'moves' all information into the lexicon. Besides the lexicon, there is only a handful of quite general rules. The important part of lexicon entries is their syntactic information. If two entries (words, morphemes, suffixes, etc.) are combined, their respective representations are unified, which is only possible if the syntactic information is compatible (Müller 2013*b*, 195–206). Despite the quite heavy technical machinery employed in HPSG, the basic working principle is really simple: the complex strings that emerge from unifying lexicon entries are 'grammatical'; everything else is 'ungrammatical'. Note, by the way, that the idea that lexical entries in HPSG represent primary meaning is not controversial (Sag & Wasow 1999, 103).

2 Meaning: Primary, Pragmatic, and Others

person with basic knowledge of German the meaning of "Frühstück" is possible by simply telling her that "Frühstück" translates to "breakfast". Accordingly, an instance of

"Frühstück" translates to / means "breakfast"

is a *paraphrase* on the view proposed here, because it is an illuminating description of how "Frühstück" is used in the community of German-speaking people. In general, it seems quite reasonable to assume that, for every meaning statement, there is a way to conceive of this statement as paraphrasing the use of a term relative to a specifiable language system (natural language; grammar theory; formal-semantic system; knowledge representation system; and so on).

The link between use and meaning statements is quite tight in everyday discourse. Of course, the *function* of a paraphrasing statement is to *tell* someone (who is otherwise competent in the relevant system) how a specific word is used relative to this system. However, the *adequacy criterion* for a paraphrase—be it a lexicon entry, a translation, or what have you—is just the reverse. That is to say, in order to determine whether a given meaning statement is correct, we would ask someone who already is familiar with the relevant language system (including the term in question)—or better: ask several such people—if this meaning statement paraphrases the use of this specific term correctly. In order to assess a given translation, one would ask a speaker who is competent in both relevant languages whether the terms on the left-hand side and on the right-hand side are used structurally similar in their respective languages.

What does "competent" mean in the above definition? It is quite common in the philosophy of language to assume 'standard' or 'average' language users (e.g. Stalnaker 1984). They are taken to be competent in a given language such as English. Normally, the notion of a 'competent speaker' is introduced by examples. A competent average user of English, for example, knows a priori that the sentence "All bachelors are unmarried" is true qua being competent in English. (Truth follows by definition.) Note, however, that this is true only if one takes for granted that the average speaker of English is familiar with the definition of, e.g., "unmarried". What about the truth of "Local supervenience implies global supervenience"? It is true by definition, hence knowable a priori. Nevertheless, one would not as-

2.1 Meaning Statements are Descriptions

sume that an average speaker knows this, for he lacks lexical knowledge of the terms in this sentence (except for "imply", maybe). The definition of a 'standard' speaker of a natural language presupposes a certain set of lexical knowledge that one would typically ascribe to such a speaker. "Unmarried" would probably be in it, "supervenience" not. For present purposes, I only need the notion of "competence", anyway. I restrict competence not to whole languages, but to words. In the Peter/Mary example, a description of "church service" along the lines of "a formalised period of communal worship" counts as a correct description iff someone who is competent in using "church service" typically associates 'formalised periods' with this word. That is, the notion of 'competence' with respect to individual words is independent from other linguistic knowledge that a speaker might (also) have.[10]

What does it mean that a language user 'associates' something with a word? I suggest that associating a word with something else can more or less be equated with understanding. This is motivated as follows: a meaning statement is typically a paraphrase of how a word is used by competent speakers. Hence, if I say that someone associates 'formalised periods of communal worship' with the concept of "church service", then this amounts to the claim that, mutatis mutandis, his use of "formalised periods of communal worship" is systematically similar to that of "church service" (though not identical). This, in turn, means that the implicit knowledge associated with the use of "church service" and "formalised periods of communal worship" is systematically similar. Hence, a competent speaker may be said to *understand* "church service" in the sense of 'formalised periods of communal worship'. This view suggests that a certain use might be indicative of understanding, while understanding is treated as knowledge of use—a view that might sound circular to some. Against this, I can only say that I am not aware of any plausible explication of 'understanding' that would lack the assumption that understanding of a given term is implicitly

---

[10] This is true if we ignore issues surrounding holism for a moment (cf. section 3.2.2). Because, roughly put, a speaker can't be *just* competent in using a given word if he is not also competent in using some other words that are meaning-related (in extreme cases, *all* other words of the relevant language). I assume in what follows that a speaker's competence in using a particular word is reasonably clear. Incorporating holism, would unnecessarily complicate matters at this point.

2 Meaning: Primary, Pragmatic, and Others

exemplified by some typical patterns of use associated with that term. I doubt that even a die-hard truth-conditional semanticist would seriously deny this.

2.1.2 Meaning Liberalism

If I now take for granted in the following that, for example, (i) 'formalised periods of communal worship' is a proper paraphrase of "church service"; that (ii) a paraphrase is appropriate if it helps competent language users to understand how a given word is used; and that (iii) from a pre-theoretic perspective, meaning statements describe implicit use knowledge, then, at first glance, it might seem that my conception of meaning is indeed quite narrow.

On the contrary, I propose to take a very liberal stance toward meaning statements. That is, I suggest defining "meaning" first of all in such a broad way as to include a broad variety of different cases. The idea behind this is to have a wide, pre-theoretic notion of "meaning" at hand that poses no ex-ante restrictions on genuine meaning statements. Philosophically more interesting are two further questions that can be accounted for independently, I think. One is the nature of meaning, which is the actual core of all philosophical (foundational/reductionistic) theories of meaning. The proper treatment of this issue, however, is unaffected by the acknowledgement that, essentially, all *existing* meaning statements are paraphrases, whose adequacy is determined relative to how well they accord with one's pre-theoretic knowledge concerning use. Another issue is the relative appropriateness of particular theories, which is just the other side of the coin. Once you 'know' the nature of meaning, you also know how to classify existing theories according to how well they fit with this conception.

Since, as I have just shown, there is an independent reason for a liberal, pre-theoretic definition of "meaning", it is the aim of the following few paragraphs to look more closely at some typical kinds of meaning statements in order to see whether they are covered by the pre-theoretic conception of meaning as 'paraphrases of implicit knowledge of use'. To this end, I shall, in particular, look at list of relevant examples that exemplify the broad range of natural-language cases that are typically discussed in the relevant literature in language philosophy. Such a list of paradigm examples would typically include the following:

Translation How is meaning conveyed by translations?

Reference What about meaning statements in terms of reference?

Discourse How do we cope with discourse representations?

Lexica Is a lexical entry a meaning description?

Formalisms Can formal representations be conceived of as paraphrases?

Trivialism If "dog" meant DOG[11], what would this mean?

Ostensive definitions Can meanings be 'paraphrased' by ostensive definitions?

Translations: A typical example of a meaning statement is when someone translates a word from one natural language into another. For example, one might say: "Schnee" means 'snow' in German, or, alternatively, "Schnee" is the German equivalent to our (English) "snow" (like in a dictionary). Similarly, we typically 'translate' words or sentences from natural languages to metalanguages, as in the notorious "'Schnee ist weiß' is true if and only if snow is white".[12] Translations are the most straightforward examples of paraphrases, as a 'normal' paraphrase is nothing but a 'translation' within

---

[11] Horwich (1998) uses capitalised words to denote meanings (see below).

[12] Note that for the present argument it does not matter whether truth conditions are sufficient descriptions of meaning. Even a use theorist might allow for T-sentences (see 4.1.3), i.e. sentences that specify at a meta-level the truth conditions of a given object-level sentence—as long as these conditions are not *identified* with meaning. The obvious reason is this: the meaning, describable in terms of use, of our own language (English/the metalanguage) is known and, in principle, explicable. It is quite a good heuristic method to assume that people with otherwise similar environment and similar psychological make-up to ourselves will use their sentence "Schnee ist weiß" in a structurally similar manner to the way we use "Snow is white", given that the truth conditions of these sentences are identical. In this sense, T-sentences are actually nothing over and above ordinary translations. Given the tight link between T-sentences and the criteria for their respective adequacy (which is use, at the end of the day), there is nothing special about usage-based theories that assign truth conditions to sentences and referential relations to terms (cf. Horwich 1998, ch. 4).

a given language. It paraphrases, in terms known to the addressee, the meaning of a given term that might be unknown to that addressee. Analogously, translations also presuppose that certain terms, namely that ones in which the translation is couched, are known to the addressee, whereas other terms, namely those that get translated, do not necessarily need to be thus known. For example, someone who says that "Schnee" means 'snow' in German presupposes that the addressee knows the meaning of "snow"; otherwise the relevant T-sentence would be *incomprehensible* to the addressee. And what he says, actually, is that the use of "Schnee" in German is structurally similar to the use of "snow" in English (plus minus the inaccuracy of our dictionaries). I emphasise 'structurally', because it is a similarity relative to *German*, of course.

If "Schnee" and "snow" have equivalent meaning, the similarity between the two in terms of use is just this: considering the correspondences between related pairs of words in German and English—e.g. the fact that "weiß" means 'white'—the tendency of competent speakers of German to apply "Schnee" and the tendency of competent speakers of English to apply "snow" is absolutely alike (all else being equal). From this point of view, translations are a paradigm example of meaning statement (i.e. paraphrases), as they are shorthand descriptions of how a given word or sentence would be used in the relevant target language. Trivially, 'intra-language translations' as well as proper translations between two languages are equally as *informative* or *illuminating* for an addressee as she is able to understand that bit of information to which the paraphrase recurs. For example, the information that "Schnee" means 'snow' in German is only informative for you, the reader, to the extent that you are competent in German (and English).

Reference: Another relevant example is reference, such as reference of proper names. It is undeniable that there must be some connection between reference and meaning. Some people in the history of philosophy of language even go as far as to say that reference *is* meaning (e.g. Mill 1916)—an idea that lives forth in truth-conditional semantics and neo-Davidsonian approaches. Others (e.g. Carnap 1956) add additional layers (intensions) in order to determine reference. These people stick to the main idea of identifying meaning with reference, because the main purpose of the intermediate level is solely to fix reference. This is an approach to semantics that continues to be developed in all strands of linguistics and philosophy related to possible worlds semantics (now classical milestones include the works of Lewis (1970, 1975, 1980), Kaplan (especially his 1989), Montague (1974),[13] and Partee (e.g. 1976, 1977)). Among more recent proponents of frameworks directly working with, or being *inspired* by possible worlds are Emma Borg (2004*b*, 2012*a*, 2012*b*), Herman Cappelen (e.g. 2004), or William Lycan (2010).[14] Still others—i.e. all those not belonging to the first two camps—are sceptical about the identification of meaning and reference (plus truth-conditional functions) but argue that it is an essential element of any serious semantic theory. At any rate, meaning and reference seem to be tightly linked.

Further evidence for a close link between reference and meaning comes from everyday discourse: very often, one can hear people saying things like "'Water' means H_2O" or "'Today' means 31 January". Professional philosophers would reformulate this and say instead: "'Water' refers to H_2O" and "'Today' refers to the 31 January" (on 31 January). In fact, this way of reformulating it is the only way to 'make sense' of these utterances. People clearly can't mean that "today" means *the same as* "on 31 January", because the referents of both terms are only alike on 31st of January. Similarly for "water": it only refers to H_2O in 'H_2O worlds' (an assumption that is commonplace in philosophy since Putnam 1975 and Burge 1979; cf. also Chalmers 2006). The close link that holds between reference and meaning

---

[13] For a quick overview on Montague semantics, I refer the reader to Janssen (2006).

[14] I emphasise "inspired" here, since possible worlds proper (i.e. model-theoretic descriptions of states of affairs) play an important role only in logic. In mainstream (that is, qualitative) philosophy of language, 'possible worlds' are often nothing more than mere labels. Still, the reason to label certain strands of theorising as being, at least, 'inspired' by possible worlds talk is the following. Frameworks such as Borg's identify meaning with certain semantic cores, namely the respective equivalents to what has been labelled "character" by Kaplan. Characters are, essentially, functions from contexts (of utterance) to contents (referents). In other words, two main ingredients from possible worlds frameworks are still at work here. Firstly, contexts of utterance (or whatever you might call them) *are* possible worlds. So, by their very construction, these frameworks presuppose talk of possible worlds. Secondly, the main purpose of introducing characters (or their corresponding equivalents) is to have some stable semantic entity that ensures, for every context of utterance, that there is a specific referent that is picked out. This, I think, justifies conceiving of these frameworks as being heavily influenced by possible worlds semantics, even though they are not possible worlds approaches in the logician's sense.

2 Meaning: Primary, Pragmatic, and Others

is exploited, so to speak, in meaning statements of the form "Term 'x' refers to entity y", in which the meaning of "x" (and hence its use) is introduced by appealing to referential 'facts'. As I will demonstrate later, referential statements need not necessarily be true—i.e. recurring to facts—in order to successfully hint at a specific use. An example of a reference statement that is used to convey meaning is the following: "'The Morning Star' refers to Venus" (said to someone who knows what Venus is). It seems plausible to regard this as paraphrasing how "The Morning Star" is used. *Depending on the background knowledge of the addressee of such a statement*, she immediately understands an important *aspect* of how "The Morning Star" is used. Remarkably enough, this knowledge concerning *use* can be conveyed simply by making statements concerning *referential facts*[15].

The "Venus" case exemplifies that appealing to referential relations may sometimes convey details about use only imperfectly. A competent speaker of English who learns that "The Morning Star" refers to Venus has learnt something about just one mode of presentation concerning Venus. "The Evening Star" is a term that is used differently, even though it shares its referent with "The Morning Star". Many philosophically important results can be drawn from this observation; in the present context, though, we are only interested in the role of reference statements (rather than in modes of presentation per se). Please note only that reference statements can be good approximations of how a given term is used. But they need not necessarily be the *best* such description. This, however, does not affect my main claim that meaning statements are paraphrases of implicit knowledge of use. This is because those aspects of ordinary reference statements that describe meaning 'correctly' are merely those aspects that recur to the use of a particular term. By the same token, reference statements like "'Water' refers to H_2O" are 'exhaustive', since they can convey—subject to the addressee's background knowledge—the entire use of a given term.

---

[15] Strictly speaking, not *facts* are important but what people *take* to be facts. If someone makes someone else familiar with the use of "water" in chemistry by saying that "water" refers to H_2O, then this 'meaning statement' in terms of reference might be successful—in the sense that the addressee has learnt how to use "water"—even if water 'turned out' to be something else (given a certain development in chemistry and given that, say, the causal-historical story about reference fixing (Kripke 1980) is true). I omit this complication in what follows and continue to talk simply about facts.

2.1 Meaning Statements are Descriptions

However, this 'ability' is not restricted to reference statements. As in the translation case, such a statement may be taken as incomplete evidence for such-and-such a use of the word in question. For instance, the addressee might infer that "The Morning Star" will be used in contexts in which planets (not stars) are relevant, given the information that "The Morning Star" refers to Venus. Yet, note that this is only an assumption. The kind of inferences the potential addressee of a reference statement will draw depends crucially on what else she already knew about the language at hand. It seems quite instructive to compare this case with a situation in which some 'non-referential' information is learnt. Say, for example, that someone learns that "slacker" is considered rude. A possible inference to draw from this is to assume that "slacker" probably will not be used in the presence of women. But this is only a first guess—similar to reference statements. Which inferences an addressee will actually draw depends crucially on what else she knew beforehand.

The bottom line is that it might indeed be referential 'facts' that convey meaning sometimes, but only *insofar* as they are abbreviated ways of imparting (partial) knowledge about uses of words. It is a well-known fact about language that co-extensional words might have diverging Fregean senses, which is to say that the corresponding use associated with each word might differ (cf. "water" and "H_2O"). This is why I emphasise "insofar" in this context.

Discourse: Discourses are notoriously hard to handle for semantic theories. One important difficulty is to model the reference relations that can be shared between different discourse units, such as the way anaphoric reference is transferred from sentence to sentence. Kamp & Reyle (1993) present a model-theoretic possibility to represent discourse. Their approach Discourse Representation Theory (DRT)—has set the standard in the field of discourse representation. Being part of the formal semantics movement, DRT covers only a limited set of discursive factors. In particular, it accounts for the *linguistic* context. DRT is thus able, for example, to represent anaphoric reference in successive sentences. A very simple representation in DRT (called 'Discourse Representation Structure'; 'DRS') might look like this:

2 Meaning: Primary, Pragmatic, and Others

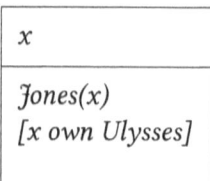

[...] Like all DRSs it consists of two components:

(i) a set of discourse referents, called the *universe* of the DRS, which will always be displayed at the top of the diagram; and

(ii) a set of DRS-conditions, typically displayed below the universe. (Kamp & Reyle 1993, 63, diagram also there)

Conceived this way, discourse representations are theoretically on a par with representations in truth-conditional semantics. Essentially, what they formalise is propositional content. It is for this reason that DRSs are not particularly illuminating concerning the natural sentences they are representations of. The representations are as illuminating as T-sentences: everyone who understands them, did so before. Their main purpose is to make *explicit* the formal relations that hold between sub-discursive units (e.g. sentences): anaphoric reference, implication, etc. That is, the explanatory aims of DRSs are, by their nature, severely limited. This generalises to all formal frameworks in semantics that confine themselves to mere truth conditions or representations of propositional content. Still, relative to the relations they formalise (e.g. anaphoric reference), discourse representations paraphrase meaning in that their adequacy is determined by how well they capture our pre-theoretic intuitions regarding these semantic relations.

Accordingly, the representations offered by DRT are clearly covered by my liberal, pre-theoretic definition of "meaning", since they reveal important aspects of language that are closely connected with use: which sentential inferences are valid; how words (e.g. personal pronouns) get and keep their referents through discourse; and so on. Still, it is equally obvious that a DRS like the one cited above is, in essence, nothing more than a very sophisticated way of saying that "Jones owns Ulysses" means that Jones owns Ulysses. It is quite clear that not all strictly formal approaches are alike in this regard. There are other, equally formal approaches to semantics that model specific semantic properties that cannot easily be read off from the natural sentences (or discourse) they are part of: see, for instance, the literature surrounding the range of possible interpretations for 'donkey sentences'[16] (e.g. Geurts 2002) or semantic theories that account for semantically validated inference patterns (Pietroski 2000). The philosophically important point, though, is not whether a given theory deals with, if you like, 'transparent' aspects of meaning like anaphoric relations or with more intricate ones like competing interpretations of donkey sentences. Rather, the point here is whether the proposed definition of "meaning" in terms of implicit knowledge of use matches with (the notion of "meaning" used in) particular theories that apparently *are* established semantic theories—of which, by the way, the above-mentioned theories are only examples. Concerning formal semantic theories such as discourse representation theory and the like, the answer is a clear "Yes."

Lexicons: Lexical entries are prototypical examples of meaning statements. In fact, a lexicon just *is* a collection of meanings of words (if meaning is nothing over and above appropriate paraphrases). It is quite clear that lexicons are covered by my initial definition only if the lexicon is *good enough*, i.e. if it consists of descriptions that help otherwise competent language users to understand particular words, i.e. the entries of a specific lexicon.

In several respects, lexicons are unique in relation to semantics. For example, the trivial aspect that lexicons contain only meaning statements—the lemmas—that are comprehensible relative to the very same linguistic system they are descriptions of. Another unique aspect of lexicons relates to what I will say below in the more theoretical chapters of this book. To anticipate a bit: below I will show that it will prove helpful to distinguish between what constitutes meaning and meaning itself (see the third part of this book). My proposal will be that word meaning is constituted by every single tokening of a word type. Meaning, in contrast, can be identified with the most general, most effective description of how that word type is used

---

[16] 'Donkey sentences' get their name from examples such as "Every farmer who owns a donkey beats it", which have two distinct readings (and hence truth conditions): every farmer who owns a donkey either beats all donkeys he owns, or he beats at least one of them.

in a specific community (see especially section 8.2). It might turn out that many lemmas actually comply quite well with this requirement. If this is true, it would have some interesting consequences. For example, one important result could be that there might be no uniform code for appropriate meaning statements. For some words, it might be most effective to summarise their use in terms of reasonable examples, or by comparing it with meanings of related words, or in terms of its conversational function, and so forth.

Formalisms: I mention formalism here in order to demonstrate very briefly that formal semantic representations fit nicely with the proposed notion of meaning. I illustrate this by using a particular theory, which I already briefly mentioned above, as an arbitrarily chosen example: head-driven phrase structure grammar (Sag & Wasow 1999). The considerations below, however, can be generalised to similar formalisms; they are independent of the niceties of this specific framework. Being a grammar theory, HPSG is not primarily concerned with semantics. Accordingly, questioning the status of semantics in HPSG seems like a cheap shot. However, semantics is not a mere by-product in HPSG. Therefore, it seems worth the effort to look at it in some more detail from the point of view of a theory of meaning. Semantic representations figure prominently in, for example, 'reference transfer'. Or, to put it differently, some syntactic features of English can only be accounted for by incorporating semantic operations, such as reference transfer, into one's grammar theory. HPSG is concerned with distinguishing grammatical from ungrammatical sentences. An example—taken from Pollard & Sag (1994)—of a problematic sentence that is classified 'grammatical' by native speakers is: "The hash browns at table six is getting angry". The problem is that the copula (singular) is incongruent in number with the subject ("hash browns"; plural). Very roughly, the solution is to say that in an 'ordering food at a restaurant' situation, reference is transferred from the actual denotation of the thing ordered (hash browns) to the person ordering it. Congruency with the copula gets then determined by the new referent (the person who ordered the hash browns). Hence, the singular form of the copula is the correct, grammatical choice in this example. What is important here is that semantics plays a crucial role, for syntactical features (singular vs plural copula) are influenced by semantic features (reference transfer).

2.1 Meaning Statements are Descriptions

$$\left\langle \text{die}, \begin{bmatrix} \textit{siv-lxm} \\ \text{ARG-ST} \quad \left\langle \; [\;]_i \; \right\rangle \\ \text{SEM} \quad \begin{bmatrix} \text{INDEX} \quad s \\ \text{RESTR} \quad \left\langle \begin{bmatrix} \text{RELN} & \text{die} \\ \text{SIT} & s \\ \text{CORPSE} & i \end{bmatrix} \right\rangle \end{bmatrix} \end{bmatrix} \right\rangle$$

Figure 2.1: Lexical entry of "die" (Sag & Wasow 1999, 394).

A lexical entry in HPSG (e.g. figure 2.1) is similar in important respects to 'normal' lexical entries like in the Oxford Dictionary or the (German) Duden. In contrast with these regular lexicons, the lexical entries of lexicon-based grammar theories focus on specific linguistic features only. This sets them apart from lexicons that contain *comprehensive* summaries of the use of given terms. However, there is no reason not to concede that theories like the HPSG model at least include important *aspects* of meaning—e.g. licensing a singular copula with plural subject in cases of reference transfer. In the example—"die"—it is quite obvious that an understanding of the meaning of "die" that goes beyond mere truth conditions is presupposed, because in the semantic part of the representation (SEM) we see that its meaning is the relation of dying (REL die). That is to say, you need to know what the relation of dying is in order to understand what the representation is a representation of. Compare this with a "die" lemma in an ordinary lexicon. The indices for CORPSE (apparently identifying the corpse) and SIT[UATION] only serve the purpose of tracking referents in the discourse (within and across sentences).

Generally speaking, when it comes to formalisms it is important which aspects are coded in the relevant representations. The most prominent information in the figure taken from Sag and Wasow is that "die" denotes the relation of dying. That is to say, it is made absolutely transparent that the

2 Meaning: Primary, Pragmatic, and Others

formal framework of (this historical variant of) HPSG is not designed to reveal any specifically semantic aspects of its lexical entries. HPSG is, to be sure, first and foremost a syntactic theory, i.e. a theory that licenses particular phrases as grammatically well-formed ones.[17] HPSG is at least not primarily concerned with semantics anyway. It comes as no surprise that the semantic features covered by the theory are therefore quite limited.[18]

Trivialism: A special case of theories that generate genuine meaning statements is what I dub 'trivialism'. A semantic theory is trivial if its meaning statements for particular words are derivable from the theory without any further knowledge about the object language. Horwich's 'use theory' can partly be seen as a theory of this kind. Consider the following quote:

> The English word "dog" means DOG. (Horwich 1998, 14)

The quote shows that the capitalised spelling of words is understood in this framework as something like a placeholder, i.e. as something denoting the yet-to-be-specified meaning of a term. Horwich adopts a 'convention of capitalizing an English expression in order to designate its meaning or

---

[17] Note that, in HPSG, a sentence is a subtype of phrases:

> A combination of a head with a further constituent is called projection of the head. A projection that involves all parts necessary to build a complete phrase is called a maximal projection. A sentence is the maximal projection of a finite verb. (Müller 2013c, 10, my translation)

So it is really just *phrases* that are licensed, even though it is equally possible to talk about *sentences* from within this framework.

HPGS is a lexicon-based approach, i.e. most of the syntactic information (and the complete semantics) is represented in lexical entries. This information is accompanied by a few general rules that specify how to combine lexical entries. Phrasal structures are licensed (that is, 'grammatical') iff their feature values are compatible. The theory builds complexes (genuine phrases and sentences) from the bottom up out of simpler units (lexical entries or simple phrases). Which units are grammatical is solely determined by the compatibility of the feature values of their constituents. The semantics does not interfere with grammaticality, i.e. its sole function in the theory is to keep track of referents (via indices) and to state which constituents provide which semantic aspects (e.g. referents for singular terms and pronouns; relations for verbs). The semantics is, if you like, 'transparent' and relies on constant meanings that are not affected by contexts: for example, "die" is semantically specified simply as [RELN die].

[18] For a modern derivative of HPSG, see, e.g., Fillmore (2013).

2.1 Meaning Statements are Descriptions

meanings' (1998, 15). It is important to bear in mind that, although Horwich's book is full of statements like "'Red' means RED", the *explanatorily relevant work* is done by means of acceptance properties (see 3.1.1). In general, trivialism is always committed to explicating what is supposed to substitute the relevant placeholders. Some forms of trivialism, incorporating no placeholders, simply *displace* the burden of explanation from one area to another, e.g. by equating the semantics of natural languages with the semantics of their corresponding concepts.

Other trivial 'theories of meaning' are similar to Horwich's use theory in important respects. These theories specify word meanings in that they postpone the problem of word meaning to other areas of research. A very popular move is to talk implicitly as if concepts and the corresponding words that express these concepts can be identified in regard to their respective meanings.[19] In this sense, then, these theories account for the meanings of words via a theory of mental representation.[20] In these theoretical frameworks, the explanatorily interesting part concerns the linkage of mental representations and semantic content (especially reference). The identification of the semantics of a given word with the semantics of the specific mental representation that is expressed by this word is typically not focused by these theories. It rather has the status of a postulation. All mentioned theories, different as they are, share a trivial core: meaning statements are derivable either by applying a capitalisation convention (e.g. that "red" means RED) or by identifying the meaning of words with the meaning of mental representations (e.g. that "red" means RED). As far as *this* part of the theory is concerned, neither case requires any object-level knowledge whatsoever.

How can 'trivial' meaning statements be reconciled with our pre-theoretic understanding of 'meaning'? The 'trivial' part apparently can't be incorporated directly, for "RED" (as such) is nothing close to a paraphrase

---

[19] Fodor, for one, even goes as far as to claim that language inherits higher-order properties (systematicity, productivity) from concepts due to meaning identity (Fodor 1998, 26–27).

[20] Interestingly, the theories of meaning listed by Horwich as alternatives to his own theory are mainly such theories of mental representation: Mental Image Theory, Informational Theory, Teleological Theory (1998, 51–54). The main proponents Horwich thinks of here are probably Hume, Dretske, and Millikan, respectively. For a similar vantage point on semantic theories cf. Godfrey-Smith (1989, esp. section II).

of how "red" is used. So whether trivial meaning statements are covered by my provisional definition of "meaning" depends on what the trivial statement is connected with. In Horwich's account, for instance, "RED" serves as a placeholder denoting the meaning of "red", whatever it is. The nontrivial part of the theory, then, gives us that the use of "red" is traceable to a specific set of acceptance properties. To wit:

> The explanatorily fundamental acceptance property underlying our use of "red" is (roughly) the disposition to apply "red" to an observed surface when and only when it is clearly red. (Horwich 1998, 45)

Here, one can see clearly that certain sorts of trivialism fit quite nicely with the proposed definition of "meaning". Because this usage theory aims at providing every single word of a language, for example English, with a general property (expressed in terms of a disposition to accept certain sets of sentences) that paraphrases its use.

In the area of theories of mental representation, 'semantic' theories include all so-called informational (/teleological) theories (Dretske (1986) is a point of reference here), or theories of 'asymmetric dependence' (Fodor 1990). From the viewpoint of natural language semantics, these theories are trivial, because in regards to words they just equate their respective meanings with the meanings of corresponding concepts. For the present purposes, it is irrelevant whether this identification itself is plausible. I am only concerned with the fact that the semantics of words and mental tokens are very often thus identified in the philosophical literature. Here are some randomly chosen examples:

> The speaker introducing the term says something like (or thinks, *it doesn't matter*), 'by "water" I mean [...]. (Levine 2010, 190, my emphasis)

> To know English is to know, for example, that the form of words 'there are cats' is standardly used to express the thought that there are cats; and that the form of words 'it's raining' is standardly used to express the thought that it's raining [...]. (Fodor 1998, 9)

2.1 Meaning Statements are Descriptions

> [T]he expression 'that sofas are more comfortable than pews' provides the content of Alfred's belief that sofas are more comfortable than pews. (Burge 1979, 101)

> If S thinks, or says, "The man in the picture was evil incarnate", whom is he referring to or thinking about: the unknown actor or Stalin himself? (Sosa 1995, 93)

> Words have meanings, and thinking has content. [...O]ften I'll move carelessly among talk of meaning and content, the meanings of words and the identity of concepts. (Gibbard 2012, 26)

By postponing the problem of accounting for the semantic basis of words, this way of talking as if words and concepts were interchangeable parallels Horwich's placeholder approach.[21]

The question as to whether theories of this type paraphrase uses of words in the relevant sense and, hence, count as genuine semantic theories (in my sense) hinges on what takes the placeholder's place. Fodorian and Dretskian accounts of mental representation, for example, emphasise the causal nexus of concepts. More precisely,

> Informational semantics generally ignores the actual history of a sign [of thought or language], and looks to what is a natural indicator of it. It is the mechanism of nomic dependence between sign and object that determines content. (Godfrey-Smith 1989, 535)

This way of approaching natural language is inspired by the 20th century dominance of truth-conditional semantics. For this reason, informational

---

[21] The parallel is even stricter than it might seem at first:

> [...] the concept DOG is most directly identified as the concept that is normally expressed in English by using the word "dog" [...] (Horwich 1998, 98).

And, further down this page:

> [...] the natural view that the meaning of an expression is the concept it expresses is quite consistent with the further claim that such concepts are identified by means of the use regularities of the words that express them.

theorists stress, for example, the alleged *referential* facts of words. Thus, we have Fodor claiming that

> The basic problem is that we want there to be conditions for the truth of a symbol over and above the conditions whose satisfaction determines what the symbol represents. (1984, 243)

Being solely concerned with truth/falsity and related concepts (reference, fulfilment), informational theories are semantic theories that focus only on specific aspects of language.[22] So, like formal semantics, the scope of at least some trivialist theories is severely limited in regard to semantic aspects.

Still, these theories are covered by my provisional definition of "meaning" insofar as, concerning natural-language semantics, they are tightly linked with non-trivial explanations such as Horwich's acceptance properties. Or, to put it another way: in the terminology of Speaks (2011), theories such as informational theory in fact belong to the area of foundational theories. On the other hand, subsuming the theories mentioned above under the heading 'trivialism' seems justified, because, in regard to the semantics of natural language (as opposed to mental representations), informational theory and similar frameworks are on a par with Horwich's capitalisation convention. The fact that "dog" is a symbol whose meaning nomologically depends on the existence of dogs is not immediately relevant to how "dog" is *used*. Therefore, informational-theoretic theorems do not illuminate the use of the expressions they are dealing with.

Ostensive Definition: Kripke's causal-historic theory of reference is another example of a theory that clearly belongs to the realm of foundational

---

[22] 'For Fodor, [semantics] is a relation between certain thoughts (beliefs, etc.) and the world, in virtue of which the thoughts are either true or false. Semantics, meaning, is about truth and falsity, period' (Dietrich 2001, 90).

theories. The famous 'baptism ceremony' of "gold", though, is ambiguous between the 'foundational' and the 'semantic' reading.[23,24] Kripke writes:

> For species, as for proper names, the way the reference of a term is fixed should not be regarded as a synonym for the term. In the case of proper names, the reference can be fixed in various ways. In an initial baptism it is typically fixed by an ostension or a description. Otherwise, the reference is usually determined by a chain, passing the name from link to link. The same observations hold for such a general term as 'gold'. If we imagine a hypothetical (admittedly somewhat artificial) baptism of the substance, we must imagine it picked out as by some such 'definition' as, 'Gold is the substance instantiated by the items over there, or at any rate, by almost all of them'. (1980, 135)

First of all, this is an explanation for *why* "gold" means what it does, i.e. it concerns its genesis. But it is also explains the *meaning* of "gold". The 'baptism ceremony' is, if you like, a special case of reference fixing, already discussed above. A speaker who performs such a ceremony commits himself to a certain use of "gold". That is, a proper *description* of the ceremony (plus Kripke's theory) is a *paraphrase* of how "gold" is used. Remember that I defined a 'paraphrase' as a description that provides competent language users with information about how the term is used. That certainly is the case for someone who is confronted with Kripke's story and is—save for the meaning of "gold"—competent in English. Note that this is a precondition for the ceremony; because if the ceremony (or a description

---

[23] Kripke's story is not meant as describing what *actually happened* when "gold" was introduced for the first time, but rather as a description that simply is *in accordance with* the actual use of that term. His claim is that the semantics of, for example, "gold" looks *as if* that word had been introduced by such a ceremony. In this sense, Kripke's approach maps exactly onto what I said above about *effective ways of summarising use*. It might be that, in fact, the *most effective* method is by way of telling a fictive story.

[24] The distinction foundational/semantic is adopted from Speaks (2011), who says that '[...] a semantic theory [...] is a theory which assigns semantic contents to expressions of a language'. In contrast, a foundational or reductionist theory is simply a theory that specifies by virtue of which underlying non-semantic properties (e.g. use) the expressions of a language have the meanings they in fact have.

thereof) did not imply a certain use, a speaker could not commit himself to a certain meaning of "water" by performing this baptism. Thus, ostensive definitions of the form "By '*x*' I mean *y* from now on" can be considered genuine paraphrases of how a term "*x*" is or will be used. They are therefore absolutely within the scope of the proposed preliminary, pre-theoretic definition of "meaning".

It is evident from this cursory list of kinds of meaning statements that my definition of 'meaning as paraphrase' is broad enough to cover very different varieties of semantic theories and semantic aspects of related theories such as grammar theory. I am not, by virtue of provisionally employing this definition of "meaning", forced to adopt a particular (philosophical) theory of meaning. I shall show in later chapters that an order among theories in terms of appropriateness can be achieved by other means. Generally, the definition is as liberal as possible. It covers a broad range of different semantic representations that can all legitimately be considered to be dealing with relevant aspects of meaning. At the same time, the discussion of the proposed definition has already hinted at some problematic areas. These include purely formal approaches, e.g. truth-conditional semantics, discourse representation theory, teleological semantics, and so forth. Theories of this kind work with a constrained notion of meaning; or, in other words, they deal only with quite specific aspects of meaning (most prominently, reference). Their theorems consist of semantic representations that hardly go beyond what can already be read off from the relevant linguistic signs they are representations of.

It goes without saying that the list of theories chosen for the above overview is incomplete. Yet it is broad enough that one extrapolate from this list that the proposed pre-theoretic definition of "meaning" is compatible with all meaning statements that figure in mainstream theories in linguistic semantics and philosophy of language.

2.1.3 Primary Meaning and Compositionality

In semantic theories in general and in philosophical semantics in particular, compositionality is a key concept. Here, I focus particularly on the relationship between compositionality and the classical conception of primary meaning in terms of reference, as both notions seem to partially justify

2.1 Meaning Statements are Descriptions

each other (see the following paragraph). The 'correct' formulation of the compositionality principle is still controversial (e.g. Gendler Szabó 2012a, Gendler Szabó 2012b). Most scholars, though, would typically subscribe to the view that compositionality is a feature of language, according to which the meaning of a complex expression is systematically determined by the meaning of its atomic parts and their mode of combination. This characterisation should suffice for present purposes; I continue discussing compositionality in 5.2.3.

Compositionality usually presupposes fixed lexical meanings of atomic parts of one's language (e.g. words). For otherwise there could be no 'mechanism' (i.e. the syntax) that, starting from meanings of words (i.e. semantics), could help determining the meaning of complete sentences. A quick argument for primary meanings could therefore run as follows: that natural languages are compositional is a widely accepted view; the compositionality principle is by far the most commonly accepted solution to compositionality; the principle is, inter alia, based on the assumption that there are fixed lexical meanings (e.g. meanings defined in terms of reference/satisfaction). Therefore, compositionality lends indirect support to the assumption of ordinary literal meanings. Independently of how this quick argument is spelled out exactly, it seems clear that there is a very close link from compositionality to literal meaning. One of the aims of this book is to argue against the common assumption that words always 'have' a literal meaning irrespective of the contexts in which they are instantiated. Accordingly, it looks like a good idea to explicate the exact nature of the relationship between literality and compositionality, for there must be something in my own theoretic framework that can serve as a substitute for literal meaning. Accordingly, I shall propose in the following a definition of "primary meaning" that, on the hand, is capable of handling literality/nonliterality issues, and, on the other hand, does without assumptions that usually go hand in hand with primary meanings (e.g. the assumption that words literally refer).

When it comes to compositionality and the justification for why we think that natural languages are compositional, Fodor (e.g. Fodor & Lepore 2002) is our first port of call. I shall briefly remind you of his main argument. Clearly, natural languages seem to be productive and systematic to a large extent.²⁵ *Productivity*, in the sense at stake here, is the phenomenon that an infinite number of well-formed complex expressions in natural languages can potentially be understood by speakers who are competent in the relevant language. In other words, there are an infinite number of grammatical sentences, all of which are potentially comprehensible for those who understand the involved semantic atoms and composition rules. *Systematicity* is the common property of languages that every competent language user who understands a given sentence and recognises its structure is similarly able to understand other grammatical sentences that result from rearranging the relevant constituents. For example, competent users of English who understand "John loves Mary" are likewise able to understand "Mary loves John". Both systematicity and productivity require— for reasons not be further examined here—a language that features atomic semantic units (e.g. Fodor & Lepore 2002).

To sum up thus far: two main reasons motivate the concept of primary meaning. Firstly, the distinction held up in linguistics as well as in philosophy of language between semantics and pragmatics.²⁶ Secondly, the compositionality of natural languages and the corresponding principle that accounts for it. It is a view on meaning widely shared by linguists and philosophers of language alike. What is important in the following examples is not that the respective arguments are based on the compositionality assumption but, rather, that the respective authors presuppose stable lexical word meanings:

> [...] it is part and parcel of the compositionality of English that the symbol 'John jumps' is complex, that it has among its constituents the symbols 'John' and 'jumps', and that its meaning (viz., *John jumps*) is inherited from the meanings of these subsentential parts. (Fodor & Lepore 2002, 1)

---

[25] Problematic cases, which seem to show that natural languages are, at least, not systematic all the way down, will come into play later on. For example, it seems that the semantic content that "white" contributes to "white wine" differs from the content it contributes to complexes such as "white Socrates" or "white wall". Suffice it to say for now that systematicity seems to be prevalent in at least large areas of natural languages.

[26] Gendler Szabó (2006), Heusinger & Turner (2006), Jaszczolt (2012).

2.1 Meaning Statements are Descriptions

[...] "dogs bark" somehow gets its meaning [...] from the meanings of the two words "dog" and "bark", from the meaning of the generalization schema "*ns v*"[27], and from the fact that the sentence results from placing those words in that schema in a certain order. (Horwich 1998, 154)

[Our hypothesis] is that the process by which a speaker interprets each of the infinitely many sentences is a compositional process in which the meaning of any syntactically compound constituent of a sentence is obtained as a function of the meanings of the parts of the constituent. (Katz 1966, 152)

The denotation of an adjective is always a function from properties to properties. [...] The standard denotations of many adjectives—for instance, ⌜green⌝ and ⌜married⌝—may be taken as intersection functions [...]. (Montague 1974, 211, emphasis omitted)

What is striking about the typical examples that theorists choose when characterising compositionality is that they are very simple. A typical sentence might be "University buildings are ugly", which, presumably, consists of four constituents, namely "university building", "-s", "be" and "ugly". The noun denotes university buildings, the suffix denotes plurality, the copula itself is, in the interpretation involved here, more or less semantically empty (basically, it functions as a syntactic device that 'enables' predication),[28] and "ugly" denotes unattractiveness. The syntax of English, in

---

[27] "*n*" is for 'noun'; "*v*" is for verb.

[28] Below I will be discussing many interesting examples of allegedly *meaningless* expressions. Depending on one's theory of meaning, copulas might also turn out to be meaningless after all, for they contribute nothing substantial to the semantic content of a complex expression. Rather, the 'meaning' of the copula seems to consist solely in its functionality: that is to say, it indicates that two *other* expressions stand in a certain relation to each other. Roughly, the copula function is to indicate that the thing denoted by the grammatical subject is among the things that has the property denoted by the predicative noun (or anything along these lines). To be sure, that *is* its meaning. But, arguably, the only way to state its meaning in these terms is in theories that recognise that the meanings of at least some terms consist solely in their function, which many philosophically interesting theories do not, after all.

2 Meaning: Primary, Pragmatic, and Others

conjunction with the meanings of the sentence constituents, gives us, or so it is claimed, the meaning of the complete sentence.

In the above example, this procedure might tell us that the property of unattractiveness is predicated of the plurality of university buildings and, hence, that the sentence is true iff university buildings are ugly. This pretty straightforward—and for ease of presentation, slightly simplified—strategy is, essentially, what truth-conditional semantics says is actually going on. I will show in the chapter after next that this way of approaching semantics is a bit *too* straightforward. Of course, it is always justified to choose a simple example in order to get one's point through without annoying the reader with unnecessary technicalities and complexity. But in the cases typically chosen in characterisations of compositionality, the simplicity is unjustified. The reason is that such a strategy only works if what is explained at the level of very simple sentences is applicable analogously to more complex sentences. This seems questionable in these cases, for reasons having to do not with the complexity or length of sentences but with the semantics of the words occurring in them.

In particular, the unjustified move is to generalise from a very limited class of words of speech to whole natural languages. Typically, the parts of speech chosen include proper names and verbs functioning as predicates. The semantics for these is then provided more or less in the style of the example above ("university building" means 'university building', and so on). All this is intuitively compelling but ignores the problem that not all of semantics can be cashed out this simply. Think of truth-valueless sentences, for instance. They clearly have meaning—if well-formed. Look, for example, at the following, still very simple example: "Hey, Mrs Robinson!" Presumably, this sentence, although well-formed, is not truth-evaluable, i.e. no truth conditions can reasonably be assigned to it. The common move here is to switch from truth conditions to 'satisfaction-conditions', because it is not the former but rather the latter that can account for some classes of non-declarative sentences such as interrogative or imperative sentences.[29] But this would not help either in cases of exclamations like the one cited. The meaning of such an exclamation is best described in terms of the conversational function associated with exclamations of this type: along the

---

[29] Although that is the probably most popular strategy, there are also alternatives.

2.1 Meaning Statements are Descriptions

lines of 'is used to express one's interest in a good social relationship'. However, it looks highly counter-intuitive to describe this function in terms of satisfaction/fulfilment, e.g. by saying that "Hey, Mrs Robinson!" is satisfied iff such-and-such conditions hold. This is because a command is, with conceptual necessity, satisfied iff the conditions specified in the command actually hold. But the analogy with exclamations breaks down 'at all levels', so to speak: the meaning of "Hey, Mrs Robinson!" remains the same, no matter whether the addressee's social relationship with the speaker alters; or whether the addressee recognised that this was the speaker's intention; or whether it indeed was her intention; and so on. So, whereas the move to satisfaction-conditions is at least consistent in the case of imperative sentences, it is implausible in the case of exclamations that regulate social status. The fact that "Hey, Mrs Robinson!" is not truth-evaluable is unproblematic as far as it goes. But the deeper problem is that, on the one hand, "Hey, Mrs Robinson!" seems intuitively compositional, whereas, on the other hand, all existing philosophical theories of meaning—from Davidson semantics to Horwich's use theory—focus on truth-evaluable sentences[30] and how these sentences derive their meaning from corresponding constituents. An established philosophical account of the meaning of purely 'functional' expressions—e.g. exclamations that clarify social status—is still missing. This is a problem that generalises to the huge class of types of sentences that, in general, lack truth-evaluable content.[31]

---

[30] For sake of simplicity, I continue to talk of sentences here. Bear in mind, though, that at least some of the problematic cases can be, strictly speaking, individuated in terms of their corresponding force, i.e. in terms of speech acts rather than sentence types. For example, interrogatives are types of sentences (they can be described formally), but wishes are types of speech acts (they can only be described with regard to accompanying intentions); what 'unites' them is that they both lack truth conditions but (probably) possess satisfaction conditions.

[31] That is to say, there is a huge class of sentences that are incapable of being 'themselves' truth-evaluable. It is possible to link expressions which lack truth value with some other expressions that do not, where the latter are supposed to express the 'right' truth conditions for the former. The theories that adopt this idea provide truth conditions for some expressions by taking into account their use conditions. Here is an example: "Hello!" might not be truth-evaluable. But of course there is a certain use condition associated with "hello". For example, 'is used to maintain social relationship'. David Kaplan, for one, proposes something along these lines (see https://www.youtube.com/watch?v=iaGRLlgPl6w, accessed: 14/01/2015).

2 Meaning: Primary, Pragmatic, and Others

To take another example, think of gestures, which must be included into an exhaustive account of natural language semantics.[32] Surely, many of them have meaning—e.g. iconic gestures. Moreover, they surely equally have meaning in the sense of 'constituents' of complex expressions. Here is an example of a complex communicated content whose meaning is 'composed' of individual meanings that are partly established by gesture (roughly, 'being annoyed' and 'I'm referring to this person'):

> In an airplane, I take my seat on the aisle. There is a woman sitting next to the window in my row. A man comes into the row behind us, talking extremely loudly and obnoxiously. I look to the woman and roll my eyes, expressing an attitude best glossed as "Ugh, this is going to be a long trip." I did not need to indicate the referent of my exasperation for her; it was clear to us both. (Tomasello 2008, 80)

It is hard to see what lexical meanings of gestures (here: rolling of the eyes) would look like, if they were such that they could then be used as a basis for an explanation of the complex meaning. A comprehensive account of compositionality must cover cases like these, since not all natural language sentences consist of simple subject-predicate structures.[33]

Truth-valueless sentences as well as gestures are two problematic areas in the field of compositionality. They indicate that the simplicity of examples typically chosen to describe how compositionality works is not just a matter of style but, rather, an unjustified simplification as regards parts of speech (or, generally, types of 'communication signs'). This, in turn, undermines the plausibility of justifying ordinary primary meanings by recurring to compositionality principles. For there must be a way to accommodate (some kind of) 'compositionality' in the cases discussed above—i.e. a strategy that does without the classical compositionality principle, which is inappropriate for gestures and sentences with specific functions (as opposed to truth-evaluable content). Prima facie, there is no need to

---

[32] I argue for this in 2.2.3 and 2.2.4.

[33] I devote a large portion of the third part of this book to a discussion of the standard reply that, for sake of simplicity, I ignore at this point: namely the worry that while pretending to talk about semantics, I actually talk about communication all the time.

assume that this modified manner of conceiving compositionality must involve primary meanings spelled out in terms of reference relations. Hence, the indirect support for primary meaning that might arise from the classical compositionality principle seems unjustified.

It is clearly not the aim of this chapter to decide this matter, nor even to suggest a possible direction between the two extremes: full-flavour primary meaning versus no primary meaning at all. Rather, the purpose of the above paragraphs was to present evidence pointing, as it were, in both directions. Save for the critique of compositionality in the very last paragraphs, all the above was 'in favour' of primary meaning. Thus, in the next section I now turn to the cons.

2.2 Constructionist Approaches to Semantics

One of the most influential paradigms in linguistics today is construction grammar. It aims at 'developing a comprehensive model of linguistic structures that is [...] a universal theory of representation, acquisition, and change of linguistic knowledge' (Ziem & Lasch 2013, 1). One of its linguistically most relevant aspects is that it starts linguistic theorising by looking at language phenomena that are conceived as peripheral from a more classical point of view (e.g. idioms). However, from a philosopher's perspective, another feature is by far more interesting: namely, construction grammar's tendency—discussed below—to neglect a clear-cut boundary between semantics and pragmatics as well the denial of such a strict boundary in the case of semantics and syntax. In construction grammar, pragmatic and syntactic information is generally represented in essentially the same framework in which semantics is represented. This development fits quite nicely with a more general tendency in philosophy of language (cf. François Recanati's work on 'truth-conditional pragmatics' (2007)) and in the research of language acquisition (cf. Michael Tomasello's work on 'joint attention' (e.g. 2009))[34] to shift the divide between semantics and pragmatics more and more towards pragmatics. In other words, in these research paradigms, semantics typically includes elements that would fall into pragmatics in more classical frameworks (cf. Recanati's treatment of

---

[34] See also Butterfill (2012) and Pacherie (2011).

'what is said'). After a very brief overview of the theoretical background, I turn to some more specific issues, in particular to multimodal compositionality, i.e. the linguistic phenomenon that many modalities contribute to utterance meaning at once.

2.2.1 Construction Grammar: From Cognitive Semantics to Philosophy

In linguistics, construction grammar (CxG) has attracted more and more attention over recent years. I shall only briefly summarise the main theses of the theory. For detailed expositions, I refer the reader to Fillmore (1993) and Goldberg (1995).[35] CxG deviates significantly from the standard. The most important thing is that no strict distinction is drawn anymore between the lexicon and the syntax.[36] Lexical and syntactical information is still encoded (and differentiated), but both 'kinds' of information are handled in largely the same manner, i.e. both are represented in the form of constructions. Constructions are form–meaning pairings, the simplest of which are morphemes. Accordingly, all linguistic information is stored, not in the lexicon and the grammar, but in what is often called the 'constructicon' (Goldberg 1995, 5). In similar fashion, construction grammar dismisses the semantics/pragmatics distinction. This is particularly important for the present discussion, because of the close relationship between this very distinction on the one hand and primary and derived/pragmatic meaning on the other hand.

One of CxG's major principles is that every sign is a form–meaning pair. Interestingly, syntactic constructions are treated as bearing their own meanings—contrary to all alternative approaches in which syntactic rules map meanings of lower-level constituents (morphemes, words, phrases) onto complex meanings. Such rules usually do not bear their own meanings, the meaning of a complex expression—eventually, the meaning of a

---

[35] The list of obligatory standard references includes: Croft (2001), Fillmore (1988, 1988), Goldberg (1995, 2006), Langacker (1987), Lakoff (1987, 467–858). Comprehensive overviews can be found in: Fischer & Stefanowitsch (2007), Lasch & Ziem (2011), Lasch & Ziem (2014), Stefanowitsch & Fischer (2008), and Ziem & Lasch (2013).

[36] Besides the mentioned standard references, the presentation developed here and in the following is heavily inspired by the comprehensive overview in Ziem & Lasch (2013).

2.2 Constructionist Approaches to Semantics

sentence—depends solely on the meanings of its parts (Tomasello 2003a). In CxG, all form–meaning pairs are constructions: from words to particular syntactic arrangements. A construction is recursively defined as follows:[37]

> C is a construction iff C is a form–meaning pair $\langle F_i, S_i \rangle$ such that some aspect of F_i or some aspect of S_i is not strictly predictable from C's component parts or from other previously established constructions. (Goldberg 1995, 4)

Before I turn to the discussion, let me just very briefly give you an impression of what a constructionist representation of linguistic information looks like. The formal apparatus of (some theory families of) CxG stems from head-driven phrase structure grammar. Although there are, as far as linguistic analysis is concerned, subtle differences between HPSG and CxG, they are similar and often even equivalent in regards to their representation format (Müller 2013b, 248–253).[38] The details do not matter here, this is just to give you the flavour of what we are talking about. The most important thing is that both grammars represent linguistic information as attribute-value matrices. The attributes encompass both syntactic and semantic information. The respective representations license certain structures in such a way that a complex expression (a phrase, a sentence) is grammatical iff the corresponding attribute-value matrices of its parts are compatible. They are compatible, basically, if their values match, or, otherwise, if one of two corresponding values is left unspecified. A simple example would be a case in which you already have a representation of a verb phrase that lacks only a subject to form a complete sentence. The verb

---

[37] This is the 'standard definition'. A newer version, also from Goldberg, is broadened in that entrenchment is explicitly allowed as a sufficient criterion for constructions, even in cases in which their meaning is otherwise predictable from other constructions (Goldberg 2006, 5). Linguistically, this difference is significant; from a philosophical point of view, it is not particularly relevant in the present context. Here I am primarily interested in whether the research paradigm of construction grammar is compatible with established theories of meaning in philosophy. As far as that compatibility is concerned, there does not seem to be a difference between Goldberg's two definitions of "construction".

[38] Other CxG variants that are less inspired by HPSG are sometimes characterised as 'cognitive' (Ziem & Lasch 2013). If not indicated otherwise, the differences between individual construction grammars are irrelevant for my argumentation.

$$\begin{bmatrix} & \textit{Transitive Construction} \\ \text{SYN} & \begin{bmatrix} \text{CAT} & v \\ \text{VOICE} & \textit{active} \end{bmatrix} \\ \text{VAL} & \left\{ \begin{bmatrix} \text{ROLE} & \begin{bmatrix} \text{GF} & \textit{obj} \\ \text{DA} & - \end{bmatrix} \end{bmatrix} \right\} \end{bmatrix}$$

Figure 2.2: Representation of Transitive Construction (Müller 2013b, 242).

phrase, then, constrains the possible values of the subject. For instance, it might demand a noun phrase that meets certain requirements. The result of applying a compatible noun phrase to the verb phrase is a sentence licensed by the grammar (assuming that the verb phrase was constructed accordingly). To put it more generally, the grammatical sentences in CxG are exactly those constructions that are built up from compatible lower-level constructions, with morphemes probably being at the lowest level.

As I already noted, in construction grammar everything from words to syntactic structures is represented as constructions. The 'Transitive Construction', for instance, might look like figure 2.2.

Here you can see the representation of linguistic information by means of attribute-value matrices. The function, so to speak, of the construction is to restrict the possible values of certain attributes. In this case, it restricts the value of 'DA' (distinguished argument) to '–', which just means that it is that argument that would not be the subject of the sentence in active voice. All these linguistic details do not matter for the moment. What is important to note is that the grammaticality of complex constructions is determined according to the values of lower-level constructions. Plus, syntactic restrictions are encoded on a par with semantic information.

When it comes to semantic theories in philosophy, the discussions often develop independently from actual linguistic theories. This holds in particular for grammar theory. The thing is, though, that developments in linguistics need to be taken into account by philosophers of language working in semantics—a truism, actually. Otherwise, one's theory is likely to lack empirical underpinning. This is a general point that not only concerns semantics but also, for example, language acquisition. You might think that philosophers are dealing only with non-empirical questions and, therefore, issues negotiated in philosophy of language are largely independent of findings in the sciences, in particular in linguistics. This is fine as far as it goes. It is fine if the claim is only that there need be no 'direct' connection between both theories in such a way that the results of one theory are deployed in the respective other theory.[39] This is so because there is no data that we would need to account for by combining philosophical and linguistic views on semantics.

However, if the claim is that both areas are completely independent, then it is probably false. Generally, philosophical theories in semantics must be *compatible* with results produced in empirical disciplines such as linguistics, psychology, anthropology, etc., i.e. these theories and their philosophical counterparts should not contradict each other (cf. also 7.1.3). Some general considerations justify this claim. The most general background assumption is that one's (philosophical) theory calls for psychological (/linguistic) reality. Let us first have a look at language acquisition theories. In philosophical terms, acquisition theories belong to the realm of foundational (or reductive) theories, i.e. they are theories that explicate the underlying properties that constitute semantic properties (Speaks 2011). In this case, they explicate the underlying properties that amount to the ontogeny of semantic competency. For example, a foundational theory would explain the origin of the relationship that holds between, for example, (the word type) "apple" and its corresponding meaning, i.e. 'apple'. A given theory of meaning must be compatible with one existing acquisition theory—this will typically be the currently accepted theory—for the following reason.

Assume it were incompatible with all acquisition theories. The latter describe how we, human beings, come to speak a language with certain features. If both theories were incompatible, two cases may be distinguished. First case: either of the theories might be false. If the semantic theory were false, that would be bad news anyway. So we may ignore this case. To assume—all else equal—that the psychological theory could be false be-

---

[39] Like when the laws of optics and of physics are combined to interpret observations of the Sun via telescopes.

cause of its assumed incompatibility with a competing philosophical theory is highly implausible. For "false" in this context may be taken to mean, roughly, 'empirically falsified'. Ex hypothesi, the psychological theory is the only empirically informed theory (of the two). To take incompatibility with a non-empirical theory as evidence for empirical inadequacy is unjustified. One is therefore justified in excluding this option. The second case is: the philosophical theory might not call for psychological reality. This option would allow for contradiction between the theories in question, since *however language actually is acquired* according to the psychological theory, the philosophical theory might be just one way of accounting for the available data. This looks like a possible strategy, but is has an evident drawback. Since language acquisition theories are the only theories that explain how natural languages are acquired, every theory that is incompatible with these theories and that denies any call for psychological reality could not possibly be a theory of *our* language (e.g. English). It might be a theory of something similar (i.e. grammar-wise superficially similar, but acquired differently); however, finding a theory of meaning that fits with actual language use is an 'all-or-nothing game', as it were. Explaining something 'similar' to natural language is not explaining natural language at all.

Mutatis mutandis, the same reasoning applies to the relation between philosophical and linguistic theories of *meaning*. They also need to be compatible. The only case in which they could end up being incompatible is when the philosophical theory is a product of 'armchair philosophy', i.e. the result of (and only of) a priori methods. For if both are empirically informed and both deal with the same subject matter, then there can't be any 'competing' theories, strictly speaking. As a matter of fact, it should always be possible in such cases to favour one theory over the other on the basis of objective criteria of theory choice (simplicity, universality, elegance, etc.). Naïvely speaking, there can always be only one *best* theory in the empirical realm (in the long run), in which case there is no actual 'competition'. In real life, this is a bit more complicated, because, for example, people tend to disagree about the appropriate set of theory choice criteria, or they disagree about how to apply them to a particular case. Be that as it may, if any of the two approaches is empirically adequate, it is the linguistic theory. As above, no matter what the philosophical theory is

2.2 Constructionist Approaches to Semantics

dealing with in such a case, it is not English (or, for that matter, any other natural language). Therefore, if one wants to account for the semantics of natural language, one better ensure that the philosophy fits in with current linguistics.

Another background assumption is that empirical evidence is a means of theory choice. All else equal, if two competing philosophical theories are to be evaluated, one of which contradicts current linguistic theories, then the respective other theory is better off. Conformity of philosophical theories with empirical theories can always be regarded as indirect evidence for empirical adequacy, for the scientific success of the latter heavily depends on *their* adequacy. A final important background assumption concerns contradictions between theories. Firstly, theories within semantics differ significantly as towards the notion of 'meaning' they involve. Secondly, there are huge differences in regard to the semantic descriptions in philosophical theories and scientific theories. One assumption needed in order to establish the claim that theories of both kinds must be compatible is that there is a way of how to verify whether this is the case or not. Without further argument, I assume that this can be done. I shall show in what follows that this is unproblematic.

This digression serves the purpose of preparing an argument for the rather strong connection between empirical and philosophical theories. The important thing to note is that if you claim your theory to be about the semantics of natural languages in the form they are actually used, you better make sure it is compatible with the relevant empirical theories. This is where CxG comes into play. This is, for obvious reasons, not the right place for a detailed discussion of the status of CxG within linguistics.[40] Of course, the argument to follow ultimately depends on the success of construction grammar, since there is no apparent incongruence between the assumption of primary meanings and other grammar theories (in particular, Chomskian generative grammar). So, the argument against primary meaning at hand hinges on the empirical plausibility of CxG. Be that as it may, there will always be competing theories and CxG is just one of many.

---

[40] Müller (2013*b*, 237–258) reviews the current state of construction grammar and provides a comprehensive bibliography on the subject matter. Stefanowitsch & Fischer (2008) is an introductory textbook focusing solely on CxG. The most recent overview in English is Michaelis (2006). Again, the most recent overview is Ziem & Lasch (2013).

2 Meaning: Primary, Pragmatic, and Others

In a nutshell, the weakest claim to be defended in the following is this: all else equal, a philosophical theory of meaning is better off if it dispenses with the ordinary notion of primary meaning explicated in terms of reference.[41]

Given the recent popularity of construction grammar in linguistics, it is worth the effort to see whether the theory is compatible with established philosophical (semantic) theories. For the moment, though, I will focus on a particular aspect of the theory, namely its connection to ordinary primary meaning. The success of CxG might be interpreted as evidence against referential semantics, this is because there is no place within the theory for any such notions as reference relations and truth-conditional functions (se also above). The most obvious counter-evidence is that one of the arguments *for* primary meaning can be reversed: I have shown that the semantics/pragmatics distinction justifies primary meanings, because, very roughly put, pragmatic meaning 'derives' from stable lexical meaning (i.e. primary meaning). In construction grammar, on the other hand, the semantics/pragmatics distinction vanishes. 'Officially', it is still there, i.e. the values of constructions are labelled accordingly. But no principled distinction is made any longer; the pragmatic 'principles' are handled as if they were semantic information:

> It seems appropriate to allow the notion of compositionality to comprise [...] 'pragmatic' instructions embedded in the grammar that provide the addressee with a certain semantic structure and instruct him or her to find content in the context that satisfies that structure. Consider utterance of a sentence like [the following]:
>
>> Kim won't (even) get question eight right let alone Sandy get question nine.
>
> [...] In this example, we have to think that the problems can be arranged on a scale (presumably of difficulty) and students arranged on a scale (presumably of ability) where the scales are interrelated in such a way that a more able student will

---
[41] Here I am tacitly assuming that this leaves compatibility with other grammar theories unaffected.

answer correctly any problem that a less able one will and a less able student will miss any problem that a more able one misses. (Kay & Michaelis 2012, 2283–2284)

It is no trivial matter where exactly to draw the distinction between semantics and pragmatics.[42] In any case, though, semantics is the study of meanings. Or, more precisely, semantics is the study of lexical, context-independent meaning[43], if you single out the meanings of particular utterances in particular circumstances as an independent field of study (which would then be pragmatics). Interestingly, you need not be exactly clear about where to draw the line between semantics and pragmatics in order to establish the claim that in construction grammar, the distinction is more or less obsolete.[44] This is because CxG still employs meanings in its 'lexical' representations of constructions. That is to say, by their very definition, constructions are form–meaning pairings and, therefore, they all have meaning. No matter what you take pragmatics to be, it certainly encompasses a distinct class of pragmatic 'principles'[45]. These principles or pragmatic regularities, however, are incorporated into constructionists' meaning representations (see Kay & Michaelis (2012) and Ziem & Lasch (2013, 14, 25–26), for example).

To be fair, many constructionist analyses ignore pragmatic issues to a large extent. These are either left out completely (e.g. Michaelis 2006), or they are mentioned only in passing (e.g. Kay & Michaelis 2012).[46] Still, if pragmatics is part of one's analysis, then the findings are modelled as

---

[42] See Gendler Szabó (2006) for a review.

[43] Note that the context independence of meanings is independent from the context *dependence* of the expressions modelled. For instance, a formal-semantic description of the meaning of "this" might essentially be 'context-dependent' in that it describes how the referent of "this" depends on context. The meaning itself, though, is independent from any such context (e.g. 'refers to what's most salient in the relevant context').

[44] 'More or less' because, judging from the terminology used by construction grammarians, one may easily get the impression that the distinction still plays a role.

[45] In particular, principles that involve references to intentional explanations—e.g. 'If the speaker utters something obviously false, he must mean something different'. Classically, Gricean maxims count as paradigm examples of pragmatic principles.

[46] Cf. also Östman (2005, 125):
Very little has been done on pragmatics proper and discourse proper in relation to Construction Grammar. It is often recognized that there is 'some-

2 Meaning: Primary, Pragmatic, and Others

part of the construction in just the same way as semantic information is represented:[47]

> The CxG notation relies on three major devices:[48] boxes-within-boxes diagrams for representing constituent structure, feature structures for detailed grammatical information, and co-indexation for keeping track of unification relations. [...]
>
> syn [...]
>
> prag constructional pragmatics & information-structure specifications
>
> val semantics of the construction
>
> phon [...] (Fried & Östman 2004, 25–26)

In similar fashion, some constructionist approaches combine CxG representations with data drawn from conversational analysis. This is relevant to our present discussion for the very same reason as in the case of pragmatics proper: normally, one would want to explain the meaning of a given term in a particular conversational situation by referring to primary meanings. However, this strategy is again unavailable here because conversational aspects of meaning are already included in the constructions from which sentence meaning is derived in the first place. As before, this makes it seem rather implausible to assume that one's basic semantic units can have primary meaning in the sense of mere reference relations.[49] Here

---

> thing' more out there, but what it is has largely remained a waste-paper basket.

[47] Cf. also Wide (2009, 131). Fried & Östman (2004) discuss the format of construction specifications more generally (see especially pp. 25–76).

[48] In this general form, this claim is probably untenable. For one thing, this might be correct for HPSG derivatives of CxG (cf. their mentioning 'unification relations' here), but it is certainly false for most 'informal' sketches of construction grammar, especially those in the tradition of spoken-language research.

[49] The reader who is worried that I might confuse issues of communication with issues of semantics is asked to have a look at chapter 8 before reading further.

is an example of how conversational aspects are modelled within a CxG framework:

form:
> communication partner: turn (TRP)   speaker: PM
> *but*-clause

meaning:
> topic continuity
> successful contact, perception, understanding
> acceptance of contribution
> solidary interpersonal function (Fischer 2013, 200)

The 'Turn-initial Pragmatic Marker' Construction[50]

It is irrelevant for the argument at hand that not all varieties of construction grammar incorporate pragmatic or conversational aspects. Even those approaches that focus solely on semantics, largely ignoring the actual communication situation, acknowledge the role played by context. It is just that this aspect is often left out of the analysis. In principle, contextual factors may be modelled in all variants of the CxG family. Moreover, in the case of formal varieties such as sign-based CxG (Michaelis 2013) or fluid CxG (Steels 2011), pragmatics is often excluded for reasons of convenience, although its relevance is widely accepted in principle.

This means that, if one wants to stick to the semantics/pragmatics distinction, pragmatics becomes—at best—part of semantics, i.e. roughly in the sense that semantics would be the study of meanings, while pragmatics would deal with a certain subclass of them. Apparently, such a weak notion of pragmatics is, in fact, not solid enough to back the idea of cashing out primary meaning in terms of reference relations. In the argument

---

[50] "TRP" is short for "transition relevance place", "PM" stands for "pragmatic marker" (like "yeah" or "okay"). The terminology of the items listed under 'meaning' stems from conversational analysis and is more or less self-explanatory. "Solidary interpersonal function" refers to what is usually known as 'face-saving strategy', i.e. communication acts that serve the purpose of signalling politeness against the interlocutor, the one from whom the turn had been taken.

for primary meaning that is based on the semantics/pragmatics distinction, pragmatics plays the following role: starting with mere preference relations, the pragmatic principles are functions from contexts to meanings in context. Such a procedure presupposes stable lexical meanings. In CxG, however, although there is still pragmatics, there are no such relevant 'principles', i.e. nothing that takes meaning (plus x) as input and yields (other) meaning as output. Accordingly, the way pragmatic information is handled in construction grammar is inappropriate to support the ordinary notion of primary meaning recurring to relations of reference.

This is not to say that a theory framework such as construction grammar, which does not allow for a principled distinction between semantics proper and pragmatics, still allows semantic information to play the same role as in other frameworks. Semantics can only be the input of pragmatic rules if indeed there *were* such rules. For example, if the intonation of "a is F" were such that it triggered an ironic interpretation, then that interpretation would be that 'a is non-F'. Conversely, if there were no such rules, there is no need for semantic information to serve as 'input' to such processes. Hence, no matter what the distinction between semantic and pragmatic information in constructionist theories (other than being labelled 'semantic' and 'pragmatic', respectively), it is not the traditional one—that information of the former kind serves as input to processes of the latter kind.

2.2.2 The Tomasellian Programme

Another argument against primary meaning stems from developmental psychology. Tomasello and colleagues have stressed repeatedly the importance of gestures for the ability of (human) animals to develop a language (e.g. Tomasello 2008). Developing gestures as simple communication signs is an initial but very important step towards this end, they claim. At first sight, this seems quite irrelevant for the question at hand. But it is not, as I will show in a moment. One important background assumption in what follows is that when it comes to semantics, gestures and other communication signs—typically, words and sentences—are handled on a par, i.e. no *principled* distinction is or can be drawn between them with respect to their 'ability' to contribute to complete utterances. From this, one may infer that if there are primary meanings, gestures have them (assuming primary meaning is a universal feature of natural language signs). Thus, if we are able to show that gestures do not exhibit primary meaning, this allows us to infer that gestures provide counter-evidence against primary meaning. Therefore, the task is to show that this is actually the case: gestures can hardly have primary meaning, if primary meanings are supposed to represent relations from signs to the world.

For a start, consider the following randomly chosen examples:

> A man in a bar wants another drink; he waits until the bartender looks at him and then points to his empty shotglass. *Gloss*: Attend to the emptiness of the glass; please fill it up with liquor. (Tomasello 2008, 63)

> At a loud construction site, one worker pantomimes to another ten meters away as if he were using a chainsaw. *Gloss*: Imagine me doing this; bring me the thing I need to do it. (68)

The examples are supposed to show two things: firstly, the 'meaning' of a given gestural sign varies enormously from one occasion to the other; secondly, no formally specifiable context dependency can account for this. The first observation, I take it, is more or less clear. So, let me concentrate on the second.

In all of the following, I take for granted that this is not the right place to defend the merits of Tomasello's research agenda. For the most part, I will restrict myself to merely reporting on his view—and to draw those conclusions that are relevant to philosophical theorising, *given* the results established by Tomasello and his colleagues. Given this, let us return to the question why there are many gestures for which it seems impossible to trace back their meaning to some formally specifiable context dependency. Why not assume gestures work like indexicals? you might ask. We have theories of how to handle indexicals, so there is no problem with gestures.[51] If the context sensitivity of gestures could be captured by characters,[52] nothing could prevent us from saying their meanings were primary.

---

[51] There is a massive amount of literature solely dealing with indexicals. The locus classicus in this context is Kaplan (1989).

[52] "Character" is Kaplan's now-classical term for a function from contexts of utterance to truth-conditional content. The basic idea here is that the meaning (as opposed to its se-

2 Meaning: Primary, Pragmatic, and Others

Granted, their primary meanings are not lexical meanings, strictly speaking, but the same holds for the meanings of usual indexicals like "this". Just provide a context of utterance and you immediately get full-blown meaning including reference, which then may be used, relative to a given set of pragmatic rules, to derive meanings in context. This strategy suffers from the following shortcoming: in a nutshell, it is impossible to state appropriate characters of gestures.

Let me explain. The character of a term or gesture—i.e. meaning minus contextual values—must be describable in such a way as to cover all possible cases. That is to say, its semantic description needs to be weakened so as to be applicable to all counterfactual circumstances (contexts) in which the term may be applied. This sounds a bit abstract; a simple example will help to clarify the idea. A term with a 'normal' (complete) meaning is "Chris", for instance. It simply denotes the person called 'Chris'. A term like "he" might be described as already 'weakened' in the following sense: although we do not know, independently from context, its complete meaning (at least not its (actual) reference), what we do know is quite a lot. Namely that, in all contexts, "he" would usually denote the last male person mentioned in the discourse (be it a conversation, a text, or whatever). This meaning is fixed (I assume) and fairly complete. Even 'weaker', then, is the semantic description we have of a term like "this". As with "he", we do not know (in advance) its reference. But this time we actually know even less, as linguistic rules alone do not suffice in this case to determine the actual referent. The contextual information must include also non-linguistic data: information about pointing gestures, for instance.

Primary meaning is the information about an atomic semantic unit of our language that we have *prior* to encountering specific instances. The semantic information is, as I have just demonstrated, relatively limited in

---

mantic value in specific contexts of utterance) can be defined or characterised in terms of token-reflexive rules. For instance, "I" gets associated with a rule such as "The semantic value of an instance of 'I' in a given context is the speaker of 'I' in that context". The 'token-reflexivity' lies in the fact that the meaning of a given token of an indexical expression can't be stated without referring to the same token again. Defining the character of "I" is comparatively easy; "here" and "now" (and cognates) are significantly harder to define, as their actual referents (relative to contexts of utterance) arguably depend on a variety of background assumptions shared between speaker and hearer (e.g. world knowledge). The locus classicus for indexicals more generally is Perry (1986).

the case of "this" compared to "Chris". Nevertheless, it is there. It might be characterised thus: "this" designates the object that is contextually most salient, with salience being determined by the linguistic context and a corresponding pointing gesture.

The point is that, when it comes to gestures as such, it is questionable whether it really makes sense any more to speak of meanings proper (though it is not completely incomprehensible to do so). I have shown that in order to determine the complete meaning of (a token of) "this", one needs to know its character (e.g. 'the most salient object in the vicinity') plus further linguistic information (the discourse into which the token is embedded) plus contextual information (information about bodily movements of the speaker)[53]. The 'character' of a gesture is, in the sense described above, even weaker, i.e. *almost no* information about the meaning of a gesture tokening is available beforehand. The relevant information thus always needs to be read off the specific situation in which a gesture gets instantiated. This is apparent if one takes a look at Tomasello's examples. In addition to all the information necessary in the case of indexicals, one needs to know the 'common ground' shared between the relevant interlocutors. Common ground is knowledge about the situation that is shared by the participants of a given situation (Tomasello 2008, ch. 3).[54] The cited examples strongly suggest that the stable, lexical part of meaning (i.e. meaning minus context minus linguistic information minus common ground) would be so thin that it seems absurd to take this for the 'primary meaning' of a given gesture.

If you assume that the primary meaning of a pointing gesture is *that which is contextually salient depending on the linguistic embedding, the context including bodily movements of the speaker, and the common ground of the participating speakers*, then this amounts to saying that you know hardly anything in advance. It could be just anything. Contrary to "this", one does not even know for sure that the referent is a (concrete) object of

---

[53] If you find pointing gestures or bodily movements unconvincing, you may amend the list of contextual information that is necessary to compute the whole meaning of a term, in particular its referent. This just complicates the issue but does not affect the point at hand.

[54] Horton (2005), Liebal (2009).

2 Meaning: Primary, Pragmatic, and Others

any sort. The gesture might even denote a situation. For example, consider the following scenario:

> Suppose that I and you are walking to the library, and out of the blue I point for you in the direction of some bicycles leaning against the library wall. Your reaction will very likely be "Huh?," as you have no idea which aspect of the situation I am indicating or why I am doing so, since, by itself, pointing means nothing. But if some days earlier you broke up with your boyfriend in a particularly nasty way, and we both know this mutually, and one of the bicycles is his, which we also both know mutually, then the exact same pointing gesture in the exact same physical situation might mean something very complex like "Your boyfriend's already at the library (so perhaps we should skip it)." On the other hand, if one of the bicycles is the one that we both know mutually was stolen from you recently, then the exact same pointing gesture will mean something completely different. Or perhaps we have been wondering together if the library is open at this late hour, and I am indicating the presence of many bicycles outside as a sign that it is. (Tomasello 2008, 3)

So one interpretation offered by Tomasello is that the pointing means 'Look! Your boyfriend is still in the library!' (given appropriate background assumptions). Notably, there are an infinite number of possible interpretations and, hence, objects, in the broadest sense, that might be denoted by particular gestures, because there is an infinite stock of background knowledge that might be shared by the participants in a discourse. As I already said, this is no conclusive argument against the ordinary way of conceiving of primary meaning. It is just supposed to show that *if* you are ready to call this 'primary meaning', you must be defending a very weak notion of lexical meaning that allows for some atomic signs to possibly denote almost anything.

Besides, the assumed 'meaning' of a pointing gesture is incomplete anyway, I suppose. Because even if it worked, the only thing it would do is determining the reference. While being one of the major components of meanings, it is at least questionable whether reference really is everything interesting about semantics. Note also that some important details have been skipped over by subsuming different things under the heading 'pointing gesture'. The second example ('construction site') involves so-called 'iconic gestures', which contribute (propositional) content that goes beyond mere reference. The question, then, is how to individuate *different* gestures. How many are there? When are two gestures type-distinct? Are the meanings of all types of gestures learnt separately? These are non-trivial questions, which one needs to answer if gestures are supposed to have primary meaning.

To sum up, gestures represent a second example of empirical evidence against primary meaning conceived of as reference relations, given that gestures are treated on a par with words. According to Davidson's distinction between a prior theory and a passing theory (Davidson 1986), what enters into the former are primary meanings, the things we know about the meaning of a sign prior to a situation in which it is used. I have shown that in the case of gestures this amounts to saying that primary meanings could be so thin as to allow for just any denotation. Therefore, the quintessence of the evidence collected above in regard to Davidson's 'prior/passing theory' distinction is that one's 'prior theory', i.e. the kind of information available before one enters into a specific communication situation, can't possibly consist solely of knowledge of reference relations and truth-conditional functions.

2.2.3 Multimodality

Keeping the above discussion of gestures in mind, it seems natural to link these results with the discussion of compositionality. The semantic framework that will emerge throughout this book is based on the assumption that utterance meaning, as opposed to mere 'sentence meaning', plays a crucial role in semantics. In this view, describing the mechanism by virtue of which *actual* referents of referring expression are determined is part and parcel of a theory of meaning. In this regard, gestures figure prominently, as they 'contribute' essentially to utterance meaning. More importantly, gestures contribute to utterance meaning in virtue of having specifiable meaning. In light of these considerations, there seems to be an interesting link from compositionality back to gestures, which will be discussed be-

2 Meaning: Primary, Pragmatic, and Others

low by contrasting it with classical views about reference fixing. Gestures thus far have played a very marginal role in linguistic semantics and especially in philosophy of language.[55] The only theme occurring from time to time in work on indexicals is indeed *reference fixing*.[56] A typical instance of which would be:

> That <pointing gesture> is a table.

Actually, starting from pointing gestures used to fix reference gives me a good opportunity to motivate the relevance of gestures for semantics in general. In the above example, a pointing gesture—which deliberately is not specified any further—serves the purpose of singling out an entity in the immediate visual vicinity. The semantics of indexicals is commonly given in terms of a token-reflexive description along the lines of

> "This" used in context c refers to the entity that, when "this" is uttered, is the most salient entity in c.

The means employed to 'achieve' salience are diverse. In the easiest cases, the linguistic context (i.e. usually the immediately preceding sentences) uniquely qualifies a specific entity as the most salient one relative to this particular context. In cases where the linguistic context does not suffice to disambiguate "this", reference is typically fixed by accompanying gestures, normally a pointing gesture. A third possibility, of course, is that a given entity is the most salient one in a context even without being made so either by verbal nor non-verbal signs. A simple example of this variant would be a thunderstorm suddenly approaching in an otherwise average situation: for example, two people standing on a meadow on a sunny afternoon when one of them, shortly after a loud noise, gives a quizzical look. If, in such a situation, the other person were to say "That's a thunderstorm",

---

[55] Though see Gärdenfors & Warglien (2013).
[56] For example, Newen (1996) points out that

> If one of a variety of equally salient objects is highlighted by a pointing gesture of the speaker, then the deictic expression occurring in a corresponding demonstrative utterance refers to that object that is highlighted by this pointing gesture. (1996, 87, my translation)

2.2 Constructionist Approaches to Semantics

the reference of "that" would not need to be fixed by any extra means, be it verbal or non-verbal. The context makes the thunder salient all by itself.

All this, to be sure, requires a lot of additional theory 'in the background' in order to work properly. Most importantly, one would need to have an account of 'standard contexts', which is hard to get anyway. Also, the mechanisms by which entities 'increase' their salience relative to contexts are not sufficiently clear up to now. Most remarks in the literature are suggestive at best in this regard. For instance, if the context is altered accordingly, it is not that clear any more that a pointing gesture to a table, executed by the current speaker, makes the table the most salient entity. Altering the context means altering the standards according to which something counts as more or less salient. Besides the issues involved with standard contexts and salience, it is, in general, unclear whether the object referred to is the most salient one in the first place. For example, Borg (2004b) discusses the relevance of speaker intentions in determining referents. Her conclusions differ from my own, since, for example, reference fixing for her is not a proper aspect of semantics.[57] Be that as it may, reference fixing seems to involve a lot of different aspects: standard assumptions, salience, speaker intentions.[58] However, all these background assumptions are not particularly relevant for the present issue. For the moment, allow me to just take for granted that some account or other can be developed that can handle these problems.

A pointing gesture can be conceived as bearing its own semantics. Seeing pointing gestures (and other gestures) that way helps in understanding how they figure in human communication and is indeed a necessary con-

---

[57] Her basic idea here is that establishing *actual* referents is a matter of utterances and, hence, important only for communication. Actual reference, in her view, can only be resolved 'post-semantically' via intention-reading processes. The realm of semantics is restricted to just those aspects of meaning that are 'available' independently from contexts of utterance, i.e., roughly, Kaplanian characters. In the present context, what is relevant is that Borg acknowledges that, still, actual referents are determined by contexts, broadly construed (including intentions and intention ascriptions).

[58] Whereby I do not want to invoke the impression that speaker intentions can directly alter meaning (as in Humpty Dumpty scenarios). Rather, the claim is that the use of indexicals can only be *explained* by assuming that speakers are guided by certain intentions (and assumptions about which intentions are recognisable by typical interlocutors, and so on), and that hearers' interpretations are intention-guided as well. I return to this in 8.3.

dition for understanding gestures at all. To see what we are getting at, let me first recapitulate how pointing gestures figure in classical semantic theories in philosophy. The meaning of "this", as I illustrated above, can be determined independently from what exactly determines salience in a context. Its meaning can be stated in terms of a rule that relativises its reference to a particular context. The pointing gesture, on the other hand, contributes to the semantics of the overall utterance only by chance: any other means that similarly would have increased salience in that context would have had the very same effect.

Compare this with the semantics of "() is a table", which arguably in most philosophical accounts of meaning is an open sentence which requires only one more constituent, which determines the reference, to make a full sentence. Truth-theoretically speaking, "() is a table" is true iff the entity to which the expression that fills the argument position refers is a table. The pointing gesture does not contribute to the semantic value in any reasonable sense. The only thing it 'does' is make some entity or other *salient* (or more salient at any rate). The semantic contribution needed to turn "() is a table" into a complete sentence—and hence, in a particular context, into a complete utterance—is the one by "this".

This view underestimates the semantic contribution of gestures to the semantics of whole utterances. The thing is that many gestures are significantly more complex than mere pointing gestures (Mittelberg & Waugh 2009, Müller 2013a). Many gestures even have properties that are typically considered defining features of verbal signs (e.g. conventionality). Gestures interact in very different ways with verbal signs and contribute in interesting ways to the semantics of utterances. Still, let me start with pointing gestures first. Pointing gestures are never used without communication intentions. Classifying *arm movements* as 'pointing gestures' implies that these arm movements serve certain purposes.[59] It might even be true that their main purpose *is* increasing the salience of particular objects in given contexts (the ones pointed to, probably). Be that as it may, pointing ges-

---

[59] For the moment I will be focusing specifically on arm movements. These are the most important pointing gestures. It is possible to point to some entity by using other parts of the body, e.g. by moving one's eyes or legs. For sake of simplicity, I restrict myself to arm movements though. Everything I shall say is intended to equally apply to other bodily movements.

tures, qua being pointing gestures, do not occur outside of communication contexts. In other words, classifying something as a pointing gesture implies that what matters is communication.

2.2.4 Compositionality Applied to Multimodality

My above comments are based on the assumption that different types of semantic units (words, gestures, intonations, postures, facial expressions, and so on) share a common sense in which they are meaningful. Put another way, since meanings are ultimately nothing over and above descriptions, meaning statements concerning different meaningful types are theoretically on a par.

Ultimately, the objects of study of a theory of meaning are utterances.[60] Several types of 'signals' contribute to the overall meaning of utterances. This aspect of semantics is called multimodality. A problem arises as soon as one tries to link multimodality with compositionality. In classical theories of meaning, the meaning of a word like "pet" (i.e. 'pet'), when it gets compositionally combined with the meaning of "fish" (i.e. 'fish'), must be 'pet fish' (that is, the meaning of "pet fish"). Considerations like these normally serve the purpose of defeating particular theories of meaning: since, for example, a prototypical pet is a dog and a prototypical fish is plaice, the prototype theory is claimed to be false (Fodor & Lepore 1996), for a prototypical pet fish is a goldfish.[61] For the present purposes, these considerations are irrelevant though. The point is just the following: "pet" and "fish" belong to the same domain (linguistic signs). So it is relatively straightforward to see how they can be combined to form larger units. When it comes to *multimodal* compositionality, however, the question is: how can semantic descriptions of different modal domains be integrated into one compositionally combined semantic description of a full utterance?

---

[60] This is highly controversial. I give a detailed justification in 8.2.3 and 8.3.

[61] There are a lot of tacit assumptions at work here, all of which, however, are irrelevant in the present context. For example, one central assumption in the argument is that compositionality ensures that, e.g., prototypes combine compositionally: the meaning of a compound expression is, or so the argument goes, the 'sum' of meanings of its constituents. I ignore these niceties here, as 'ordinary' examples of compositionality are mentioned here only to serve as a starting point for my discussion of gestures.

2 Meaning: Primary, Pragmatic, and Others

The only reasonable solution seems to be reverse engineering, because the only available information to start with is utterance meaning, i.e. the 'end product' of communication processes.

Reverse engineering is a method of ascertaining the production process of an object by deconstructing the end product. For example, (there are people who think that) Chinese engineers copy German cars (e.g. Mercedes's GL) by first *trying to find out how the end product was built*. They have no access to the relevant construction plans; they are thus forced to work with the car itself as their only source of evidence. In the present case, the end product is utterance meaning; the construction plans are the atomic semantic constituents and their mode of composition. Reverse engineering applied to linguistics means: deconstructing utterance meaning—which is given—into its constituents. In the case at hand, the task is 'simplified' by the fact that parts of the 'construction plans' are already known. We know the meaning of the *verbal* constituents of multimodally composed utterances. This amounts to saying that in these cases, the meaning contributed by a gesture must be utterance meaning minus verbal aspects.

Here is a toy example that illustrates this. Instantiations of "that" in conjunction with a particular pointing gesture have (relative to specific background assumptions) a determinate referent. Typically—though not necessarily—the object referred to is the object pointed at. Notably, establishing reference is achieved by combining the interpretations of pointing gestures and of the word "that". Reference is an integral part of semantic theories; therefore, assigning interpretations to gesture and verbal sign in such a way that their combination can uniquely determine a particular reference is primarily a semantic task (and does not belong to pragmatics). Given that the reference is known, determining the semantic contribution of verbal and gestural sign means finding two appropriate interpretations that, if combined, yield the desired output (the object referred to, which, by assumption, is given).

The solution along the lines of classical theories in philosophy is quite boring, though illuminating. It will serve as my starting point. Semantic theories that are particularly designed to handle indexicals often use indexes (see above). In indexicalist accounts, indexicals are expressions with certain indices (of which the obvious ones are time, place, speaker).[62] The index values determine the context of utterance. The indexical "that" is a function from contexts of utterances to extensions. In natural language, the character of "that" can be characterised thus:

> "That", uttered by speaker S, usually refers to the entity that is most salient in the relevant conversational context.[63]

In this reading, "that" is a term whose semantics is somehow unsaturated. In particular, one is in a position to figure out its referent only relative to the relevant contextual cues.[64] The semantics of "that" *in conjunction with the semantics of the pointing gesture* determine the semantic value of a particular "that" utterance. Accordingly, the semantics of a pointing gesture thus must be something like the following:

---

[62] In fact, time, place, speaker, and anaphoric reference are typically the only contextual features that get incorporated into a formal theory of meaning. Borg (2004b, e.g. pp. 52–62) stresses that intentions, in particular, are difficult to handle in formal approaches. I think, though, that her reservations apply, in effect, to all potentially 'interesting' contextual cues such as common ground, world knowledge, plausibility assumptions, default assumptions, co-text, knowledge concerning one's interlocutors, social conventions, and so on (i.e. interesting in that they are relevant for fixing actual reference).

[63] For ease of presentation, I omit other potentially relevant contextual factors such as time and place. Also, I simply take for granted here that "salience" can be defined rigorously. This, of course, is a topic on its own.

[64] Cf., for instance, Higginbotham (1994, 92–93):

> [...] the truth conditions of sentences with context-dependent elements are themselves conditional, dependent upon the satisfaction of conditions that are not in general represented in utterances of those sentences. Consider an utterance with demonstrative 'this' in subject position, a form that places no categorial limits upon the referent, and is limited in context only by the requirement that the referent be appropriately proximate. If the utterance is, say, 'This is red' then (ignoring tense) the conditional truth conditions are [as follows]:
>
>> If the speaker of 'this is red' refers with the utterance of 'this' therein to x and to nothing else, then that utterance is true if and only if x is red.

A pointing gesture, in the majority of cases, serves the purpose of increasing the salience of the object towards which it is directed.

This leads to the intermediate result that an instance of "that" plus pointing gesture towards object x supposedly refers, ceteris paribus, to x.[65] Note two things: firstly, my description of how "that" gets its reference can be considered to be more or less uncontroversial, for everything said thus far is just making explicit what is implicit in, e.g., Kaplanian semantics, anyway. Secondly, it is not particularly difficult to 'combine' two descriptions, although they concern two totally different domains (linguistic sign vs gesture). I will illustrate below how easily this generalises to other cases.

Crucially, the effect of executing a pointing gesture can sometimes be achieved by linguistic means. One could just equally increase the salience of an entity by, for example, describing it. Still, it is important to bear in mind that modal-specific signs are not equivalent in meaning to the linguistic expressions that are their corresponding descriptions. An immediately evident example is irony. Metaphorically speaking, irony 'reverses'

---

[65] The CP clause is required here because the 'meaning' of a pointing gesture is, by its nature, underspecified. That is, the salience of which object exactly is increased by a given instance of a pointing gesture necessarily depends on further, potentially unknown, factors. To take a variant of Borg's (2004b, 178) example: if I point at a CD cover, whereby I increase, very roughly, the salience of this cover, the addressee still does not know to which *object* my corresponding "that" tokening *refers*. Exactly this is at stake here: the meaning of pointing gesture in conjunction with an indexical. I could be referring to the CD cover, the artist, the picture, the music style, and so forth. All of which depends on my—the speaker's—intentions, and the recognition thereof. In this particular example, there are arguably two further 'classes' of information that might be relevant. One is the question as to which kind of thing is salient in this particular context anyway—independently from the pointing gesture as such. For instance, which topics did I mention in the previous conversation? Another one is the basis for my decision to consider this specific pointing gesture an appropriate means of directing the addressee's attention to a particular object (cover, music style, etc.). For example, am I familiar with the addressee's background knowledge ('world knowledge'), and am I justified in thinking that, on the basis of this knowledge, the addressee is likely to be able to figure out the actual referent? So there are a variety of factors that influence the actual referent of an indexical in conjunction with gestures, which are at least partly underdetermined by the two clearly identifiable constituents. In other words, the process of reference fixing of indexicals is context-dependent in a way that goes beyond those features of contexts of utterance that are formally specifiable such as time, place, and speaker.

the propositional content that is expressed 'literally'. There are certain typical triggers for irony, one of which is intonation. A linguist might describe the meaning of an intonational pattern that typically triggers ironic readings by saying that this particular pattern means 'What I'm saying is meant ironically'. Everyone would understand such a description. And everyone would understand, *based on this description*, the use of the intonational pattern at hand. However, saying that 'what I'm saying is meant ironically' has quite a different effect on one's audience than using this pattern.

Hence, although gestures and the like sometimes substitute linguistic signs, they are definitely not equivalent to them all the time. The linguistic description is always just an approximation. The better my interlocutor is able to understand a gesture (or the like), based on how I describe its meaning, the better the description. Which is to say that the problem of compositionality in the domain of multimodality can't be solved by simply 'substituting' the gesture with a semantic description that corresponds to or approximates it. Gestures, in other words, have their own semantics.

Salience as the link in reference fixing between the semantics of indexicals and the corresponding 'contribution' of gestures is just one option among many. For instance, Borg (2004*b*, passim) repeatedly emphasises that finding out about actual reference is a matter of communication (not semantics), in particular a matter of reading and ascribing intentions. In regard to indexicals, she defends the view that '[c]ontext-dependent expressions have a lexical entry which merely specifies a rule for generating a token expression's truth-conditional contribution' (2004*b*, 166). This works quite well for her own example, "I": if x utters "I", then this token refers to x. It is also relatively straightforward for the case of "that" relativised to salience: if x is the apparently most salient object in the vicinity of a speaker uttering "that", then this token refers to x. By itself, the assumption that determining reference is primarily a matter of intention-reading[66] seems very plausible to me. The problem lurking here is that one needs to specify the 'conditionalised T-sentence' for "that" (analogously to "I"). In particular, if *intentions* are the pragmatically relevant factor in determining the actual referent in a specific context, then the conditionalised semantic rule associated with "that" must inevitably recur to intentions as well. Roughly,

---

[66] See, e.g., Borg (2004*b*, 209).

along the following lines: if x is the object an utterer of "that" wanted to refer to, then this token refers to x. In this case, the 'contribution' of a pointing gesture might not be increasing salience (as such), but rather to indicate the particular object to which the speaker wanted to refer.[67] At this point, I only want to span the logical space of possibilities. So I shall leave the detailed discussions to later chapters. Let me just note here that this example already shows that incorporating gestures into one's semantics is far from trivial.

For compositionality to start off, a *common format* of meaning representation is required. This common format might be descriptions of use in natural language. I showed how straightforward it is to 'compose' utterance meaning, given the context-related, underspecified meanings of "that" and pointing gestures. On the other hand, it is hard to imagine alternative, more sophisticated possibilities that would not recur to use. I have concentrated on the simplest possible case, and even in this case, use plays *the* essential role in that it determines which factors increase salience and thereby fix the relevant reference. It is even clear that this salience-increasing factor is implicitly taken for granted in classical theories of meaning, which lends further support to it.

Now for more complicated cases. Examples include:

- Emphasis (gesture, pause, intonation) (e.g. Bartels 1999)

- Referential/iconic gestures (e.g. Indefrey & Gullberg 2010)

- Code-switching sign language/natural language (e.g. Emmorey, Borinstein & Thompson 2005)

- Multimodality in general (e.g. Cienki & Müller 2008, Müller, Cienki, Fricke, Ladewig, McNeill & Teßendorf 2013)

- Gestures expressing propositions (e.g. Streeck 2009)

In prefaces, introductions, and the like, people very often declare that their respective theories only deal with 'meaning' in a specific, limited sense. The above list of examples of cases of multimodal compositionality is likely

---

[67] To be sure, increasing salience is *one* way of doing this.

to invoke the impression that 'meaning' is understood here in a sense that deviates from this standard. The worry could be that the present proposal might be too permissive. Accordingly, my aim in the following is to show that the way I employ the term "meaning" crucially accords with the established practice.

To be sure, showing this amounts to nothing less than saying a few words about what a semantic theory *is* in the first place. First and foremost, a semantic theory is a theory that is about the meaning of communicative acts (cf. section 7.2.1). Accordingly, without even defining "meaning" more precisely, one may already exclude cases like "This means the end of the Cold War", which clearly involve the metaphorical sense of "meaning". The really interesting cases concern, for example, facial expression. I want to defend the view that facial expressions have meaning *in exactly the same sense* as words have meaning. This is, to say the least, not obvious. However, the refusal to accept anything as meaningful units other than words, sentences, phrases, and morphemes, for example, is rooted in biases, I think. The three most important ones are probably: focus on declaratives; focus on written language; focus on literal meaning. Focussing on these three elements gives a distorted picture of which underlying properties one expects to find in the area of semantics.

From a pre-theoretic stance, the central notions of modern theories of meaning—intension/extension, truth-evaluability, inferential validity, etc.— look somewhat counter-intuitive. At least pre-theoretically, one would think that a theory of meaning should cover the whole range of available evidence in the realm of meaningful entities. That is to say, a theory (i) should be guided by all available evidence and (ii) should account for all observable phenomena in the semantic domain. An unbiased view on language includes, among other things, recognising that a large amount of human communication takes place orally; that a great portion of human communication is non-verbal; that truth-evaluability is relevant for a minority of cases even in written language; and that language use is, to a large extent, often imperfect, rhetorical, ad hoc, etc. This is pretty close to a moral that Tarski drew in his classic 1944 paper, in which we read that:

> *The problem of the definition of truth obtains a precise meaning and can be solved in a rigorous way only for those languages*

2 Meaning: Primary, Pragmatic, and Others

> *whose structure has been exactly specified.* For other languages—thus, for all natural, "spoken" languages—the meaning of the problem is more or less vague, and its solution can have only an approximate character. Roughly speaking, the approximation consists in replacing a natural language (or a portion of it in which we are interested) by one whose structure is exactly specified, and which diverges from the given language "as little as possible." (Tarski 1944, 347)

The crucial point in this polemic is that he acknowledges that he considers his theory to be fundamentally inapplicable to natural languages (in their present form). For a start, English seemingly contains 'its own' truth predicate, i.e. a predicate that is applicable to sentences of the *very same* language it itself belongs to. In this sense, Davidson's project of turning a Tarskian theory of truth into a Davidsonian theory of meaning seems to contradict one of Tarski's most basic assumptions. The problem is not just that the 'natural' truth predicate differs from the one envisaged by Tarski. The more fundamental problem is that even the most basic theoretical ingredients—the meaning stipulations for singular terms and predicates—are disentangled from natural language semantics.

A quite illustrative example is vagueness. The 'base clause' for "chair", for example, is: x satisfies "() is a chair" if and only if x is a chair. But whether that is actually the case in English depends on which objects people actually apply "chair" to, i.e. it depends on use. Probably, the verbal behaviour of many people diverges with respect to "chair" and chairs. That is to say, whether the cited base clause is accurate depends on whether the meaning we as theoreticians attach to its right-hand side matches the meaning of "chair" in the idiolect of that person to whom knowledge of the base clause is ascribed. Davidson assumes that features like productivity can only be accounted for if we assume that people have implicit knowledge of Tarskian theorems.[68] Davidson's solution to this, namely to posit

---

[68] In Davidson's own terms:

> [...] a theory of meaning for a language L shows "how the meanings of sentences depend upon the meanings of words" if it contains a (recursive) definition of truth-in-L. And, so far at least, we have no other idea how to turn the trick. (1967, 310)

2.2 Constructionist Approaches to Semantics

that both sides of the T-biconditionals are semantically equivalent by definition (Davidson 1967, 314–318)—i.e. to say that we are dealing with *interpreted* sentences—amounts to saying that we are not dealing with (actual) natural language after all. This is because only formal languages are interpreted languages in the relevant sense.[69] People just have passed on certain expectations that shape their definition of "meaning". My justification for taking a more liberal stance towards this definition is: we need to clarify the appropriate order first. That is: let us examine the phenomena first, then start theorising, not the other way around. The phenomena—some of which I just listed—simply *require* that we recognise that certain elements have meaning.[70]

Consider the following example: someone says "Nice weather!" By making an accompanying facial expression, she indicates irony. Accordingly, her respective interlocutor would understand that she, the speaker, is under the impression that the weather is bad (here and today). The facial expression *must* mean 'Attention, irony!' because if the whole utterance means 'Bad weather!' (as it does by assumption) and "nice" and "weather" can't be *solely* responsible for this (which, again, they can't by assumption, since "nice" plus "weather" means, all else equal, 'nice weather'), then something else must be in charge of eliciting this interpretation. Nothing is simpler than assuming that the meaning at hand is composed of the meanings of "nice", "weather", and the facial expression.

Thus, in the conception of "meaning" defended here, people, when they *understand* other peoples' signals, do nothing more than implicitly associate a certain use with these signals. Building on this understanding, it is not hard to see how people 'compose' meaning across several modalities. They just use facial expressions to indicate, e.g., irony, just as they would use any other means with which they could achieve the same aim, including utterances of the form "I mean this ironically". Concerning multimodality, the original problem is thus not solved but postponed. Since description of use already *is* a common format of meaning representation, it is not more prob-

---

[69] I am assuming "interpreted sentences" defined along the lines of, e.g., Stalnaker (1999, 36).

[70] Chapter 8 is devoted to a detailed discussion of this.

2 Meaning: Primary, Pragmatic, and Others

lematic to combine different intermodal descriptions than it is to combine ones from the same modality.

2.2.5 Constructionist Primary Meaning: The Case of Malapropisms

Taken together, there are theoretical considerations that speak in favour of 'ordinary' primary meanings (e.g. in referential terms), while at the same time empirical evidence suggests the contrary. This means: on the one hand, I should incorporate into my theory of meaning the theoretical intuitions that lead to the assumption of primary meaning. On the other hand, however, I should try to avoid doing this by actually postulating reference relations (and related 'meanings'), because the empirical evidence speaks against it. The first thing to do, therefore, seems to be to examine pragmatics and compositionality more closely in order to find out whether there is any *other* way of accommodating both features. In other words, the task is to do without ordinary primary meanings and, at the same time, to answer the intuitions that give rise to them in the first place. In the case of the semantics/pragmatics distinction, people typically—albeit implicitly—assume that this—omitting primary meaning—is in fact impossible (as the distinction requires lexical word meaning). Regarding compositionality, many theorists take for granted that there are no alternative ways to conceive of compositionality (especially Fodor).

Showing that an alternative approach, which does not involve reference postulates, is achievable amounts to presenting a framework for a new account of meaning. In the next section, I will be discussing particular cases that can't be handled appropriately within classical frameworks. The discussion will be particularly focused on the semantics/pragmatics distinction. Compositionality will be dealt with separately; here I only need to show that compositionality is compatible with my own approach. In order to keep things simple, I stick to the terminology I already introduced above. That is, instead of doing away with 'primary meaning' altogether, I propose a *redefinition* that is capable of accommodating the empirical results that I have discussed above.

Malapropisms will serve as a starting point for the following discussion. Here is an example of a (German) malapropism:

2.2 Constructionist Approaches to Semantics

(2.1) Wir sollten hier ein Exemplar stationieren.
We should here a sample position.
'We should do something as a warning.'

The classical picture sees the intended meaning as parasitic on the conventional meanings of the expressions used. In comic terms the story goes like this: the hearer of the utterance computes the meaning of the sentence on the basis of the meanings of its parts. This literal interpretation is: 'We should position a sample here', which hardly makes any sense (under normal circumstances). The hearer then figures out that by replacing the phonetically similar "Exempel" for "Exemplar" and "statuieren" for "stationieren", the sentence would make perfect sense. Given certain background assumptions (in particular concerning world knowledge), the hearer, therefore, is able to figure out that 'We should do something as a warning' is the most reasonable interpretation of the sentence. This meaning of the whole sentence is computed from the parts of the sentence (and their possible combinations) exactly as in the case of the first 'try', save for replacing the two 'inappropriate' terms with the 'correct' ones and assuming *their* primary meanings instead.[71]

The classical source for such inferentialist, neo-Gricean approaches to semantics/pragmatics is Bach & Harnish (1979). Their framework takes classical primary meaning for granted; the relevant inferences they posit operate on the full content 'literally' conveyed by a given speaker. Thus we read:

> We view linguistic communication as an inferential process. The speaker provides, *by what he says, a basis for the hearer to infer what the speaker intends* to be thereby doing. [...] In general, the inference the hearer makes and takes himself to be intended to make is based [...] on mutual contextual beliefs [...], as we call such salient contextual information. (Bach & Harnish 1979, 4–5, my emphasis)

The idea here is that whatever language users de facto convey, their conveying something at all is always parasitic on their competency in a lan-

---
[71] Malapropisms became famous in philosophy of language due to the 'later' Davidson, who discussed them extensively in his *A Nice Derangement of Epitaphs* (1986).

guage (i.e. lexical knowledge), their interlocutors' corresponding competency, and their shared beliefs about these competencies. For instance, hearers are said to rely on the so-called 'presumption of literalness', which is

> The mutual belief in the linguistic community C_L that whenever any member S utters any e in L to any other member H, if S could (under the circumstances) be speaking literally, then S is speaking literally. (Bach & Harnish 1979, 12)

In general, the *basis* of inferentialist approaches to utterance meaning is always 'literal', i.e. context-independently specifiable sentence meaning.

First evidence supporting the claim that there must be an alternative way of how we arrive at the meaning of an utterance without the detour via reference postulates comes from the observation that the procedure just described is simply not applicable across the board. There are cases of successful human communication that do not seem to operate on sentential meaning. This suffices to establish the claim that there must be an alternative route. To begin with, the example above is somewhere in the middle on a continuum of cases to which the classical picture is more or less applicable. For example, the obvious inappropriateness of "Exemplar" could trigger the relevant inferences. Irony is another very good example of cases where one could easily get the impression that the classical picture gets at least something right. This is because the intended reading of an ironic utterance is the 'opposite' of the literal meaning. In the "Exemplar" example, the strategy seems still quite plausible, because world knowledge can be exploited in finding out that "Exemplar" is used inappropriately here, which, in conjunction with the phonetic similarity of "Exemplar" and "Exempel", might cause the hearer to conclude that the speaker mixed up the two. So the gist is this: there are cases (e.g. irony) in which inferentialist strategies work quite well and others (e.g. a slip of the tongue) in which they work fairly well. Accordingly, the most interesting cases are those in which people are able to determine utterance meaning *without* accessing the alleged literal sentence meaning.[72]

---

[72] This is an area of research in which people seek answers on the basis of empirical data. Typically, the underlying idea here is that shorter reaction times for specific interpretations of sentences (e.g. Recanati's minimal proposition) indicate that language users

2.2 Constructionist Approaches to Semantics

To see what is actually happening, it will help to look at examples in which the goings-on are not obscured by contingencies like phonetic similarity. That is, examples which resemble malapropism, irony, etc. in that their pragmatic meaning is recognisable; but in which that fact can't be explained in terms of primary meaning. The idea here is: if recognition of pragmatic meaning can be explained sufficiently for these cases, the same strategy—which by assumption must be a strategy that does not recur to primary meaning—might be similarly applicable to other cases. The following example will serve as a starting point for the discussion:

(2.2) Das Wetter ist heute aber usellig.
The weather is today however cold.
'It is cold today.'

The peculiarity here is the word "usellig", which is unknown in Standard German (unknown, at least, beyond the borders of the Ruhr area). In a context in which speaker and hearer are debating the weather, and in which it is obvious to both of them that the weather is bad (and obvious that this is obvious to the respective other, etc.), an otherwise competent speaker of German is able to recognise the meaning of "usellig" in this specific conversational context. Of course, this is partly due to the fact that the hearer understands "Das Wetter ist heute aber ___". But the relevant point here is that, by assumption, "usellig" (and hence the whole utterance) can't be understood by the hearer on the basis of its primary meaning (for this would require this meaning to be known in advance).

Following Horwich here, to understand a word is to implicitly know its use. Understanding in actual communication situations has, trivially, two aspects: the hearer's and the speaker's perspective. From the hearer's point of view, understanding lies in the ability to recognise the speaker's use of a given term in a given context (e.g. to recognise that "usellig" means 'cold', 'unpleasant', 'misty'). It is the speaker's 'responsibility' to enable such understanding—e.g. by taking into account what is common ground between them. Which sources, so to speak, enable the hearer to understand

---

'access' these interpretations more directly—vice versa for longer reaction times. For some (more or less) recent research in this area, see Nicolle & Clark (1999) and Noveck & Reboul (2008).

2 Meaning: Primary, Pragmatic, and Others

a given utterance is secondary from the theoretician's perspective, as long as understanding can be established. In the malapropism case, it is possible to give an inferentialist explanation for how understanding is established (due to phonetic similarities). In the "usellig" example, this possibility is no longer given, since "usellig" is unknown to the hearer and shares no commonalities with familiar words.[73] Which is to say: *if* there were any inferential processes involved (in order to arrive at the intended interpretation), these are not processes operating on "usellig". What the Tomasellian programme, quite plausibly, suggests here is that a hearer is able to understand the utterance in question because the involved interlocutors engage in a cooperative activity (e.g. informing the other about one's impression regarding the weather outside).

So even if *certain* classes of linguistic effects—like malapropisms—can be explained *in terms of primary meaning*, namely by recognising the *inappropriateness* of the term actually uttered, there remain other cases for which such an explanation is unavailable. This, in turn, might be interpreted as indirect evidence against primary meaning even in the former cases. Because the latter kind of explanation—which, to be sure, is up to now only a *sketch* of an explanation—is equally applicable to malapropisms and the like. This is an issue I will return to in 8.3. In the present context, let me just note that if one tries to explain malapropisms (and similar effects) without ordinary primary meaning, the relevance of cues such as phonetic similarities does not vanish. In other words, the inferential processes that lead from, say, "Konifere" to "Koryphäe" must and can be kept in a modified framework. The upshot is this: there seem to be cases in which hearers know what a speaker meant, although they do not primarily rely on primary meaning, i.e. on what is literally said. In fact, in these cases pragmatic meaning seems to be retrievable without any prior knowledge of the primary meaning of relevant constituents. A satisfying theory of meaning has to accommodate this result.

Thus far I have really only hinted at a solution to the problem of how hearers achieve understanding in cases where they can't rely on their prior semantic knowledge. A more detailed picture will emerge in the course of

---

[73] Save for the hearer's syntactic bootstrapping capacities (Gleitman 1990). For example, the ending "-ig" signals that "usellig" might be an adjective.

this book. The purpose of the present chapter, rather, is to present a range of examples that question the status of primary meaning in semantic theory. The above discussion was focused on primary meaning in general. However, primary meaning in terms of reference/satisfaction is specifically relevant for varieties of truth-conditional approaches to semantics; they *require* reference, whereas usage-based theories *contingently* employ referential terms. This severely limits TCS's explanatory resources. A very illustrative case at hand in this regard is language acquisition, an issue to which I shall turn now.

2.2.6 Constructionist Language Acquisition

Language acquisition is a difficult issue for Davidsonian and neo-Davidsonian approaches, since these frameworks are first and foremost theories that are specifically designed to handle competencies of fluent natural language speakers. Remember, one major motivation for Davidson is the problem of explaining productivity, which, in his view, can only be solved by assuming that people master recursively defined rules that compute sentence meaning from given atomic meanings of the relevant constituents. This explanation, however, concerns what people allegedly know *now*. It is blind as to how they learnt to 'associate' word forms with meaning. For example, it is silent on the obviously learnt ability of human communicators to associate "bank" with either 'riverbank' or 'financial institution'. There are many problematic aspects in this context that TCS faces, one of which is that the relevant base clauses (e.g. that "snow" refers to snow) are either known or unknown. Spelling out semantic knowledge in terms of knowledge of reference relations does not allow for intermediate steps in the ontogeny of semantic abilities (i.e. degrees of knowledge).

Emma Borg, in a recent attempt to defend neo-Davidsonian semantics,[74] addresses the problem of learnability very briefly. She says: word learning seems to be intimately bound to one's mindreading ability, i.e. one's ability to recognise others' mental states, in particular intentions (Borg 2004*b*). This, it seems, contradicts her own theoretical framework insofar as she assumes that semantic competence is completely disentangled from inten-

---

[74] Her most relevant works include: Borg (2004*b*, 2004*a*, 2012*a*, 2012*b*).

tions and the speaker's or hearer's ability to ascribe or recognise them. But, she claims, this apparent conflict may be solved thus:

> Any appeal to intentionality as a fundamental element in acquiring a lexicon is, I believe, compatible with a modular theory of linguistic (and specifically semantic) understanding which claims that appeal to speaker intentions is not necessary in order to grasp literal linguistic meaning. This is because the conditions necessary to set up the linguistic system in the first place need not be the same as the conditions subsequently required to be in place for the proper functioning of that system after it has been set up. Even if we ultimately decide that language acquisition *is* an essentially inferential process requiring sensitivity to speaker intentions, there is no direct move from this idea to the claim that linguistic understanding *per se* is such an inferential process, appealing to such a sensitivity. (Borg 2004*b*, 139, emphasis original)

The crucial step here is the claim that 'there is no direct move from this idea [language acquisition requires usage-based explanation] to the claim that linguistic understanding per se is such an inferential process'. Trivially, that is true in the sense that the concession concerning language acquisition does not *imply* TCS's falsity. However, it does reveal that there is a huge explanatory gap, which is not easy to bridge.

In the quoted passage, Borg concedes that some plausible current theories of word learning make usage-based assumptions.[75] Although, in fact, there is no 'direct move' from this concession to a usage-based theory of meaning (in contrast to, for example, a usage-based theory of word learning), it places the burden of proof on the formal semanticist's or minimalist's side. Two reasons are especially relevant in this context. Firstly, if usage-based explanations are already required for language acquisition,

---

[75] More precisely, she talks about intention-reading capacities and hearers' inferential processes operating on those capacities. I think it is legitimate to call the approaches that she summarises here 'usage-based', as the philosophically relevant point is that children associate a given word with a particular meaning *only due to the acquaintance with that word type in specific contexts of utterance*. See, for example, Borg's quotations from Bloom (2000).

there must be *really* good reasons to give an alternative, potentially contradictory explanation for 'linguistic understanding per se'. Secondly, without further support there is absolutely no reason to think that suddenly—in the blink of an eye—understanding develops from being based on mindreading capacities to being based on knowledge of reference relations.

Here is one small argument in support of the last claim. Suppose that Borg is right in assuming a fundamental distinction between understanding in language acquisition and understanding per se. Then there are two possibilities for diachronic meaning shifts. One is that meaning shifts involve abilities different from mindreading capacities; which is absurd, for that would further complicate the picture. Or meaning shifts rely on the very same abilities that are employed in language acquisition (e.g. mindreading); which is also implausible, for in this case the minimalist explanation of 'linguistic understanding per se' would become even more superfluous. Either way, one quite severe problem with Borg's picture seems to be the idea that word learning lies in recognising which word forms belong to which referents—lexical knowledge which is fixed, once it is learnt.

More generally, the problem seems to be Borg's deep conviction that semantics is an area of study that is ultimately disentangled from the study of communication and utterance comprehension.[76] She acknowledges without much hesitation that utterance comprehension clearly involves pragmatic processes. As just seen, she even goes as far as to acknowledge that language acquisition recurs to essentially the same mechanisms that are relevant for utterance comprehension in general. Here, I think, Borg underestimates the scope of her 'no direct move' claim. The problem is that, in effect, her thesis is this: understanding in word learning contexts involves only pragmatic processes; but once word meaning is learnt, the very same processes are not sufficient any more for understanding. This is implausible, if anything is. Let me elaborate a bit. For conceptual reasons, language acquisition must be possible without semantic knowledge regarding the words the acquisition process is concerned with. (Otherwise it is not word learning.) Crucially, Borg—rightly, I think—assumes that the acquisition of lexical knowledge depends on one's ability to comprehend utterances in which the relevant word occurs (cf. her short review of Bloom's

---

[76] See especially the second chapter of her 2004 book and her 2012 book, respectively.

experiment; Borg (2004b, 136–138)). Taken as a whole, this amounts to saying that the areas of language learning and language application essentially require usage-based explanations; but *what* is learnt (i.e. what constitutes understanding) is not (knowledge of) use but (knowledge of) usage-independent reference relations.

It is important at this point to remember that usage-based theories do not deny that competent speakers rely on lexical knowledge. Horwich, for example, would be perfectly happy to acknowledge that the meaning of "snow", for example, depends on snow (e.g. due to the frequency with which people use the word "snow" in the presence of snow). He would even claim that his theory is able to explain, in usage-based terms though, why and how "snow" *refers* to snow. The point here is that lexical knowledge—knowledge concerning stable word meaning—is a central ingredient of mainstream usage-based theories. Bearing this in mind, Borg's conviction that usage-based explanations are required for language acquisition and communication but that nevertheless lexical knowledge is usage-independent looks even more implausible.[77] The underlying problem is that evidence in favour of Borg's conclusion that is based solely on the observation that human behaviour is specifically guided by lexical knowledge is unavailable, as the rival theory (usage-based semantics) posits lexical knowledge too. The only remaining option that I see here is to argue that the *explanation* of lexical knowledge itself fares better in truth-conditional terms than in usage-based terms. I do not see this. On the contrary, there is good reason to assume the opposite: if language acquisition and communication require usage-based explanations—as the minimalist acknowledges—*and* lexical semantics can be accounted for in terms of use as well, then the by far most elegant explanation is based on the assumption that lexical knowledge lies in implicit knowledge of use.

---

[77] To be sure, talking about 'usage-independent' here is a bit tricky. Borg certainly does not want to say that what terms actually mean is independent from use (after all, use determines that "bank" means either 'riverbank' or 'financial institution'). Furthermore, she certainly also does not want to say that lexical knowledge as such is use-independent (e.g. acquiring lexical knowledge involves mindreading capabilities). Rather, her claim is that the lexical knowledge people have, once they acquired it, is use-independent in the sense that they know something about the meaning of a given term, independently of how it is applied in specific communication situations (e.g. the knowledge that "snow" refers to snow).

2.2 Constructionist Approaches to Semantics

A related worry in the context of language acquisition is that neo-Davidsonians who acknowledge that acquiring lexical knowledge is facilitated by utterance comprehension face the following difficulty. Toddlers are able to comprehend whole utterances, but they do so by treating them (first) as unanalysable units. This phenomenon is usually labelled 'holophrase' or 'frozen phrase'. The basic idea here is that although toddlers can *understand* and *apply* these phrases in accordance with their interlocutors' use, they do not see the underlying (lexical and syntactic) structure of these phrases. From a philosophical point of view, the problem here is that this obviously undermines Davidson's conviction that the human ability to understand well-formed complexes is tightly linked with one's prior knowledge of recursive rules. Tomasello (2003*a*) summarises his view as follows:

> [...] children's early one-word utterances may be thought as 'holophrases' that convey a holistic, undifferentiated communicative intention, *most often the same communicative intention as that of the adult expressions* from which they were learnt [...]. [In the case of frozen phrases] there is different syntactic work to do if the child is to *extract productive linguistic elements* that can be used appropriately in other utterances, in other linguistic contexts, in the future. For this the child must engage in a process of segmentation, with regard not only to the speech stream but also to the communicative intention involved—so as to determine *which components of the speech stream* go with which components of the underlying communicative intention. (36 and 38, all emphases mine)

Such a view is perfectly compatible with what Borg, for example, says about word learning, i.e. that it crucially involves being capable of reading minds. However, this is incompatible with the Davidsonian ideas in at least two respects. Firstly, it undermines Davidson's view that language comprehension proceeds from the bottom up, so to speak. Rather, in the view advocated by Tomasello, language comprehension is primarily a top-down process, i.e. children *first* understand utterances in context and *then* begin to deconstruct utterance meaning into its (context-independent) lexical and syntactic constituents. Secondly, Tomasello's remarks on holophrases and frozen phrases also question the idea that the *result* of such abstraction processes might be anything like (knowledge of) the Tarskian base clauses that, Davidson thinks, underlie adults' cognitive abilities. To summarise, language acquisition is, in several respects, highly problematic for Davidson and his disciples. The fundamental issue is that, with conceptual necessity, language acquisition (as opposed to language application) requires that *structures* (i.e. constructions at several levels of description, especially words and syntactic structures) are learnt on the basis of a *prior understanding of the complexes that are built according to those structures.* That is to say, language acquisition must primarily be explained in terms of abstraction. But if Davidson's story about utterance comprehension fails in the case of the acquisition process, then there is no reason to assume it will fare any better in the 'ordinary' cases of regular language use.

3 Usage-based Theories of Meaning

The central idea underlying this book is that usage-based approaches in the philosophy of language are worthy of being reconsidered for two opposed reasons. On the one hand, recent developments in relevant empirical disciplines clearly support a usage-based approach to semantics—either by being based on usage-based assumptions themselves, or by implicitly assuming such a theory framework. On the other hand, the currently by far most successful theory in that area—Paul Horwich's 'use theory'—is being severely challenged due to its restriction to truth-evaluable content. In simple terms, the most reasonable strategy, therefore, seems to be to take the 'use theory' as a starting point and suggest possible improvements with respect to classes of words (sentences) that hitherto have been hard to handle in that theory (effectively, all classes of words that lack truth-evaluable content).[1]

I divided this chapter into two and a half sections. First, I shall introduce the basic idea of accounting for meaning in terms of use (3.1). This also includes a very brief overview of Wittgenstein's private-language argument and Kripke's interpretation thereof, the reason for this being the relationship between acceptance properties and private-language. In 3.2, I briefly explicate Horwich's notion of 'understanding', as that will become highly relevant in the following chapters. The main section, then, is the third (3.3), in which I shall highlight some obstacles to clarifying the claim that 'meaning is use'. As I already mentioned in the Introduction, I reserve the term "use theory" exclusively for Horwich's approach; the umbrella term for his and related theories is "usage-based theories" (and their cognates).

---

[1] The only alternative here is to propose an all-new theory, which for obvious reasons is beyond the scope of this book.

3 Usage-based Theories of Meaning

3.1 Use

Famously, the later Wittgenstein is known for having popularised the idea that meaning is use. In the *Philosophical Investigations*, he says:

> One cannot guess how a word functions. One has to *look* at its application and learn from that. (Wittgenstein 2009, 116e, emphasis original)

All mainstream theories in philosophy that consider themselves 'usage-based' see Wittgenstein as their most relevant predecessor. The common assumption of all these theories is easy to state: meaning is use. The difficulties arise when it comes to specifying what this claim amounts to. I would like to keep this chapter very focused. So there are several things that I *will not try to do* here. Most importantly, I will not delve into exegetical issues.[2] Furthermore, I will omit a detailed discussion of usage-based approaches other than Horwich's. For instance, inferentialism (à la Brandom) is a very influential theory of meaning and a prominent exponent of the usage-based camp (Brandom 1994, 2001). However, instead of giving a comprehensive overview of usage-based approaches, I would rather focus on one specific theory in order to discuss some more details. Anyway, Horwich's theory is pretty much in line with my own view that I outline in chapters 6, 7, and 8. Discussing his theory will therefore serve as a backdrop against which I can present my own ideas by explicating important differences. In 3.1.1, I will introduce Horwich's main thesis that the use of a word can be traced back to some underlying acceptance property. Then, in 3.1.2 and 3.1.3, I discuss some critical aspects of this view.

3.1.1 U Equals A(x)

> The overall use of each word stems from its possession of a basic acceptance property. For each word there is a small set of simple properties which (in conjunction with other factors and with the basic properties of other words) explain total

---

[2] I refer the interested reader to the impressive work of Peter M. S. Hacker, which is an invaluable source in this regard (e.g. Hacker 2013).

linguistic behaviour with respect to that word. [...F]or each word, w, there is a regularity of the form

> All uses of w stem from its possession of acceptance property A(x),

where A(x) gives the circumstances in which certain specified sentences containing w are accepted. (Horwich 1998, 44 and 45, emphasis omitted)

The basic idea in so-called 'usage-based' accounts of meaning is that the meaning of a given term is—in a sense to be specified—constituted by how the term is used (in a given language community). In slogan form: meaning is use. This, of course, is misleading. Clearly, not all aspects of a term's use can alter its meaning. But the simplified slogan helps to see what is common to all usage-based theories, namely that they all acknowledge that language is first and foremost a means of communication.[3] And that therefore,

---

[3] This might sound a bit trivial but it has been widely neglected (and denied) in much of the history of philosophy of language. The study of language as a philosophical sub-discipline has always been the study of (context-free) declarative sentences, detached from concrete situations, in which they could possibly be uttered or asserted: 'The mainstream approach to semantics—*almost universally accepted amongst linguists and philosophers*—is truth-theoretic' (Horwich 2008a, 233, my emphasis). Interestingly, proponents from both camps consider themselves lonesome heroes defending the minority view. For example, Borg (2004b, 15) begins her discussion of truth-conditional semantics with this:

> What kind of thing must an agent know to be a competent language user and what kind of cognitive architecture might lie behind our linguistic abilities? The answer I want to give [...] *is not, perhaps, especially fashionable at the moment*. For I want to argue for a kind of formal approach to the study of language, which [...] continues through into such approaches as the truth-conditional theory of meaning of Davidson et al., and the model-theoretic approach championed by Kaplan and others. (My emphasis)

Philosophically speaking, it is relatively unimportant which side is correct here. Based on the number of publications and prominent current proponents, I have the impression that Horwich is right in this regard. What is more important is that the (real or merely felt) dominance of TCS has left its mark with respect to what people think semantics is all about: context-free specifiable meaning of word/sentence types. This influence is present even in theoretical frameworks that are subsumed under the heading 'usage-based' such as Horwich's use theory or Brandom's conceptual role semantics. In chapter 7, I shall be defending the following two claims: (i) that philosophy of language as an

3 Usage-based Theories of Meaning

roughly speaking, meanings are determined according to how they figure in actual communication situations, i.e. how they are in fact used.

Particular theories differ in the way they cash out the idea that meaning is use. So, in order to get to grips with what is meant by saying this, I shall, by way of example, examine Paul Horwich's view on the matter. This will then serve as a good starting point to develop the basis of a new framework, as Horwich incorporates many correct insights into his theory. Yet, the use theory suffers from some specific difficulties. These difficulties, however, can be handled without omitting the general idea of Horwich's theory.[4] First of all, Horwich introduces, as a theoretical device, a 'capitalisation convention', according to which the meaning of "dog" is DOG, the meaning of "tea" is TEA, and, generally, the meaning of a term can be referred to by writing the word in capital letters.[5] It is important to bear in mind that a capitalised word is nothing more than a name. By definition, this name denotes a meaning. If you were asked 'What is the meaning of "dog"?', the answer "DOG" would be perfectly correct. Yet, the capitalisation convention is only a means of metalinguistic description. It goes without saying that one who is able to apply this tool does not, by virtue of this ability, automatically know the meaning of the term to which it is applied. This is the point of introducing the convention in the first place. It enables us theoreticians to refer to specific meanings, irrespective of how they can be individuated.

Writing words in capital letters is a way of *referring* to meanings, but the interesting question is how to *determine* them (in principle). Horwich pursues a two-step strategy in this regard. Firstly, he claims that meaning properties are constituted by use properties. Secondly, he then goes

---

independent discipline is better off if it focuses on actual communication rather than on the corresponding abstractions thereof; and (ii) that language is primarily a means of communication and, hence, its theoretically most interesting aspect is use. For the time being, I take the results of this discussion for granted.

[4] The most important resource here, in which the so-called 'use theory' is presented in full detail, is his 1998 book *Meaning*. Further elaborations of particular objections raised against this theory are collected in Horwich (2004, 2005, 2010). Horwich's most recent defence of (parts of) the use theory is his 2012 book.

[5] In accordance with Horwich's style, I use capital letters to indicate placeholders for meaning—but only in quotes and paraphrases from Horwich. See also the Terminological Preliminaries (1.2).

3.1 Use

on to say that the use properties of a given word are determined by certain acceptance properties associated with sentences in which that word occurs. Actually, Horwich's line of argument is a three-step strategy, for his intermediate thesis is that, ultimately, the meaning of natural-language expressions can be identified with the corresponding concepts (1998, 44). Horwich treats the term "means" as approximately synonymous to "indicates". Thus the use of "dog" by a given speaker indicates the presence of (the concept) DOG in the speaker's mind. Mutatis mutandis, for any other word of the speaker's idiolect. The other two steps of this 'three-step account' are exactly the same as in the two-step version. Some avoidable difficulties are incurred by choosing the three-step strategy. This is why I read Horwich as actually defending the simpler picture.

If meanings are concepts, then concepts either play an explanatory role in one's theory of meaning or they do not. If they do, then what one is doing in specifying the underlying non-semantic properties that constitute meanings (read: concepts) is specifying a theory of mental representation (and the origin of these) rather than a theory of meaning proper. Horwich himself suggests this reading by comparing his theory of *meaning* with, for example, the 'Informational Theory' (see Dretske 1986) or the 'Teleological Theory' (see Millikan 1989) (Horwich 1998, 52). Taken seriously, this amounts to saying that what a term means, in the sense of specifying the underlying properties of meaning, is determined by a theory of mental representation. This, I think, obscures the debate at best. Even if, in the end, utterances of words 'indicate' the presence of corresponding concepts in the speaker's mind, this should be largely independent from one's theory of meaning. Otherwise the question of the underlying (non-semantic) features of meanings is simply moved from the philosophy of language to the philosophy of mind. At worst, this strategy might even be completely misleading, because it is dubious whether there really is such a simple one-to-one connection between concepts and the corresponding words usually used to express them. On the other hand, if concepts play no explanatory role in the theory of meaning, then to identify them with meanings seems superfluous. For even if such an identification may be relevant to make one's theory compatible with certain theories of mental representation, the identification of meanings with concepts, if it is explanatorily insignificant, is irrelevant to a theory of meaning *as such*. In such a case, it

3 Usage-based Theories of Meaning

seems strange to include the 'identity thesis'—meanings are concepts—into the list of the theory's main principles (as is done in chapter 2 of Horwich 1998).

I shall briefly summarise in somewhat more detail what it means to reduce use properties to acceptance properties. First of all, the notion of 'constitution' applied here means that both properties are co-extensional, but that their corresponding predicates are not synonymous (Horwich 1998, 18–27; in particular p. 25, n. 8). So, to say that meaning properties are constituted by use properties is just a very careful way of expressing the idea that 'meaning is use' or that 'what a word means is determined by how it is used'. The more interesting thing is how use properties can be characterised appropriately. The solution developed by Horwich is unique to his account. It is worth taking a look at how it works in greater detail.

'Use properties' are really only placeholders in the use theory of meaning. The explanatory work is done by those properties with which use properties are identified, i.e. by acceptance properties. Now, what are acceptance properties? The basic idea is this: there is, for each word, a basic acceptance property that can be expressed by a single sentence (maybe a complicated conjunction) which is normally accepted by speakers of a given language and in which the word in question occurs. The acceptance of other sentences in which this very word occurs can be explained on the basis of acceptance of the former sentence. This is why it is called the 'basic' use property. Specifying his use of "use", Horwich explains that the use property is

> [...] some property of a word type. This property is specified by a generalization about tokens of that type—by the claim that they are all explained in terms of a certain acceptance property, a property specifying the circumstances in which designated sentences containing the word are held true. [...For example,] that we have the disposition to assert "That is red" in the presence of evidently red things [...]. (Horwich 1998, 57–58, emphasis omitted)[6]

---

[6] Please note the apparent similarity between Horwich's way of spelling out acceptance properties and Peacocke's remarks on concept possession:

Taken together, the main thesis of Horwich's use theory of meaning is that meaning properties (of word types) are constituted by acceptance properties (of the same word types). I will be discussing the postulated close connection between use and acceptance further down. For now, I end the exposition of Horwich's theory and turn to some characteristics of it that might seem problematic. In the process I focus on those features that are of general interest for my own framework. In particular, I shall briefly present Wittgenstein's famous private language argument, as Horwich's explication of 'use' along the lines of 'privately accepted sentences' seems to be at odds with the impossibility of private language.

3.1.2 The Private Language Argument

> The [use theory of meaning] is focused on the semantic feature of a word. The distinctive form of that feature is that it designates the circumstances in which certain specified sentences containing the word are accepted [...]. For example, it may be that
>
>> the acceptance property that governs *a speaker's overall use* of "and" is (roughly) *his tendency to accept "p and q" if and only if he accepts both "p" and "q"* [...].

> A possession condition for a particular concept specifies a role that individuates that concept. The possession condition will mention the role of the concept in certain transitions that the thinker is willing to make. These will be transitions that involve complete propositional thoughts involving the concept. In some cases they are inferential transitions; in others they are transitions from initial states involving perceptual experience. (1992, 107)

Which, if applied to an example, gives us that

> For a thinker to possess the concept *square* (C) [...] he must be willing to believe the thought Cm_1 where m_1 is a perceptual demonstrative, when he is taking his experience at face value, the object of the demonstrative m_1 is presented in an apparently square region of his environment, and he experiences that region as having equal sides and as symmetrical about the bisectors of its sides [...]. (108)

3 Usage-based Theories of Meaning

> [...] Think of all the facts regarding *a person's linguistic behaviour*—the sum of everything he will say, and in what circumstances. [...] It is not implausible that something like [this regularity is] what explain[s] *our overall use* of the [word] "and" [...]. (Horwich 1998, 45, emphasis added)

The highlighted passages of this quote indicate that the theoretical scope of the use theory of meaning is to account for the linguistic behaviour of linguistic communities (and thereby to state the meaning of the words deployed by that community) by listing the acceptance properties of the individual speakers. This by itself—the switch from speakers to language communities—may be questioned. It involves some important background assumptions that would need to be justified independently. For instance, one would need to assume that dispositions to accept certain sentences are distributed more or less homogeneously among individuals that belong to one single linguistic community. Also, one would need to allow for differences in dispositions that reflect no corresponding differences in meaning: when, for example, a blind person is not disposed 'to apply "red" to an observed surface when and only when it is clearly red'.[7] All this will be largely ignored in what follows. Instead, I would like to focus on the question: doesn't this fly in the face of Wittgenstein's famous 'private language argument'?

To begin with, the private language argument might be considered problematic for a usage-based account (formulated in terms of acceptance properties) because, as is shown by the above example, acceptance properties are individuated in terms of individual dispositions to accept certain sentences. According to a popular reading of the later Wittgenstein, this can't

---

[7] "Red" is Horwich's favourite example. Note, however, that colour predicates are a particularly difficult class. You might want to argue that the semantics of "red", used by a blind person, differs indeed—even if only slightly—from its ordinary semantics. In this case, replace "red" with a proper name: intuitively, the meaning of a proper name like "Aristotle" can't have a different meaning in the mouth of a seeing person compared with a blind one. Either, then, you still want to maintain the claim that meanings correspond one-to-one to dispositions, which would result in plentiful new meaning postulates (e.g. dispositions of blind people to apply a given term as opposed to allegedly different dispositions of seeing people), or you make sure your dispositional descriptions are as general as to be applicable to seeing and blinded people alike (to name just two groups). Theoretically, disjunctive analysis might be a third, viable option.

be right.[8] An individual speaker can't tell a case where he follows a rule—say, to accept "p and q" only when he also accepts "p" and "q"—from the case where it only *seems* to him as he would follow this rule (although he actually follows a different rule or no rule at all). In Wittgenstein's terms, following a rule and thinking to follow a rule fall into one and the same category in regard to private language. This means that an individual speaker as such would not know whether he follows a 'rule' correctly.

The original argument, in the *Philosophical Investigations*, is presented in §§ 243 and following. The literature on the topic is fairly independent from the actual source, i.e. the literature on *the* private language argument is not just exegetical but also, to a large extent, concerned with the content, with the pros and cons of the possibility of private language per se (Stern 2011). This holds in particular for the most famous and most influential interpretation by Saul Kripke in his *Wittgenstein on Rules and Private Language* (1982). The interpretation of Wittgenstein's work that Kripke offers is sometimes considered to be fairly independent of the original, which is why it usually goes under the name "Kripkenstein". Kripke describes Wittgenstein's worries in terms of *dispositions that match past use*. The basic idea is that if one takes into account one's whole past use of a given term, then there is no fact of the matter as to whether this term had the meaning that one typically thinks it actually has (now and in the past). This is because there are always many competing rules that accord with past use. Here is Kripke:

> Given [...] that everything in my mental history is compatible both with the conclusion that [by "plus"] I meant plus and with the conclusion that I meant quus [i.e. answer "5" for all summands greater than 57], it is clear that the sceptical challenge is not really an epistemological one [i.e. rooted in insufficient available data]. It [i.e the problem] purports to show that nothing in my mental history or past behavior – not even what an omniscient God would know – could establish whether I meant plus or quus. But then it appears to follow that there

---

[8] The Wittgenstein works that are most relevant here include his *Philosophical Investigations* (Wittgenstein 2009) and *Remarks on the Foundations of Mathematics* (Wittgenstein 1967).

> was no *fact* about me that constituted my having meant plus rather than quus. [...] There can be no fact as to what I mean by 'plus', or any other word at any time. (1982, 21)

So, Kripke's worries seem to be even more relevant for Horwich's acceptance-based approach, as there seems to be no way to determine whether *any* dispositional analysis of the meaning of a given term is ever correct.

3.1.3 Acceptance in Usage-based Theories

For our present purposes, I largely ignore exegetical issues. The main aim of this chapter is to give a rough overview of the possibilities and limitations of usage-based theories of meaning. A discussion of Wittgenstein's and Kripke's contribution to the rule-following problem is a good starting point, as there is reason to think that dispositions will figure prominently in any promising philosophical account of usage-based semantics. In other words, there is simply no other reasonable way than to spell out usage-based semantics in terms of the relevant dispositional analyses. Therefore, it will be worth looking more closely at how these two thinkers, Wittgenstein and Kripke, influence contemporary discussions in the field. Specifically, two questions or concerns are relevant in the present context:

(1) Following Kripke, one might want to say that it is impossible to 'read off' particular dispositions that one (supposedly) had in the past from the facts alone, i.e. a given past use of a term is always compatible with a variety of dispositional analyses. In other words, there is more than just one 'correct' interpretation of past use.

(2) Similarly, Wittgenstein emphasises that one can't follow a rule privately, for in that case rule-following and attempting to follow a specific rule would fall into one. This seems to contradict Horwich's approach, for Horwich construes the analysis of core use properties in terms of privately accepted sentences.

Discussing these two 'aspects' of Wittgenstein's criticism will help to illuminate one of the most crucial challenges that today's usage-based theories still face.

3.1 Use

Ad (1): In Horwich's version of the use theory of meaning, use properties are constituted by acceptance properties. In the sense in which water may be identified with H_2O, use properties may be identified with acceptance properties. Acceptance properties, again, are stated in terms of dispositions: they are 'tendencies to accept' specific sentences. Tendencies are dispositions. But then, it seems, Kripke's interpretation of Wittgenstein can be read as a direct criticism of the use theory.

Consider the word "plus". The use theory of meaning tells us that the acceptance properties (disposition) associated with "plus" determine all uses of that word (except occasional mistakes). Suppose, for the sake of argument, that this procedure works in principle. In particular, suppose that if we—linguists, philosophers of language—know the exact acceptance properties of "plus", we would know how the word is used.[9] The upshot of Kripke's argument, if correct, is that all this is compatible with the claim that "plus" might mean something completely different. Because the adequacy constraint on dispositional analyses is dependent on conformity with the available evidence, which is past applications in this case. The problem here is that, even if the theorems of the use theory are correct in this sense—i.e. if they conform with past verbal behaviour of members of a given language community—a broad variety of competing analyses are *also* still correct. However the use theorist analyses the alleged acceptance properties that constitute one's overall usage, Kripke could always—given the plausibility of his argument—claim that "plus" might mean 'quus' instead.

To be sure, it *may* be that "plus" means addition. It is just that we can not know. Even God does not know this, or so Kripke claims. This is my reply: well, maybe we can't tell from our past dispositions that by "plus" we mean addition (now). So Kripke is right in claiming that these past dispositions do not uniquely fix the meaning of the term. But it is an *apparent phenomenon* that we mean addition by "plus". In order to show this, one may, for example, take a look at how Kripke himself describes the situation:

---

[9] Which is to say that all tokenings of "plus" can be traced back to a person's basic tendency to apply "plus" to such-and-such things in such-and-such circumstances.

3 Usage-based Theories of Meaning

> I, like almost all English speakers, use the word 'plus' and the symbol '+' to denote a well-known mathematical function, addition. (1982, 7)

This quote is from the opening paragraphs of Kripke's essay. It illustrates quite nicely what Kripke explicitly admits in a later section: that his scepticism in regards to dispositional analyses of usage concerns not our present dispositions but our convictions about the dispositions we had in the past.

What is interesting about this passage is that Kripke is using the only available possibility to formulate one major premise of his argument here: the premise that "plus" in English means 'plus'. The only way to achieve this is by referring to 'a well-known function'. The point I should like to emphasise is that this reveals something important about the status of a 'theory' in philosophy. The 'theory' of meaning, whatever its precise form, is not supposed to show that, say, "plus" means 'plus'. Rather, it is just the other way around. "Plus" de facto means 'plus'—*this* is the fact the philosophical theory needs to account for. In other words, the question is not, *which* dispositional analysis is correct (irrespective of whether it concerns past or present use) but *why* a particular one is correct. To be sure, this view per se is not sufficient to *argue* against Kripke's Wittgenstein or Quine's (1960) inscrutability of reference. My point here, rather, is that, *given one's specific intellectual interests*—e.g. designing an empirically validated, philosophically informed theory of meaning—certain problems can simply be bracketed out. Given that we want a theory that fits with our pre-theoretic assumption that "plus" means 'plus', we do not need to consider scenarios in which it meant 'quus'. Given that we want a theory that fits with out pre-theoretic assumption that "rabbit" refers to rabbits, we do not need to consider scenarios in which it referred to undetached rabbit parts.

Ad (2): A related obstacle, which, in particular, applies to the specific variant of usage-based semantics defended by Horwich, is Wittgenstein's observation that one can't follow a rule privately. The way Horwich formulates his idea of 'core use properties' sounds as if his account could fall prey to the Wittgensteinian objection:

> The regularities of use that (I am suggesting) constitute the meanings of words concern the circumstances in which spe-

cified sentences are privately accepted (i.e. uttered assertively to oneself). (Horwich 1998, 94, emphasis omitted)

The gist of Wittgenstein's private language argument is that 'private' rule-following is not rule-following after all. Proper rule-following requires a corrective; e.g. a language community that 'sanctions' obvious deviant behaviour. According to the Wittgensteinian argument, one can't privately accept sentences and thereby conform to a particular regularity. Applied to the use theory, the argument amounts to saying that there can't be regularities like Horwich's 'tendencies' that explain the overall use of a given word by a given speaker. This is because all competing dispositional analyses could be just as correct.

It is not exactly clear what the private language argument is an argument against. In a natural reading, it is an argument against the possibility of a 'private language', where this is a language of a single individual. This affects the quoted aspect of Horwich's theory only insofar as we conceive of it (i) as being concerned with the meanings of words *as they are used by individual language users* and (ii) as referring only to individuals when it comes to meaning constitution. Neither condition is met in the present case. Firstly, although the quoted passage suggests an individualistic reading, it is clear from the outset that the use theory of meaning is a general theory about natural language. It is not directly concerned with idiolects (only to the extent that they affect semantics within language communities). A fortiori, it is not concerned with languages independently from the communities in which they are embedded. It is, if you like, merely a stylistic choice to state the properties that constitute the use of a given word in terms of individual dispositions. This does not affect the fact that the theory applies only to complete natural languages, and, hence, its adequacy is measured relative to them. One idea behind the 'individualistic' formulation of Horwich's dispositional analysis is surely the following. There is a very close link between individual tendencies to accept certain sentences and meaning in language communities, because the relevant dispositions are clearly shared by a significant proportion of people. In this respect, it makes sense to say that meaning is constituted by individual tendencies (had they been different, the relevant meaning would have been different as well); but the meaning to which this analysis applies is still meaning in communities. Within a community, people share particular tendencies such as the tendency to apply "red" to red objects.

A second relevant clarification in this context is the following. Although the sentences Horwich talks about are *privately accepted* sentences, the relevant tendency is *determined* and *corrected* by the language community that the person who accepts sentences participates in. So, although it is surely correct, and in fact quite accurate, to say that the basic disposition that constitutes my overall use of the term "red" is my tendency to apply it to red objects, my motivation behind this use—i.e. the corrective at play here—is that other members of my language community have a similar tendency. From this point of view, Horwich's dispositional analyses in terms of privately accepted sentences concern language use in communities. For this very reason, Horwich's appeal to privately accepted sentences is immune to Wittgensteinian private language objections. In a similar fashion, Kripke himself notices that

> What is really denied [with the private-language argument] is what might be called the 'private model' of rule following, that the notion of a person following a given rule is to be analyzed simply in terms of facts about the rule follower and the rule follower alone, without reference to his membership in a wider community. (Kripke 1982, 109)

Applied to the use theory of meaning, this amounts to the following: meanings are constituted by individual dispositions to accept certain sentences. These dispositions, in turn, are influenced by the language community in which the individual speaker participates.[10] In this sense, the private language argument is no threat to the use theory of meaning, since it is a the-

---

[10] In the passage quoted above, Kripke is dealing with meaning ascriptions, rather than meaning itself. But there is an immediate link between our actual ascription practice and meaning constitution. Due to this link, Kripke's remarks are immediately relevant also for meaning constitution. If a given community ascribes certain meanings to the words used by a given speaker whenever he is following a particular rule (and refrains from doing so otherwise), then the person in question, if he wants to be understood, will try to *conform* to the behavioural expectations of others. For example, when the language community expects me to apply "red" only to evidently red things (under appropriate conditions), and I recognise this expectation, then I will—on the whole—make sure that I apply "red" accordingly, i.e. I will, normally, apply it only to red things. The mean-

ory about language communities. This ensures that individual speakers *do not privately follow rules (i.e. conform to specific dispositions), although they privately accept certain sentences.*

In light of this specification, the problem with Horwich's core use properties—as far as the private language argument is concerned—seems to be that it invokes an unjustified individualistic reading of his examples. However, this weakness might be repaired quite easily by emphasising the two issues that I just mentioned. Given these, one could say that the meaning of a word is determined by the set of acceptance dispositions that an individual speaker has with regard to certain sentences in which that word occurs. Words have meaning only relative to language communities: in particular, the respective sets of dispositions are, on the whole, distributed homogeneously among a community. They are accommodated by speakers according to the behavioural expectations of others. Of all possible word meanings that are in accordance with the set of 'compatible' dispositions (e.g. 'plus' vs 'quus'), a word *de facto has just that meaning that is also in accordance with the ascription practice within the relevant language community.* This last proviso answers Kripke's worry that there might be competing dispositional analyses that accord with past use. However, Kripke himself acknowledges that in regard to *present* usage we all seem to agree that by "plus" we mean 'plus' (as opposed to 'quus'). If that is correct, then, by the same token, the same is true of past use—since we all agree that we meant 'plus' in the past. The sceptical philosophical reply—'You can't know for certain that this is the correct interpretation of your past dispositions!'—is inadequate here, for the alleged 'epistemological' problem is a rhetoric trick. We *know* which interpretation of past applications of "plus" is correct (just as we know which interpretation is correct concerning present use); so, if Kripke's argument indeed shows that this fact can't be captured by certain dispositional analyses, then there is indeed a need to improve the relevant analysis. But there is no need to worry whether our interpretation, on which we agree anyway, was correct in the first place.

---

ing ascriptions of other participants of a language community thus constantly influence one's dispositions to apply certain words.

3 Usage-based Theories of Meaning

Independently from the plausibility of construing a usage-based theory of meaning in terms of acceptance properties, in this section it has been shown that such an account can be defended against objections that focus on the private language argument. Basically, it is just a matter of precise formulation. A clear answer to the question whether private-language arguments are capable of undermining the plausibility of Horwich's theory depends on the exact formulation of acceptance conditions. If it is appropriately relativised to linguistic communities, roughly like in the above formulation, then the argument does no harm to the theory. Nevertheless, this intermediate result leaves it entirely open at this point whether there could be any further problems associated with acceptance-based approaches in general. I return to this question in section 6.2.2.

3.2 Understanding

"Understanding" is a notoriously vague term. In Horwich's theory, it means to have implicit knowledge of the use associated with a given term. I adopt this view in what follows. Therefore, I shall discuss this notion at some more detail in this section.

3.2.1 Understanding and Knowing the Meaning

Now I should like to look in detail at how a use theory in the spirit of Horwich's can be combined with the apparent conceptual equivalence between 'knowing the meaning of x' and 'understanding x'. Both concepts are closely linked, and examining their exact relationship will reveal important aspects of the notion of 'understanding', which figures prominently in usage-based semantics in general, and in the 'use theory' in particular.

'Knowing the meaning of a term' implies understanding it. To see this, it is crucial to first look more closely at the two involved notions, "knowing (a meaning)" and "understanding", respectively. Horwich's suggestion, which I shall adopt in the following, is that to 'understand a term' is to know how it is used. For instance, if the relevant term is in my active vocabulary, I know how to use it, or else, I would know how other speakers use the term. 'Knowing how to use a term' implies, in turn, that one knows the term's inferential role; that one's use is roughly in accordance with the established use within the corresponding community (i.e. that it is correct);[11,12] that one is able to answer appropriately if asked for the meaning of the term; and maybe a bit more, depending on the theory-specific notion of 'use' involved.

To state when exactly somebody can be said to 'know the meaning of "x"' is slightly more complicated. On a very natural, albeit somewhat naïve, reading, it might mean that one is simply able to state the meaning of "x". This is surely one important aspect. True as it is, without further restrictions this is essentially valueless. To name but one problem here, whether statements are appropriate meaning statements depends crucially on the semantic theories considered. In general, there at least as many permissible variants to state the meaning of a given terms as there are semantic theories. What is required here is a theory-independent notion of semantic knowledge. Such a theory-independent conception is likely to be pretty similar to the description of 'understanding' explicated above. Because knowledge of meaning involves essentially knowledge that manifests itself in observable verbal behaviour: which inferences one draws from which sets of premises; which answers one gives to certain questions; how one behaves non-verbally in response to others' behaviour; and so forth. Pressed in this direction, one easily gets the impression that understanding is indeed very similar to semantic knowledge, and that the only thing that is undoubtedly very dissimilar is explicit knowledge of the underlying prop-

---

[11] In this sense, I agree with Horwich that understanding comes in degrees (see Horwich 1998, 17–18).

[12] The idea that understanding a term implies that a speaker's use of that term is roughly in conformity with how the word is used within her language community (or by 'the experts') goes back to Putnam (1975). He discusses this restriction in the context of reference fixing. Horwich expands this restriction and relates it to meaning (as opposed to mere reference); he sees agreement (of use) with the group of 'experts' as a measurement of understanding. In general, a person fully understands a given term when his use is 'correct' in the sense that it is in accordance with the experts' use. The other end is marked by the threshold at which a person can be said to use the same word type as his language community. It is a difficult matter to determine where exactly to drawn the line here. If someone uses "tiger" and does not know that a tiger is an animal, this would surely be below the threshold (Putnam 1975). Still, the threshold for what is appropriate might in fact be substantially low, so that, if one is asked what the meaning of "democracy" is, "a kind of regime" might already count a sufficiently informed answer (in the sense that one 'talks about the same').

erties of meaning. In other words, the expression "knowledge of meaning" in the former sense, in which every competent language user knows the meaning of the terms that he masters, is by its very nature tightly linked to the use associated with the term, i.e. tightly linked to understanding.

3.2.2 Horwich on Understanding

The niceties that are relevant in the area of understanding are worth discussing, since they reveal important aspects of Horwich's use theory. So just like before, when Wittgenstein's rule-following argument served as the starting point for the discussion, understanding and knowledge of meaning will now be vehicles by which I would like to present some details of the theory at stake. The most problematic aspect of Horwich's theory in the context of 'understanding' surely is the so-called capitalisation convention. Because as has already become clear above, it is quite 'easy' to tell the meaning of a word (in a very weak sense of "telling"). If really only *naming* is concerned, it is sufficient to master the convention. The tension between his account and the closely connected concepts of knowing the meaning of a term and understanding it forces Horwich to admit some ambiguity when it comes to what it is to 'know the meaning of a term'. Officially, the meaning of "dog" is just DOG, which in turn is specified in terms of a use property u. However, since no understanding of "dog" is required in getting there, this can't be the whole story, of course. Accordingly, in the passages dealing with understanding, Horwich specifies his notion of 'knowing the meaning of a term' in such a way as to directly referring to use properties, instead of taking the route via meaning properties:

> The degree to which an individual understands a word is constituted by the degree of similarity between what it means in his idiolect and what it means in the communal language. And this degree of similarity in meaning is in turn constituted by the degree of similarity between the explanatorily basic use property, $u(x)$, that determines the word's overall deployment in the community and the use property that determines its deployment by the individual. (Horwich 1998, 17–18)

3.2 Understanding

These facts concerning use properties are known only implicitly, Horwich claims. This allows him to say that somebody can understand a given term, without being able to explicitly state more than the obvious fact that "dog" means DOG, which, in principle, is knowable independently from understanding.

But there is a problem lurking here, because in Horwich's account, evidence to the contrary notwithstanding, 'understanding' and 'knowing the meaning' must fall apart. Horwich seems to admit that there is a very close connection between the two, in particular that, as we assume, knowledge of meaning implies understanding (no matter whether the reverse holds). He claims that 'those who do not understand the word (i.e. do not know what "dog" means) ... [do such and such]', and that there is a 'conceptual equivalence of "understanding a word" with "knowing what it means"' (1998, 16 and 18, respectively). So, in a way he treats both notions as synonymous or approximately synonymous. It makes sense to take Horwich as having the everyday notion of semantic knowledge in mind here. This is, as I said above, distinct from the knowledge associated with the constitutive properties of meaning.

In Horwich's account, almost all knowledge concerning meaning that he discusses in his work is implicit knowledge. The only meaning facts explicitly known (if any) are those about capitalised expressions, i.e. what a speaker might know explicitly is the *name* of the meaning of a given term, *but not the meaning itself.* This allows him to equate understanding with knowledge of meanings: investigation into meanings (for example, by analysing uses in order to list relevant acceptance properties) does not affect one's understanding. Understanding varies with the degree of similarity between one's own use of a given term and how it is used within the corresponding community—and so does knowledge.

So there are at least two senses in which one can be said to know the meaning of a given term. One is the usual, implicit understanding of the notion. On the other reading, 'knowledge of meaning' concerns the metalinguistic knowledge philosophers and linguists try to gather when they examine the constitutive basis of semantics. It seems plausible that the former notion can't be dissolved from the notion of "understanding", for, as already indicated above, they share a common evidence basis: use. In a usage-based understanding of meaning, then, *use* is the commonality

3 Usage-based Theories of Meaning

between the two notions. If I investigate the use that constitutes the semantics of my own language, I explicate—provided I work accurately—a body of information that I already knew implicitly before.

There is just one problematic aspect of Horwich's theory that I would like to mention in the present context. His favourite example of a meaning statement that is based on acceptance properties is this: 'that our use of "red" can be explained in terms of 'the disposition to apply "red" to an observed surface when and only when it is clearly red' (Horwich 1998, 45). This itself is surely correct, or at least very close to the truth. But the example term "red" oversimplifies things here, since its meaning can be analysed—as the example illustrates—largely independently from the meaning of related terms. Semantic holism in its simplest form is the claim that the meaning of a given term is dependent on (or can't be stated independently from) the meanings of other terms that are 'linked' to it (cf. Devitt 1993). The idea here is that language is a 'semantic net' into which all meaningful expressions are embedded. In this view, the meaning of a term changes as soon as any other term in the semantic net is altered (provided they are linked appropriately). Holism is a relatively old idea; its most influential proponent in 20th century philosophy was probably Quine, who famously claimed 'that our statements about the external world face the tribunal of sense experience not individually but only as a corporate body' (1951, 38). Today, there is a variety of different distinctions in the area of holism, none of which, however, is particularly relevant to my point here. "Red", being a colour term, is a word whose meaning is—even if semantics is a holistic enterprise—explicable more or less independently from what related terms mean. This, in turn, means that the 'knowledge of meaning' involved here is in fact quite self-contained. Other examples will probably turn out to be far more complicated than this one.

By way of summary, it seems—in light of the previous discussion—reasonable to define "knowledge of meaning" and "understanding" as follows. A person *knows (explicitly) the meaning* of a given word iff that person is able to state the circumstances in which that word may be applied in conformity with the standards of the respective language community. A person *understands* a given word iff that person knows its use, i.e. she knows how to use it 'correctly' herself (ability of correct application) or how it is used by others (ability of correct interpretation). This knowledge includes:

(i) knowledge of the inferential role of the word; (ii) the ability to use the word roughly in accordance with how the word is used within one's language community; and (iii) the ability to answer (more or less appropriately) questions regarding the meaning of the word.

3.2.3 Understanding and Knowledge Covary

The above discussion, hopefully, shows two things. Firstly, that understanding and semantic knowledge are indeed tightly linked notions. Secondly, that there are several readings of 'knowledge of meaning' at work. Let me summarise the argument by recapitulating these two issues.

The phrase "knowledge of meaning" is ambiguous, it seems, in several respects. One important differentiation proposed by Horwich is between implicit and explicit knowledge. This, however, is problematic insofar as it presupposes a theory-bound understanding of the body of information that is implicit (e.g. knowledge of conceptual role). I think the direction of Horwich's line of argument is basically right, but it should better be formulated in epistemological terms. The *implicit* knowledge concerning meaning simply corresponds to 'understanding'. Understanding is the ability to employ one's implicit knowledge of applying or interpreting particular words, sentences, theories, and so on. This connection seems independent from the semantic knowledge itself. For instance, it could consist of (knowledge of) Tarskian truth conditions. *Explicit* semantic knowledge is knowledge about the constitutive basis of meaning: e.g. knowledge that the meaning of "red" is essentially determined by a tendency to accept the sentence "That's red" in the presence of red objects, or knowledge that "red" refers to a specific colour. Irrespective of one's favourite theory of meaning (i.e. irrespective of whether the postulated explicit knowledge gets formulated in usage-based terms), the touchstone of both implicit and explicit semantic knowledge is observable behaviour. Understanding is an ability, as I just said. Abilities are ascribed on the basis of what people who seem to have this ability in fact *do*.

So, what Horwich does when he claims that he only makes explicit the implicit knowledge that every competent language user has anyway is skipping one step in the above argument. He would need to claim that the explicit knowledge that he postulates (e.g. sets of acceptance proper-

3 Usage-based Theories of Meaning

ties) best explains the behavioural patterns that competent language users show and which we take as evidence for their ability to understand. Summing this up in simple terms, use is not the common factor of implicit and explicit semantic knowledge but it is the common factor in an epistemological sense, namely in the sense that the very same behavioural patterns that justify ascriptions of understanding also justify assumptions concerning a specific constitutive basis of meaning.

In light of these considerations, the link between understanding and knowledge of meaning seems obvious. Understanding is just implicit knowledge of usage-based facts, i.e. knowledge of how words (and the like) are applied and interpreted. One's ability to understand a term is reflected in one's overall linguistic (and non-linguistic) behaviour, but it is *constituted* by one's implicit knowledge of the use properties of that word. Given this, Horwich's proposal for 'measuring' understanding in terms of the similarity of one's use of a term with the overall employment of that term in the corresponding linguistic society seems quite reasonable.[13] For this allows us to say, independently of any theory, some people understand certain words better than others.

3.3 Explicating the Claim

The basic idea behind usage-based semantic theories is that 'meaning is use'. This, to be sure, is a motto or slogan at best. So, one step toward a semantic framework whose value might be assessed appropriately is to make clear what this claim amounts to, once it is spelled out. This is what I would like to do in this section.

3.3.1 Core Use Properties

One argument against usage-based accounts of meaning focuses on the apparent fact that *if* meaning were use (as such), then with every change in

---

[13] Provided the involved background assumptions are plausible. In particular, one would need to justify the assumption that *complete* understanding consists in perfect compliance with the overall use in a given society.

3.3 Explicating the Claim

use, a word would alter its meaning.[14] This is an undesired consequence, for it is contrary to our intuitions. Intuitively speaking, not every new instance affects the meaning of a term. Suppose, just for the sake of argument, that we spell out use properties in terms of acceptance properties. In 2012, one would accept the sentence "Dr Angela Merkel is Germany's current chancellor". A few years later, this sentence wouldn't be accepted any more. Now, if the meaning of "Dr Angela Merkel" depends on all its uses (instantiations of the relevant type) and, hence, can be explained by listing all accepted sentences in which that term occurs, then its meaning has changed somewhere around the time of Merkel's de-selection as chancellor. Rather than accepting this radical result, we would want to explain the difference in use in terms of different facts in 2012 and, say, 2017.

Irrespective of whether one wants to define use in terms of acceptance properties, one needs an answer to this problem. Somehow, therefore, I need to restrict the scope of "use" in my definition of "meaning". On the other hand, I certainly should allow that even small changes in use 'result' in altered meanings. The most obvious case is in which the change is based on a new definition of the term. I shall illustrate this by the example of "planet". On planets, Horwich writes that

> [...] if a planet beyond Pluto were discovered, and we started to say "There are ten planets", we would not thereby have given the word "planet" a new use. [...] [The opponent will then ask in reply], what is the basis of the distinction that is being assumed here between the use facts (like, perhaps, our disposition to accept "Planets orbit stars") which could plausibly be held to constitute *the use* of "planet", and other use facts (like our disposition to accept "There are nine planets") which surely could not? (1998, 59–60)

---

[14] The details depend on the particular theory. For example, according to Horwich's account, a word would—if the objection were correct—change its meaning if the change in use resulted in a corresponding change of the list of accepted sentences (in which that word occurs). See Horwich (1998, 59–60) for a—very short—reply to this objection. The basic idea is to restrict the list of accepted sentences to those necessary to account for all sentences in which the particular word occurs.

3 Usage-based Theories of Meaning

There may be *other* reasons to decline acceptance of "There are nine planets" than the discovery of a tenth planet. In 2006, the definition of "planet" was modified, so that according to the new definition, Pluto is not a planet any more.[15] This, of course, altered 'our disposition to accept "There are nine planets"' (now there are eight planets in the solar system). Horwich is surely right in noting that our disposition to accept "There are nine planets" is, if you like, an inessential aspect of our use of "planet". However, we are certainly inclined to say that our altered dispositions in the case of redefinition is due to a change in meaning. Redefinitions are paradigm examples of altered meanings.

While Horwich's example shows that acceptance properties may differ with constant meaning, the redefinition of "planet" illustrates that, *in regard to the very same acceptance properties*, altered dispositions may also be the result of corresponding changes in meaning. This in itself does not undermine the claim that this disposition does not constitute *the use* of "planet". But it shows that what makes this a case of irrelevant dispositions is *not*—as is suggested by the example—that an empirical observation was involved. It is true that such observations do not directly affect meaning.[16] This, however, is not what sets *these* dispositions apart from others like the disposition to accept "Planets orbit stars". Horwich's point is that he wants to reanimate the analytic/synthetic distinction: our disposition to accept "Planets orbit stars" is left unaffected by any minor redefinitions (e.g. the redefinition that excludes Pluto) or empirical observations. In other words, "Planets orbit stars" is an analytic truth about planets and therefore our disposition to accept this sentence is among the essential dispositions that constitute our use of "planet". The basic idea here is that as long as the analytic truths associated with a given word remain, its core use properties remain the same as well.

It goes without saying that there are alternatives to the Horwichian approach. For example, instead of positing *one* word type "planet", one could acknowledge that there were two different words, before and after 2006.

---

[15] See 'IAU 2006 General Assembly: Result of the IAU Resolution votes', http://www.iau.org/public_press/news/detail/iau0603/, accessed on: 18/06/2012.

[16] Yet they might do so indirectly, as new observations might make a redefinition of terms necessary.

3.3 Explicating the Claim

This, however, would lead to further consequences beyond the scope of this chapter. Many words alter their meaning more or less continuously; compare, for instance, the semantic 'stability' of words like "because/'cuz" or "war" on the one hand and "Aristotle" or "twenty-three" on the other hand. It certainly seems implausible to posit arbitrarily new types here. Accordingly, I shall leave all this aside and focus on the theoretical motivation for core use properties, rather than on their exact design.

Core use properties are, in fact, essential to any usage-based theory of meaning. The mere claim that 'meaning is use' is so abstract and general that, if it were true, it were vacuously true.[17] One respect in which the claim that 'meaning is use' must be specified concerns the apparent fact, discussed above, that primary meaning—or its theory-specific equivalent—plays an important role in a variety of linguistic effects such as irony, metaphor, implicature, etc. For example, the potential of "It's nice weather today" to mean 'The weather is quite bad' in certain circumstances seems to be parasitic on the quite different potential of this particular phrase to mean 'It's nice weather today' in most other circumstances (what is commonly called 'under standard conditions'). Now, if one takes the claim that 'meaning is use' all too seriously, then the problem is that *the* use of a term simply seems to be the totality of all word type instantiations, among them instances of, say, "nice" that mean 'bad', or 'interesting, or 'misplaced', or what have you. Yet, the potential of "nice" to mean 'bad' seems to be rooted *solely* in the fact that "nice" primarily means 'nice', and nothing more. In other words, usage-based theories of meaning are required to systematise use in the sense that they need to distinguish a *core* of use properties that accounts for use tout court (e.g. the core use property that constitutes the potential of "nice" to mean 'nice').

More generally, semantics is not just the study of meaning of natural-language expressions but also of abstractions thereof. Accordingly, semantics not only explains that and why, for example, "nice" might mean 'nice' in a particular situation, and 'bad', or 'interesting', or 'misplaced' in others. It also explains (or should at least be compatible with accompany-

---

[17] Even proponents of truth-conditional semantics or formal semantics potentially agree that use plays *some* role in determining meaning—e.g. they might allow that the type-difference between "bank", referring to an institution, and "bank", referring to a special parts of rivers, is rooted in differences in use.

3 Usage-based Theories of Meaning

ing frameworks that explain) why the interpretation 'nice' is a particularly relevant one and why other interpretations are derivative or peripheral. The idea here is that core use properties can serve as a basis for explanations that generalise over the totality of use. In Horwich's theory, core use properties are identified with distinct acceptance properties, where the latter are stated in terms of dispositional analyses: the core use properties of a given term can, so argues Horwich, be stated by specifying a (singleton) set of sentences which a competent language user would accept under appropriate conditions. For instance, a competent user tends to accept "That's red" in the presence of red objects. This explains his overall employment of the term "red". In this sense, the 'theory' is able to account both for literal as well as peripheral, non-literal word-type instantiations.

The list of sentences the acceptance of which constitute one's (core) use of a particular word needs to be restricted somehow. As should be clear at this point, sentences involving empirical claims certainly need to be excluded; that is, those sentences the acceptance or rejection of which can be explained away by referring to empirical facts are inessential to meaning constitution. In the first example, the acceptance of "Dr Angela Merkel is Germany's current chancellor" depends on whether Merkel is taken to be the current German chancellor. Similarly, for the first "planet" example. In the case of a redefinition, there is no empirical fact (in the relevant sense) that decides the matter. In other words, there must be some non-empirical facts that distinguish essential dispositions from inessential ones. Or, in Horwich's own words: '[…] the way to pick out the particular use property of a word that comprises what we call "the use" is to find the use property that provides the best explanation of all the others' (Horwich 1998, 60). Far from being an answer, this is more like a re-description of the initial problem.

An obvious alternative would be to bite the bullet and accept that *the use* of a word really is the totality of its use. This option, however, runs counter to our intuitions. Consider the redefinition case again: "planet" changed its meaning *and* we modified our use of it ('How many planets are there?' 'Eight!'). But this is not the whole story. We, language users of English, have accommodated our use just because the meaning of "planet" has changed. And this is incompatible with the claim that the total use of "planets"—including our disposition to accept "There are eight planets"—

constitutes its meaning. The interim conclusion, then, is something like this: on the one hand, I can't consistently maintain that the total use of a term constitutes its meaning; on the other hand, there is no conclusive solution yet as to where to draw the line between the dispositions considered essential and the rest.[18]

Another, admittedly less obvious alternative is to give up the idea that (explanatory basic) use properties of a word can be individuated on the basis of acceptance properties. This is because the whole problem concerns only the quite specific issue of how to separate the use-constituting sentences from the class of all accepted sentences. If I would omit acceptance properties, I could also simply ignore the corresponding dispositions. This solution has one further, important advantage. I have already mentioned the problem that a usage-based account that focuses merely on acceptance properties leaves out the huge class of truth-valueless sentences (or words that do not contribute truth-evaluable content). Can we reasonably say that in such-and-such circumstances sentences like "Hello!" or "What the f**k?!" are *accepted*? The words occurring in these sentences surely have their respective meanings, and it is likely that these are determined by how the words are used as constituents in, inter alia, the cited sentences. But you can't accept "Hello!" in appropriate situations in a similar way that you accept the application of "red" in the presence of an object that is clearly red (if you do). Accordingly, in light of the problems facing 'acceptance-based' accounts, I suggest spelling out use properties not in terms of acceptance properties but somehow more broadly (see chapter 6).

This strategy serves two distinct purposes. Firstly, it leaves open the possibility to generalise one's theory of meaning to truth-valueless sentences and words occurring in them. Secondly, it sets issues of meaning apart from the discussion of the analytic/synthetic distinction. The former is a welcome result because it frees me from the need for yet another theory that would then account for truth-valueless sentences. The latter is a

---

[18] The solution that I suggest in part three of this book is to distinguish between semantic descriptions and constitutive bases of meaning. The latter (total use) leaves the relative 'stability' of the former (dispositional analysis) intact, as it were. Typically, when we are talking about 'meaning', what we mean is semantic descriptions, which is why the intuition that total use does not affect meaning directly is indeed correct.

virtue because this is an unsettled debate, and you better play safe and not base your theory of meaning on such a controversial distinction.

3.3.2 Linguistic-Philosophical Terminology

Several disciplines contribute to the project of a 'theory of meaning', among them philosophy of language, philosophy of mind, some branches of linguistics, anthropology, cognitive psychology, etc. They all differ in their theoretical aims and with respect to the 'methods' they employ. When it comes to broad classifications of semantic theories, several distinctions are drawn, of which the distinction 'truth-conditional approaches vs usage-based approaches' is just one.[19]

The term "usage-based" figures prominently across the literature of several professions. The last common ancestor of "usage-based" and its cognates is the work of the later Wittgenstein, especially the *Philosophical Investigations*. This suggests that usage-based theories in different disciplines have a set of basic assumptions they share. Still, "usage-based" as a technical term shows subtle differences in meaning in philosophical and non-philosophical literature. I should say a few words here about those subtle differences.

First, philosophy. In philosophy, usage-based approaches start with the assumption that the meaning of a word *is identical with its use*. Accordingly, a very simple and popular paraphrase of what use theories of meaning claim is, in effect: meaning is use (see above). Of course, this slogan form of the main axiom obscures many important details of the actual theory. For example, take the 'type vs token' issue that is highly relevant in usage-based considerations (see 8.2). I do not want to go into these niceties here but rather illustrate the broader picture. Roughly, when philosophers say that meaning is use they are making a programmatic claim. What they mean is that, in principle, given enough cognitive resources, memory, and information about the world and its history, it is possible to determine (i.e. to state) the meaning of a given word. Philosophers are not particularly concerned with finding out how a word is actually used. Their programmatic claim is merely meant as a contrast to the view according to which

---

[19] Other relevant distinctions are 'semantic theories vs foundational theories' (Speaks 2011) or 'theories of semantic content vs theories of communication' (Borg 2004*b*).

meanings of words are fixed and can be stated without taking into account particular situations in which language is actually applied. That is to say, usage-based theories are counterparts to theories that approach semantics independently from communication concerns.

What is at stake will become even clearer when I take into account some example cases.[20] Here is Horwich (1997b), talking this time about vague predicates:

> [The use-regularities of vague predicates] do not derive from stipulation, but are implicit in our linguistic practice (insofar as they provide the best explanation of that practice). (933)

And

> [...] the explanatorily fundamental regularity in our use of [the vague predicate] "H" is approximated by a partial function A(H) which specifies the subjective probability of its applying as a function of the underlying parameter n (i.e. 'number of grains' for "heap", 'number of dollars' for "rich", etc.) [...] Such a use-regularity results from our having learned, regarding various different values of the parameter n, that they constitute clear instances of "H", somewhat less clear instances, cases in which "H" is definitely not applied, and slightly less certain cases of inapplicability. [...I]nsofar as A(H) is really the *complete* articulation of the basic regularity governing our use of "H", then no matter what else is discovered, it cannot imply a confident application of either "H" or "¬H" to the borderline objects. (933–934, emphasis original)

Again Horwich, this time talking about meaning more generally:

> The overall use of each word stems from its possession of a basic acceptance property. For each word there is a small set

---

[20] The theories listed in the following differ significantly from each other. Here, however, I am currently concerned only with the distinction 'usage-based semantics vs truth-conditional, formal semantics'. Keeping this distinction in mind, different theories—e.g. conceptual role semantics (e.g. Block 1986) and the later Wittgenstein—are theoretically on a par, as they all rest on the assumption that meaning is effectively determined by how language is actually applied.

3 Usage-based Theories of Meaning

> of simple properties which (in conjunction with other factors and with the basic properties of other words) explain total linguistic behaviour with respect to that word. [...] The present theory is focused on the semantic feature of a word. The distinctive form of that feature is that it designates the circumstances in which certain specified sentences containing the word are accepted; and the primary explanatory role of a word's acceptance property is to account for the acceptance of other sentences containing the word. (1998, 44–45, emphasis omitted)

Greenberg & Harman (2006, 242), discussing conceptual role semantics, say that

> Conceptual Role Semantics (CRS) is the view that the meanings of expressions of a language (or other symbol system) or the contents of mental states are determined or explained by the role of the expressions or mental states in thinking. The theory can be taken to be applicable to language in the ordinary sense [...].

And further down in the same article:

> One way to investigate the contribution of use to meaning is to consider how a thinker describes certain imaginary possibilities. For example, one aspect of Mabal's use of concepts is her firm belief that all cats are animals. Other aspects include her firm beliefs that there are cats now, there have been cats in the past, and there will be cats in the future. Another aspect is the way she applies the concept *cat* to particular things. (305–306)

Block (1986), an early proponent of conceptual role semantics, summarises his view thus:

> The internal factor [as opposed to not further specified external factors], conceptual role, is a matter of the causal role of the expression in reasoning and deliberation and, in general, in

3.3 Explicating the Claim

> the way the expression combines and interacts with other expressions so as to mediate between sensory inputs and behavioural outputs. A crucial component of a sentence's conceptual role is a matter of how it participates in inductive and deductive inferences. A word's conceptual role is a matter of its contribution to the role of sentences. [...E]lements of language have a total causal role, including, say, the effect of newsprint on whatever people wrap in it. Conceptual role abstracts away from all causal relations except the ones that mediate inferences, inductive or deductive, decision making, and the like. (628)

Wittgenstein, characterising the notion of a language game, asks:

> Are "there" and "this" also taught ostensively? – Imagine how one might perhaps teach their use. One will point at places and things, but in this case the pointing occurs in the *use* of the words too and not merely in learning the use. – [...] Now what do the words of this language *signify*? – How is what they signify supposed to come out other than in the kind of use they have? And we have already described that. (2009, 9e)

And in his *Remarks on the Foundations of Mathematics* he remarks that

> The *point* of the word "all" is that it admits no exception.— True, that is the point of its use in our language; but the kinds of use we feel to be the 'point' are connected with the role that such-and-such a use has in our whole life. (1967, 8e)

This cursory list of core aspects of different use theories is supposed to show that no philosopher of language seriously intends to *state* the properties that constitute meaning. What most use theorists do is specify the 'register', if you like, in which such properties might be articulated best. Horwich likes to have meaning properties articulated in terms of acceptance properties.[21] Greenberg and Harman consider several possibilities for

---
[21] Interestingly enough, this motif shines through even when the topic is vagueness (see above).

123

3 Usage-based Theories of Meaning

narrowing down conceptual roles, one of which is conceivability. Block, who fancies a narrower variant of conceptual role semantics, tries to capture them in terms of inferential relations. Wittgenstein leaves the question entirely open. This list can probably be extended ad libitum. The point is: the commonality between all these different theoretical frames is that they all try to narrow down the all too trivial slogan that 'meaning is use'.

One key aspect of philosophical theories of meaning is that they draw a general, abstract picture of how meaning statements are possible; real-life meaning statements are not of primary concern here. A second key aspect is that, in contrast to linguistic and psychological theories, specifically philosophical theories of meaning are not designed to be especially useful. To borrow Tarski's phrase here, '[semantics] has no pretensions of being a universal patent-medicine for all the ills and diseases of mankind, whether imaginary or real' (1944, 345). Theories in formal semantics, for example, are typically meant to be implemented one way or other in computer programs (for the purpose of translation, searchability in semantic nets, voice input, etc.), theories in cognitive grammar are motivated by the search for an integrated theory of cognitive capacities of which language is just one aspect (such that one main purpose is that the theory is compatible with related theories in cognitive science). There is no such practical motivation behind semantic theories in philosophy.[22] They follow their own, self-referential rules: typical marks of adequacy are naturalism, generality, uniformity, and so on.

Eventually, a third key aspect of usage-based approaches to semantics in philosophy is this: the notion of 'use/usage' employed in these theories is rather abstract, so to say. What philosophers mean when they say that their theory is usage-based is not that they examine uses of a word in order to find out what it means. What a word means is—to philosophers at least—*always clear* pre-theoretically. In case of doubt, they will *tell* you what a word means. In this respect, meaning statements in philosophy of language inherit an important feature from the thought experiments in which they appear. In thought experiments, there is no epistemological barrier between the reader and the described situation. In order to find out

---

[22] The later Wittgenstein is a bit of an exception in this regard, as he stressed the therapeutic aspect of his work.

what is the case in a given thought experiment, one only needs to read the description carefully. It describes all the relevant facts, or else leaves them unspecified.[23] Philosophers often construct thought experiments that take a certain *semantic* interpretation for granted.[24] Assignment of semantic values often times depends on tacit assumptions in these cases.[25] The claim that 'meaning is use' is a programmatic or methodological statement: if one wants to find out what a word means, the best option is to scrutinise its use (instead of its alleged reference relations). But the examples that are used to underpin this programmatic claim typically presuppose a specific interpretation that is only valid given certain specific background assumptions.

I shall briefly contrast this notion of "usage-based" with the one employed in linguistics and related fields. When linguists claim their theory is usage-based, what they typically mean is (i) that their research is corpus-driven; (ii) that meaning is a social phenomenon, determined by interacting language users; (iii) that the meaning of a word is constituted by its instances; and (iv) that meaning can only be fully comprehended by considering the situational context of utterances (Tomasello 2003a). To be sure, all this is compatible with more philosophically minded use theories. Philosophical and empirical theories alike originate in Wittgenstein's later work. Yet, linguists' and philosophers' respective interests differ. Proponents of usage-based linguistics emphasise that they utilise 'real' data. i.e. actual *use* instead of armchair examples. Philosophers, on the other hand, hardly ever need to recur to real conversations in order to qualify as 'usage-based' theorists.

The gist is this: the term "usage-based" (and its cognates) is a technical term both in philosophy and in linguistics. Although there is allegedly a common origin, both terms differ significantly in current theorising. Roughly speaking, in linguistics the term is more or less synonymous to "corpus-driven", i.e. it expresses the idea that language must be scrutin-

---

[23] Often, most things are specified, because most thought experiments include a clause that says 'this and that is different in the imagined situation; everything else is the same as in the actual world'.

[24] Indeed, there are also a lot of philosophers these days that argue by means of linguistic data (cf. the so-called 'X-Phi movement').

[25] For example, a relatively typical background assumption is that the laws posited by the sciences are, by and large, correct.

3 Usage-based Theories of Meaning

ised in relation to specific situations in which it is applied. In philosophy, "usage-based" is an umbrella term for theories that deviate from the mainstream idea of reducing semantics to reference relations and related notions such as satisfaction, truth, etc. Crucially, though, the two research agendas complement each other. In fact, philosophical theories of meaning can reasonably be conceived as philosophically informed foundations of the empirical theories to which they correspond.

4 Truth-conditional Theories of Meaning

Basically, there are a large number of dividing lines that can be drawn with respect to competing theories of meaning. Here, I would like to focus on just one possible divide; namely the distinctive characteristics of, on the one hand, usage-based theories and, on the other hand, truth-conditional semantics (TCS, henceforth). For the most part, I am going to concentrate on neo-Davidsonian approaches to semantics. I think, though, that most of my critical remarks concerning TCS apply equally to all similar approaches that take explanations of *referential relations* of linguistic expressions to be the hallmark of success in semantics. I have divided the present chapter into two sections. In the first of these two sections (4.1), I will be presenting the general idea behind truth-conditional semantics, which is, roughly speaking, that specifying a sentence's truth conditions is one way of stating its meaning. My plan is to introduce the main motivation *in favour of TCS* by taking a reconstruction of Davidson's famous argument concerning sentence comprehension as my starting point. I discuss this argument in detail by distinguishing between two theoretically independent issues: Novelty[1] and compositionality. The former is, roughly, competent language users' ability to comprehend sentences that they have not heard before. The latter is a well-known feature of natural languages, i.e. the (apparent) fact that the semantic value of a sentence is a composition of the semantic values of its constituents.

In the second part of this chapter (4.2), I explain why TCS is supposed to be the theory that seems to fit the bill with respect to Novelty. My criti-

---

[1] In contrast to compositionality, Novelty is a phenomenon that is seldom discussed. Whenever I refer to it, I use a capitalised word to indicate that I mean the particular characterisation that I give below. I tend to call Novelty a 'problem', which is a shorthand description for 'the problem to explain how it is possible that Novelty holds'.

cism will be based on a detailed evaluation of arguments pro TCS. Finally, I will argue that usage-based approaches are not only *also* able to account for human comprehension competencies, but that they are, in fact, *better* suited for this purpose. This anticipates a methodological argument that I present in the third part of this book (in 7.1.1 and 7.2.2)—an argument to the effect that *phenomena* (as opposed to their corresponding abstractions) have epistemological primacy. Applied to language comprehension, this amounts to saying that *sentence* understanding can only be accounted for in terms of understanding of *utterances*, and not, as the truth-conditional semanticist is likely to suppose, the other way around.

4.1 Donald Davidson et al.

In this section, I give a short overview of truth-conditional semantics by way of presenting one highly influential argument in its favour. By far the most important figure in this area is, of course, Donald Davidson. The major part of the presentation below draws on his early writings, especially *Truth and Meaning*. I am going to assume for the rest of the chapter that my main target in this area is not Davidson's theory per se but what his heirs made of it, i.e. neo-Davidson semantics. Davidson's work on meaning is based on Tarski's prior work on *truth* in formalised languages. Accordingly, I shall briefly present this framework as well. Many more recent theories in philosophical semantics are inspired or directly influenced by Davidson's early work. However, the main idea behind Davidsonian semantics has remained unmodified since then: explaining linguistic capacities in terms of postulates that correspond to the 'rules of composition' and 'reference postulates' in a Tarski-style theory of truth.[2] Therefore, I think it is safe to say that my general critique of TCS applies across the board, so to speak, although it critically engages specifically with one aspect of Davidson's original argumentation.

---

[2] Note that in modern theories in philosophy of language and in formal semantics, the term "refers" replaces what was "fulfils" in Tarski's truth theory.

4.1.1 Introduction to the Framework

The most relevant alternative to usage-based approaches to meaning is truth-conditional semantics.[3] Its most prominent proponent is Donald Davidson, who elaborated and defended his theory of meaning in a number of articles.[4] In summarising the main ideas of truth-conditional semantics, I shall mainly focus on the early Davidsonian way of presenting it.[5] Why is Davidson's theory relevant for the present purposes? This is simply because TCS, in general, is a theory that is well suited to account for one specific problem: sentence comprehension. And, as will turn out in due course, this problem is particularly hard to tackle from *outside* truth-conditional approaches.

The problem, in short, is this: language users can understand and produce (in the respective languages that they master) a potentially unlimited number of sentences, and they do so with only limited cognitive resources (in particular, severely limited memory). The problem is how best to account for this astonishing ability. Most significantly, competent language users have (in fact, *can have*) only limited knowledge in regard to the meanings of atomic expressions (words, morphemes, and so on). More precisely,

---

[3] As already indicated above, a classification system of established theories always involves some simplification. Insofar as this is true for *all* classifications, I am not particularly worried by the simplifications that I presuppose here. I think it is fair to say that *if* one puts all broadly 'usage-based' frameworks into one group, then the most obvious contrast group is theories that take *reference* to be the central semantic notion. In this sense, (neo-)Davidsonian semantics seems indeed the most relevant rival theory.

[4] The most important essays are collected in Davidson (1985). Out of these, *Truth and Meaning* (Davidson 1967) is the central point of reference. Regarding his philosophy of language, Davidson (2005) is another relevant collection. Therein, the reprints that are most relevant to our present subject matter include: Davidson (1986, 1994). The earlier works of Davidson differ in some respects from his later work. Besides the three articles just mentioned, Davidson (1990) gives a comprehensive overview of his 'later' position.

[5] The most influential neo-Davidsonians are Ernest Lepore and Kirk Ludwig (e.g. Lepore (2006), Lepore & Ludwig (2005, 2006)). There are some strands both in linguistics and philosophy that, although not dealing with Davidsonian philosophy itself, are heavily influenced by the core insights of truth-conditional semantics. Among others, these include: Bar-On, Horisk & Lycan (2000), Borg (2004b, 2012a), Fodor & Lepore (2002), Heck (2007), Lycan (2010). A very comprehensive, critical interpretation of Davidson's earlier work is Hoeltje (2012), who argues, essentially, that Davidson's conviction that a truth theory can serve as a basis for one's theory of meaning is not well justified.

4 Truth-conditional Theories of Meaning

the number of meaningful atomic expressions in a given natural language is always restricted, whereas the range of propositional content that can be expressed by means of language never is. Still, competent speakers know what a given sentence means independently from whether they have heard or read this sentence before (subject to their familiarity with all constituents and the relevant syntactic structure). Here is an example that illustrates this ability:

> During the 2012 Olympic Games, Boris Johnson, then mayor of London, cried out loud 'Mother is the best' before he jumped head-first into the Thames.

Chances are quite high that you never have read this sentence before. However, you are able to comprehend its content (I assume). You understand that this sentence says *that during the 2012 Olympic Games, Boris Johnson, then mayor of London, cried out loud 'Mother is the best' before he jumped head-first into the Thames*. Truth-conditional semantics is highly relevant for the purposes of this chapter, because it sets out to provide an explanation for this astonishing ability.

In fact, you hardly ever come across a theoretic justification of truth-conditional semantics that would not refer to this specific ability. In light of this, I think it makes sense to take this as an appropriate starting point for a general discussion of the framework. For obvious reasons, this overview will be kept relatively short.[6]

4.1.2 Understanding Sentences

When it comes to truth-conditional semantics and its advantages, two issues must be kept apart. The first is the phenomenon just described: the ability of language users to comprehend potentially any novel sentence in their language.[7] The other important observation that TCS accounts for is

---

[6] For a comprehensive, in-depth analysis of Davidson's semantic programme, I refer the interested reader to Lepore (2006).

[7] This holds, given some—more or less uncontroversial—background assumptions. For example, natural language sentences may be infinitely long, i.e. the recursive character of languages allows for sentences of any length. Particular sentences are always finite, though. Human beings with their limited cognitive resources, however, can only under-

4.1 Donald Davidson et al.

that natural languages seem to be compositional—which, from Davidson's own perspective, is just the other side of the coin. There are several ways of conceiving of compositionality,[8] but the following definition will do for our purposes. A language is compositional iff the meaning of a sentence is determined by the meanings of its atomic parts (words, morphemes, ...) and the way the sentence is structured. To take a simple example: the (literal) meaning of "Snow is white" is (fully) determined by the meanings of "snow", "is", and "white" and the syntactic structure of the sentence, i.e.

---

stand sentences up to a certain length (depending on their memory). If one ignores these limitations for a moment, one may say that language users can potentially understand an unlimited number of sentences (all grammatical sentences of that language). Roughly put, they may *in principle* understand every grammatical sentence of their language. Davidson mentions some further important assumptions:

> When we can regard the meaning of each sentence as a function of a finite number of features of the sentence, we have an insight not only into what there is to be learned; we also understand how an infinite aptitude can be encompassed by finite accomplishments. For suppose that a language lacks this feature; then no matter how many sentences a would-be speaker learns to produce and understand, there will remain others whose meanings are not given by the rules already mastered. It is natural to say such a language is *unlearnable*. This argument depends, of course, on a number of empirical assumptions: for example, that we do not at some point suddenly acquire an ability to intuit the meanings of sentences on no rule at all; that each new item of vocabulary, or new grammatical rule, takes some finite time to be learned; that man is mortal. (Davidson 1965, pp. 8–9 of the reprint)

A further issue, that I will briefly touch upon below, is that Davidson and contemporary scholars speak of *sentences* instead of *utterances*. The problem here is that, prima facie, only utterances can be understood, since they are the relevant type of entity that plays a role in understanding. On the other hand, utterances mean a variety of different things in different situations and *sentence meaning* is just one factor that potentially influences utterance meaning. Taken together, the most plausible reading here is that utterance comprehension always—i.e. independent from specific contexts of utterance—rests upon one's ability to comprehend the 'literal' sentential meaning first. And for *this* ability (neo-)Davidsonian semantics is supposed to provide the corresponding interpretations. I will return to this in 7.2.2.

[8] See Gendler Szabó (2012a) for a review. See also Pagin & Westerståhl (2010a, 2010b), who give a nice, comparatively non-technical introduction to the topic. Cf. also Fulop & Keenan (2002), Grandy (1990), Groenendijk & Stokhof (2005), Pelletier (1994, 2003), and Robbins (2001). For a decidedly pro-TCS argumentation in the context of compositionality, see Higginbotham (2007).

4 Truth-conditional Theories of Meaning

the meaning that is, for lack of a better description, 'produced' by writing a noun, followed by a copula plus an adjective.[9]

To be better able to refer to the two topics just summarised, I suggest the following characterisations:

Novelty Competent language users are typically able to understand sentences that they have never read or heard before, given (i) that they are familiar with the words and syntactic structures occurring in a given sentence, (ii) that the length and complexity of the sentence does not exceed the subject's cognitive resources.

Compositionality Complex natural language sentences seem to be semantically compositional in that the meaning of the whole complex is exhaustively determined by the meanings of the atomic parts the complex consists of ('lexical meaning') and the way in which these parts form a complex ('syntax'), provided the resulting complex is well-formed.

Both issues are closely related, of course. Let me elaborate in some more detail how. The overall picture seems to be this: Novelty is a fact, compositionality is not. The former is usually explained in terms of the latter. Therefore, by construing an account of compositionality, you already indirectly provide an explanation for the Novelty problem. Two further things need to be noted that are implied by what I have said thus far. Firstly, there are different possible explanations, or, to be more precise, there are at least as many explanations for Novelty as for compositionality. And, secondly, if something else explains Novelty, then there is no apparent need to account for compositionality, since compositionality itself is no apparent fact at all (at least not in virtue of the arguments put forth in favour of Novelty).

Why is Novelty a fact and compositionality not? I take it that it is pretty obvious that competent speakers understand novel sentences.[10] Concerning compositionality, things are a bit more complicated. At least it *seems*

---

[9] The underlying idea of setting up the procedure this way is probably that, eventually, we may end up with a (possibly hierarchically ordered) inventory of sentence structures that all uniquely determine sentence meaning, given the meanings of their atoms.

[10] If the 'Boris Johnson' example does not move you, think of *any* other grammatically well-formed English sentence and test it on your departmental colleagues.

4.1 Donald Davidson et al.

that English sentences are compositional. Especially if—as was common practice in early modern philosophy of language—one focuses on simply structured declarative sentences. Certainly, you might think, the fact that "Socrates is white" means what it does depends, inter alia, on the further fact that "Socrates" stands for Socrates; that "white" denotes a certain colour; and that the syntactic structure of copula sentences somehow ensures that the whole expression ascribes the property denoted by the predicative to the subject of the sentence (or something reasonably similar). This seems natural and is quite plausible indeed. Philosophically speaking, however, the crucial point here is this: whether natural languages such as English really *are* compositional in the sense just sketched is an empirical question. Compositionality does not *follow* from the fact that Novelty holds.[11] The status of Novelty, on the other hand, is not similarly challengeable. For it describes only a phenomenon, not an explanation. Novelty refers to people's alleged ability to understand. Of course, one could imagine a scenario in which the observable phenomena are alike but in which no understanding occurs, as we conceive of it. Still, this does not undermine my present claim, since the relevant *understanding* referred to in the description is itself part of the phenomenon. For example, people respond to questions by giving certain kinds of answers; they execute certain types of actions in response to commands; they infer specific conclusions from sets of premises; and so forth. *This* is what we—other speakers of the language community—are able to observe and what we combine with our prior knowledge of semantics and syntax. Therefore, the status of Novelty can't be challenged analogously to compositionality, for it is only about what is observable independently of the theories anyway.

A variety of relevant examples that question the status of compositionality have been discussed in the current literature. The following two are quite illustrative in this respect. Assume that the 'semantic content' of "white wine" is composed of the semantic values of, respectively, "white" and "wine" (just as the semantic value of "snow is white" is composed of the semantic values of its constituents). Then there is a *specific* 'part' of the

---

[11] Note that here and in what follows I do not presuppose that natural languages are *not* compositional. My argument specifically attacks the alleged justificatory relation from Novelty to compositionality (and nothing else).

133

4 Truth-conditional Theories of Meaning

semantic value of the complex expression—i.e. that it means, say, 'white wine'—that stems from the meaning of "white". The relevant part, obviously, seems to be the alleged fact that "white" means 'white' (irrespective of how this gets spelled out in specific theories). Now compare this with the complex expression "white wall".[12] Apparently, although the expression is complex (and, in fact, looks as if its semantic content were composed of the semantic content of, respectively, "white" and "wall"), the contribution, so to say, that "white" makes to the first complex seems to be different from the contribution it makes to the second one. From this, many authors derive the conclusion that the lexical semantics of, say, "white" must be such that it suits both complexes.

An even more impressive example is the genitive construction. To wit:

> To understand what is said by 'He has bought John's book', one must identify the referent of 'he', of 'John' and (perhaps) of 'John's book'. But one must also identify the relation that is supposed to hold between John and the book. [...] 'John's book [...] means something like 'the book that bears relation x to John'. To understand what is said by means of a sentence in which 'John's book' occurs, this meaning must be contextually enriched by instantiating the variable 'x'. (Recanati 1989, 297–298)

The basic idea here is that the semantic content that the genitive construction contributes to the overall content of a noun phrase is seriously underdetermined. Philosophers of language with a refentialist bent are forced to adopt the view that the genitive construction ⌜x's y⌝ conveys only the 'information' that x stands in some contextually specifiable relation to y. But then the further problem is that this does not specify a specific *truth-evaluable* content, if the context that could serve to disambiguate between different relations is left out. The context *must* be left out, since a context that were 'rich' enough so as to specify a particular relation would entail features that are explicitly forbidden in neo-Davidsonian accounts such

---

[12] By the way, note that nothing hinges on whether we examine noun phrases, whole sentences, or, indeed, any other type of complex expression. We could just as easily run the example with "That is white wine" and "That is a white wall".

as common ground, intention-reading abilities, world knowledge, and so forth. However, truth-evaluability is the most relevant threshold in truth-conditional accounts (e.g. Borg 2004*b*, 33, note 25). From a formal semanticist's perspective, then, the problem is that one is forced to admit that the genitive construction contributes specific content to the overall sentential content, but in order to determine *which content* one would need to refer to contextual features beyond those typically considered (e.g. intention-reading abilities). To put it differently, the crucial aspect of the genitive construction is not its underspecification per se but rather the fact that no truth-evaluable content seems to be retrievable solely on the basis of the sentence. To achieve truth-evaluability, one would need to know which relation is *actually* claimed to hold between x and y, which obviously requires ascriptions of speaker intentions in many cases.

I only cite these examples here in order to illustrate that, in the linguistic and philosophical literature alike, the exact status of compositionality is controversial. In particular, it is controversial whether *all* areas of natural languages are semantically compositional, or whether some areas— e.g. 'peripheral' phenomena like sayings—are non-compositional after all. I do not argue for either side. My point is that Novelty is the problem one needs to account for. And with respect to *this* problem, the argumentative step from here to compositionality is only valid under the assumption that there could be no alternative explanation.[13] The cited examples can be interpreted as undermining the plausibility of this assumption. Both the semantics of compound expression such as "white wine" versus "white wall" as well as the semantics of the genitive construction, for example, suggest that compositionality is at least not as straightforward as many people think it is. There are examples that are supposed to show that languages are non-compositional in certain respects (e.g. idiomatic expressions such as "jemandem auf die Finger schauen"; Ziem & Staffeldt (2011)). In con-

---

[13] Davidson (1967, 23) is quite explicit about this; i.e. for him, no such alternative seems possible:

> [A] theory of meaning for a language L shows 'how the meanings of sentences depend upon the meanings of words' if it contains a (recursive) definition of truth-in-L. And, so far at least, we have no other idea how to turn the trick.

trast, the examples I just cited here do not undermine the claim that natural languages are (entirely) compositional. Nevertheless, they show that the lexical meaning must sometimes be specified in such a minimal way that—irrespective of 'actual' pragmatic processes (e.g. Gricean inferences)—the (truth-evaluable) meaning of a sentence can only be determined relative to full conversational contexts.

The issues surrounding compositionality indirectly affect a related issue that I have already touched upon in chapter 2: primary meaning. A compositional language requires stable, lexical meanings of its atomic elements.[14] Otherwise the semantic content of its well-formed complex expressions (e.g. sentences) can't be *determined* on the basis of their atomic constituents. In other words, primary meanings, attached to words, are the starting point for semantically compositional complexes like sentences. As I see things, there are basically two solutions here. One is to completely abandon compositionality.[15] The other option is to preserve a (redefined) notion of "primary meaning" that is capable of accounting for compositionality, but which at the same time does not presuppose a neo-Davidsonian conception in terms of reference relations à la Kirk, Ludwig, Lepore, etc. I will come back to this below.

4.1.3 Truth-Conditional Semantics

When it comes to truth-conditional semantics, two names are particularly relevant. The first is Donald Davidson, who 'invented' and popularised truth-conditional semantics in the second half of the last century.[16] The other highly important figure in this context is Alfred Tarski. His work is the basis for a great deal of Davidson's own work, especially Tarski's highly influential articles *The Semantic Conception of Truth* (1944) and *Der Wahrheitsbegriff in den formalisierten Sprachen* (1935). For sake of simplicity, I mainly use the term "truth-conditional semantics" in this chapter

---

[14] '[T]he interpretation [of sentences] in terms of truth values requires the existence of tight boundaries […] between literal and non-literal meaning' (Kayser 2003, 1262).

[15] Which seems highly implausible, as most areas of language *do* seem to be compositional. This even holds for problematic aspects such as underdetermination that I have just mentioned.

[16] See the references in note 4, page 129.

when referring to the theory sketched in *Truth and Meaning*. Other terms used in the literature include "truth-functional semantics", "truth-theoretic semantics", "referential semantics", or simply "(neo-)Davidsonian semantics".[17]

Being a logician and mathematician, Tarski was interested in defining the notion of 'truth' for formal languages, and in particular in developing adequacy constraints for such projects, most notably Convention T (see below). Although his way of defining "truth" is often referred to as a 'theory of truth', his aims differed from the typical aims of current truth theories (clarifying the nature of truth; exhaustively describing the term "true" in natural languages; accounting for truth with respect to related notions like realism, scientific success, etc.; justifying the choice of particular primary bearers of truth; and so on). From the perspective of today's theories of truth, Tarski's theory is concerned only with a tiny area of what modern theories are dealing with. For example, Tarski was not primarily concerned with the layman's use of "truth", nor did he try to explain *why* natural languages tend to develop a truth predicate in the first place (questions that are paradigmatic examples of what one would typically expect these days from a theory of truth).[18] Be that as it may, Tarski's 'truth theory' was highly influential and is influential still. Most importantly, Tarski's theory

---

[17] "Davidsonian semantics" is self-explanatory. "Truth-conditional" emphasises that neo-Davidsonian approaches to semantics aim at (i) showing that stating the truth conditions of a sentence is a way of stating its meaning and (ii) demonstrating how sentential semantic content (truth condition) systematically depends on atomic semantic content (reference relation). "Truth-*functional*" might be a bit misleading here, since, strictly speaking, only *connectives* can be truth-functional: the truth value of a sentence containing a connective is a function of the truth values of the sentences connected. "Truth-*theoretic*" and "referential", in contrast, do not invoke this connotation.

[18] Tarski explicitly denies that his theory aims at being in accordance with natural languages:

> [...] the very possibility of a consistent use of the expression "true sentence" which is in harmony with the laws of logic and the spirit of everyday language seems to be very questionable, and consequently the same doubt attaches to the possibility of constructing a correct definition of this expression. (Tarski 1935, 279, quoted according to the translation by J. H. Woodger (1983) *in* J. Corcoran, ed.,'Logic, Semantics, Metamathematics', Hackett, Indianapolis, p. 165.)

4 Truth-conditional Theories of Meaning

lay the ground for Davidson's work, which is based on the assumption that a Tarski-style theory of truth can be 'converted' into a theory of meaning (Kölbel 2001, Newen & Schrenk 2008).

Central to Tarski's work is the so-called Convention T, which is the requirement that the theorems of one's truth theory should take the form of instances of the following schema:[19]

(T) "p" is true iff p.

Let me first very briefly explain how it works. First of all, with (T) comes the distinction between object language and metalanguage. Let German be the object language, i.e. the language we talk about in the following statements. Then a simple instance of (T) is

(T_1) "Schnee ist weiß" is true iff snow is white.

The corresponding metalanguage, then, is the language one uses to talk about sentences of the object language (here: English sentences that deal with the truth conditions of German sentences). Notably, (T_1) *as a whole* is written in our metalanguage, English. The expression

"Schnee ist weiß"[20]

is part of English, it is a *name*[21] for the *German* sentence "Schnee ist weiß". Much confusion in regard to the schema stems from many authors' tendency to use English both as their metalanguage and object language. Things are far easier to explain if one chooses different (natural) languages for the respective purposes. Especially since we actually use a meta-metalanguage when we describe the relationship between the 'lower' two languages.

I said that

"Schnee ist weiß"

---

[19] The schema is called 'T-schema', its instances are 'T-sentences'.

[20] Note my use of meta-metalanguage here.

[21] I emphasise "name" here, because competent speakers of a natural language (in particular, speakers who master German) often times can't help themselves seeing a structure here. But this is misleading. The quoted expression is technically just a name, i.e. a non-decomposable semantic atom.

i.e. the result of writing double quotation marks, followed by the sentence "Schnee ist weiß", and again followed by double quotation marks is a *name* (in the metalanguage) for the German sentence that says that snow is white. There are other ways of referring to object-level sentences. Using quotation marks and the 'original' sentence of the object language is the most convenient and usual one, however.[22] Another option would be to say that the German sentence built by writing the sequence of letters (and spaces) "S", "c", "h", ..., "e", "i", and "ß" is true in German iff snow is white. That is to say, one could employ a structural description of the sentence at hand (in terms of German letters). This is the method originally suggested by Tarski. All this, in any case, is part of the metalanguage. The underlying idea that everything expressible at the object-level must also be expressible at the meta-level is often expressed by saying that the metalanguage must 'contain' the object language.[23] Using two *different* natural languages when describing what is going on helps understanding the difficulties.

An example will illustrate this. Suppose now that I use English both at the object-level and at the meta-level. The probably most often quoted instance of the T-schema then reads:

(T_2) "Snow is white" is true iff snow is white.

This is misleading, because there is actually no structural similarity between the right-hand side and left-hand side of this instance. This was somehow transparent in T_1, but in T_2 it seems that "Snow is white" occurs two times actually. This is not the case, since the expression on the left-hand side of the copula is an unstructured entity, a name for an object-level expression. So, since instances of "Snow is white" at both levels express the proposition <snow is white> (as they do by assumption), the meta-level sentence must be a step-by-step translation of the object-level sentence. This is what Putnam means when he says that when we determine Eng-

---

[22] It is clear what I mean here; yet, strictly speaking, it is not the *original* German sentence that I use here, for the whole expression in question is in the present metalanguage.

[23] A bit more precisely formulated: (i) it must contain the relevant part, i.e. translations of the sentences one wants to insert into the schema; (ii) it must contain names of the relevant object-level sentences (or otherwise a method of referring to these sentences, e.g. structural descriptions); (iii) it must contain a certain amount of logic, "iff" in particular. In sum, it must be 'semantically richer'.

4 Truth-conditional Theories of Meaning

lish to serve a double-purpose as both metalanguage and object language we '[decide implicitly] that each sentence of [object-level English] is to be translated "homophonically" into [metalevel English]' (1985, 69).

It is in the same paper that Putnam claims that Tarski's theory fails to be an account of our colloquial "true" (as if that were Tarski's intention):

> Now, pay close attention, please! This is just where, it seems to me, philosophers have been asleep at the opera for a long time! Since (2) [(for any sentence X) If X is spelled S-N-O-W-SPACE-I-S-SPACE-W-H-I-T-E, then X is true in L if and only if snow is white] is a *theorem of logic* in meta-L (if we accept the definition—given by Tarski—of "true-in-L"), since no axioms are needed for the proof of (2) except axioms of logic and axioms about spelling, (2) holds in all possible worlds. In particular, since no assumptions about the *use* of the expressions of L are used in the proof of (2), (2) holds true in worlds in which the sentence "Snow is white" does not mean that snow is white. In fact, "true-in-L," as defined by Tarski, is a notion which involves only the primitive notions of L itself [...]. So if L does not have notions which refer to the *use of linguistic expressions*, there is no way in which "true-in-L," or, rather, the notion to which Tarski gives that name, *could* involve the *use* of expressions in any way. The property to which Tarski gives the name "true-in-L" is a property that the sentence "Snow is white" has in every possible world in which snow is white, *including worlds in which what it means is that snow is green.* (Putnam 1985, 63–64)

The controversial bit is the very last claim; that a sentence like T_2 is a theorem of Tarski's theory in all worlds. That would be disastrous for the theory, even if it is not designed to capture ordinary uses of the truth predicate. I will now show that Putnam is mistaken here.

Suppose you open any good textbook on astronomy. In the introductory paragraphs you read this:

> A position on the Earth is usually given by two spherical coordinates.[24]

---

[24] Karttunen et al. (1994), *Fundamental Astronomy*, Springer, Berlin, page 13.

Now, if this sentence meant that 'Hansel and Gretel went into the forest to fetch some wood', then the book you would be looking at would contain rather a fairy tale than basic astronomical knowledge. In order to ensure a 'standard' interpretation of his remarks, the author of this book needs to do *nothing*. The same goes for books on truth. The whole description of the theory (including the description of meta-L and how to derive *theorems* in meta-L) is given in a meta-metalanguage, which is English in this case. In this language, "white" denotes whiteness, "snow" denotes snow, and so forth. This is precisely the interpretation that is in accordance with how *we*, writers and readers of English, use these terms. Like the astronomer, Tarski does not need, therefore, enforce this interpretation explicitly. So when we read (in meta-meta-English) that the object-level expression "snow" refers to snow (cf. the 'base clauses' in Glanzberg 2013), this is enough to make sure that "snow" at the object level is used to refer to snow. When Putnam talks about 'worlds in which what "Snow is white" means is that snow is green', the most straightforward answer to the problem he posits is this: if the only thing that deviates from the actual world is that "white" refers to the colour green, then in the metalanguage *for this version of English*

"Snow is white" is true iff snow is white

would no longer be a theorem of the truth theory, since the axiom

"white" refers to the colour white

would be 'replaced' in that theory by the axiom

"white" refers to the colour green

and, hence,

"Snow is white" is true iff snow is green

would turn out true in that modified theory.[25] Which, by any standards, is an unproblematic theorem relative to the assumptions mentioned above.

---

[25] Cf. Patterson (2012, 136):

> If the intuitive meaning of an expression of the object language changes, Tarski's definition needs to be reworked to capture the concept of truth for the language so re-interpreted. This is a consequence of the fact that intuitive meaning is an "off table" matter to be kept in mind of the users of the theory [...].

4 Truth-conditional Theories of Meaning

Note that something like the substitute axiom must come into play somewhere, for this is how the deviant variant of English is *defined* by Putnam in the first place. He notes that in this specific world he is talking about 'it [the snow sentence] means that snow is green', which is one way of expressing the idea that specific axioms hold for the semantics of that word (e.g. "'white' refers to the colour green"). Considering other worlds—worlds in which words function differently—is to allow for a different set of T-sentences.

Another important thing to note in regard to (T) is that there are at least a handful of varieties of how to state the schema.[26] Different 'stylistic' variants of the schema are for the most part motivated by technical niceties, most of which do not concern me here. The most important technical problem is this: in (T), I applied regular quotation marks; so, strictly speaking, I quoted "p". But "p" is a sentence variable, to be substituted by a declarative sentence of the object language. *This* occurrence then gets quoted. When I moved from the schema to a particular instance—i.e. from

"p" is true iff p

to

"Schnee ist weiß" is true iff snow is white

—I immediately applied the 'intended' reading of the schema. Some theorists circumvent this problem by using quasi-quotation; others use—like Tarski—structural descriptions to denote sentences. Having said this, I shall use the simple notation in what follows.

Last comment on (T): Tarski's method introduces a hierarchy of truth predicates. Truth, that is, may only be attributed to sentences at a lower semantic level. This gives me a further reason to not use English both as metalevel and object-level language (even if only for pedagogical reasons). Suppose I did. Then the question *Does English have a truth predicate?* would become ambiguous. Yes, it does, if used as a metalanguage. But as an object language it does not, at least not the one needed to attribute truth *to its own sentences*.[27] This is obscured by sentences like

---

[26] Cf., e.g., Priest's (2006, 17).

[27] The reason that in a Tarskian framework "true" is not applicable to sentences that belong to the same (level of) language as "true" itself belongs is that this would lead us to para-

4.1 Donald Davidson et al.

"Snow is white" is true iff snow is white

because such examples suggest that we may say *in English* that the *English sentence* "Snow is white" is true, but we can't if we accept the Tarskian idea of hierarchically ordered languages. Whether this idea itself is plausible is irrelevant for the present considerations. I am only interested in truth to the extent that it affects theories of meaning. In this section, in particular, I am only interested in truth to the extent that it affects Davidson's and neo-Davidsonians' theory of meaning. If only to avoid unnecessary confusion, it is worth employing at least two natural languages; one as object language, and a different one as metalanguage (and meta-metalanguage).

Back, then, to where I began. I gave only a very brief overview of Tarski's work.[28] What is most important in the present context is that Tarski takes certain semantic notions for granted: "refers" and "satisfies". One might say that he presupposed a theory of meaning (as reference and satisfaction can only be defined in terms of meaning), and built a 'theory of truth' on it (i.e. he kind of reversed the Davidsonian programme). For example, we read that

> In view of the situation [i.e. in view of the need for a recursive definition of "truth"], there is no method with which it would be possible to recursively define the investigated notion. On the other hand, it is possible to introduce a general concept that is applied to arbitrarily many propositional functions, that is recursively definable, and that leads us immediately to truth, if applied to propositions ['Aussagen']. It is the notion of satisfaction of a given propositional function by given entities—in the case at hand, satisfaction by classes of individuals—that meets these requirements. (Tarski 1935, 307)[29]

---

doxes, most prominently the liar paradox. For a possible solution of how to reconcile a hierarchical solution to the liar paradox with the intuition that natural languages have (each) just one truth predicate, see Horwich (2010, 87–91).

[28] For a closer look, see Patterson (2012).

[29] My translation (of the German version), spacing omitted. The original publication in 1933 was in Polish. The German translation reads:

> Angesichts dieser Sachlage lässt sich keine Methode angeben, welche es erlauben würde, den untersuchten Begriff unmittelbar auf rekursivem Wege

4 Truth-conditional Theories of Meaning

Tarski's groundbreaking idea is to omit a full-blown *definition* of "truth". He circumvented the problem of providing such a definition by saying, roughly, that all T-sentences of a given language that comply with Convention T are *partial* definitions of the concept of truth. Patterson (2012) summarises Tarski's strategy as follows:

> [...] what we find is that an expression for which the T-sentences are theorems is, given the conventions governing the object language and the metalanguage, forced to express the content of the concept of truth as construed in the semantical definition [for all x, x is a true sentence if and only if, for a certain p, x is identical with 'p' and p]. Since the language of the metatheory has intuitive meaning just as much as does the object language [...], each T-sentence is meaningful [...] in accordance with linguistic usage. In particular, a T-sentence like:
>
> > ["snow is white" is true iff snow is white
>
> means that "snow is white" is true iff snow is white][30]. Now, though the T-sentence itself says nothing of its own *saying* that something is the case, a party to the conventions governing the metalanguage will recognize that in fact the T-sentence does say [...] exactly that. (119)

Mutatis mutandis, the same holds for 'a party to the convention governing the object language'. Thus, the basic idea that Tarski put forward is that someone who masters both object language and metalanguage will accept T-sentences in such a way that the applicability of "true" corres-

---

    zu definieren. Es ergibt sich aber die Möglichkeit, einen Begriff von allgemeinerem Charakter einzuführen, welcher bei beliebigen Aussagefunktionen Anwendung findet, sich schon rekursiv definieren lässt und, auf Aussagen angewendet, uns mittelbar zum Begriff der Wahrheit führt; diesen Bedingungen genügt nämlich der Begriff des Erfülltseins der gegebenen Aussagefunktion durch gegebene Gegenstände und im vorliegenden Falle – durch gegebene Klassen von Individuen.

[30] I substituted the example sentence in order to simplify at this point.

ponds perfectly to our pre-theoretic understanding of the truth predicate (Patterson 2012, 117–122).

Davidson now reverses this order, or so many interpret him. For him, truth is a self-evident, transparent concept (Newen & Schrenk 2008). In other words, one does not need, says Davidson, other concepts (in the relevant sense) to understand the meaning of "true". One is asked to take its meaning for granted and base a theory of meaning on it. A very clear way of saying where we are getting at here is to say that Davidson's claim is that a Tarski-style theory of truth *is* a theory of meaning (cf. Lepore 2006). My task in the following paragraphs is to explain what this methodological dogma amounts to.

Tarski told us how to build a theory of truth for specific formalised languages (and how to test its adequacy). Its axioms determine the extensions of all 'atomic parts' of this component of English. Thus, in regard to names, for example, we might have a list that relates them to individual objects; we might have another list that relates predicates to n-tuples of individuals; and we have recursively formulated rules that determine the extensions of all well-formed sentences as functions of extensions of the atomic parts of the sentence in question. Here is an example to illustrate this: if "Aristotle" refers to Aristotle (which is settled in an axiom list for names) and "x is a human" is satisfied iff the substitution instance of "x" refers to an entity that belongs to the class of humans (again, set by an axiomatic list for predicates), then the sentence "Aristotle is a human" is true iff Aristotle is a human (i.e. actually true, if the formal theory is accurate).

Here is how Glanzberg (2013) summarises Tarski's approach somewhat more generally:

> Tarski notes that truth for each atomic sentence can be defined in terms of two closely related notions: reference and satisfaction. Let us consider a language **L′**, just like **L** [i.e. a language containing two specific well-formed sentences] except that instead of simply having two atomic sentences, **L′** breaks atomic sentences into terms and predicates. **L′** contains terms 'snow' and 'grass' (let us engage in the idealization that these are simply singular terms), and predicates 'is white' and 'is

green'. So **L′** is like **L**, but also contains the sentences 'Snow is green' and 'Grass is white'.

We can define truth for atomic sentences of **L′** in the following way.

1. Base clauses:
    1. 'Snow' refers to snow.
    2. 'Grass' refers to grass.
    3. a satisfies 'is white' if and only if a is white.
    4. a satisfies 'is green' if and only if a is green.
2. For any atomic sentence $\ulcorner t$ is $P \urcorner$: $\ulcorner t$ is $P \urcorner$ is true if and only if the referent of $\ulcorner t \urcorner$ satisfies $\ulcorner P \urcorner$. (Emphasis omitted)

We see here that it is possible to construe a Tarski-style truth theory for a small, formalised fragment of English, i.e. a theory that produces, for all well-formed sentences of that fragment of English, T-sentences that specify truth conditions for these sentences. 'Davidson is known for having reinterpreted Tarski's theory of truth as a theory of meaning, and for applying it to ordinary language' (Newen & Schrenk 2008, 56, my translation). Instead of taking semantic notions for granted (e.g. "satisfies") and 'explaining' truth in terms of these notions, Davidson did just the opposite by taking 'truth' for granted in order to explain meaning. The idea here is that the body of knowledge that *we theoreticians* need to postulate when trying to account for competent language users' comprehension abilities must resemble the structure of a Tarski-style 'truth theory'.

4.2 Truth-Conditional Semantics at Work

In the previous section, I presented the main ingredients of truth-conditional semantics by showing two things. Firstly, in preparation of this section and the discussion in the next chapter I said a few words about one major argument employed by Davidson (the argument from sentence comprehension). Then, secondly, I discussed the—admittedly, *highly* simplified— Davidsonian programme of transforming a Tarski-style 'theory of truth' into a theory of meaning. Accordingly, the aim of the present section is to apply this framework to the initial problem (sentence comprehension). Again, I would like to show two things here. On the one hand, TCS seem *particularly* likely to be a possible solution to the cited 'problem', i.e. people's capability to comprehend any well-formed sentence of their respective languages. Showing why this seems to be the case is one of my aims. On the other hand, there are good reasons to suppose that Davidson's central claim—which is that his proposal is in effect the only possible solution to the problem—is false. That is to say, there are viable alternatives. Moreover, for reasons emerging throughout the book (especially in the methodological part), the alternatives are the preferred options. Let me now first turn to the pros of truth-conditional semantics.

4.2.1 Linking Novelty and Compositionality

A closer look at why compositionality and Novelty are discussed together in one chapter and why truth-conditional semantics seems adequate to account for both will help us to see the major advantages of this approach. These advantages set the threshold for potential alternatives. According to TCS, a theory that produces infinitely many sentences of the form "'p' is true iff p" can be regarded a theory of meaning.[31] Davidson says that what an adequate natural language semantics should be able to do is stating truth conditions for all well-formed sentences of the relevant target language.[32] It can be considered controversial whether truth conditions represent all there is to know about the meaning of a sentence. The classical passage on this issue reads as if Davidson thought this were the case:

> There is no need to suppress, of course, the obvious connection between a definition of truth of the kind Tarski has shown how to construct, and the concept of meaning. It is this: the

---

[31] Save for some exegetical niceties that I waive here: e.g. Davidson's contention that truth conditions and meaning are not the same, but that 'giving the truth conditions of a sentence' is one way of stating its meaning.

[32] See Davidson (1967, 34–35) for some remarks on demonstratives and, accordingly, on what roles utterances might play in his account. Even if we would take into account sentences relativized to formally specifiable contexts of utterance, we would still leave out most semantically relevant aspects of utterances that I mentioned above.

4 Truth-conditional Theories of Meaning

> definition works by giving necessary and sufficient conditions for the truth of every sentence, and *to give truth conditions is a way of giving the meaning of a sentence.* (Davidson 1967, 310, emphasis added)[33]

The following, I think, is uncontroversial: firstly, it is true that a theory of meaning should at least be compatible with Convention T, or more specifically, with the view that every sentence somehow 'indicates' its own truth conditions ('sentences bear their truth conditions on their sleeves', as it is often put). Secondly, truth conditions are important aspects of meaning that are relevant in many areas of theorising. Thirdly, everyone who understands a particular T-sentence knows something, albeit very little, about the meaning of that sentence.[34] I deny, however, that it is a necessary condition for an adequate theory of meaning that it entails all, or indeed any, relevant T-sentences.

Moreover, it can be doubted that truth conditions are *all* there is to know about the meaning of sentences. To argue for this is to say something about when one is usually satisfied with an answer to the questions of the type "What does sentence *x* mean?" Suppose you learn that "Snow is white" is true iff snow is white. Essentially, two possibilities are available here: either you knew in advance what "snow", "is", "white", and the syntactic structure 'S-C-P' (S=subject; C=copula; P=predicative) mean, or you did not. In the first case, you did not 'learn' anything because you already knew

---

[33] The widespread conviction that Davidson *identifies* meaning with truth conditions probably stems from this passage. It seems natural to interpret this paragraph accordingly (cf., e.g., Saka 2007).

[34] This holds with certain provisos: (a) Here I assume the Horwichian understanding of "understanding", namely that "understanding" means, roughly, 'to know how to use'; (b) furthermore, I presuppose that T-sentences are wholly formulated in a metalanguage, i.e. that a sentence like " 'Το χιόνι είναι λευκό' is true iff snow is white" is—in its entirety—an *English* sentence; (c) I assume further that, e.g., one who merely understands this sentence understands the Greek "Το χιόνι είναι λευκό" *only to the extent that he knows that in Greek this sentence corresponds to the English "Snow is white"* (and, hence, has such-and-such truth conditions), which is to say that he does *not* know, from that bit of information alone, how "Το χιόνι είναι λευκό" is used in Greek. This is because "Το χιόνι είναι λευκό" plus quotation marks is an English name, and because of this everyone who masters English and is familiar with the T-schema does not need any further competence in order to understand the 'Greek T-sentence'.

the truth conditions of "snow is white" anyway (hence, asking would be superfluous). In the second case, you do not learn anything either because you are unable to understand the proposed explanation.

The natural reply by truth-conditional semanticists is to say: 'Actually, I never claimed that T-sentences are in any way "interesting" or that you learn anything about meaning with the help of my theory. I only say that my theory provides meanings for all sentences—and this is what we expect of such a theory.' Not quite. If T-sentences were all we could come to know about sentence meanings, then the fact that "What does x mean?" is a common question and normally demands an illuminating answer would be inexplicable. For it is far too trivial for many grammatical sentences in natural languages to work out their respective truth conditions. No one would ever think of asking such questions if the only answers solely consisted in truth-condition statements.

To be sure, this little argument is far from being conclusive. Neither Davidson nor his followers are particularly concerned with the role of meaning inquiries in layman's usage. Still, the notion of 'meaning' that Davidson is after can't be conceived *completely* independently of the folk notion it originates from, for this would render his whole argumentation implausible. Remember that the key step in *Truth and Meaning* is the presumption that "is true" is an extensionally correct *substitute* for the allegedly obscure "means that".[35] By the same token, it seems justified to *require* of Davidson's theory that, as far as non-metaphorical use of "meaning" is concerned, it should resemble the folk notion as far as possible. And it is a commonplace that locutions such as "What does x mean?" and their corresponding answers are among the most central applications of the notion of 'meaning'—locutions that seem incompatible with an understanding of meaning based merely on truth conditions.

---

[35] By which I do not want to suggest that Davidson aimed at replacing meaning by truth conditions. I am only referring to the well-known, often-cited passage in which he says:

> As a final bold step, let us try treating the position occupied by 'p' extensionally: to implement this, *sweep away the obscure 'means that', provide the sentence that replaces 'p' with a proper sentential connective, and supply the description that replaces ' with its own predicate.* The plausible result is
>
> (T) s is T if and only if p. (Davidson 1967, 23, emphasis added)

4 Truth-conditional Theories of Meaning

What, then, is the alternative? In an abstract sense, the answer is simple: one is typically satisfied with a 'meaning statement' if the corresponding answer illuminates one's understanding of the sentence in question, or, otherwise, if it conforms with what one knows about the sentence's meaning anyway. This amounts to saying that we tend to be satisfied with answers to meaning inquiries whenever they help us to see how the sentence in question is (typically) used.

Here are a few examples. First example: if you do not know German, then the (English) explanation "'Schnee ist weiß' is true iff snow is white" (read: "Schnee ist weiß" *means* 'Snow is white') helps you to understand (i.e. indicates how to use) "Schnee ist weiß" to the extent that you would fully understand it once you understood related sentences.[36] Second example: if two people are in front of a library and one of them says "This is Tom's bicycle" and I say to you, describing this situation, that this *means* that the guy wants the girl to know that her ex-boyfriend is in the library, then you probably understand this sentence (ceteris paribus). That is to say, you would come to know that it is used to say something about the whereabouts of Tom, albeit that the sentence is 'about' a bicycle and its literal truth conditions do not depend on Tom.[37] Last example: if you are an

---

[36] This last proviso is essential. Only when you know the use of *all* related sentences of "Schnee ist weiß", then you fully understand the sentence itself. If you learn only this individual fact—that "Schnee ist weiß" means 'Snow is white'—then your knowledge of the use of "Schnee ist weiß" is, so to speak, potential knowledge. That is, you do not *really* associate a particular use with this sentence, because you are unable to connect this bit of information with other relevant knowledge. In the case of "Schnee ist weiß", the immediately 'related' sentences might be "Das ist Schnee" and "Das ist weiß", for example (cf. also Davidson 1967, 26, note 10).

[37] This is essentially Tomasello's example (from his 2008, page 3). The point of this example is that it illustrates (for arguments, see below) that the context that determines content is often times very wide. In this particular case, for instance, this content would have been different two weeks earlier, or with another interlocutor, and so on. Generally, the content would have been different with different shared background knowledge. In Tomasello's own words:

> It is easy to say that what carries the meaning in these different examples [i.e. variations of the one above] is "context," but that is not very helpful since all of the physical features of the immediate communicative context were (by stipulation) identical in the various scenarios. The only difference was our shared experience beforehand [...]. (2008, 3–4)

otherwise competent speaker of English but do not know the word "apple", and you're told that "apple" *means* 'a round fruit with firm juicy flesh',[38] then you understand will "apple" (or sentences containing "apple', for that matter), because you know how it is used in sentences whose other constituents you are already familiar with, like "This is an apple", "Apple is good for making cakes", "I like apples" and so forth.

One possible reply is to point out that this way of arguing mixes up the distinction between semantics and pragmatics, and that, in particular, too much pragmatics enters into the presented examples. The argument here would be along the lines of: the *central* locutions in which "means" occurs is when semantics is at stake; which is clearly not the case in, for example, Tomasellian common-ground scenarios. But this is grist to my mill, for as I argued already in section 2.2, this distinction is blurred (at least) in recent empirical work in construction grammar. Moreover, to say that semantics covers only truth conditions is clearly an exaggeration, for many much more 'conservative' approaches comprise (quasi-)pragmatic aspects as well. See, for example, Recanati's contextualism (e.g. Recanati 2007).

A further objection might be this: the semantic approach that is suggested by the above examples implies that one can't know the meaning of a term or sentence tout court but that understanding essentially comes in degrees. True, but this is actually a virtue of my view. Here, again, I can offer no waterproof armchair argument; I only say that this is the most plausible way to make sense of our de facto 'meaning discourse'. It is perfectly reasonable to say things like "She has only a vague idea of what we are talking about"; "More and more he understood what they said"; "I don't know what it means precisely", etc. If meaning were an all-or-nothing game, this part of our discourse would not be intelligible at all. Also, meaning holism already suggests that people learn word meanings one step at a time.[39]

---

[38] Hornby, A. S. (1995), *Oxford Advanced Learner's Dictionary*, Oxford University Press, London, p. 46.

[39] Meaning holism is here understood as the thesis that the meaning of a word depends on the meanings of other words of the same language. There is a vast range of theoretical possibilities when it comes to holism, most of which I will simply neglect at this stage. For a concise overview, the reader is asked to consult Pagin (2006). There are also some illuminating passages in Horwich, or in Fodor, or in Quine. The main idea, though, is

4 Truth-conditional Theories of Meaning

Competent speakers know the meaning of a term only to the extent that they are familiar with (more or less) related terms. Since one can't learn a whole language at one go, people improve their knowledge as they learn more and more words (or, in general, broaden their linguistic competence). Eventually, natural language speakers' way of dealing with technical terms also shows that knowledge of meaning comes in degrees. Think of a term like "full employment": probably every competent language user of English knows the meaning of this term in the sense that he is able to use it appropriately and knows how others typically will (potentially) use it. Very few of us, however, are familiar with the available exact definitions of "full employment" and that, hence, the term varies in its extension depending on the particular theoretical background applied. So, if an average speaker is not sure as to whether "full employment" applies to a situation where, say, 3 % of a particular population are unemployed, then this uncertainty is neither due to vagueness (all *definitions* of "full employment" have strict boundaries), nor due to incompetence (he would know that "full employment" means 'that almost all are employed'), but due to his restricted knowledge as regards the relevant meaning. That is to say, he knows the meaning of the term merely *to a certain extent*, which is to say that his semantic understanding comes in degrees.

4.2.2 Truth-conditional Semantics Does the Trick

For the reasons I pointed out in the previous subsection, TCS seems to be particularly well-suited to account both for the Novelty problem as well as for compositionality. The simple reason is that both issues are basically treated as two sides of the same coin: since Novelty can *only* be explained via referring to compositionality (or so Davidson argues), providing a solution for the latter means solving the former as well. Now I would like so show in some more detail why this seems so. First of all, I assume for

---

simple and always remains the same: given meaning holism, it is impossible to assign meaning to atomic elements of a given language independently of the meanings that get assigned to related elements of the same language. In this sense, learning a language stepwise and holism always come together: holism implies the epistemic constraint that knowledge of the meaning of a particular term depends on one's potentially restricted knowledge of the meanings of related terms.

4.2 Truth-Conditional Semantics at Work

the sake of argument that the following holds: (i) meanings are truth conditions, i.e. there is no semantic information of a given sentence exceeding its propositional content; (ii) truth-conditional semantics 'works', i.e. a broadly neo-Davidsonian approach can be applied to a reasonable sample of natural English.

The compositionality principle requires us to provide a mechanism that computes the meaning of a sentence, given the meanings of its atomic parts and the way they are put together. By assumption, TCS—certainly so in neo-Davidsonian approaches—is a theory that connects words of English with meanings.[40] Furthermore, a Tarski-style theory of truth tells us in which way the truth conditions of any well-formed sentence depend on the meanings of its parts. Here is a simple example. I begin with meaning statements for atomic units of a given language:[41]

r_1 "Snow" refers to snow;

r_2 "Socrates" refers to Socrates;

...

f_1 "x is white" is a function that is satisfied if x is white, otherwise false;[42]

...

c_1 A sentence of the form "x is F" is true iff x satisfies "x is F".

...

A brief look at the relevant complex sentence "Snow is white" reveals that one can easily combine the above basic information. The result is

---

[40] These meanings are referents in the case of names, functions in the case of predicates, and so on. The two above assumptions ensure that all (or a significant portion of all) English words are covered and that the kind of meaning provided captures the full meaning of a term.

[41] The presentation of these 'base clauses' in a Tarski-style framework is adopted from Glanzberg (2013). Again, I do without quasi quotation.

[42] For ease of presentation, I simplify a bit. For example, one would actually need to first state the meaning of "white" and then explicate the meaning of predication (or "be" when used as a full verb). The combination of the two is the meaning of "x is white".

"Snow is white" is true iff snow is white

which is, relative to the above assumptions, an *exhaustive* description of the meaning of "Snow is white". In short, it is relatively obvious that it is a direct consequence of my second assumption ('TCS works') that truth-conditional semantics can successfully handle compositionality issues.

Things get a bit more complicated when I now turn to Novelty. The problem is that there is a discrepancy between the potential *infinity* of well-formed (grammatical) sentences of natural languages that language users are basically able to understand and the *finitude* of cognitive resources that can explain this. To bridge this gap, says Davidson, one needs recursion/recursiveness. Tarski's apparatus that I employed above when demonstrating how the meaning of a sentence depends on its parts essentially involves a recursive strategy. The rules for determining the meaning (truth conditions) of complexes may be applied ad libitum. In particular, the rules may be applied several times in building sentence meanings. This ensures that by using this method, one is able to determine the meaning of declarative sentences of any length.

To account for the fact that language users are typically able to understand sentences they have never encountered before, truth-conditional semanticists assume that a competent speaker (implicitly) knows such recursive rules roughly as described by Tarski.[43] The meaning of *any* complex sentence can be built recursively with these rules. By analogy, the same mechanism is supposed to explain language users' ability to comprehend novel sentences. All this is pretty straightforward and well established, so there is no need to go too much into the details. Especially so, since what is really interesting is not the argument as such but rather the plausibility of its main premises. The two premises that, for the sake of argument, I assumed above were these: (i) meanings are truth conditions; (ii) truth-conditional semantics is a successful enterprise. I shall now consider both premises in turn and argue that they are unwarranted.

---

[43] To be fair, this is, to my knowledge, never stated explicitly. But this is the only way I can think of to make sense of Davidson's claim that his semantic theory provides the *only* solution to the problem that natural languages must be learnable (Davidson 1965). Note, though, that the status of Davidson's project as aiming at psychological reality is at least debatable (Röska-Hardy 2005).

4.2 Truth-Conditional Semantics at Work

Ad (ii): I start with the claim that TCS is *successful*. To be sure, there are many relevant respects in which theories can be more or less successful. I shall here concentrate on one particular mark of adequacy: a theory should *in fact* be able to explain all phenomena that it officially *says* it is applicable to. Semantics is the study of meanings of sentences.[44] If you like, you may even add the restriction that semantics proper is solely concerned with sentence meanings irrespective of context. This problem can be bracketed out for the moment. Yet, semantics supposedly is the study of *all* sentences. One crucial deficit of TCS is its initial restriction to a particular class of sentences, namely declaratives.[45] There are quite a lot of attempts to enlarge the class of sentences covered by classical truth-conditional or broadly formal semantics. This holds in particular for formal treatments of questions.[46] The central difficulty remains, though, namely that all broadly formalist approaches to the semantics of non-declaratives are attempts to *extend* a theory designed for declaratives to other forms (not like usage-based theories, which are intended to apply across the board from the very beginning). The simple reason for excluding other types of sentences is that only *truth-evaluable* sentences can have truth conditions.

It can be considered uncontroversial that declarative sentences is the only class of truth-evaluable sentences, i.e. only sentences belonging to that class can reasonably be assigned truth values. Think of questions, exclamations, emotional expressions, imperatives, and the like. They can hardly be said to have truth-evaluable content, although much ink has been spilt—

---

[44] This, at least, is probably the most widespread position in philosophy and certainly an undisputed truism in linguistics. As usual, there are people who deny even truisms:

> Syntax studies sentences, semantics studies propositions. Pragmatics is the study of linguistic acts and the contexts in which they are performed. (Stalnaker 1970, 275)
> According to this characterization of semantics [i.e. semantics as the study of propositions], then, the subject has no essential connection with languages at all, either natural or artificial. (274)

[45] I ignore for the moment that within this restricted class there are probably further areas that are not accounted for satisfactorily in Davidsonian semantics; e.g. underdetermination as exemplified by the genitive construction discussed above.

[46] Belnap (1982), Higginbotham (1996), Krifka (2007, 2012).

4 Truth-conditional Theories of Meaning

especially in linguistics—on complementing truth conditions with conditions of fulfilment or use conditions.[47] So, at best, TCS covers a wide range of sentences but is at the very least not *directly* applicable to many other types of sentences. If this is right, an alternative semantics for the remaining sentences is required. Prima facie, there is no reason to suppose that this alternative would lack the resources to account for declarative sentences, too. To be sure, the status of TCS as a semantic theory of declarative sentences remains unclear as long as there is no reasonable alternative. But if there were such an alternative, the restriction of truth-conditional semantics to a particular class of sentences would speak against the theory.

Otherwise, truth-conditional semanticists might want to argue that they conceive of their theory as a universal semantic theory. It is just that so far no one has fully worked out the details for sentences that involve non-truth-evaluable content. This seems equally problematic, for why should we think that the existing theory sketch would be applicable to questions, imperatives, and the like? In fact, there is ample reason to doubt this. Questions will serve as an example. Similar reasoning could be applied to other types of sentences though. Propositions are the primary bearers of truth and hence determine the corresponding truth conditions for sentences that are used to express them.[48] In this view, declarative sentences are truth-evaluable because they express propositions. Consider the question "Is red

---

[47] Classically, propositions are considered primary bearers of truth. Declarative sentences are said to express propositions. In this view, declaratives are truth-evaluable derivatively: they directly inherit their truth values / truth conditions from the propositions they are used to express. For example, "snow is white" expresses the proposition <snow is white>. Questions do not *express* propositions in this sense, hence they lack truth value, which, however, is not to deny that questions do not relate to propositional content. It is just that there is no 1-to-1 correspondence as in the case of declaratives. Hence, the mechanism, if any, that relates propositional content ("that p") to the semantic content of a question (e.g. "Is it the case that p?") must be something different. Be that as it may, no matter what the exact relation is here, due to conceptual reasons questions as such can't be truth-evaluable. The same holds for commands, etc., which can only be satisfied but can't be true.

[48] At least, I will assume this in what follows. See Horwich (1998, 16–17, 86–90) for a justification. The argument, however, is independent of specific views on truth; it may easily be redescribed in terms of sentences as primary truth bearers.

4.2 Truth-Conditional Semantics at Work

Tom's favourite colour?" What would be an appropriate way to associate this question with a proposition?

Irrespective of *how* we might connect the question with a corresponding proposition and, by doing so, with its alleged 'truth conditions', the obvious candidate for this job is the proposition <red is Tom's favourite colour>. But whereas the sentence "Red is Tom's favourite colour" is (as per TCS) true iff red is Tom's favourite colour, things get slightly more complicated when we now turn to questions. What *actually does have* truth conditions (or is truth-evaluable) is the answer to the question. Roughly put, an affirmative answer is true iff <red is Tom's favourite colour> is true, false otherwise, and vice versa for negative answers. The problem, though, is that if we associate answers in this way with truth conditions, we still do not know the truth conditions for the question itself (for there is none). Even worse, if we take wh-questions into account, we not only do not know the truth conditions for the question itself (as opposed to the corresponding answer); we do not even know how to associate a question with a (set of) proposition(s) at all. As in the case of yes-or-no questions, the theory would need to refer to the answer. But since there are infinitely many (or at least a whole lot of reasonable) answers for specific wh-questions, the theory would need to 'build' truth conditions out of 'the question' and 'the answer' (i.e. the relevant parts thereof). Roughly along the following lines: the answer "Red" to the question "What is Tom's favourite colour?" is true iff red is Tom's favourite colour; the answer "White" to this question is true iff white is Tom's favourite colour; and so on ad libitum. As of today, Davidson-inspired semantics for non-declarative types of sentences still tends to be a rather unsatisfying endeavour.

Ad (i): I have shown that there are good reasons to question the general success of the truth-conditional paradigm. This undermines the plausibility of the second of the two original assumptions. It is now time to turn to the first assumption (meaning is truth condition). Likewise, I shall now demonstrate that this assumption is also unwarranted. Truth conditions are an important aspect of meaning, but only *aspects*, nevertheless. Many other aspects of meaning are not covered by theories that, like TCS, focus solely on truth conditions. There are even many circumstances in which it seems *irrelevant* what the truth conditions of sentences are (or the referential 'facts' concerning singular terms, for that matter).

4 Truth-conditional Theories of Meaning

All different varieties of truth-conditional semantics seem so attractive because of their purity and technical rigour. If the meaning of "snow is white" is that it is true iff snow is white, what else, then, can you ask for, if your main aim is clarity in meaning statements? The concepts employed by TCS are unambiguous: a word "w" either *refers* to its referent or it does not; a sentence "s" is either true in such-and-such circumstances or it is not; a predicate "F" either denotes a certain set of individuals or it does not; a proposition <p> is either true or it is not. Language is different. Language is vague, not only in regard to a concept like "bald" but in general. Language is, as we have known since Wittgenstein, vague in regard to "chair", for example, which is a term that serves not exactly as a paradigm example in the literature on vagueness. People's disposition to apply "chair" to a given entity develops over time, it varies between individuals, and it is context-dependent. Unlike truth conditions: "This is a chair" is either true or false if applied to a given object, and it is true only if the entity referred to by "this" is actually a chair.

To be sure, sentences seems to wear their truth conditions on their sleeves. That is to say, even if the meaning of "chair" is not a fixed set of individuals (the chairs) but varies with certain contextual factors including time, idiolect, conversational situation, etc., then "This is a chair" is still true iff this is a *chair* (corrected for time, idiolect, situation, etc.).[49] So the problem is not epistemological in nature. Rather, the problem is that the only plausible explanation for the varying meaning of "chair" is a corresponding variety of use in speakers. (Neo-)Davidson semantics is strictly bound to the Tarski-style framework summarised above. In this framework, the referents of individual terms and general terms are fixed (as in "'Aristotle' refers to Aristotle"). This implies that, for each new meaning of a term, one would need a new 'base rule' stating its meaning, which amounts to an all new theory.[50] This is implausible if TCS is put forward as a solution

---

[49] The theory that most explicitly denies such a stance on truth conditions is called occassionalism (Travis 2008). That is clearly a minority view.

[50] Actually, the underlying problem of formal approaches to semantics is that the meaning-determining context is particularly wide, as exemplified by Tomasello's 'Tom's bicycle' case (see above). For example, it may include common ground, world knowledge, speaker intentions, etc. Formal approaches may cope with some specific contextual factors such as time, place, and speaker, but it is virtually impossible for them to formally specify

to the Novelty problem, as it is far easier to assume that people's ability to understand new sentences derives from their implicit knowledge of how the terms occurring in them are used than it is to assume that this ability derives from their learning new theories every now and then.

4.2.3 Novelty and Usage-Based Theories of Meaning

The basic idea defended in the present chapter is that compositionality and Novelty are, in effect, two completely distinct issues. In particular, I have argued that the immediate step from Novelty to compositionality is unwarranted, i.e. that the alleged compositionality of natural languages is not the only option when it comes to reasonable solutions to the Novelty problem. In a way, this line of reasoning might seem anti-compositional. Although nowhere in my argument do I presuppose that languages are not compositional, I at least assume that one crucial argument in favour of the compositionality of natural languages fails. Anyway, the received view of how Novelty is to be explained is in terms of compositionality. Hence, denying the alleged strict relation between the two issues eventually leads to a certain tension between the two explanatory needs.

Here is not the right place to formulate a fully fledged alternative to the received view. Rather, I would like to highlight some methodological concerns and roughly indicate a possible solution to the problem just sketched. One potential problem in Davidson's own argumentation seems to be this. From the (apparently correct) observation that people understand any instantiation of a well-formed sentence (of a language that they master), Davidson more or less directly concludes that TCS holds. This line of reasoning essentially relies on the strategy of explaining abilities concerning sentence comprehension in terms of lexical and syntactic capabilities. Crucially, this kind of argument amounts to saying that sentence comprehension involves knowledge of composition rules and recursion. The thing is that this argument *as such* does not favour TCS nor, in fact, any other theory. An opponent of TCS could perfectly well accept the whole argument (up to this point) and argue that composition rules and recursion might be accounted

---

contexts in regards to, e.g., the knowledge shared by hearer and speaker. Accordingly, such frameworks would typically emphasise that these 'non-formal' features of context do not affect literally expressed content of sentences (e.g. Borg 2004, 2012).

4 Truth-conditional Theories of Meaning

for somewhat differently (e.g. in terms of usage-based facts). Which is to say that there is no direct step from the assumption that natural languages are organised recursively to the denial of usage-based semantics.

Another potential problem is that people—for no obvious reason—tend to think that usage-based approaches to semantics are incompatible with the compositionality principle. From this perspective, then, it looks pretty straightforward to directly infer from Novelty that some form or other of truth-conditional semantics must hold. Throughout this book, I continue to distinguish, in terms of the philosophy of language, only between two broadly construed camps: usage-based vs truth-conditional. Although this distinction, as any categorisation in philosophy, simplifies things a bit, I think it is reasonable to suppose that it does not *over*simplify. If you buy into this distinction, then the claim that usage-based approaches are incompatible with the compositionality principle amounts to saying that all compositionality-involving explanations (e.g. with regard to Novelty) must be essentially truth-conditional. An example that nicely illustrates this position can be found in Fodor & Lepore (2002, 3–4):

> The line of our argument is that since mental representation and linguistic meaning are *de facto* compositional, we can reject out of hand any theory that says that concepts(/word meanings) are Xs unless Xs are the sorts of things for which compositionality holds. That is, there must be a distinction between primitive and complex Xs, and the syntactic/semantic properties of the latter must be inherited from the syntactic/semantic properties of the former. [...] It's our belief that [...] only very few [candidates]—perhaps only one—can meet this compositionality condition; it's the bull in almost everybody's china shop.

With the above methodological considerations in mind, there are now two theoretical possibilities available to a usage-based theoretician who wants to refute the Davidsonian learnability argument. One option is to deny the assumption that usage-based approaches are incompatible with the compositionality principle. In other words, one could concede the major portion of the argument up to the intermediate conclusion that Novelty can only be explained in terms of composition rules and recursion (or, that this at least holds for the majority of cases). Accordingly, one would then need to show that usage-based accounts can be construed compositionally/recursively[51]. There are indeed some explicit attempts to reconcile the compositionality principle with usage-based semantics (e.g. Horwich 1997a). So this seems to be a viable strategy indeed.

A further option is to object to the line of reasoning one step earlier. The way I presented the argument is supposed to show that only Novelty has the status of a *phenomenon*, which is to say that it is indisputable in a way. It would require some really weird assumptions to describe the objectively observable phenomena in such a way that people, in fact, do not understand each other. Compositionality, on the other hand, is not equally immune; the fact that we typically describe languages as being fully compositional might be an artefact of academic training. Even if some (or most) parts of natural languages *are* compositional, some might be non-compositional. In effect, Construction Grammar suggests something along these lines. Importantly, in this case the whole learnability argument fails. If people are able to understand some classes of semantically non-compositional complexes (e.g. holophrases, sayings, certain syntactic constructions, idioms, etc.), then, by all means, compositionality can't account for Novelty in the way suggested. This would undermine that argument as a whole, since the *point* of invoking compositionality considerations is to account for Novelty tout court.

Here I can only very briefly indicate the basic direction that such a strategy would need to take take. In general, the claim that understanding is possible in cases in which the alleged knowledge of recursively defined composition rules plays no role whatsoever can be established quite easily. A highly pertinent example in this context is holophrases:

> [...] most children begin language acquisition by learning some unparsed adult expressions as holophrases—such expressions as *I-wanna-do-it*, *Lemme-see*, and *Where-the-bottle*. (Tomasello 2003a, 38)

---

[51] Here, I do not discuss recursiveness and compositionality separately, because the learnability argument itself presupposes that the relevant composition rules get formulated recursively (for otherwise they could not help explaining the human ability to understand an *infinity* of well-formed expressions).

4 Truth-conditional Theories of Meaning

Holophrases show that phrases that are semantically compositional from the adult's perspective (and are supposedly construed with that knowledge in mind) can be understood by children who lack the relevant syntactic knowledge (in appropriate circumstances, that is). From a philosophical point of view, two questions are especially pressing. What is the relationship between the (non-compositional) understanding of holophrases in children and the (supposedly compositional) rules that adults employ in uttering them? What is it that explains comprehension abilities if not the familiarity with composition rules?

In line with the Tomasellian paradigm, I suggest pursuing the following strategy. As regards the first question, holophrases are particularly interesting in two respects. They not only pose a problem for explanations (of Novelty) that recur to compositionality/recursion. Moreover, they themselves hint at the solution to the problem they pose (if that much metaphor is okay). Let me explain. Postulating knowledge of composition rules is not only the alleged solution to the Novelty problem but elicits further problems: namely the problem that the postulated body of information must be *acquired* in the first place.

A plausible solution here is to suppose that language learners learn composition rules by experiencing them instantiated. Simply put, the only way for learners to figure out the 'workings' of recursively defined composition rules (e.g. the semantics of relative clauses) is by observing how they are used. Holophrases are a particularly illustrative example in this context because they are interpreted non-compositionally by definition.[52] However, the basic mechanism of utterance interpretation is probably alike in all cases of language comprehension. The strategy that gets employed when inferring composition rules from a given set of utterances is, of course, well-known: abstraction (cf. Tomasello 2003a). What mechanism, other than abstraction, could explain language learners' ability to acquire syntactic knowledge?[53] This argument does not even presuppose a specific un-

---

[52] If you assume that children who understand holophrases apply rules of composition you are either redefining "holophrase" or changing the subject matter.

[53] I mean, supplemented with further constraints. Abstraction per se (whatever that is) does not help here, for one first needs to 'guess' what the relevant entities were relative to which one needs to abstract from contexts of utterance. For example, it helps if you have reasons to suppose that a particular verb is a *verb*, that a particular noun is a *noun*,

4.2 Truth-Conditional Semantics at Work

derstanding of 'abstraction'; for the purpose of this short section, it suffices to say that abstraction is one's ability to recognise commonalities between contexts and infer generalisations on the basis of this ability.

Remarkably enough, most of the entities that theories of meaning deal with are abstract entities such as propositions, sentence types, lexical meaning, inference rules, conceptual roles, semantic nets, etc. That is remarkable insofar as this coerces language learners to familiarise themselves with abstract entities (e.g. sentence types) by examining concrete objects (e.g. utterances). Given the degree of abstractness that linguistic descriptions have, it is no wonder that people argue about issues like the bottleneck problem (e.g. Kirby 2002), the poverty of the stimulus argument (e.g. Chomsky 1965), language faculty in the broad sense and in the narrow sense (Hauser, Chomsky & Fitch 2002), e-language and i-language (Chomsky 1986), and the like. More importantly, given that the only available data for learners is utterances (i.e. context-bound instantiations of sentence types), they have no other choice than to use that data to determine the semantics of the abstract entities they are supposed to learn. For example, language learners might infer that "chair" refers to chairs from the observation that most of their already competent interlocutors use "chair" to refer to chairs.

The above argument strongly suggest the following interpretation of language acquisition: rather than relying on knowledge of composition rules in order to interpret utterances, learners seem to do just the opposite. They are forced to acquire linguistic knowledge, including knowledge concerning recursive composition rules, on the basis of their *prior understanding of utterances*. In this view, the error in explaining Novelty in terms of compositionality lies in the negligence of the fact that the composition rules at hand must be acquired first. As I have shown, the possibilities are rare here. One option is to assume they are innate, which seems implaus-

---

etc.; it helps if you can narrow down the logical space for novel semantics by taking into account known semantics (Ferguson, Graf & Waxman 2014); it helps if you are able to delineate word boundaries (Tomasello 2003a, 59–61); it helps if you can tell whether it is a particular (absent) object that your interlocutor is focusing on (Liszkowski, Schäfer, Carpenter & Tomasello 2009); it helps if you are capable of recognising syntactic structures (Brent 1994); and so on and so forth.

4 Truth-conditional Theories of Meaning

ible for a variety of reasons.[54] The alternative is that they are learnt. However, if they are learnt, they are learnt on the basis of the available data. And the source data is utterances, which—from a metatheoretic perspective—are compositional complexes.

One of the currently most influential neo-Davidsonians, in discussing mindreading abilities, frames the problem thus:

> A first point we need to consider concerns how the nascent language user acquires their lexicon initially. That is to say, since presumably normal speakers are not born with a dictionary-like body of knowledge, pairing natural language words with their meanings, we need to explain how competent language users come to learn such information. [...I]n order to learn a language in the first place (*for example, to find out which publicly available sign one's linguistic community has chosen to attach to which object or property*) it may well be that a grasp of speaker intentions is necessary. [...] Yet all that the modular theory [Fodorian modularism, upon which Borg's Minimalism is based] is committed to claiming is that *once this system is in place*, that is, once a lexical item has been acquired, then the use of this item no longer need rest on recognition of any kind of speaker intention. (Borg 2004b, 136 and 139, both italics mine)

The problem that Borg discusses here is that there seems to be no place in her theory for intention ascriptions and mindreading abilities. Let us ignore this issue for the moment. I identify at least three important points in the quoted passage. Firstly, Borg acknowledges that although semantics 'takes place', so to speak, at the level of types (in particular, lexical meaning), acquisition of (alleged) semantic facts necessarily takes place at the

---

[54] For example, one insurmountable problem in this context is the speed with which meaning shifts, grammaticalisation processes and the like take place. At both the syntactic and the semantic level, natural languages morph within periods of time that are incompatible with innateness theses. It might be that the processes that constitute language acquisition are innate to a large extent (e.g. things like gaze-following ability; cf. Brooks & Meltzoff (2005)). Innateness of these processes does not affect the present argument though.

4.2 Truth-Conditional Semantics at Work

level of tokenings. This is tantamount to saying that language learners face the problem of simultaneously abstracting away from *all* factors that contribute towards utterance meaning, e.g. from speaker intentions. Secondly, Borg indicates here that she wants to defend a rather naïve conception of the continuity of natural-language semantics. Describing the problem of word learning along the lines of finding out which words 'one's linguistic community has chosen to attach' to particular objects clearly neglects the dynamics of actual language use. I will return to this in a minute.

Thirdly, Borg suggests a strict boundary between semantics and language acquisition.[55] I think this last point and the second one are, effectively, two sides of the same coin. If you think that word semantics works as if it were written down in a social contract, then you probably also think that word learning processes are completed once they are finished. Such a strict boundary seems unwarranted, given the rapidity with which, for example, words change their meaning in actual linguistic societies. It seems far more plausible to assume instead that the mechanisms underlying language acquisition keep being used even in competent speakers. This picture is, to a surprisingly large extent, congruent with Borg's view; the only difference being that I would assume that language 'acquisition' is not completed at some point but is rather a continuous process. Simply put, word learning—or, in general, learning of new constructions—is a process that happens with each acquaintance with a particular instantiation. It is just that *most* words have a relatively stable lexical meaning which might invoke the impression that learning processes concerning

---

[55] In other parts of the book, she also distinguishes between semantics and language use (i.e. communication). This enables her to allow for things like mindreading abilities not only in language acquisition but also in language use, although they are not allowed in her actual theory. That is to say, mindreading abilities (and the like; e.g. plausibility considerations, world knowledge, cotext, default assumptions, etc.) *do affect* language acquisition and language use, but, in her view, they do not affect semantics proper. For the specific relevance of default assumptions in semantics, the reader may consult the work of Jaszczolt, who says that

> Starting with *salient* meanings of lexical items [...], interlocutors proceed to the interpretation of larger units either assigning meanings to them automatically or processing them through conscious inference, depending on contextual factors. (2011, 14)

See also Jaszczolt (2005).

these words are finished at some predefined point in time, i.e. once one had 'found out' which words attach to which objects (cf. the use of "and" today and five-hundred years ago). However, other words change their meaning rather rapidly, which undermines the claim that learning processes regarding them (or, in fact, any other term) can be completed once and for all (cf. the use of "to twitter" today (2014) and ten years ago).

There is one more general worry that I would like to raise in regard to the above quotation. The passage clearly invokes the impression that *any* specific semantic theory could be reconciled with just about *any* theory of word learning. The basic idea seems to be that allowing for mindreading (and the like) at the level of acquisition does not affect the plausibility of denying that such capacities play an explanatory role at the level of semantics. Again, '[e]ven if we ultimately decide that language acquisition *is* an essentially inferential process [...], there is no direct move from this idea to the claim that linguistic understanding *per se* is such an inferential process [...]' (Borg 2004b, 139, emphases hers). But this seems problematic as the *object* of the relevant acquisition processes are the abstract entities postulated by semantics (e.g. sentence meaning as opposed to utterance meaning). So the link between the two realms is rather tight. Borg explicitly characterises herself as neo-Davidsonian (2004b, ch. 1, passim). By virtue of this conviction, the basic elements postulated by her theory must concern knowledge of referential relations, for the simple reason that these relations are the defining feature of Davidsonian semantics.

This implies, though, that a theory of word learning (or, generally, an acquisition theory) is compatible with Borg's minimalism only to the extent that the objects postulated by the former theory comply with the objects postulated by the latter theory. I begin with the latter theory (Borg's). Being a neo-Davidsonian approach, the basic elements postulated correspond to the so-called Tarskian 'base clauses' discussed above ("'snow' refers to snow"; "x satisfies 'is white' if and only if x is white"; et cetera). I dub these 'referential facts'. If one combines all this, the following picture emerges. Firstly, Borg herself suggests that word learning can only be explained in terms of use. Secondly, a strict boundary between acquisition theories and semantics seems unwarranted, since 'word learning' is an ongoing process. You can't delineate the class of cases in which you learn from the class of cases in which you merely interpret. Hence, word learning is usage-based and it is not clearly separable from mere semantic interpretation. Given this, it seems highly unlikely that the theoretical objects that a theory of language acquisition should postulate are beliefs concerning *referential facts* rather than beliefs concerning *usage-based facts*.

This concludes my discussion of the relationship between theories of acquisition and theories of meaning. A related worry that I already raised above concerns relevant alternatives: what kind of explanation accounts for Novelty if not ascription of knowledge about recursive rules of compositions à la Davidson? Here, my answer will be even more tentative (i.e. shorter), as this question actually requires a book-long treatment. I think Davidson's strategy is to combine the two problems reflected in compositionality and what I call Novelty. His proposal, essentially, is to provide a single solution for both issues. Given all the reasons cited above in favour of the distinction, I accordingly suggest that an answer to the question at hand involves distinguishing between these two projects first. That is to say, the *alternative explanation* we are after primarily concerns Novelty, not compositionality.

Presumably, competent language users construe their utterances partly on the basis of the rules of composition that they master. This, however, does not imply that language *learners* employ the very same rules in order to interpret those utterances. Nor does it imply that language *users* employ *only* those rules in conjunction with lexical knowledge whenever they interpret (for what hearers potentially understand is utterances, not sentences). Which mechanisms play a role in interpretation is, at the end of the day, an empirical question. It thus does not concern me here. Davidson, I think, is quite right in noting that the ability of competent language users to interpret novel 'sentences' is somehow rooted in their prior linguistic understanding. Yet, as the above discussion shows, this does not speak (solely) in favour of his theory. The very same 'correlation' between prior linguistic knowledge and understanding could be explained relative to the assumption that the recursive rules of composition get formulated in usage-based terms. The above argument concerning language acquisition (and the continuous process of 'acquisition' due to the dynamics of natural languages) suggest that, in fact, those rules (as well as lexical knowledge) should be thus formulated.

4 Truth-conditional Theories of Meaning

The philosophically most relevant point in this context is, I think, that language learning reveals a general constraint on how the Novelty problem should be best approached. Language learners (e.g. children) understand 'novel sentences' just like we do. In contrast to competent speakers, they do this despite their lack of prior linguistic knowledge. In Borg's terms, they do not know yet which expression has been chosen by the society to attach to which object or property. Fortunately, the ascription of *understanding* is fairly independent from what we suppose constitutes this understanding. Whether we are justified in ascribing understanding concerning a given utterance to a given child in a given situation depends on the overall observable behavioural patterns that the child shows. This is essentially independent from the linguistic knowledge that we typically presuppose in adults. By assumption, children lack this kind of knowledge. Given that, nevertheless, they are able to understand (which is justifiable on the basis of what they *do*), something else must explain their abilities.

As I said, I will not try to give a comprehensive answer here. The philosophically relevant point is just that whatever one's explanation might be, *it can be given independently from the fact that the 'thing' that is supposedly understood (i.e. an utterance) is semantically compositional from the point of view of competent speakers or theoreticians*. For example, "Gimme-it!" seems compositional from the adult's perspective. But typical evidence for a child's understanding of that expression would be its satisfaction when it receives the object that it asked for. This holds even if we had independent reason to assume that the child does not understand the underlying compositional structure of the expression (for example, if we knew independently that the it does not understand or apply "give" in other linguistic contexts).

These considerations are essentially methodological. The interesting issue still remains: what explains understanding if not prior linguistic knowledge? The currently by far most influential paradigm in the area of language acquisition is Tomasello's. The basic idea is to shift the theoretical focus from language as such to the social settings in which language takes place. More precisely, the Tomasellian idea—put in philosophical prose—is to focus on human cooperative behaviour by viewing language as one means among others that enable or foster cooperation in the first place. In contrast to the Gricean paradigm, language is not conceived as a cooperative endeavour but as a *means* to achieve cooperative goals.[56] This suggests the direction that a plausible answer to the present question would need to take. A theory of meaning starts with a theory of communication, as communication is the point of having a language. What cognitive agents are primarily interested in is achieving their respective ends. Using language 'correctly' is only interesting insofar as it fosters success in achieving these ends. According to Tomasello, language is basically a means that helps achieving goals in cooperative settings (Tomasello 2008).

When it comes to language acquisition, the question accordingly is not: why do children understand certain utterances? Rather, the relevant question is: by which means do humans achieve cooperative goals *in general*? Or, rather, what are the prerequisites under which cooperation occurs? Applied to the holophrase example, the idea then is to first explain the prerequisites for the achievement of particular goals (here: 'getting it'). Such an explanation probably recurs to common ground, joint attention, mindreading capacities, and related notions, i.e. notions that are not primarily designed to explain language but cooperation. *Semantic* explanations would then start, if you like, from the 'communication-theoretic' fact that the child is able to recognise *the specific meaning of "Gimme-it!" in particular situations* (i.e. in situations that are such that uttering "Gimme-it!" leads to 'getting it'). Generally, approaching language comprehension this way makes it possible to explain the quite counter-intuitive effect that it seems possible to understand utterances without 'understanding' the instantiated sentence type in advance. This is what actually happens in language acquisition. In a final step, the *semantic explanation in the strict sense* (i.e. explanations concerning lexical and syntactical knowledge[57]) presumably recur to the child's abstraction abilities (whose exact nature is, again, an empirical question). For example, in order to acquire knowledge of lexical meanings, a child needs to recognise similarities between the semantic contributions of the same word across different conversational contexts.

---

[56] This is my supervisor's way of putting it.

[57] Remember that construction grammar—the theoretical framework that serves as a backdrop for this book—assumes that syntactic constructions bear their own meaning, which is why I list them here in the context of semantics.

Part II

Disposition

5 Theories of Truth & Meaning

This chapter draws directly on the results of the previous chapter. There, I proposed that we distinguish clearly between genuine phenomena and their corresponding theoretical explications, which, by their very nature, lack the specific—indisputable—epistemic status of the former. The Novelty issue, I suggested, is such a phenomenon. It can't possibly be explained away. There is really a *need* to account for it. Prima facie, compositionality looks like a phenomenon, too. In contrast to Novelty, though, this seems wrong-headed. I argued that impressions to the contrary stem from theoreticians' tendency to present the Novelty problem in such a way as if it concerned compositionality itself. People understand complex expressions due to their underlying compositional structure. Therefore, it seems that what we need, first and foremost, is an account of compositionality. However, compositionality is (i) primarily a feature of language, not of communication (as such it is a *phenomenon* only in the derivative sense in that it is exemplified in communication)[1] and, therefore, (ii) it is a *means* to account for certain abilities (i.e. comprehension capacities), rather than itself something that gets 'discovered' and requires explanation.

---

[1] This, again, anticipates my reasoning in the methodological part. The basic idea here is simply this: of course, there is a tight link between language and communication to the extent that some features of the latter can only be explained with recourse to the former. Crucially, though, language is an abstract system that involves the postulation of entities that are not 'out there in the world' (e.g. sentence types). This implies that the entities (and features; e.g. compositionality) postulated with respect to that abstract system are not themselves phenomena but merely means to account for the actual phenomena out there. As regards communication, the phenomenon is *utterance* comprehension. Postulation of knowledge concerning the semantics of *sentences* (including knowledge concerning recursive rules of composition) is only required to the extent that it helps explaining utterance comprehension. This is because there is no independent reason to assume that people understand sentences irrespective of our evidence that they understand certain utterances (written or verbal).

5 Theories of Truth & Meaning

My aim in the present chapter is to underpin these claims by relating them to a critical discussion of the prevalent conviction in philosophy that the *literal* meaning of words and sentences is the primary object of study in a theory of meaning. In particular, I am going to question the widespread assumption that the relevant property of referring expressions is their *referring* to something (i.e. singular terms refer to objects, predicates to classes thereof), where "relevant" means that this property is required to explain certain features of language (especially non-literality). On the contrary, my argument in this chapter is that all that is required to fulfil the job of ordinary 'primary meaning' defined in terms of reference relations is an alternative definition of the term that operates only on expectations. I explicate my re-definition of the term "primary meaning" by proposing to reverse the order of explanation in semantics and pragmatics. Fundamentally, meaning in context (arguably a matter of pragmatics) can explain context-independent meaning (semantic meaning). For example, people would argue that "cold" means 'cold', and that *by virtue of that property* "cold" might mean something else, given appropriate circumstances. I argue instead that what people always understand (if they understand) is pragmatic meaning, i.e. meaning in context. The expectations that they arrive at *by virtue of their ability to understand pragmatic meaning* is enough to account for linguistic features that require a literal/non-literal distinction (like irony). Looking at it that way, the explanations for non-literality might, in the end, be very similar to the original explanation (e.g. Grice's), for the expectations that one would typically acquire arguably very much resemble the 'primary meanings' ordinarily postulated (e.g. people would typically expect that "Aristotle" is used to refer to Aristotle, and so on).

All this is the topic of section 5.1. In section 5.2, I then discuss compositionality and recursiveness[2] in the context of construction grammar, especially with respect to Tomasello's work on language acquisition. The motivation behind this is this: if I argue—as I do in the present chapter and the previous one—against Davidson's ideas regarding primary meaning and compositionality, I should rather show that an alternative (constructional) account of compositionality is viable and indeed worth pursuing. In effect, I will argue that Tomasello's framework based on the notion

---

[2] I use "recursiveness" and "recursion" as stylistic variations of each other.

of *cooperation* is already a good basis upon which an account of utterance comprehension can be built.

5.1 Literal/Non-Literal Interface

The foregoing chapter was, to a certain extent, anti-Davidsonian in that it criticised major elements of truth-conditional semantics. Undeniably, though, there seems to be a rather strong connection between *truth* and *meaning*. What is the connection between these two notions if one assumes a usage-based approach to meaning? Obviously, there are differences to TCS. For example, in truth-conditional semantics one would suppose that the meaning of a singular term is its reference, i.e. one would assume that, for example, the meaning of "Aristotle" is (the person) Aristotle.[3] One would also assume that the meaning of a predicate like "() is wise" is a function from possible worlds to a set of individuals (or just a set, if one takes into account only the actual world). Then a complex expression like "Aristotle is wise" would be *true* (for "is true iff" 'replaces' the ordinary "means that") if and only if the individual denoted by "Aristotle" (Aristotle) is among the individuals in the set of things denoted by "() is wise" (the wise entities). In short, "Aristotle is wise" is true if and only if Aristotle is wise.

Truth is a property of propositions, or, derivatively, of sentences (see above). It is not ascribable to atomic expressions. In truth-conditional semantics, the role played by truth at sentential level is fulfilled by (other) extensions at sub-sentential level. In the orthodox view, truth values are extensions of sentences. So, the meaning which "Aristotle" contributes to the meaning of a sentence is the fact (if any) that it *refers* to Aristotle. The meaning which "() is wise" contributes is the fact (if any) that it *refers* to a set of individuals (or that it is a function from worlds to sets of individuals). In other words, reference at the sub-sentential level corresponds to truth at sentence level.

Among the commonplaces in the philosophy of language is the assumption that almost all (non-logical) elements of natural languages, if they are

---
[3] More precisely, one would need to say that one way of stating the meaning of "Aristotle" is by saying that "Aristotle" refers to Aristotle.

5 Theories of Truth & Meaning

meaningful at all, have a literal meaning. Atomic as well as complex elements (typically, words and sentences) have, it is claimed, a type-specifiable meaning that can be studied more or less independently from the tokenings of these elements. Davidson (1986) defines "first meaning" as 'what should be found by consulting a dictionary based on actual usage' (159), given certain standard conditions. Knowledge about 'first meanings' in this sense belongs to one's 'prior theory', i.e. roughly the theory that one has before entering a conversation. There is a huge variety of notions related to "first meaning" that all more or less serve the same purpose, including "semantic meaning", "literal meaning", "truth-evaluable content", "actual meaning", "lexical meaning", and so forth. For what follows, I shall use the term "primary meaning" only (as above). I call the opposite concept "pragmatic meaning". Normally, the distinction between the two is presented in terms of the intuitively compelling dichotomy of what is said versus what is meant. What is said by using a certain sentence is what this particular sentence means, given the 'standard' interpretation of all terms occurring in it. Before I continue with a rough characterisation of what is meant by a particular sentence, let me look at some examples first. My plan in what follows is this: first, I present some examples and discuss the ordinary notion of 'primary meaning' in the sense of literal meanings as they are assumed in truth-conditional semantics. Then I argue that a refined definition of "primary meaning" that is solely based on expectations (i.e. is defined use-theoretically) is capable of accounting for those phenomena that typically motivate the assumption of a literal/non-literal divide. Since there is no reason to assume this divide other than the classical examples (e.g. irony, metaphor, etc.), I conclude that my redefined notion of "primary meaning" is theoretically adequate.

Here is the first example. Suppose that a speaker of an utterance of "James is waiting at the corner" thinks that Will is called "James" and therefore intends to refer to Will by uttering "James", then the 'literal meaning' of "James" nevertheless is 'James'. Hence, the sentence means that he, James, is waiting at the corner. The speaker's intentions, if any, come into play only when it comes to pragmatic meaning. Given the assumptions, one common interpretation of the sentence as regards what is meant is *that Will is waiting at the corner*. And the explanation for this is that *this* is the intended interpretation of the speaker. Literal meanings are taken to determine the truth conditions of a sentence. If so, "James is waiting at the corner" is true iff James is waiting at the corner, irrespective of the speaker's intentions (and beliefs, for that matter). Although there is also some evidence to the contrary, it seems reasonable to suppose that the usual view on this matter is that—save for obvious candidates for context sensitivity, especially indexicals—the truth conditions of a given sentence can be determined without any further world knowledge such as speaker intentions, world knowledge, belief ascriptions, etc.

For the sake of argument, I need to assume provisionally the distinction between literal/primary/lexical meaning and derived/pragmatic/utterance meaning. Accordingly, I sometimes speak as if words really have primary meaning in the traditional sense, e.g. in terms of reference.[4] Following the classical Gricean example (Grice 1989), the assumption of some plausible background assumptions ensures that the non-literal meaning of "It's cold in here, isn't it?" could—under appropriate circumstances—be paraphrased as 'Could you close the window, please?' (or something reasonably similar). This view, usually referred to as 'two-step' or 'inferentialist', will be explained in some more detail in the next section. The idea of two-step strategies is to delineate between two distinct interpretative processes. Roughly, the first process is semantic interpretation, which computes sentential meaning on the basis of sub-sentential elements. The non-literal meaning is then *inferred* on the basis of the literal interpretation derived at the first stage (i.e. by recognising that maxims of conversation (Grice 1975) have been violated). From the current perspective, two-step interpretations of non-literal meaning are highly relevant as they presuppose that sentential *primary meaning* can serve as 'input' to the actual inferential process that allegedly guides utterance interpretation.

5.1.1 Intuitive Propositional Content

This first overview of the distinction between primary and pragmatic meaning should suffice for present purposes. I do not want to go too much

---

[4] For most of this book, I adopt an established convention from linguistics when I talk about derived meaning. In linguistics, people tend to use *single quotes* to indicate paraphrases, i.e. rough characterisations of the most probable non-literal interpretation of utterances. I do the same in what follows.

5 Theories of Truth & Meaning

into the details at this stage. What is important to note here is that the last example hints at the very close connection that exists between pragmatic meaning and pragmatics. The textbook story runs like this:[5] primary meanings are fixed, so "John" refers to (the person) John, etc. When confronted with a given utterance, a hearer interprets the utterance against the backdrop of general pragmatic principles (e.g. Grice's maxims). Given the literal meaning of the utterance plus pragmatic principles plus a little world knowledge, the hearer is eventually able to infer what is meant.

When it comes to pragmatic and primary meaning and to the motivation for that distinction, a reasonable strategy seems to go just the other way around. It makes sense to start with the observation that pragmatics abound in everyday conversations. You have irony, metaphor, socioculturally determined word choice and what not. There must, therefore, be something that explains these phenomena. Semantics deals with literal meaning (I assume for the sake of argument). But these meanings can't explain the relevant phenomena. So there must be something else— namely 'pragmatic principles'—that account for these phenomena, or so most people claim. So far the easiest way for pragmatics to achieve an explanation is to take primary meanings as starting points, because they exist anyway (says the semanticist). The job of pragmatics then is just to explain how what is meant can be determined on the basis of literal meanings. What is relevant from the current perspective is that if all this is a successful strategy, then the distinction semantics/pragmatics seems to justify the distinction literal/non-literal meaning.

One of the most striking examples in regard to the connection between primary and pragmatic meaning is irony. The meaning of an ironic utterance is, people typically assume, *just the opposite* of what the expression would 'actually' mean. For instance, "This is a nice building!" means, according to the inferentialist' interpretation, that this is a nice building. However, if one knew that it was stated in an ironic manner (whatever the evidence might be), then one would also know that *in this case* it means

---

[5] For example, Akmajian, Demers, Farmer & Harnish (1995). They provide a neo-Gricean explanation of how pragmatic meaning is derived. The explanation starts with primary meanings and, if certain 'presumptions' are violated, ends up with some derived meaning or other, depending on the 'strategies' (irony, metaphor) involved. The 'classic' in this area is Bach & Harnish (1979).

5.1 Literal/Non-Literal Interface

(non-literally) that this is not a nice building at all. Prima facie, it seems that pragmatic meaning is *parasitic* on literal meaning. Therefore, the former kind of meaning seems to presuppose the latter.[6]

This admittedly very brief overview of two-step approaches to utterance meaning shows that an important motivation for primary meaning is a certain underlying conviction about the boundaries of semantics and pragmatics. The distinction is not undisputed but widely accepted. By the same token, many people accept the assumption of primary meaning as well. Taken together with the undisputed acceptance of the compositionality principle, the following picture seems to emerge. Two main reasons seem to support the classical conception of primary meaning. One is compositionality, which apparently requires that words have a stable, lexical meaning that can serve as the basis for a composition process (more on this in the next section). Another reason obviously is a prevailing idea of the semantics/pragmatics divide that is underlying particular approaches to pragmatics, especially neo-Gricean paradigms. These convictions concerning a clear-cut semantics/pragmatics divide and formally identifiable primary meanings (i.e. the idea that words 'wear their meanings on their sleeves') fit nicely with neo-Davidsonian approaches to semantics. For example, Borg repeatedly emphasises that her theory is not at all concerned with communication; hers is a semantic view that perfectly maps onto a broadly Gricean conception of pragmatics. Hence, questioning the status of these just-mentioned convictions implies questioning the status of truth-conditional semantics in general. In the following section, I shall go into the details of Davidson's 'sentence comprehension' argument. I will argue that his assumption that sentence comprehension can only be explained by recurring to compositionality and recursiveness is unwarranted. This argument is based on the idea that 'primary meaning' need not be spelt out, as Davidson assumes, in terms of referential relations but, rather, might

---

[6] The debate between contextualists (e.g. Recanati) and minimalists (e.g. Borg) is, to a certain extent, a debate about whether formally described meaning statements accord with the 'intuitive' propositional content that a typical language user would ascribe to a given utterance (see Borg 2004*b*, ch. 4.3). Borg's view contrasts nicely with Recanati's so-called Availability Principle, according to which there is a 'level at which we find both what is said and what is implied, which level is characterized by conscious accessibility' (2004, 13).

5 Theories of Truth & Meaning

simply be spelt out in terms of expectations. Accordingly, I propose a redefinition of this term that fits these purposes.

5.1.2 Functions of Primary Meaning

Classical primary meaning is taken for granted by virtually everyone in philosophy and linguistics. The reasons in its favour are legion. On closer examination, it seems that most arguments boil down to mere plausibility considerations. Most of these arguments, again, derive their plausibility from the plausibility of the more fundamental compositionality principle and arguments for recursion in natural language.[7] The argument for primary meaning remains implicit. Still, it falls off as a by-product if the argument for recursiveness in natural languages is construed roughly as follows:[8]

(i) Humans are able to comprehend any new sentence they hear or read (empirical observation);[9]

---

[7] The historically relevant source for the notion of 'recursion' is Bar-Hillel (1953). A fairly recent overview article is Clark (2006).

[8] Davidson hints at such a strategy in *Theories of Meaning and Learnable Languages* (1965), when he says that '[supposing that language lacks recursion]; then no matter how many sentences a would-be speaker learns to produce and understand, there will remain others whose meanings are not given by the rules already mastered' (388). In this context, cf. also Patterson (2005). However, I need to emphasise here that the presented argument is a straw man that first and foremost serves the purpose of showing that I have a viable alternative to classical primary meaning. An alternative, that is, which is applicable to the Novelty problem discussed in the previous chapter, i.e. the 'problem' that competent speakers are able to comprehend unknown, well-formed sentences in the language they have mastered. Note that in the argument reconstruction (construction, rather) I keep using "sentence" instead of "utterance", although, of course, only the latter can be *understood* or *comprehended* by speakers/hearers (cf. also my remarks on understanding in the previous chapter). However, this way of speaking accords quite nicely with the Davidsonian jargon. The idea here is that since sentences (like words) are supposed to have a stable meaning that can be assigned to them relative to contexts of utterances (e.g. in order to resolve indexicals), but independently of conversational situations (e.g. irrespective of intentions), these *sentence meanings* can be understood (Borg 2004b). In line with this assumption, I continue to speak of 'sentences' in this chapter.

[9] Provided (a) they are competent in a natural language L, (b) the sentence at stake is a sentence of L and is grammatically well-formed, (c) the sentence consists only of words and syntactic operations the hearer is familiar with, and (d) no constraints in regards

5.1 Literal/Non-Literal Interface

(ii) Humans have only limited cognitive resources (empirical observation);[10]

(iii) Comprehending sentences of any length with finite means is only possible via recursively defined rules (assumption);

(iv) Recursively defined rules in the sense of functions from atoms to sentence meaning operate on literal meaning (analytic truth);

(v) The only way to account for humans' linguistic abilities is via primary meaning (from (iii) and (iv)).

(i) is uncontroversial.[11] (ii) is equally uncontroversial as (i) (probably even more plausible). (iii) is the 'only game in town' assumption that I will be discussing at length below. (iv) must be an analytic truth, since functions have determinate values for certain arguments. Take, for example, the function "$f(x) = 3x$". This is the function it de facto is because it yields the value 3 for the argument 1, the value 6 for the argument 2, and so forth. This is why it is the $3x$ function. If it 'behaved' differently, it would not be the $3x$ function any more. It yields certain values because the values of the arguments are fixed, i.e. "1" means 1, "2" means 2, and so forth. No fixed values, no function. The same holds for 'functions' in

---

to computational power and time apply. Note that the last constraint is not essential to the argument. Reformulating the argument without it would just complicate matters unnecessarily, roughly along the following lines: Suppose there is a limiting number of symbols per sentence people can comprehend (or maybe an absolute length limit of sentences). Then, still, people are able to comprehend *almost* infinitely many sentences (because there are almost infinitely many ways to construe words with the resources of the alphabet, and almost infinitely many ways to combine words). But it is similarly implausible to assume that people use (almost) infinitely many different ways to link symbols with meanings, i.e. even in languages with such a sentence length limit speakers would probably rely on the very same resources to compose meanings as in languages without such limits. That is, they would also employ recursively defined rules (according to the present argument).

[10] That is to say, limited resources in regards to the number of 'rules' they employ for linking symbols with meanings, not with respect to computational power and time (cf. previous footnote).

[11] You may convince yourself by continuing to read this book.

Tarski's framework.[12] "() is white", for example, yields the value True for the argument "snow", False otherwise. If this is so, it is because "snow" and "white" have fixed meanings. "Snow" means snow; and snow, let us suppose, is white (in a given theory). The theory could not have yielded the value True for "Snow is white" if "snow" (or "white", for that matter) were interpreted in other ways or had somehow 'indeterminate' content (whatever that would mean here). So, if the above is conceived as a Davidsonian argument for Tarskian recursion (that is, for the idea that semantic knowledge is implemented in humans in a way that corresponds to the recursive rules in Tarski's theory of truth), then this implies an argument for stable, primary meaning as well. Only stable meanings can serve as input to recursive rules of composition.

Given these considerations, it seems relatively hopeless to question the validity of the argument.[13] I acknowledge that it leaves some aspects underspecified: for example, I could possibly specify more precisely what it means to be able to comprehend a sentence (or utterance, for that matter). In particular, I should probably say a bit more about what counts as evidence in this context. Be that as it may, it seems reasonable to suppose, with Davidson, that people obviously have *some such ability*, if only for the sake of argument. Also, the premises all look pretty plausible. From my perspective, the only premise that can reasonably be attacked here is the third, i.e. the assumption (or intermediate conclusion) that only recur-

---

[12] The 'recursively defined rules' are often identified with rules in Tarski's truth theory (see Davidson).

[13] I mean, valid if you allow that I omit some obvious intermediate steps. For instance, it would be logically invalid to take the step from (i) and (ii) to (iii). But this can be repaired quite easily by further assuming that recursive rules *are* in fact a plausible solution for the Novelty problem and that they are the *only* available solution. Fiddling with the validity of the argument unnecessarily complicates matters. What is really interesting from a philosophical point of view is whether the premises are true. Actually, ensuring validity in an argument is really cheap. For example, it is always possible to transform an invalid argument into a valid one by introducing further premises: "A; ergo B" is invalid, "A; when A then B; ergo B" is not. So, if the 'missing' premises are obvious enough (as they presumably are in my reconstruction), then, I think, it seems reasonable to simplify as far as possible.

sion can account for human comprehension abilities.[14,15] To begin with, it is an observable fact that the ability of language users to understand novel sentences correlates strongly[16] with their familiarity with the words occurring in those sentences (plus syntactic knowledge). Or, reversely, if someone is ignorant with regard to the words (or syntax) that constitute a sentence, she is unlikely to understand it—even if she is otherwise completely competent concerning, in general, the language used and, in particular, the syntactic structure (or words) employed. This suggests—and it is often concluded—that someone's ability to understand a simple declar-

---

[14] In line with Davidson's argumentation in *Truth and Meaning*, I suppose that the 're-cursively defined rules' we are talking about correspond to Tarskian composition rules that specify truth conditions of sentences on the basis of the atomic meanings of their constituents.

[15] Basically all semantic accounts that base their justification on considerations concerning human comprehension capacities do so by invoking 'classical' primary meanings in terms of reference relations. For example, the ability to understand "That's an apple" is, or so the arguments go, partly determined by my knowledge that "apple" refers to apples.
One might argue that my criticism of the third premise does not apply to Fodor's language of thought, since semantic values of sentences are traceable to their syntactic structures. Therefore, the atomic parts of sentences do not need to have primary meaning (e.g. in terms of reference); in fact, they need not have meaning at all. (Alexandros Tillas pointed out to me this possibility.) However, Fodor points out several times that, regarding the view on the semantics of words, he advocates just the position that is at stake here. We read:

> [...] the assumptions we have been defending can be abbreviated as: learning [a natural language] L involves (at least) learning its truth definition. Now, one way of formulating a truth definition [...] is this: We distinguish between a finite set of *elementary* predicates of L, for each of which the appropriate determination is actually *listed* [...]. (Fodor 1975, 79)
>
> Consonant with the general methodology of this study, I shall endure what I don't know how to cure. In particular, I shall continue to assume that learning a natural language is learning the rules which determine the extensions of its predicates [...]. (82)

[16] Although not strictly, as proven by children's ability to understand holophrases, for example.

ative sentence like, say, "Snow is white" is parasitic on her understanding of "Snow", "to be", "white", and the 'copula sentence structure'.[17]

As a matter of fact, it would be absurd to deny this correlation. However, two further independent claims may be questioned. One is the step from mere correlation between word knowledge (knowing the meaning of a given word) and sentence comprehension (being able to understand novel sentences) to the claim that sentence meaning is a function of word meanings. The other is the implicit assumption that a Tarskian framework is the only reasonable solution for going from word meaning to sentence meaning, where the important part is, of course, that a Tarski-style theory is fleshed out in terms of reference, satisfaction, and truth conditions (as being, respectively, the meaning of singular terms, predicates, and sentences). Since I have already criticised some general elements of truth-conditional semantics in the previous chapter (4), the focus in this chapter lies on the role 'primary meanings' play in my own framework. In particular, I would like to show in the following which role the redefined notion of 'primary meaning' can play in the task of relating atomic meanings with complex meanings.

The intuition that the (conventional/literal) meaning of "cold" is coldness seems very strong. Interestingly, this intuition seems to persist irrespective of the sentential context in which "cold" occurs. In the famous Gricean example, it is shown that an instantiation of (α) "It's cold in here" can be used to express a particular wish or command (under appropriate circumstances). The mentioned intuition is relevant, since the pragmatic meaning—for instance, 'Please close the window!'—can, Griceans say, only be 'inferred' by hearers if they have a prior understanding of α's constituents. But the intended/conveyed meaning (roughly, 'what is meant'[18]) is

---

[17] This, of course, is just a reprise of a well-known theme in Davidson (especially 1965 and 1967).

[18] "What is meant", like "what is said", is a notoriously controversial notion. I will try to avoid using both in what follows as far as possible. The phrase "what is meant" (in Grice's terminology) corresponds to what I call pragmatic (or conveyed) meaning in this chapter. I particularly like the term "conveyed" in this context, as it bears the connotation that the intention to get a particular meaning across is *fulfilled* or *successful*—a connotation that "what is meant" lacks. That is, in my terminology pragmatic meaning depends on what people actually do in their effort to coordinate their behaviour. The phrase "what is said" is especially problematic since Recanati's proposal to conceive of what is said in

5.1 Literal/Non-Literal Interface

not in any reasonable sense made up of the components "It's", "cold", "in", and "here" (plus syntactic structure). Rather, or so the classical story goes, what is meant is inferred *from the meaning of the complete expression "It's cold in here"* plus world knowledge (and more), i.e. the important intermediate step is to compute the complete literal meaning first before going to what is actually meant in a specific context. If one accepts that there are good reasons against primary meaning (as I do), then one needs to provide an explanation for why people are inclined to have the intuition in question. Prima facie, you can't directly go from hearing "It's", "cold", "in", and "here" to the interpretation 'Close the window!' without the intermediate interpretation 'It's cold in here'. I shall talk about this intuition first and come back to word/sentence meaning below.[19]

The explanation I am going to present is simple. I take it that the reason why people come to think words have primary meaning is because they commit a kind of statistical fallacy. The fallacy is triggered by the circumstance that pragmatic meaning (i.e. the actual content of a given utterance) is, *in the vast majority of cases*, identical with primary meaning. For instance, most of the time "dog" really means 'dog', i.e. it is used to talk about dogs (or dog-like entities). There is no better way to express this, I am afraid. Note that the claim is not that the literal meaning of "dog" is that it refers to dogs (or doghood). Rather, it is a claim about how "dog" is standardly used. This has nothing *directly* to do with reference, although standardly "dog" *is* in fact used to refer to dogs (or dog-like entities). Lastly, note that I am not assuming, as Fodor does (1975, esp. ch. 2, 1987, ch. 4, 1994), that there is a fundamental difference between the two cases of failed vs successful reference (in the sense that the meaning of 'unsuccessful' tokenings of DOG (and hence of "dog") is asymmetrically dependent on 'successful' ones). Natural language semantics is concerned with how language is actually used. And in the actual world, tokenings of "dog" are triggered by dog-like entities (which, again, usually happen to

---

terms of intuitively available propositional content (cf. his Availability Principle, cited above).

[19] Today, there is a whole industry devoted to questions such as whether people first interpret 'literal' meanings and then metaphors, enriched propositions, implicatures, implicitures, indirect speech acts, etc. Cf., e.g., Nicolle & Clark (1999), Noveck & Reboul (2008), and Noveck & Sperber (2007).

be dogs). A usage-based theory that accounts for the actual use of "dog" should not posit any differences between successful and unsuccessful uses (read: referentially successful), unless this alleged difference indicates certain regularities in the use of "dog" that are not graspable otherwise. The fundamental importance of successfully referring with "dog" to dogs lies in its contribution to the truth (falsity) of an utterance (or proposition, for that matter). But truth (falsity) is not needed in order to exhaustively describe the use associated with "dog". To put this point even more cautiously, whether truth (falsity) is a concept that has explanatory value regarding language use is eventually an empirical matter. My modest claim at this point is merely this: by saying that the use of "dog" is such that most of the time it is used to refer to actual dogs, I am not, by virtue of this claim alone, committed to the view that the meaning of "dog" is that it refers to dogs.

From the point of view of the use-theoretic framework defended in this book, the dichotomy between ordinary primary meaning and pragmatic meaning is misleading. Because sentences have only meaning in context, *all sentences pragmatically mean something*, e.g. under appropriate circumstances (an utterance of the sentence) "It's cold in here" might mean, for example, that it is cold in here. In this view, 'primary meaning' is a very special subset of pragmatic meaning. I therefore propose to define the term "primary meaning" thus: primary meaning, in my view, is the meaning that utterances have if the sentence used is used standardly, with 'standard uses' being the homogeneous majority of uses (if any) averaged over all actual instantiations of a given word/sentence type.

I now go through the details of this definition step by step. To begin with, the reason I emphasise that all sentences *pragmatically* mean something is that they also have 'pragmatic meaning' (if you want to talk that way) in cases where primary and pragmatic meaning 'fall into one'. To see where this is getting at, let me briefly take a look at how this admittedly marginal point—indeed, superficially this looks like a terminological concern—is handled classically. Standard semantic theories in philosophy would say things like: "It's cold in here" means (literally) that it is cold in here. If someone uses the sentence in order to express the corresponding proposition <It is cold in here>, they use the sentence *literally* (i.e. 'what

5.1 Literal/Non-Literal Interface

is said' corresponds to the conveyed meaning).[20] In certain other cases, given certain background conditions, a speaker might express their wish to close the window by uttering the very same sentence type. In these cases, it is said, the sentence literally means the same as before but, since it is used non-literally, now also means (on top, so to speak) 'Please close the window!' In this view, all sentences have literal meaning (what is said is always the same), but they have non-literal meaning 'on top' under certain circumstances. That is, literal sentence meaning is what sentences wear on their sleeves; "snow is white" means 'snow is white', etc.

In contrast, in the view advocated here, pragmatic meaning is explanatorily basic. The alleged primary meaning of linguistic signs will be ex-

---

[20] Generally, I try to avoid talk about propositions as far as possible in this chapter. Propositions are a useful means in many fields (King, Soames & Speaks 2014). For example in the area of truth theories, propositions are often justified thus: if person a thinks that p is the case and person b thinks that it is not, then there is something—namely <p>—about whose status (truth value) a and b disagree. These reasons are perfectly legitimate, I think. In philosophy of language, propositions are often justified analogously, e.g. in regard to translations. If "snow is white" expresses the proposition <snow is white> and "Schnee ist weiß" does as well, then "snow is white" is a good translation of "Schnee ist weiß", and vice versa. And just here lies the crux with propositions in theories of meaning. They can easily invoke the misleading impression that there is an intimate relation between sentence types and the corresponding propositions that they express. In fact, however, people disagree widely about which propositions are expressed by which sentences ("snow is white" being an exception here). For instance, truth-evaluability is often considered to be a threshold for the content that is literally expressed by sentence types (cf. the treatment of indexicals by, e.g., Borg (2004b)). Roughly, the idea is to say that the most minimal content that is truth-evaluable is that content literally expressed by a given sentence. But this strategy leads to further problems. One is that this minimal content is often times by default trivially true (false), hence the explanatory advantage of truth-evaluability seems dubious here (cf. the classical example "Jill can't continue"). Another one is that minimal content does not always match with the propositional content that must be known in order to determine the truth value of a given sentence, hence the worry is that minimal content involves a somewhat misleading notion of truth evaluability (cf. the Kaplanian character of "here" (e.g. the place of the speaker), which leaves the relevant place particularly underspecified). In order to avoid these difficulties, I stick to my strategy of indicating meanings with single quotes, which by definition can't be off the mark. If someone means 'snow is white' by a given utterance, then he means that content (whatever it is) he typically expresses by uttering "snow is white"; irrespective of whether <snow is white> is typically the content that he expresses by utterances of this type. This strategy is pretty similar to Horwich's placeholder approach (capitalisation convention), which also can't go wrong.

plained in terms of pragmatic meaning, rather than the other way around. Utterances show a certain systematics in what they mean. Principally, sentences can (under given circumstances) virtually mean anything. For example, "It's cold in here" might mean 'Please close the window!' or 'Store the food in this room!' or whatever. In most cases, "It's cold in here" means simply that it is cold in here. This peculiarity of language—that within the class of *all* utterances of a sentence there is a specific subset of uses in which a sentence always means the same—leads to the impression that this is the literal meaning of this sentence, with "literal" indicating that other uses derive their meaning from this standard. However, the class of uses of α in which it means that it is cold in here is just a very frequently recurring, entrenched variant that is theoretically on a par with other uses. Note that this does not imply that the regularity among uses of α is arbitrary. Many words (and sentences) have one *core* of uses that can be singled out. Others—homonyms and homophones—have two or more cores; they are therefore two word types.

There are even words (or, generally, signs) for which no *clear* core use can be singled out. A rule of thumb might be: the more technical a term, the more clearly determinable its core use properties. For example, "alkaline phosphatase" is probably *only* used to denote alkaline phosphatase.[21] So, its core use is pretty quickly determined: no variation in regards to meaning, all occurrences considered. On the other hand, certain gestures (see sections 2.2.3 and 2.2.4) have a 'semantics' that is so indeterminate that it hardly makes any sense at all to speak of primary meaning any more. Most cases, however, lie in between these two extremes. These symbols have a core meaning; yet sometimes the actual meaning deviates from this core. For instance, "cold" (I guess) is used most of the time to denote coldness (i.e. in sentences like "I think it's cold in this room"; "Yesterday it was colder than it is today", etc.), whereas sometimes it is used, given some background conditions, in sentences that can express one's wish to close a window. It is not within the scope of a philosophical theory of meaning to determine the core use properties of words.[22] It *is*, however, philosoph-

---

[21] Exceptions might prove the rule.

[22] There are interesting findings by, e.g., Bonini, Osherson, Viale & Williamson (1999) in the context of vagueness about the exact demarcation line for applying "tall" to people. They found out that native speakers of English tend to apply "tall" to people above 181.49 cm

ically important to note that core use properties are not what constitutes the meaning of words across all instances (as in Horwich's account). Core use properties are just a particular, surely important, subset of overall use properties of a word. What is typically called 'meaning' is constituted by the latter, i.e. determined by total use.

At present, it does not matter in which 'register' the core use properties are formulated. What is important is this: there is what I call a 'homogeneous majority of uses', e.g. the tokenings of "cold" used to refer to coldness. However, this core use does not fully predetermine the meaning of 'non-literal' uses. If the majority of uses of a term forms no theoretically prior class, then, you might ask, what is the reason for having such a core at all? To put it simply, why is it that "dog" is almost always used to refer to dogs, i.e. is used 'literally'? Here I can offer no conclusive answer but neither can truth-conditional semanticists. The likely explanation is that this has something to do with speakers' expectations. People typically have successfully referred to dogs in the past by using "dog" (let's suppose). Their inclination to use "dog", if they need to talk about dogs, is relatively high—due to their past success in using "dog" and their expectations about others.[23] The fundamental reason why there is no theoretically important difference between core uses of "dog" and 'deviant' uses is that both can equally well be described by paraphrasing particular uses in more familiar terms (as described above). The fundamental difference, again, between "dog" and "alkaline phosphatase" is that the latter is used relatively seldom, and, hence, the contexts in which speakers are able to expect particular reactions from their respective hearers by uttering this word are rare. This explains why technical terms are used standardly most of the time. This is not to say that there *can't* be deviant uses. Here is a very simple example. Suppose John is a chemist, Mary is a literary scholar.

---

of height. These results are astonishing, but their philosophical significance is rather marginal. What is relevant in the discussion about vagueness, and in philosophy of language more generally, is whether, for any vague predicate, there *is* such a strict line or not. (Some say Yes, some say No.) Where to draw this line is of no help, because it does not explain anything of philosophical relevance.

[23] This is, of course, basically Lewis's (1969) story about how conventions get established. See Millikan (2008) for some interesting remarks on how Lewis's work fits in with the basic ideas of CxG.

5 Theories of Truth & Meaning

> John: Look here! I use alkaline phosphatase to make this liquid start bubbling. Nice, innit?
>
> Mary: Yeah, John, I also *always* use alkaline phosphatase to do this.

Mary, let's further suppose, means 'I don't understand a single word', or 'Whatever', or some such. It does not matter; further information about the context would tell. By assumption, she does not mean that she also uses alkaline phosphatase, a fortiori she does not refer to alkaline phosphatase by uttering "alkaline phosphatase". Nor does the pragmatic meaning (e.g. 'I don't understand what you're saying') derive its 'content' from the alleged literal content of the words she is using. Much the same conversation could have taken place if John had replaced "alkaline phosphatase" by a similar term (similar with respect to its 'sounds technical' potential) that he just made up. The truth conditions of both sentences would have been different, but this does not matter in this context. Mary's conveyed meaning depends on her successfully mirroring the utterance of a technical term that John understands and Mary does not. In order to convey the meaning she de facto conveys, Mary does not need to presuppose that "alkaline phosphatase" means 'alkaline phosphatase', nor does John need to assume this. Pragmatic meaning is established as soon as the hearer (John) understands what the speaker (Mary) wants him to understand (here: 'I don't understand'). In the example, relevant contextual cues might be intonation, information about Mary's academic background, co-text, etc. The literal content of the utterance, however, plays no role here in determining pragmatic meaning. Hence, given certain circumstances, it is possible to successfully convey a specific pragmatic meaning independently from any assumption about literal content.

If I now try to delineate primary meaning from pragmatic meaning by recurring to homogeneity, I immediately face the problem that—since there are infinitely many ways to individuate conversational contexts—all word type instantiations are similar in at least some respects. This would make it seem impossible to single out a homogeneous subset of instantiations that could qualify as exemplifying primary meaning. That is, in fact, problematic for the current account, but only insofar as it is problematic for *all* semantic theories. The distinction 'literal/non-literal' (like 'primary/non-primary') is merely presupposed in the literature, and I shall simply do the same in what follows. When a theorist describes tokenings of words as 'metaphorical', 'ironic', 'misapplication', and so on, he is always presupposing the complementary set to these uses, i.e. the standard use—and that the reader is able to recognise them as such. The situation is similar here: I also presuppose such a distinction and I assume that the reader is able to recognise it. For example, I assume that the reader is able to see that the tokenings of "dog" that are used to talk about dogs form a homogeneous majority of uses in that they are similar in respects that account for their ability to refer to dogs and dissimilar in other respects. Therefore, relying on pre-theoretic understanding in order to tell primary from non-primary meaning seems unproblematic. This is less clear when it comes to another controversial notion involved in the characterisation of "primary meaning" given above: "instantiation".

The alleged problem is that one can't simply 'count instantiations'. For example, it is obviously the case that the conversational context is highly relevant to what word/sentence type instantiations actually mean. Accordingly, the worry would be here that it is unclear how much 'context' I assume needs to be included in counting instantiations. If there were, say, 5 billion instantiations of the word type "dog" and in 4.7 billion cases the tokenings referred to dogs, then I would arguably be committed to the claim that the primary meaning of "dog" is that it is used to refer to dogs. But this will not help, for I said above that language users derive primary meaning on the basis of pragmatic meaning by *identifying homogeneous sets of instantiations.* That is to say, the description of instantiations of "dog" must necessarily include a description of those contextual features that were *relevant* for the reference to dogs in 4.7 billion cases. Ultimately, these features justify talk of homogeneity here. I think that this worry can be relatively easily met. The relevant contextual features that need to be included in 'counting' instantiations are simply those features an otherwise competent speaker would consider when forming his dispositions to apply a given term on the basis of what he learnt how the term functioned in previous cases. In section 6.2.1, I will introduce the notion of 'ideal dispositions', i.e. that disposition a language user would arrive at if he were familiar with all previous instantiations of a given word type. Thus, the principle according to which contextual features need to be mentioned in

5 Theories of Truth & Meaning

a description of tokenings can be stated schematically: exactly those features of conversational contexts of a given set of tokenings are relevant that an otherwise competent language user would consider as being relevant in deriving dispositions on the basis of familiarity with that set.

People sometimes remark that it can't be actual tokenings/instantiations of a word that constitute its meaning; one reason for this being that meaning would be indeterminate a concept then. The present account is based on just the opposite assumption: that it is actual use—more accurately, *all uses* of a word taken together (specifications, see below)—that determine the semantic content of a word. That sounds counter-intuitive at first but has indeed some neat advantages over its rivals. Firstly, unrealised tokens of "dog" have, or so one might argue, the same meaning as actual ones. Accordingly, it is the type that has meaning, the instantiations of "dog" have meaning qua being tokenings of that type. But this can't be right on a usage-based account of meaning,[24] for if meaning is determined by (or is) use, then the dispositional power of possible tokenings of "dog" to mean 'dog' (or whatever) depends on the meaning (i.e. use) of actual "dog" tokens. Metaphorically speaking, non-actual tokens are never used. The same holds for types.

Secondly, the alleged disadvantage that meaning changes with every new token of a word is, on closer examination, actually an advantage. It allows me to say why meaning change over time (on diachronic scales) occurs: because the instantiations of one word type in 1450, for example, differ from its instantiations today. Furthermore, it allows me to say why the meaning of *one and the same term* in different social groups, in different registers, on different occasions, and so forth sometimes differs in meaning: because actual tokenings of these words have occurred and still do occur with systematic differences relative to social groups and other factors.[25] On a related note, it explains why meaning is sometimes indeterminate *within* a given group, when, due to a very limited number of actual instantiations of a word type, no statistically relevant core has evolved yet.[26]

---

[24] Assume for the sake of argument that the theoretical superiority of usage-based theories has already been shown independently.

[25] I return to this point in 6.2.1.

[26] Example: the use of the verb "wulffen" in German during the first two months (or so) after the beginning of the so-called 'Wulff affair' in Germany in December 2011.

5.1 Literal/Non-Literal Interface

Thirdly, the assumption that the meaning of a given word is constituted by all its actual tokenings explains why "meaning" is such a vague notion. I said that the standard use of a word is the homogeneous majority of uses averaged over *all uses*, read: instantiations of that word type. No one can know all tokenings of a word. Therefore, no one can know the exact meaning of a word.[27] That is how it is. Semantic theories that suggest otherwise obscure matters. The clearest case is theories that (plus minus some modification) identify meaning with reference. Meaning would be an easy business if meaning were reference, since a term x either refers or it does not, and x refers definitely either to y or to z but nothing in between. Unfortunately, meaning is not reference (as Frege, to name but one illustrious name, already told us). Of course, one might base one's semantic theory of meaning on the notion of reference. But that is just replacing the problematic term with a well-defined technical term.[28] Such a clear-cut notion of meaning is an illusion. A similar example would be Horwich's capitalisation convention: *up to the point* where he needs to redeem the placeholder in form of a capitalised word, the meaning of a word is, albeit vacuously, nameable: e.g. "dog" means DOG. But this kind of technical elegance is artificial. The actual statement of acceptance properties that goes in for the placeholder is not that clear-cut any more.[29]

---

[27] To be sure, one can know the meaning of a just-coined word, or of names, or of technical terms, and so on. That is, the exceptions that prove the rule are terms whose use is significantly restricted.

[28] Note Davidson's choice of words in this often-cited, crucial passage in 'Truth and Meaning':

> As a final bold step, let us try treating the position occupied by 'p' [i.e. the right-hand side of the T-schema] extensionally: to implement this, sweep away the obscure 'means that', provide the sentence that replaces 'p' with a proper sentential connective, and supply the description that replaces 's' [accordingly, the left-hand side of the schema] with its own predicate. (1967, 309)

[29] Acceptance properties are first introduced in Horwich (1998, 94–96). An example—already cited above—would be: 'the explanatorily fundamental acceptance property underlying our use of "red" is (roughly) the disposition to apply "red" to an observed surface when and only when it is clearly red' (Horwich 1998, 45). The difference in terms of technical rigour between this and "'red' means RED" should be obvious.

5 Theories of Truth & Meaning

These, then, are the reasons that speak in favour of my modified definition of "primary meaning". In the following section, I shall use this definition in order to argue against (the reconstruction of what I think is) Davidson's argument for recursion. This argument operates on classically defined primary meaning. Accordingly, by arguing against recursiveness I show that one important reason for assuming classical primary meanings is unwarranted.

5.1.3 Novelty Only Via Recursion

Accordingly, it is now time to return to the issues surrounding recursiveness. In my short argument (re-)construction above, it was the third premise that I said seemed dubious: the only way to comprehend sentences of any length with finite means is via recursively defined rules. The empirical data from a range of disciplines suggests otherwise. On the contrary, the data shows that very often language users *are* able to understand sentences the meaning of which they can't have determined on a 'words and rules' basis.[30] In philosophical terms, recursively defined rules operating on atomic semantic units can't account for all cases of language users' ability to comprehend sentences. At least sometimes they understand sentences by different mechanisms, e.g. during language acquisition.

My argument against recursion is twofold. One main claim, to be defended further below, is that communication is not itself a cooperative activity—as most theorists assume—but instead a means to enable and foster cooperative behaviour. This subtle difference partially explains our ability to understand other people's utterances: because implicit agreement about common goals is established previously and can be taken to be commonly known (see below for details). The other main claim is that the 'recursive explanation' is on the wrong track even in cases where, judging from the knowledge about word meaning and syntax available to the subject, such an explanation would accord with the evidence. In slogan form, sentence comprehension goes top-down, not bottom-up.

For a start, this line of thought is partly motivated by holophrases and frozen phrases. In these cases, children hear—and apparently understand—

---

[30] For some general critical remarks on 'words and rules' approaches in semantics, see Ziem & Lasch (2013, 90–95).

utterances of sentences they have never heard before. The reason why they are called 'holophrases' (as opposed to normal sentences that contingently happen to consist of just one word) is that they are syntactically complex[31] from the point of view of descriptive linguistics. Here is an example from Tomasello (2003a, 38): "I-wanna-do-it!" Call this sentence β. If one looks naïvely at at the data, one sees—simplifying a bit—the following situation. A child understands β (all else equal). β is syntactically complex, i.e. its overall meaning can be traced back to atomic meanings plus syntax. As per the argument above, the child must have learnt the words and the rules *beforehand* in order to be able to understand the sentence. Judging from the available empirical evidence, this is not the case. Even more important, explaining the child's abilities in terms of knowledge of syntax would only be necessary if that were the only option. This is often assumed to be indisputable (see especially Fodor). If, however, an alternative explanation were indeed possible, then, without further ado, this would qualify as the preferred explanation, for there is no independent evidence that the assumed syntactical knowledge is available to children in advance (they need to *acquire* their language first).[32]

It is the aim of this section to establish such an alternative view. The basic idea, supported by the cited evidence, is that the hearer of an utterance infers the meaning of an uttered sentence from contextual factors that are available to him. In this sense, a hearer knows the meaning of an uttered sentence *immediately*—as soon as enough information is at hand. What I would like to do now is this: by applying my own definition of "primary meaning" to another group of cases that have been discussed extensively by Davidson (malapropisms), I show that it is possible to account for sentence comprehension—the crucial factor in the argument for

---

[31] Keep in mind that I am formulating this in a way that it would get formulated classically. Whether a sentence that would be classified as syntactically complex counts as complex in CxG as well, where different 'rules' probably apply, is unimportant in the present context. Simply put, "syntactically complex" here means 'syntactically complex from most theoreticians' point of view'.

[32] To be sure, this claim concerning preferred explanation assumes that people typically aspire for what is called 'psychological reality'. If you are not primarily interested in psychological reality, then the alternative does not qualify as the preferred option all by itself. Note that 'particular constructionist approaches differ in [...] the degree of emphasis on usage and psychological reality' (Goldberg 2006, 18).

5 Theories of Truth & Meaning

recursiveness—without the assumption that words always in fact *have* their conventional meaning. Malapropisms only serve as an example here. Other examples would do just as well. The important point, though, is that if it can be shown that sentence comprehension is independent from primary meaning, then Davidson's argument for recursiveness fails. This is because it relies crucially on the assumption that sentence comprehension can *only* be explained by means of recursion.

The philosophically interesting aspect of malapropisms is that language users are able to comprehend sentences that involve unknown words, or words, at least, that do not 'fit' with the rest of a sentence or a whole context.[33] Example: "Er ist eine Konifere auf seinem Gebiet" (literally: 'He is a conifer in his subject'; likely interpretation: 'He is an expert', where the German counterpart of "coryphaeus" is used to denote experts). The classical, intuitively plausible, explanation is along the following lines: in a given (average) context, saying that someone is a conifer in his area is nonsense. A typical hearer would appreciate this. He would know that there is a phonetically very similar word to "Konifere": "Koryphäe". Exchanging the two words would render the utterance plausible. Therefore, the typical hearer's 'passing theory' (Davidson 1986) is that for the speaker the word "Konifere" has the same meaning as has "Koryphäe" for him, the hearer. Hence, the hearer infers that what the speaker meant was that someone is an expert in his subject. That is the 'classical' view defended by Davidson (1986). In promoting this view, Davidson seems to be motivated by preserving the distinction between what he calls 'first meaning' and conveyed meaning.[34] Without this distinction, one is confronted with the problem of how a hearer can understand the utterance, if it is conceded that what he understands is that some person or other is an expert. This problem is especially pressing due to the fact that this ability is somehow parasitic on the phonetic similarity between "Konifere" and "Koryphäe".[35]

---

[33] See also section 2.2.4, where I first discuss malapropisms.

[34] At least in his earlier account (e.g. his 1965 and 1967), "Er ist eine Konifere auf seinem Gebiet" means that he is a conifer in his area.

[35] I do not argue that, in general, phonetic similarity is a necessary prerequisite for retrieving the intended meaning in malapropisms. However, I would argue that in this particular example, phonetic similarity undoubtedly is important.

5.1 Literal/Non-Literal Interface

To state the alleged problem clearly: in the account advocated here, "Konifere" in the example above means 'Koryphäe', i.e. is used as "Koryphäe" would be used in other contexts (as per Davidson's framework) but does *not* (contra Davidson) literally mean 'Konifere' in *this* context. How is it that hearers are still able to understand the sentence in question? Before I proceed with an answer to this question, let me emphasise that in this part of the overall argument I am not concerned with the plausibility of usage-based theories as such. Rather, I am only concerned with the question as to whether there is a usage-based explanation to the problem of malapropisms. Having said that, I admit that the solution will look *very similar* to Davidson's. In fact, the only significant difference is that it foregoes primary meaning and the distinction 'prior/passing theory'. In the example, "Konifere" is used like "Koryphäe" would be used in other contexts, which is uncontroversial. Meaning *in use-based theories* is use. In my view, meaning is nothing over and above a paraphrase that allows otherwise competent speakers to understand how the word in question (i.e. the word for which a meaning statement is given) is used. A 'legitimate' such paraphrase was just given. There is no need to posit reference relations. But that is just one part of the explanation, as it is still unclear why the hearer is able to understand "Konifere" in the sense of 'expert'. Assume, for the sake of argument, that Davidson's explanation is correct in supposing that the hearer's inference exploits the phonetic similarities of the two terms.[36] Assume further that the semantic content that the speaker wants to express is that what Davidson's passing theory says, namely that someone ('he') is an expert in his area.

It seems natural to suggest that the speaker *wants to express this by saying that he is an expert in his area*. What he utters, though, is "Konifere". There are several possibilities why he might do this, most of which are mentioned by Davidson himself. These reasons are irrelevant for present concerns. The important point here is that the relevant explanations for how hearers determine conveyed meaning do not presuppose a prior theory that would involve knowledge of referential facts. My suggestion would be that we

---

[36] The argument, though, does not depend on that assumption. Anyway, since the opposition's argument works on that presumption, it seems likely that the opponent will not, at least, argue against *this* part of the argument. Besides, as I said already, the assumption looks undeniably plausible.

only need to recur to *expectations*, i.e. knowledge of usage-based facts—a suggestion that I have only briefly hinted at in the above; I shall pick it up again in 6.1.1.

5.2 Cooperative Contexts

At the core of the present chapter lies Davidson's argument—especially in *Truth and Meaning*—that the only way to make sense of the human ability to understand unknown sentences is by way of recurring to knowledge of recursively defined rules of composition. In the foregoing section, I argued that Davidson's premise that there is no viable alternative to this seems unjustified. There are alternatives. One prominent alternative proposal is to start investigating utterance comprehension by looking at the preconditions that led to the development of human communication in the first place. Arguably, the most innovative and influential proposal in this area comes from Tomasello, who argues, roughly speaking, that the drive to act cooperatively and achieve common goals is the key to understanding human communication (i.e. language). In this view, language is primarily a *tool* to foster success in language-independent areas. Utterance comprehension, therefore, must not be viewed *independently* of extralinguistic, cooperative aims. Quite on the contrary, an appropriate *basis* for an explanation of utterance comprehension is presumably the insight that—first and foremost—language users acknowledge that their respective interlocutors try to achieve some common goal *by means of using language.* In other words, the crucial step towards determining the meaning of a given utterance is *not* to understand its underlying syntactic structure, *but* to understand the extralinguistic aims that a given speaker is trying to achieve. In the present section in general and in subsection 5.2.4 in particular, I discuss some details of such an approach to language understanding.

5.2.1 Playing Unfair

In many cooperative contexts, utterance meaning can be 'read off', as it were, from the relevant context. This is the basis of my claim that language users immediately understand utterances of sentences if they are otherwise competent. A natural response would be to say that all this presupposes genuine cooperative contexts. Imagine a scenario in which a mother teaches colour terms to her daughter. In such a situation, a *cooperative* context would require that the mother really aims at teaching her daughter the colour terms 'correctly' (as she herself would use them). The mother, however, could play foul and teach her child the terms in an 'unconventional' way. She could, for example, point to clearly yellow objects and say "That's blue" (assuming she correctly recognises yellow as yellow). Would that alter the meaning of "blue" (as used by the child/as used by the society)? Doesn't this show that nothing in the proposed account ensures that language acquisition is successful? Doesn't this presuppose that everyone acts cooperatively? How can someone 'immediately understand' wrongly used sentences in the first place?

I hope to clarify my account by answering these questions in turn. Firstly, would 'incorrect' applications of "blue" by the mother alter the meaning of the term? Yes and no. As used by the child, "blue" means 'yellow', because, by assumption, the child systematically learns to associate "blue" with the property yellow. Relative to the society the child is part of (i.e. the English-speaking community), the term "blue" is used to denote the colour blue (even by the mother). Relative to this reference class, the child is simply an exception. Of course, one might argue about how many children it would take to alter the meaning of "blue" with respect to societies, but let us bracket this for the moment. Given that the child is the only exception, "blue" means 'blue' relative to the society, even if uttered by the child.

Secondly, nothing in the proposed word-learning scenario ensures successful language acquisition. That is how it is. Language acquisition normally *is* successful, to be sure. But to explain this fact is not necessarily part of a theory of meaning. Even more importantly, most of the time people do de facto act cooperatively—especially mothers teaching colour terms to their children. Given this, a (framework for a) theory of meaning that presupposes that language acquisition is successful, and that it is successful due to the cooperative efforts of all language users is, ipso facto, *not an idealised framework* relying on implausible assumptions. Rather, it only relies on the assumption that, all else equal, people act cooperatively in contexts of language acquisition. If the accusation is that, in this case, the theory works only for the actual world, a reasonable reply seems to be: a theory that works for the actual world—this is what I am aiming at.

5 Theories of Truth & Meaning

Thirdly, the account presented here is not entirely incompatible with the Gricean idea that *once the language system is in place*, it is possible to act 'cooperatively' in a merely linguistic sense. Every otherwise absolutely uncooperative person could be 'linguistically cooperative' in this sense. Consider the most uncooperative context you can think of; say, a bank robbery. The robber says "Put the money in here!" (as is likely in a bank robbery). "Over my dead body!" the bank assistant replies. Now, this is clearly a quite uncooperative context, in the original sense of the term. The respective (non-linguistic) aims of the robber and of the assistant are incompatible. Linguistically, however, robber and assistant 'cooperate': their communicative aims converge in that both want to be understood and want to understand. The most reasonable step to take for the robber in order to make clear that he wants the money is by uttering "Put the money in here!" (or anything). Conversely, the assistant *confirms* to the robber that his choice of words was appropriate (relative to his aims) in this context. In Wittgenstein's terms, they are playing the same language games. They thereby strengthen (or entrench) the meanings of "to put", "money", etc. Note that this line of reasoning does not necessarily require that "money", for example, *conventionally* means 'money'. In other words, it is not required that the assistant recognises the robber's intent on the basis of their alleged conventional meanings. Rather, "money" could mean virtually anything (given particular contexts). It is just that in this context, the overwhelmingly most plausible assumption is that by "money" the robber indeed means 'money'.

To take a less exciting example, consider a mother who is, in interaction with her child, uncooperative most of the time by rejecting most of the child's wishes. The mother does not feed the child when it asks; she does not hug the child when it wants to be hugged; and so on. The mother is, if you like, perfectly uncooperative. From time to time, though, the mother hugs the child, feeds it, and so on. Also, there are other people who regularly take care of the child and behave in a more friendly manner towards it. When the child asks its mother for something, most of the time the mother replies "No!" The important point is that concerning the semantics of "no", the mother is absolutely cooperative. The child learns (not unlike the bank robber) that the words (or actions) chosen to express its wishes were appropriate, because the mother refuses to give what was asked for after uttering "no" (and the child's 'working hypothesis' is that "no" means 'no'). Others fulfil the child's wishes after uttering "okay" (or whatever). Thereby, the child learns that, for example, uttering "I want food" is an appropriate strategy to ask for food, *even in uncooperative contexts in which request for food remains unsuccessful*. Along the same lines, one can argue that the child thereby learns that "no" means 'no' (i.e. is used to express refusal of a request). Assuming that the child's working hypothesis is that "I want food" means 'I want food', it will notice the correlation between "no" utterances and refusals—especially in uncooperative contexts. Generally, it is hard not to be cooperative when it comes to semantics.

Fourthly, "to understand" is a success verb. An objection to the proposal then would be: how can the child immediately *understand* "blue", as taught by her mother, given that "blue" actually means 'blue' (i.e. denotes the colour blue)? The answer is quite simple: the child *is* successful, because in the envisaged situation (mother–child interaction) the linguistic community consists, for the time being, of the mother and the child. Relative to the cues available for figuring out the meaning of "blue", the only option for the child is to assume that it means 'yellow'. In this situation, "blue", if uttered by the child, really means 'yellow', since the child uses it this way and the mother understands her child accordingly. Still, it is unproblematic that "blue" in the whole English-speaking community means 'blue'. There are enough counterbalances in the form of other participants in the language game that ensure that apparently 'deviant' uses would be corrected. Those deviant uses that are not corrected accordingly are called 'language change'.

5.2.2 Good and Bad Reasons for Primary Meanings

I have already mentioned some general concerns about classical conceptions of 'primary meaning' in the Introduction and in the previous chapter. Taken together with my reservations voiced in this chapter, the picture emerges that primary meaning in the classical sense of knowledge of reference relations seem to be poorly justified. However, it is important to note that they are typically not merely postulated. Quite on the contrary, they are very well motivated. Above I construed Davidson's argument for recursion as an indirect argument for primary meaning. I argued that it

5 Theories of Truth & Meaning

fails eventually, as its central premise (only recursion can explain sentence comprehension) seems unjustified. Yet, the problem remains that primary meaning can't be simply abandoned but rather has to be replaced by an alternative notion. It remains to be shown that my expectation-based alternative possesses the right explanatory capacities. This is what I demonstrate in this and the following two subsections.

If one were simply to abandon primary meaning without substitution, the *systematic success in using particular words if a particular interpretation is intended* would remain obscure. In general, the alternative proposal must be able to account for all systematic effects that rely on the distinction between primary/non-primary meaning: e.g. metaphor, irony, etc. For instance, the fact that people are (given a certain context) particularly successful in evoking the interpretation 'Please close the window!' by instantiating the sentence type "It's cold in here" demands an explanation. Gricean approaches suggest here that the potential of "It's cold in here" to mean 'Close the window!' is parasitic on its primary meaning 'It's cold in here'. I argued above that it is possible to give an alternative explanation. This alternative would necessarily involve a systematic regularity of core meanings that can (potentially) be ascribed to the majority of uses, all instantiations considered.[37] This sounds more or less similar to classical (inferentialist) conceptions, since the meaning of "red", for example, would still be 'red' in most cases (i.e. in 'standard contexts'). However, the above argument shows that the assumption of reference relations and satisfaction conditions is superfluous in terms of the explanation. The same effects in regard to malapropisms, irony, etc. can be explained by 'primary meanings' that merely refer to 'core use properties' (Horwich 1998) instead of reference.

The three most important features that differentiate core use properties from ordinary primary meanings are the following. Core use properties are universally applicable. For instance, gestures commonly have a very wide applicability with varying semantics in different contexts. The semantic variety of gestures suggests that many gestures have virtually no

---

[37] The proviso "potentially" covers the case for words that lack such a core meaning. The meaning of such words can only be accounted for in terms of their conversational function; e.g. placeholders ("thing"), caring for social relations ("hello"), etc. I return to this below.

stable lexical meaning at all. In my framework, this can be accounted for by the absence of any homogeneous majority of uses. Moreover, core use properties are perfectly compatible with the fact that in many situations people are able to infer the intended reading of an utterance without acknowledging the alleged primary meaning first. Lastly, core use properties make it possible to explain why, in principle, any word can be used to mean anything, given the correct context. At the same time, not all meanings (or, more precisely, utterance interpretations) are equally probable. The probability for a word like "and" to be used as a conjunction is very high (though not certain), because the 'homogeneous majority of uses' covers virtually all instances.

The gist is this: there is place in semantic theories for a certain semantic core in order to explain why word choice is often systematic, strict, and successful. However, positing (ordinary) primary meanings in the sense of semantic knowledge comprising reference relations is neither necessary (as shown by core use properties) nor supported by the data (as shown, for example, by frozen phrases). This concludes my discussion of primary meaning. I now return to the overarching topic of the present chapter: sentence comprehension. Before I discuss compositionality in the context of CxG frameworks in 5.2.4, I *very* briefly make sure that we are all on the same page regarding compositionality as such.

5.2.3 A Very Brief Overview of Compositionality

Compositionality is one of the most central concepts in philosophy of language. For obvious reasons my discussion of compositionality will be rather brief. I just want to make sure that my background assumptions concerning compositionality are sufficiently transparent. Especially because, in the next chapter, I shall say a few words on recursion, which is an issue that is tightly linked with compositionality. Moreover, since this whole book is more or less in favour of construction grammar and construction grammar is sometimes characterised as being partly non-compositional, I need to clarify the relationship between CxG and compositionality as well. Good overview articles are (Gendler Szabó 2012*b*) and Pagin & Westerståhl (2010*a*). The standard textbook on compositionality is Werning, Hinzen &

Machery (2012).[38] A comprehensive collection of some rather tentative articles on this topic is Fodor & Lepore (2002).

As a first approximation, compositionality is an alleged feature of natural languages that posits that the meaning of a complex expression is determined by the meanings associated with its syntactical constituents (lexical meaning) and the way these are put together (syntactic composition). This approximation is more than sufficient for present purposes. To say the least, more rigorously defined formulations of the principle will be variants of this approximation, i.e. the basic idea is always the same. When it comes to compositionality, there are some subtle differences between linguistics and philosophy. For instance, non-compositionality (e.g. idioms) is an area that is widely neglected in philosophical areas, whereas it plays a crucial role in linguistics. On the other hand, philosophers are concerned with issues such as reverse compositionality,[39] which, in turn, is a topic that seems less prominent in linguistic circles.

In section 5.1.2, in which I presented my reconstruction of Davidson's argument regarding utterance/sentence comprehension, I mostly talked about recursiveness. I assume that the connection to compositionality is relatively obvious: the 'recursively defined rules' discussed there make sense only if they are understood as 'rules of composition' that take atomic meaning as input and give complex meaning as output. Recursiveness per se is comparatively uninteresting in the context of language comprehension. So, although recursiveness and compositionality should not be identified, there is still ample reason to discuss them together here.

From the point of view of CxG, the most relevant objection in the context of compositionality is that, in general, usage-based approaches are said to be unable to incorporate compositionality into their respective frameworks (Fodor & Lepore 2002). For instance, Fodor & Lepore (1991, 334) claim that:

> It turns out that compositionality is an embarrassment for the kind of New Testament semantics [conceptual role semantics à la Block 1986] that identifies the meaning of an expression with its inferential role. In particular, it invites the following kind of *prima facie* argument:

---

[38] See also Werning (2005).

[39] Johnson (2006), Patterson (2005), Robbins (2005).

- meanings are compositional
- but inferential roles are *not* compositional
- so meanings can't be inferential roles.

Conceptual role semantics exemplarily represents usage-based approaches here; the structure of the argument may easily be adopted to construe objections against related theories (cf. Fodor & Lepore 2002). Hence, the underlying concern is that usage-based approaches in general lack the resources to account for compositionality. In contrast, it is, as I have shown, quite easy to incorporate compositionality in truth-conditional semantics (or, for that matter, any other framework based on reference relations). So, if denying compositionality is not a viable option, one would need to show that usage-based approaches can indeed be construed compositionally. This, I take it, is beyond the scope of this book project. At this point, I refer the interested reader to Horwich (1998, ch. 7). There, Horwich convincingly shows that the compositionality principle is compatible with just any kind of property that could possibly constitute meaning (e.g. some kind of use property). In general, the framework he proposes takes the following form:

> Consider an arbitrary complex expression "e", and suppose that it is constructed by combining certain primitive terms (some of which are schemata) in a certain order. That is,
>
> > "e" is the result of applying combinatorial procedure P to the primitives $\langle "w_1", \ldots, "w_n" \rangle$
>
> My proposal is that the meaning property of "e"—namely, 'x means E'—is constituted by the construction property
>
> > x results from applying procedure P to primitives whose meanings are $\langle W_1, \ldots, W_n \rangle$
>
> (where W_1 is the meaning of "w_1", etc.). Assuming this constitution thesis, it is clear how [...] we can explain why "e" means what it does from the facts about what its primitive constituents mean and from the fact about how it is constructed from those primitives. (Horwich 1998, 158)

There is thus good reason to suppose that the general concern directed against usage-based theories that they can't incorporate compositionality is de facto unjustified. In the following subsection (5.2.4), I shall strengthen this position by arguing that, since usage-based approaches offer the only plausible theory about what it means to *acquire* knowledge of rules of composition, there is some plausibility in the claim that this kind of knowledge, in turn, is essentially associated with use.

5.2.4 Sentence Comprehension & CxG

Construction grammar in general and Tomasello's theory of language acquisition in particular take for granted that sentence comprehension works fundamentally differently than assumed in many established philosophical theories of meaning. Just to remind you of the background of the discussion above concerning recursion: Davidson repeatedly claims that one important, if not *the* major phenomenon regarding language is that people understand infinitely many well-formed sentences. This is one major argument in favour of truth-conditional semantics. Given my criticism of this argument in 5.1.2, it makes sense to now take a look at what we are getting at with use oriented approaches with respect to the Novelty issue.

The starting premise is: given some background conditions (memory, cognitive resources, mastery of a language, etc.), language users are able to understand any utterance of a well-formed sentence they have never heard before. From a philosophical point of view, the problem is not to find an explanation for *this*. The explanations are legion in the empirical literature, especially in the work done and inspired by Michael Tomasello. Rather, the actual problem is that virtually no existing *philosophical* theory of meaning seems to be compatible with Tomasello's theoretical framework, or, in fact, with construction grammar in general. I aim to show that the framework that evolves throughout this book fits nicely with what I call the Tomasellian paradigm. Accordingly, it is essential to briefly introduce the basic ideas of this framework here. This is what I would like to turn to now. I concentrate on the bits of the theory that are particularly relevant for philosophical theories of meaning, especially on recursiveness.

Fundamentally, the empirical data suggests that philosophers have been wrong in assuming that a certain set of capacities must explain the ability to comprehend novel sentences. The alternative is to take just the opposite direction. In other words: people *first* are able to understand novel sentences; *then*, later on in their psychological development, they acquire the capacities that classically have been reckoned to be responsible for this ability (e.g. knowledge concerning composition rules). Besides being able to comprehend novel sentences, people surely are *also* able to state the composition rules according to which the semantics of a sentence can be computed from the semantics of its constituents (or, alternatively, they know these 'rules' implicitly). It therefore seems natural to assume that the very same ability might account for the ability to understand novel sentences, if combined with appropriate lexical knowledge. This simple picture is no longer tenable in light of the increasing success of construction grammar, which is a movement of which Tomasello's work is an integral part (Ibbotson, Theakston, Lieven & Tomasello 2012). People do in fact know (if only implicitly) the ways in which the meaning (or semantic value) of a sentence depends upon the meaning of its parts (or their respective values). From an empirical point of view, though, this knowledge is posterior to their ability to comprehend sentences (Tomasello 2003a). Accordingly, one step towards an empirically informed philosophical theory of meaning is to solve the Novelty problem independently of composition rules. Interestingly enough, this leaves explanations of compositionality mostly unaffected, as I shall demonstrate later on.

It is a fact that young children understand sentences. From their ability to understand sentences with unknown words one can infer that sentence comprehension at least sometimes does not rely on knowledge about composition rules. For the latter require that one is familiar with the words 'stuck into' those rules. Hence, something else must account for it. In Tomasello's account, it is the children's mindreading abilities—more specifically, their ability to recognise intentions—that account for their ability to understand sentences. Here's Tomasello's own summary:

> The evolutionary adaptation for understanding others as intentional agents like the self becomes manifest in human ontogeny today at around 9–12 months of age. [...A]t around their first birthdays infants become able to:

5 Theories of Truth & Meaning

- establish with adults various *joint attentional frames* that create a common intersubjective ground for communication;
- within these frames, *understand communicative intentions* as they are expressed in utterances; and
- engage in *role reversal imitation* to acquire symbolic conventions first used toward them in these frames. (2003a, 40–41)

Davidson's theory is a very straightforward explanation for how people (children) comprehend complex expressions. *If* one takes for granted that the meaning of sentences is indeed determined compositionally, then it is hard to believe that children, who lack this knowledge, can understand these sentences. Two things help here. Firstly, compositionality is an aspect of language that can be accounted for within a constructional framework. I will come back to this in a minute. Secondly, compositionality as such, as already indicated in 4.1.2, is not a genuine phenomenon that exists in the real world. Rather, it might be an artefact of how professional linguists describe certain things like utterances. In any case, it is in fact possible to account for Novelty without taking the route via compositionality.

It is quite unproblematic to determine when people understand an utterance. It manifests in their behaviour, including their verbal and non-verbal behaviour. In contrast, it is relatively hard to argue that the available linguistic evidence suggests that language is compositional (ignoring formal language). The fact that (at least parts of) natural languages can be *described* compositionally does not make them so. Regarding understanding, there does not seem to be an analogue to this. If a person's behaviour is such that one would describe that person as understanding a specific thing, then there is no other evidence that could possibly undermine that claim (save for further behavioural evidence). Whereas in the case of compositionality, there might be such evidence. For example, if it is possible to 'linguistically' characterise a language as compositional, then there could still be psychological evidence that might suggest otherwise; e.g. if the composition rules thus posited do not fit with what we know about what competent speakers are in fact able to know.

5.2 Cooperative Contexts

Bearing this in mind, the constructional language acquisition story does not look that mysterious any more. It is *obviously* the case that children at a certain age understand utterances. Explaining this in terms of composition rules *is just one option among a variety of alternatives*. The constructionalist explains understanding in terms of mindreading (this, at least, is what Tomasello does). Children develop the crucial capacities for language comprehension a few months before their first birthday (see above quote); at around their first birthday they understand first utterances (Tomasello 2003a). An important piece of evidence in favour of this view is that they seem to regard some complex sentences as unanalysable units, whereas they are still able to comprehend its content. Another, more philosophically minded reason is that in order to learn the meaning of words, children must first understand them in sentential (and situational) contexts. One reason for this is that they seldom hear individual words in isolation but rather almost always embedded in sentences, i.e. as parts of utterances. It takes them some time to 'isolate' words in sentences, and they use quite sophisticated methods to do this: among them information about typical distributional patterns of phonology; information about the sound of known words; information about intonation and emphasis (Tomasello 2003a, ch. 3). They utilise prior semantic knowledge in order to narrow down the possibilities of the semantics of unknown words (Ferguson et al. 2014).[40] Being confronted with whole utterances, a child's first task is therefore to determine the meaning of sentences (in contexts). According to the theoretical framework relied upon here, this is tantamount to saying that, to a large extent, finding out about the type-level meanings of words involves determining the intentions of communicative partners first.

Compositionality fits in nicely with this view of language. First of all, if natural languages really are compositional, this does not by itself require language users to be familiar with composition rules in order to determine the meaning of complex expressions. Their competency in understanding new sentences might still rely primarily on their intention-reading skills. Moreover, compositionality is built into the Tomasellian account of language acquisition in two ways: (i) it explains how language learners ac-

---

[40] Cf. also the vast literature on bootstrapping: e.g. Gleitman (1990), Pinker (1994), and, relatedly, Steels & Kaplan (2002).

quire composition rules, and (ii) it is perfectly compatible with the view that once *competent* speakers have successfully acquired those rules, they then, of course, use them both for comprehension and for production.

Ad (i): As a psychologist, Tomasello is highly interested in aiming at 'psychologically real' descriptions, i.e. descriptions that do not merely make sense of a certain phenomenon but which pick out real cognitive capacities of speaker-hearers. He thus argues ardently against approaches that assign meaning to atomic constituents and conceive of compositionality as functions from these semantic atoms to complex units. His general worry is that

> [...] formal linguistic approaches [...] characterize natural languages in terms of formal languages, using as basic theoretical primitives meaningless algebraic rules and meaningful linguistic elements that serve as variables in the rules. [...F]or usage-based theorists the fundamental reality of language is people making utterances to one another on particular occasion of use. When people repeatedly use the same particular and concrete linguistic symbols to make utterances to one another in "similar" situations, what may emerge over time is a pattern of language use, schematized in the minds of users [...]. (2003a, 98–99)

Hence, my above claim that the Tomasellian paradigm can explain how language users acquire the relevant rules of composition seems, strictly speaking, wrong. At least, that is, if it is understood as referring to the very same *kind* of rules, i.e. otherwise meaningless rules that have meaning only in virtue of mapping simple (or simpler) semantic units onto complex (or more complex) semantic complexes. For our present concerns, though, the slightly more interesting aspect is whether 'rules of composition' in general fit with Tomasello's framework. And here the answer is a clear 'Yes'. Thus,

> [The] construction grammar perspective provides a more plausible account of the interaction between the concrete and the abstract [e.g. syntactic construction] in language development— because it focuses on *abstractions across whole utterances*—than

does a lexical rules approach in which all depends on the meaning of the particular verbs involved [...]. The current proposal [of how children construct abstract constructions] is that they do this using the pattern-finding skill of analogy, which basically categorizes together complex wholes on the basis of commonalities in their relational structures. It is very important to emphasize that abstract analogies—for example between two structures that have no elements in common—can only be drawn if children use their *intention-reading skills to discern the function of those elements in the larger structure*. It is only by doing this that children may align the elements that correspond to one another—the elements that do the same communicative job—across the two structures [...]. (Tomasello 2003a, 193, my italics)

So, Tomasello is absolutely fine with a semantic theory that postulates recursively defined rules, or, generally, rules of composition. For these simply fall under the heading 'abstract construction'. The thing is, though, that the mechanisms that, according to him, underlie the acquisition of syntactic constructions are radically different to mechanisms compatible with TCS such as innateness. As the above quotation demonstrates, Tomasello conceives of language development as essentially token-based, abstraction-based, and—most crucially—intention-based. Syntactic constructions (i.e. the 'rules of composition' in CxG) are learnt only on the basis of understanding in particular instances of their application how they work, which involves being able to attribute appropriate intentions to one's respective interlocutors.

Ad (ii): Thus, intention-reading is a possibility for children (or language users generally) to circumvent the problem of determining the content of utterances at stages of their development at which they lack relevant knowledge of word meaning and formal rules of composition. Over time, children's knowledge of constructions increases, including knowledge about *syntactical constructions*. Syntactical constructions are, in a way, the component of construction grammar that corresponds to syntactical *rules* in more classical grammar theories. Eventually, these rules determine the way in which the semantic value of a particular sentence structurally depends on the semantic values of the atomic sentential parts. 'Like words, constructions are symbolic entities in which a particular meaning or function is mapped onto a particular form (i.e., a particular configuration of structural and/or lexical elements)' (Diessel 2013, 349). Many relevant features of compositionality can be covered in construction grammar by simply incorporating them into (or equating them with) syntactic constructions.[41] Here is an example that illustrates this:

> Consider the sentence *What did Michael send Miriam?*, which involves the combination of a number of different constructions; first, each of the five words are constructions; then there are the VP construction, the NP construction, a Subject-Auxiliary Inversion construction, the *wh*-construction, and the Ditransitive construction. [...W]hile the VP and the NP Constructions combine larger phrases out of individual words (constructions), the *wh*-construction licenses the argument of the verb *what* in sentence-initial position, and the Ditransitive construction is understood to encode the grammatical relations by pairing a particular form/function with a particular meaning. (Boas 2013, 240–241)

When it comes to meaning, the explanatory 'dead end' in a broadly Tomasellian framework of language comprehension is intention-reading, i.e. the basis for explanations in the area of semantics (pragmatics) would be the observation that infant humans have the ability to attribute intentional states to their (prospective) interlocutors. In this respect, Tomasello's work

---

[41] I formulate this cautiously because compositionality plays a different role in construction grammar than it plays in other theories. Firstly, language is not fully compositional according to construction grammar (Ziem & Lasch 2013). Secondly, in Goldberg's first formulation (Goldberg 1995, 4) non-compositionality is employed as a feature that singles out constructions (cf. also section 2.2):

> According to Construction Grammar, a distinct construction is defined to exist if one or more of its properties are not strictly predictable from the knowledge of other constructions existing in the grammar.

This definition is widened in more recent publications as to cover constructions that *are* thus predictable but which at the same time are sufficiently *entrenched*, i.e. used regularly and invariably.

is theoretically on a par with, for example, Davidsonian accounts that see meaning rooted in reference and truth conditions (which are also explanatory dead ends in their semantic frameworks). Neither account is itself an 'ultimate' explanation of the semantics of sentences: both explanations again call for further explanation in related research areas. I now briefly summarise what I think are the three main reasons for questioning the Davidsonian framework in this context.

Firstly, Davidson (like his adherents) has no developmental story to tell about how children learn the prerequisites necessary to determine sentential truth conditions (i.e. meaning). It seems implausible to assume that they have an inborn interest in learning reference relations (e.g. that "dog" refers to dogs). Secondly, even if they had such an interest—which is unlikely since 'referential knowledge' *as such* is of no help to them—it probably would be fostered by their actual, underlying interest in understanding others (in which case we are back where we started). Besides, although Davidson's main motivation for truth-conditional semantics, mentioned repeatedly in his work, is a *psychological* fact, he is never explicit about claims concerning what is commonly called 'psychological reality', i.e. the status that knowledge about reference has remains unclear. Lastly, the only possible way for children to learn facts regarding reference and rules of composition is via *utterances*, since these are the only data available to start with. In other words, abstract types can, with nomological necessity, only be learnt on the basis of context-bound tokenings of that type, which, again, derive their semantic values not just from formally specifiable 'contexts of utterance' (time, place, speaker), but also essentially from contextual factors beyond the reach of formal theories (world knowledge, intention ascriptions, common ground, etc.).[42] But, from a Davidsonian perspective, it is exactly the other way around—for which case, however, there is no plausible developmental story. Assuming that knowledge about reference and rules of composition is not innate, a Davidsonian theory of meaning looks pretty much unlearnable.

I should say a few words about why it is particularly easy to decide whether a person understands, whereas it is relatively problematic to argue for compositionality (/recursiveness) as the underlying cause of under-

---

[42] See also section 7.2.2.

5 Theories of Truth & Meaning

standing. In philosophy, "understanding" is sometimes used as a technical term. In that case it is understood as a counterpart to "explaining", emphasising the difference between the two. I bracket this discussion here. For present purposes, 'understanding' is simply a certain ability, a knowledge-how.[43] It is the ability to show appropriate behavioural responses to specific situations. In linguistic contexts, these responses paradigmatically include *verbal behaviour*, e.g., answering questions in a certain way.[44] Although verbal behaviour is indeed important in some context, the ultimate mark of correctness for understanding is overall behaviour. Generally, overall behaviour is the mark of correctness in any social ascription practice. If, for example, a caregiver says to her child "Please give me the red ball!", and the child responds by giving the red ball to the caregiver, then it seems reasonable—all things considered—to assume that the child understood the command (maybe after the child repeatedly showed structurally alike behavioural patterns in similar situations). So, understanding is quite straightforwardly ascribable. Note that an attribution of understanding is *always revisable only on the basis of new evidence*. In the case of the child, evidence might be that you find out that she gave back the red ball by chance (she would have given just any ball in the vicinity).

The gist is this: revising the attribution of understanding requires further evidence. This is different when it comes to recursion. The classical (Davidsonian) explanation for why children can, in principle, understand "Please give me the red ball!" is because this sentence consists of individual words, which have their own meaning (e.g. "ball" refers to balls, "x is red" is satisfied iff x is red, etc.). These words are put together in such a way that there is a corresponding set of recursively defined syntactic rules which compute the semantic value of the whole sentence based on the semantic values of its constituents. This is, from the (neo-)Davidsonian point of view, a plausible explanation for understanding. As opposed to understanding,

---

[43] The following explanations demand certain charity on the reader's side. I shall keep the examples short, and therefore omit some more or less obvious niceties. The same holds for my characterisation of "understanding", which involves the notoriously vague notion "appropriate". I think, though, that the examples are sufficiently clear to get the basic idea. For 'knowledge-how', cf. Jung & Newen (2010).

[44] Cf. Gibbs (2002, 2005), Gibbs & Perlman (2010), Gibbs & Tendahl (2006), Nicolle & Clark (1999), and Noveck & Sperber (2007).

5.2 Cooperative Contexts

however, recursiveness is not warranted by the observable phenomena as such. That is, an attribution of knowledge of recursive rules can be revised *without further evidence*[45]. This concession was already implicit in Davidson's own formulation of the argument: he construed it as an inference to the best explanation based on the assumption that *no other* solution to the Novelty problem was available apart from his own (see especially *Learnable Languages*).

So, Davidson's argument in favour of recursiveness is threatened from two ends. Firstly, his 'only game in town' assumption seems rather dubious (see section 5.1.3). Secondly, not only *is* there a relevant alternative; this alternative even seems to be the only serious contender. This is because, simply put, from a developmental perspective, children must acquire their mastery of a particular language on the basis of their prior ability to understand utterances, the constituents of which they did not know in advance (see above). Therefore, if we require of a philosophical theory of meaning that it should either involve a plausible developmental account, or, alternatively, be at least compatible with current such accounts, then Davidson's theory seems seriously threatened. The broader theoretical background that inspires my own approach to semantics, which I pursue in this book, is construction grammar. Tomasello's ideas do not really need to be *shown* to be compatible with CxG; they are *part* of the CxG movement. Hence, *this* part of motivating a particular theory of meaning—i.e. by showing that it is compatible with an established theory of language acquisition—can be dropped. Accordingly, my emphasis in this chapter was on undermining Davidson's claim that TCS is particularly likely to account for human capabilities of successful sentence comprehension. Rather, I argued, it is just the other way around: a plausible developmental theory starts with the assumption that children *lack* the abilities suggested by Davidson. They then continuously acquire semantic knowledge by first understanding utterances. The basic mechanism that they presumably employ is abstraction. The alleged semantic knowledge postulated by TCS (especially reference) comes into play *at the end* of language acquisition, if at all.

---

[45] I mean 'data' in the narrow sense of the term. Metaphorically speaking, armchair reasoning might count as one's 'new evidence' here.

6 Dispositional Analyses

Now that I have discussed language acquisition at length it is time to return to the core topic of this book: meaning. In this chapter, I indicate the rough outline of what I think an empirically validated theory of meaning in philosophy might look like. The starting point will be a brief return to primary meanings (in 6.1) and the role they play within the framework that I develop here. The major part of this chapter, then, is section 6.2. There, I will be piggybacking on Paul Horwich's idea to spell out the (relatively empty) claim that meaning is use by means of dispositional analyses. I think that this is exactly the right strategy to be dealing with use properties, i.e. the right strategy to counter the problem that constitutive use properties must eventually be *identified with something else*. Otherwise, there would be no 'access', as it were, to those use properties. In other words, if I only say that meaning is use without providing a corresponding method of *stating* the relevant use properties, I would be making a possibly true, but uninteresting claim. Associating use properties with something else (here: acceptance properties) provides an opportunity to evaluate the thesis in the first place.

Given a usage-based approach to meaning, dispositional analysis is without any alternative. However, I think that identifying use properties with *acceptance* properties is a mistake, as it easily leads to the impression that only truth-evaluable content can have meaning. One can't plausibly accept, for instance, sentences like "Hi there!" So, if one goes for a usage-based account that is supposed to be universally applicable to all areas of natural languages, one should indeed pursue dispositional analyses, but without the unnecessary constraint that *all* meaningful units have to be analysed with recourse to acceptance. This is what I will be proposing in the second half of this chapter.

6 Dispositional Analyses

6.1 The Role of the Refined Notion of Primary Meaning

The paradox that I discussed in the previous chapter was this: there are good arguments against classically defined primary meanings; yet, a semantic theory that simply does away with primary meaning (and, thereby, the literality/non-literality distinction) seems highly implausible. As I have shown, one needs 'something like' ordinary primary meanings in order to account for such systematic effects as irony. Accordingly, I proposed—in 5.1.2—a refined definition of "primary meaning" that is acceptable from the point of view of CxG and usage-based approaches more generally, but which at the same time can be utilised in explaining literal/non-literal effects. There is some similarity between my 'primary meanings' and Horwich's 'core use properties', which are those 'explanatory basic properties' (Horwich 1998, 60) that account for the overall use of a term. The basic idea in both cases is that there must be *some* sufficiently general description of the meaning of a given term that can capture how this term gets employed, all things considered. This section is about how primary meanings figure in my own theoretic framework.

6.1.1 Again, The Case of Malapropisms

The core of the classical Davidsonian strategy of explaining the inferential mechanisms involved in processing malapropisms can be kept in my theory framework. Instead of truth-conditional knowledge (concerning referential relations), the current proposal is based on expectations. But the overall strategy is still pretty similar to Davidson's, i.e. starting from (the equivalent to) primary meaning, it ends with the very same 'pragmatic meaning'. For example, my proposal allows that one's ability to interpret a particular instance of "conifer" in terms of 'coryphaeus' is at least partly rooted in semantic knowledge regarding "conifer", that is, knowledge regarding 'literal' meaning. An obvious worry in light of these similarities concerns my original motivation for giving up truth-referential meaning in the first place. In the new framework, the inferential process requires, or so it seems, that its basis is primary meaning again: only expectations concerning primary meaning can *go wrong*. I shall first explain briefly why

6.1 The Role of the Refined Notion of Primary Meaning

this worry is unjustified. Following this, I shall point out why the proposed framework fares better with respect to meaningless expressions.

The problem, discussed in 5.1.3, was this: in order for the inferential process to get off the ground, it is necessary that there are expectations about the use of the 'wrong' word, for example, "Konifere". However, one argument against TCS is that there are words whose meaning is such that it can't be explained by reference or by reference analogues such as satisfaction. Most obviously, this holds for classes of words that can only be semantically characterised by acknowledging their specific conversational *function*: e.g. "hello". Then there are also words that lack meaning entirely, which, however, are still 'comprehensible'. For instance, there are cases in which malapropisms involve meaningless words, as Davidson himself notes with respect to Lewis Caroll's Jabberwocky. For conceptual reasons, people can't have any *expectations* about how these words might be used. By assumption, meaningless expressions are such that people did not use them before. To be sure, it may be that people are able to identify similarities between meaningless expressions and meaningful counterparts. For instance, they might identify certain phonetic similarities; cf. "galumphing" (a term coined by Caroll) vs "gallop" and "triumphant".[1] But if they do, they derive expectations concerning those meaningless expressions from their prior expectations concerning the meaningful counterparts. In any case, given that meaninglessness here can reasonably be equated with absence of prior use, there is nothing from which expectations possibly could have emerged.

The solution to this is simply this: the alternative proposal allows us to keep Davidson's machinery to a large extent; but this does not imply that understanding of malapropisms must always be inferential. The only thing I wanted to demonstrate above was that if sometimes understanding malapropisms involves inferences concerning, among other things, phonetic similarities between words, then this fact can be accounted for within the proposed framework. But often understanding is non-inferential or, at least, does not involve inferences concerning false expectations. Indeed,

---

[1] Cf. the Wikipedia entry on Jabberwocky, http://en.wikipedia.org/wiki/Jabberwocky\#Possible_interpretations_of_words, accessed on: 25/03/2014.

6 Dispositional Analyses

"Er ist eine Konifere auf seinem Gebiet" is quite a good example in this regard, since many people have no idea what a 'Konifere'/'conifer' is. And by this I do not mean that they are not familiar with the scientific definition. Many people do not know that a conifer is, for example, some kind of tree. To put it another way, they form no expectations whatsoever about how "conifer" might be used. Hence, if someone uses the term, their expectations can't be false. Still, many people understand (utterances of) the relevant sentence perfectly well.[2] This means that the intended interpretation ('expert') must be directly available to otherwise competent language users. In fact, this is what I want to argue for. People are able to immediately understand utterances, without necessarily considering 'literal' interpretations first.

That something roughly along these lines *must* be correct is evident from the facts. If people *who, by assumption, do not understand "Konifere" individually* are able to understand "Er ist eine Konifere auf seinem Gebiet" (call this sentence "α"), then inferences operating on the primary meaning (of "Konifere") can't be in play here. I claim that hearers *immediately* understand whole utterances, even if they are unfamiliar with certain 'parts' of it, because they engage in common cooperative activities with their interlocutors, and communication is one of the means they employ in executing these activities. In a typical situation, a speaker who utters α tries to convey the information that a particular person ('he') is an expert. The hearer, of course, uses all available information to figure out what α means. Most importantly, in a typical situation he would know (i) that the speaker intends to ascribe a 'positive' attribute to the person referred to by the pronoun "he";[3] (ii) that the construction "Er ist eine ___ auf seinem Gebiet" means that he is a(n) ___ in his area; and (iii) that, from the context of the preceding conversation, 'he' must be an expert in his area.

The third condition says, in effect, that a hearer already *expects* something like the intended interpretation. Bearing the following considera-

---

[2] To be sure, this is an empirical claim that can't be justified entirely in the current context. However, I take it that, irrespective of the particular example, this phenomenon is common enough so that the reader is able to come up with examples that work analogously.

[3] For instance, the speaker might employ an intonational pattern that suggests that a "Konifere" must be something positive. Also, the rest of the overall conversational context might exclusively support this conclusion. And so on.

6.1 The Role of the Refined Notion of Primary Meaning

tions in mind, this does not seem too implausible. Keep in mind that utterances are always embedded in contexts. If the context is 'poor', i.e. if, for example, a speaker *starts* a conversation by saying "He is a conifer in his area" (to someone who does not understand "conifer"), the context offers little evidence as to what this could mean. That is true but not in conflict with my proposal, for it is equally true in such a case that, for the hearer, the intended interpretation is hard to grasp (if not impossible). If, on the other hand, the context is 'rich', it would entail more information that the hearer could exploit in figuring out the intended reading. For instance, α might be embedded in a larger conversational context:

> Adam, you know, is a philosopher. He knows a whole lot about the meaning of life, about just societies, and about the ethical implications of animal experiments. He has written two books and forty-seven articles. Man, he's great. *He is a conifer in his area.* For real.

In this situation, one may reasonably assume that (i)–(iii) (or some reasonably similar conditions) are fulfilled and that the hearer is able to figure out the meaning ('expert') on this basis alone. In general, the overall context cuts down—for speakers and hearers alike—the range of possible interpretations of utterances. One might argue that the highlighted information in (iii) is chosen arbitrarily (by me as an informed theoretician), and that there are many more bits of information available in the abovementioned conversation that could equally qualify as relevant for a given utterance interpretation. For example, the information that Adam likes to write articles, etc. Many different kinds of information could have played the role of pointing the hearer to the most liekly interpretations. That is basically right. This, however, is not a problem for the hearer but for us as theoreticians. The problem is that it is hard to state a *general rule* that picks out the most relevant information that guides the interpretations of any specific utterance.

The general, schematic 'rule' for the hearer is simply this: pick out the interpretation that seems most probable. And given the 'data' in our little thought experiment, the hearer picks out 'expert' as the interpretation that seemed most probable. In a way, namely post hoc, the situation is similarly simple for the theoretician: given the way the hearer in fact interpreted

6 Dispositional Analyses

the utterance (an ascription that is independently justifiable on the basis of non-verbal behaviour), the information that Adam is an expert *must* have been the most salient one. The only problem, so to speak, is that one can't state a rule in advance, independently from particular conversational contexts that would uniquely determine the meaning of an utterance. But that's just fine if one accepts that a semantic theory is unable to achieve this anyway. The only thing we can hope for is a theory that explains why utterances have the meaning they in fact have. And the answer to this question is: because speaker and hearer engage in common activities with common goals, and hearers exploit all available information, in particular contextual information, to determine utterance meaning.

In my example, the assumption is that the information that Adam is an expert, which triggers the hearer's inclination to interpret "conifer" as 'expert', was already implicit in the foregoing statement. Prima facie, this seems to render my explanation trivial, for, *apparently*, most of the time the decoded information is not implied by previous statements. In the case of malapropisms, the hearer must have some cues as to how to interpret a given utterance. My hunch is that if malapropisms are interpreted successfully (i.e. as intended by the speaker), then the relevant information was already implicit in the context. If it is not to be found in the utterances preceding the one in question, then probably somewhere else. Consider the following example:

> One winter, I was looking out of my kitchen window. It was raining heavily. I turned to my friend, who was about to leave, pointed at the window and uttered (the German equivalent of) "Would you like to borrow a whisk broom?" Without hesitation, my friend pulled her umbrella from her backpack, waved it at me, and said "No, thank you, I've got one." Only after that we both realized what I had in fact said, and burst out laughing.
> (Glüer 2013, 347)

The information that was relevant for the hearer was, presumably, that she herself was about to leave and saw her friend looking through the window. Maybe Glüer also employed some more general information like that her friend is concerned about her; that the overall weather conditions were such that the hearer could easily assume that her friend could see that it

6.1 The Role of the Refined Notion of Primary Meaning

was raining outside (even if the hearer was unable to see what her friend saw); and so on. Similar to the example before, the (non-linguistic) context was rich enough as to provide sufficient information for determining the content of the utterance.

The framework developed here suggests that if the (linguistic and non-linguistic) context does not provide enough information, successful communication is hampered or impossible. Again, it is virtually impossible to state a general rule for this. In Glüer's example such a condition might be that the hearer did not see that she was looking out of the window, or if it was highly unlikely to rain that day, or what have you.

Probably the most vital source of information for expectations about how words might be used on future occasions is one's familiarity with their past instantiations. Accordingly, a very common reason for misunderstanding or unsuccessful communication is when the respective knowledge of word meanings diverge between speaker and hearer. In such cases— e.g. in conversations between a professional and a layman—the context is often too poor for the hearer to be able to interpret an utterance. The reason is that under normal conditions, a given speaker would assume (implicitly) that if the hearer shares some common semantic knowledge with the speaker, the utterance itself would provide enough contextual clues to figure out its meaning. Simply put, under normal conditions, speakers assume that their English-speaking interlocutors understand, say, "The Earth is round" as meaning that the Earth is round.

Speakers, therefore, very often accommodate their speech to ensure that the shared semantic basis between them and their interlocutors is as broad as possible.[4] Also, speakers typically ensure that this shared basis is commonly known to be thus shared. A very familiar case is when you are abroad and you speak to some random person. In order to find out about whether there is some overlap between what you think your words mean and the semantic knowledge of the other person, you would typically ask questions like "Do you speak English?" Depending on the answer, you are justified in assuming that your utterances themselves (i.e. the *linguistic*

---

[4] If they do not, their communication aim is probably not to convey the content of their utterances. For example, one might just want to sound competent and therefore use technical terms deliberately, assuming that their (exact) meaning is widely unknown to one's audience.

6 Dispositional Analyses

context) will provide enough contextual clues to figure out their meaning, without needing to provide further, non-linguistic clues such as, e.g. gestures.

To see that the relevant context for successful communication is in fact very broad, consider this. A special kind of communication is written communication. Here, many factors that in serve purposes of disambiguation oral communication are unavailable (facial expression, shared visual field, gesture, intonation, etc.). Also, the typical speaker's sources for accommodating her speech according to the hearer's reactions are missing. For this reason many things that are possible in situations of oral communication are impossible, or severely complicated, in books and articles. Irony, for example, is often accompanied in speech by certain intonational patterns. These must be substituted by descriptions thereof in written work.

It is not *always* necessary to substitute non-linguistic clues, of course. But it *is* necessary if the context is otherwise too poor to trigger a particular intended reading. Metalevel descriptions, however, is not the only means employed by writers to get their message across. Consider the following: many statements in physics textbooks are presumably true (naïvely speaking). Equally, many statements in the Sherlock Holmes Novels are probably false (save for geographical facts concerning London). Anyway, textbook authors and novel writers are both equally 'successful' in getting their messages across, i.e. their respective audiences read their works roughly as intended.[5] The example shows that even such abstract categories as text genre are part of the context and determine the conditions under which author and readership communicate with each other. Genre is one of many contextual factors that can determine a reader's expectations about how specific words or sentences might be used in what is reading.

I began with malapropisms, where the most interesting fact about this phenomenon is that readers/hearers understand sentence tokenings largely independently from the primary meaning of the falsely applied word (cf. "conifer"). My explanation for this ability was that interpretation always takes place in communication contexts in which producer and recipient

---

[5] In construction grammar, there are even attempts to conceive of discourse units or whole literacy texts as constructions, i.e. there are attempts to broaden the technical notion "construction" accordingly such that it goes beyond the the borders of sentences: e.g. Günthner (2009, 2010), Imo (2010), and Östman & Fried (2005).

participate in some common activity or share some common goal, all of which helps the hearer/reader to figure out the intended reading. The range of linguistic and non-linguistic means that speakers use to enforce a particular meaning of their utterances and that hearers employ in determining what a speaker meant—this range is so broad that it is impossible to state a universal rule for how they do this. The only valid such 'rule' is the rather non-specific: it is all down to the context.

6.1.2 Primary Meaning in the Current Framework

Before I turn to a more general discussion of dispositional analyses, let me conclude this section with a few remarks on how the redefined notion of 'primary meaning' fits into the broader picture. The slogan of usage-based semantic theories is that meaning is use. In this book, I defend a specific variant of this claim, namely that the constitutive basis of meaning is the totality of actual tokenings of a given (word, sentence, etc.) type.[6] 'Meaning', in the ordinary sense of that term, is the most appropriate descriptions thereof—for example, an analysis of relevant dispositions. Defending this claim against some objections will help to show what I mean here more generally.

It is important to stress right from the start that a whole family of objections can be forestalled by making clear that *typing* meaningful entities might involve a lot more than taking into account their formal properties plus relevant aspects of disambiguation. For instance, individuating the meaning of "bank" might involve more than just saying that tokens of that word type consists of such-and-such sequence of letters and that in certain contexts it may mean 'institution' whereas in others it could mean 'riverside'. Typing words and other meaningful entities might require relativisations to all sorts of things, including periods of time or social groups. I ask the reader to bear this in mind when I talk about 'all tokenings' of a given (word) type: this is always meant to be relativised to the appropriate (i.e. meaning-affecting) circumstances such as the relevant social group, the relevant period of time, the relevant conversational context, etc. (for this, see especially 6.2.1).

---

[6] Cf. also part three of this book.

6 Dispositional Analyses

Generally speaking, foundational theories of meaning (reductionist theories) are concerned with explicating the underlying non-semantic properties that constitute semantic properties. A theory that explains meaning (a semantic property) in terms of use (a non-semantic property) is such a theory. Understanding is typically identified with a certain ability. For example, understanding a particular word is identified with being able to apply and interpret instances of this word, i.e. to know what it means. Now, if the meaning of a word were constituted by the totality of its past instantiations, a variety of problems would arise. Firstly, there is the problem that one typically wants to assume that all members of a specific language community (e.g. the English community) are competent in that they understand what words of their particular language mean. Presumably, qua being competent speakers, they must at least implicitly know the constitutive basis of word meaning. Secondly, the claim that meaning is total use seems to imply that the constitutive basis of word meaning is de facto not specifiable. There are infinitely many ways to individuate contexts, hence there are infinitely many ways to describe the contexts in which a word is uttered. Even if there were only one plausible context per utterance, the number of actual instantiations of a given word type would be far too high to actually 'list' these instantiations. Thirdly, knowledge of all actual word type tokenings, taken by itself, seems to be valueless anyway, i.e. such knowledge as such does not foster one's understanding. Grasping the meaning of a term is essentially an ability that involves abstracting from specific instances and coming to know valid generalisations.

I think all three worries boil down to the objection that, as it stands, "total use" is massively underspecified. I emphasise the totality of actual uses due to technical reasons, some of which I will discuss in detail in the following section. From a theoretical point of view, we are of course interested in generalisations, not in mere lists of instantiations. Therefore, I think it makes sense to make clear that—within semantics—we are typically dealing with, at least, two more or less different issues. There is a divide between the constitutive basis of meaning and semantic description. Typically, when people talk about 'meaning' in the folk sense of the term, they are interested not in its constitutive basis but in adequate descriptions. Constitutive bases constrain the range of adequate semantic descriptions. This, however, does not imply that changes concerning a given basis *must*

6.1 The Role of the Refined Notion of Primary Meaning

involve corresponding changes with respect to the adequacy of semantic descriptions. Importantly, claims such as "meaning is total use" concern the properties that constitute meaning; they are thus not *directly* concerned with what is usually called 'meaning'. In this view, claims such as "meaning is total use" are abbreviated ways of expressing the thesis that 'total use determines meaning'. 'Meaning' itself is simply the most effective way of describing this constitutive basis (e.g. total use). This amounts to saying that 'meaning', as ordinarily conceived, is, strictly speaking, not total use but the most appropriate description thereof.

Concerning the three objections just mentioned, it is important to note that they oscillate between the two 'readings' of meaning. The first two objections say that equating meaning with total use prevents competent speakers from understanding and theoreticians from stating meaning. However, what is in fact unknown is only the constitutive basis of the meaning of each word. Neither ordinary speakers nor theoreticians know them. A philosophical theory might still make perfectly justifiable claims about the metaphysics of semantics. Simply put, I do not need to know individual tokenings of a word in order to justify the claim that individual tokenings alter the constitutive basis of semantics. For example, one reason is that each new tokening that a hearer/speaker is confronted with provides potentially new evidence as to what specific words might be useful in the future in order to reach specific aims (or recognise such aims in others). "Dog", for example, is used to refer dogs. This fact—assuming it is a fact— is constituted by each new "dog" tokening. As a hearer/speaker, one can infer this meaning on the basis of impoverished knowledge, without being acquainted with the whole constitutive basis.

Thus, distinguishing between semantic metaphysics and semantics in a more narrow sense helps us to see that understanding and semantic description are enterprises that are to a large extent independent of metaphysics. Similarly, the third worry—'listing uses without formulating generalisations seems valueless'—can be accounted for in terms of this metaphysics/description divide. The semantic descriptions we are dealing with *are* generalisations in the required sense (e.g. "hello" is used to greet someone). It is this type of knowledge that we would typically ascribe to competent users (as opposed to familiarity with total use). Plus, it is this type of knowledge that explains understanding in competent speakers or hearers;

6 Dispositional Analyses

e.g. someone who knows that "hello" is used to greet someone arguably understands this term. The *adequacy* of such generalisations depends on the constitutive basis of all uses. If "hello" were to be used for different purposes in the future, then the mentioned generalisation would become invalid. The ordinary hearer/speaker does not need to consider the complete metaphysical basis of meaning in order to understand. His only 'responsibility', so to speak, is to form generalisations only on the basis of the *segment of this basis with which he is familiar*, i.e. the tokenings that he uttered or heard in particular conversational contexts.

6.2 Meanings Are Dispositional Analyses

I reject the identification of use properties with acceptance properties. The alternative I propose is twofold. Firstly, I think that it is best not to place any constraint whatsoever on the form of dispositional analyses other than that it must be efficient. Evaluating the value of a dispositional analysis (of the use properties that constitute word meaning) is like evaluating a lexicon entry: it is good if it conveys a sufficiently precise idea of the use associated with the term in question. In this sense, I think that there is ample reason to acknowledge that Horwich's sketches of analyses of terms like "red" are good approximations, i.e. analyses in terms of acceptance are perfectly legitimate in some areas. Secondly, I think that the 'search' for good dispositional analyses should *start* at the *end* of communication processes. Arguably, the dispositions people usually arrive at depend crucially on their interpretation of communication situations, i.e. the way they ascribe *intentions* and the *success* of using particular linguistic expressions relative to a given set of thus ascribed intentions. In 6.2.1, I say why I think meanings are dispositional analyses. In 6.2.2, I explain the explanatory role of intentions in semantics.

Relative to what I said at the end of the previous section, the title of the present section is not to be taken all too seriously. Meanings are efficient ways of describing their underlying constitutive basis. In my view, the latter is use. And my proposal is that the most effective method in this regard is dispositional analysis. In this sense, the claim that 'meaning is dispositional analysis' is not meant as revealing some irrefutable truth about semantics. Rather, the idea is that, considering all that is known about attempts to describe use, the dispositional method—à la Horwich but without the restriction to acceptance—is probably the most efficient method currently available.

6.2.1 From Descriptions to Dispositions

Returning to the recursion issue serves as an excellent starting point for the following discussion, which will lead to a more precise understanding of what meanings are. The extensive literature centering around compositionality and recursion is all inspired by the assumption that declarative sentences are the relevant unit for studying semantics. The mainstream literature suggests that sentence types are the most important theoretical entities when it comes to language comprehension. The paradigm examples in philosophy of language are the simplest examples, consisting of just subject and predicate: "snow is white", "Socrates is wise", and so on.[7] I have already shown that such an approach is highly problematic in regard to other types of sentences (e.g. exclamations).

The appropriate solution here seems to be the following, which is radical but efficient. It does not really help to argue about sentence comprehension in terms of usage-based approaches versus truth-functional approaches, or anything like that. For they basically face the same problem in that they try to explain language comprehension in terms of semantic knowledge of constituents. I think it is a misconception to take for granted that 'sentence' is the unit that can be understood at all. Sentences (i.e. type-level, abstract units) are theoretical artefacts. Roughly put, thinking of sentences as the genuine objects of language comprehension is pretty much committing a category mistake. Borg, in particular, is likely to object at this point:

> I will see or hear a sentence as meaning what it in fact does mean regardless of other things I believe or, in general, what I hope a given speaker is going to say. If you, as an interlocutor,

---

[7] As I note repeatedly throughout this book, the more general problem in the study of semantics is that many people take written language to be their primary object of study. In philosophy, claims concerning spoken language often seem heavily influenced by the prevailing dominance of written language. For the relation between written and spoken language in linguistics see Linell (2005).

> decide to come up with the most surprising, most irrelevant utterance you can think of, it will still be the case that any sufficiently competent language user, within earshot and paying attention, could immediately interpret what the sentence you produced meant, even if they can find no relevant reason for your having spoken as you do. [...] Though I do not expect there to be an alligator in the corridor of my philosophy department, still a cry of "There's an alligator in the corridor!" means that there is an alligator in the corridor and, though I may have my doubts about the veracity of this report, it can lead me, cautiously, to investigate the matter. Yet, if semantic understanding were susceptible to expectations or to my general view of the world and my current situation, it is hard to see how this could happen. (2004b, 89–90)

As I see things, there are basically two possible counterarguments. One is short; the other is shorter. The shorter reply is the following. What is at stake here is apparently *understanding*. Ascriptions of understanding, though, are defined in terms of what people do in specific situations. In particular, understanding is defined relative to how people behave in response to particular utterances. The abstract unit 'sentence' only comes into play in order to account for what enables understanding in the first place (if at all). However, sentences are not the objects of understanding.[8] In any case, explanations of language comprehension always begin at the

---

[8] To be sure, Borg's conviction that semantics is the study of context-independent meaning is not new. In fact, she is in good company, as the following quote is supposed to show:

> The justification which permits the grammarian to study sentences in abstraction from the settings in which they have occurred or might occur is simply that the fluent speaker is able to construct and recognize syntactically well-formed sentences without recourse to information about settings, and this ability is what a grammar undertakes to reconstruct. Every facet of the fluent speaker's linguistic ability which a grammar reconstructs can be exercised independently of information about settings [...]. (Katz & Fodor 1963, 173)

A slightly modernised version of this idea reads:

> [...] what is said is determined linguistically. When a speaker utters a given sentence in a given context, the only intention that is relevant to what he is saying is his semantic intention, i.e. his intention concerning the resolution

6.2 Meanings Are Dispositional Analyses

level of utterances. Note also that it would not help either to point out that someone who only knew that someone said 'There is an alligator in the corridor' would merely know that someone said something that means that there in an alligator in the corridor. This is perfectly explicable in terms of utterance comprehension. If the subject in question only understood (or knew) what a specific utterance meant in respect of certain formal properties (e.g. that the utterance consisted of specific words), then this means that the context was so poor that the subject was only able to retrieve information from that particular utterance *on the basis of this utterance being an instantiation of a specific sentence type*. Nevertheless, it is still the utterance that is understood (or is known to have a specific meaning).

I think it also would not help to point out that here we are specifically concerned not with understanding as such, but with *semantic understanding*. Within the broader picture of Borg's theoretic framework, the comprehension of 'sentences' (i.e. instantiations thereof) is a matter of processes going on in one's 'semantic module' (cf. Borg 2004b, especially chapter 2). In this view, 'semantic understanding' is independent from 'interpretation of communicative acts' (Borg 2004b, 90). Thus, what 'semantic understanding' is is not explicable in terms of behavioural dispositions (though the above quote might be read suggesting this), but only explicable in terms of (mere) knowledge of truth conditions. That is to say, it would seem that my objection might be a bit unfair, as I presuppose that *utterances* are the only proper objects of understanding. I can only partially agree. Indeed, I presuppose—and argue for the claim—that only utterances can be understood and I have problems with seeing what it means to 'semantically' understand context-free tokenings of sentences. But I do not think that this unfair or, in any way, could possibly undermine the claim that Borg did not

---

of any ambiguities and the fixing of any indexical references. (Bach 2001, 28)

Cf. also Bach (1994). The most recent expression of the idea that semantics can be pursued completely context-independent is this:

[...] to know the meaning of a sentence δ is for there to be a type of speech-act A and a form of content ψ such that one knows that in a literal and unembedded utterance of δ the speaker is performing an act of kind A whose content is of form ψ. (Schiffer 2015, 78)

6 Dispositional Analyses

show that she is able to understand 'context-free' sentence tokenings. My general, methodological concern would be that if 'understanding' is completely detached from behavioural dispositions, as Borg suggests,[9] then it is hard to see what would potentially count as *evidence* for attributions of understanding. On the other hand, if behavioural dispositions did play a role in determining whether a given subject understood some tokening of a specific sentence type, then it is unclear why that understanding should concern merely the sentence type but not *that* specific utterance. This is because the behavioural dispositions associated with the interpretation of a given sentence type systematically depend on how utterances of that kind are typically interpreted.

More generally, Borg seems to build her framework upon a certain idealisation. The idealisation lies in the implicit assumption that competent speakers all understand the same thing when they overhear a particular utterance. And that is probably false, because what they understand depends on a variety of different factors, including (i) which meaning they associate with the particular words uttered; (ii) what they consider relevant in a given context; (iii) on their overall cognitive abilities; and so on. In general, what people *understand* generally depends on the actual utterance, not on sentence types. There are several possibilities for Borg to object to this line of reasoning (all of which I only extrapolate from her writings). Firstly, she might object that I am confused about the explanatory end of linguistics. Linguists, or more generally: empirical theorists, typically try to capture generalisations. If I now explain understanding solely at the level of tokens, I neglect the fact that competent language users have one quite general ability, namely to recognise that someone who utters something of type *x* means something that is commonly expressed by tokenings of

---

[9] Borg (2004b, 81):

> If, for example, we treat grasp of literal linguistic meaning as the canonical derivation of truth-conditions for sentences [...], then semantic understanding can form part of a genuine language module, for this is clearly a function which is encapsulated and computational. Knowledge of meaning, on this kind of account, consists of knowledge of a proprietary body of information (the lexicon of the language) and knowledge of a set of rules operating only on that information [...].

6.2 Meanings Are Dispositional Analyses

this kind (in case we were back at the level of types). One worry might be that an utterance-based (usage-based) conception of understanding might not be able to formulate generalisations (as it is individual utterances that get understood in this framework). To be sure, sentences are essential in order to formulate generalisations. But there is no contradiction here. If we want to express the idea that people who overhear "There is an alligator in the corridor" *always understand* that there is an alligator in the corridor, then we could just do this. Such an assumption (that I doubt is true) means that competent speakers of English understand utterances of this type similarly. This is a claim that would need to be justified by evidence showing that the behavioural patterns that people show as an immediate response to those utterances are sufficiently alike.

Secondly, Borg might raise the worry that although there are behavioural differences between language users when it comes to how they interpret utterances, it might still be the case that they interpret *sentences alike*. For example, people might *actually* respond differently to utterances of "There is an alligator in the corridor"; but what is common between competent speakers is that they, *qua being competent*, know that "There is an alligator in the corridor" means that there is an alligator in the corridor (which is knowledge that only partially determines their reaction). Competent speakers have different idiolects; what they 'know' about the meaning of a given sentence depends on what they 'know' about the words constituting that sentence. If competent speakers can have different idiolects, then there are two alternatives. One is to say that the phrase following the "means that" locution is interpreted relative to individual idiolects, in which case ascriptions of the form "*S* knows that instantiations of sentence type '*p*' mean that *p*" is true.[10] But this can't be true in Borg's view as this is specifically anti-Davidsonian.[11] A second option is to say that the phrase following "means that" has a stable meaning, e.g. the one ascribed according to the theoretician's standards. However, in this case the ascription "*S*

---

[10] I know that utterances of the form "There is an alligator in the corridor" (relative to my idiolect) mean that there is an alligator in the corridor (relative to my idiolect).

[11] Where by "Davidsonian" I mean that particular theory variant that takes Tarski's theory of truth as input and delivers a theory of meaning as output. As one of the readers of this book rightly pointed out to me, the 'later' Davidson (especially Davidson 1986) seems to defend the idea that, indeed, there are *only* idiolects, i.e. 'passing theories'.

6 Dispositional Analyses

knows that '*p*' means that *p*" might turn out false, since its truth depends on what people associate with a given sentence. For the sake of simplicity, assume that what people associate with a sentence can be expressed in terms of truth conditions. Then the truth conditions that people associate with "There is an alligator in the corridor" might be different, depending on what, e.g., "alligator" means in their idiolect (e.g. to which set of objects it refers). If the associated truth conditions can differ, a generic ascription such as the one proposed by Borg can't be right.

A rather radical response would be to emphasise that the proviso "sufficiently competent" ensures that the relevant semantic knowledge that language users associate with a given sentence must be sufficiently alike. For one thing, this is pretty circular, since presumably competency, again, can be defined in terms of similarity of knowledge (e.g. the knowledge that "alligator" refers to alligators). Also, if a reasonable number of speakers are to count as competent, the standards for ascribing competency must be relatively low. As already remarked repeatedly throughout this book, the differences between individual 'competent' speakers are usually obscured by philosophers' tendency to discuss all too simple examples ("There is an alligator", "Snow is white", "It's raining", etc.). If you consider more complex examples (e.g. "Democracy is a goal worth pursuing"), you see quite easily that even *competent* speakers are likely to disagree about what particular sentences *mean* (independently of particular instantiations). And it does not help either to say that *by definition* competent language users must know what particular sentences mean, i.e. along the lines of: whatever "There is an alligator in the corridor" means, competent speakers must at least know that it means that there is an alligator in the corridor. Because then you are either referring to idiolects again (which is specifically anti-Davidsonian)[12], or you are referring to competent users' ability to know that any sentence means what it de facto means, which is an ability that is fairly independent from their specific linguistic competency.

"Meaning" is a theoretical concept that refers to a particular state if it is used in expressions such as "Subject *S* grasps the meaning of '*p*' ". It refers

---

[12] Borg repeatedly remarks that her view is supposed to be a neo-Davidsonian one (e.g. 2004*b*, 3–4 and 2012*a*, 3–4). Which is to say that, until recalled, she is committed to that Davidsonian perspective.

to that very state subjects are in if and only if their behaviour correlates in a specific manner with "p" utterances.[13] What I propose, effectively, is to think of meaning as dispositional analyses. Dispositional analyses are approximations. When I say that "+" means addition, this does not mean that a given subject S *will* answer my question "What is 1000+2?" by saying "1002". However, such an answer is the one that is *most likely* (all things considered), given that the relevant subject is part of a language community in which "+" de facto means addition. Kripke, in *Wittgenstein on Rules and Private Language* (1982), discusses this at length in the context of private language.[14] As a brief reminder: the problem is that if use (i.e. meaning) is couched in terms of dispositions, then one can't ever know with any absolute certainty the 'correct' set of dispositions (associated with a particular word). Because the set of dispositions is derived from the finite set of past manifestations (of particular word types). For now, let me just note that our *actual success* in conveying meaning ultimately determines that we are talking about the same dispositions. Kripke, when he says things like that he 'uses the word "plus" to denote a well-known mathematical function' assumes that his readership understands him, thereby presupposing that he and the audience associate the correct dispositions with "addition"—for example, they would reply with "1002" rather than "1004" to the aforementioned question.

Dispositional analysis is no end in itself. Its success hinges on how well it 'summarises' the use of a given word, since the latter is what we are actually after. It is important to bear this in mind when weighing different possibilities of spelling out dispositions. For instance, dispositions must be attributed to objects.[15] The obvious candidates for this are speakers and hearers. Assuming that communication is for the most part successful (people understand each other), I see no reason to think that there is a fun-

---

[13] Or, alternatively, for words: statements of the type "Subject S grasps the meaning of 'w'" refer to the particular state subjects are in iff their behaviour correlates specifically with utterances that contain the word "w". The reasoning behind this is simply this: although utterance meaning is theoretically primary, it is reasonable to suppose that many utterances that contain a word such as "apple" are structurally similar in some respects, namely in those respects that account for the meaning of "apple".

[14] See section 3.1.2.

[15] For a general overview of dispositions, I recommend Heil (2005).

6 Dispositional Analyses

damental difference between speaker- or hearer-centered descriptions.[16] I therefore focus, as is common practice in philosophy, on the speaker in what follows. Accounting for the meaning of words in terms of the dispositions associated with its use has some neat advantages. I emphasise four of them and explicate them in turn. Dispositional analyses are (i) relativisable (to social groups, time, etc.); (ii) they are commonly accessible, which is an essential feature of meaning; (iii) they provide a framework for degrees of understanding; (iv) they can be designed in such a way that diachronic development gets incorporated very easily.

Ad (i): Dispositions can be easily relativised to different social (and other) groups and different historic times. This helps, for example, in describing the individuation of different meanings of homophones. It also allows for quite natural explanations for meaning shifts, which are difficult to handle in truth-functional frameworks and related theories. To be sure, dispositional analyses do not in *themselves* help to individuate meanings. However, they provide a quite straightforward means of modelling different meanings or meaning shifts, given that these are known. I think it is relatively fair to say that it is not the task of a decidedly philosophical theory of meaning to uncover semantic differences between homophones or shifted meanings.

---

[16] From the neo-Davidsonian point of view, the most problematic aspect of usage-based descriptions is its reference to intentions; speaker intentions in a speaker-centred scenario, mindreading in the corresponding hearer-centred framework. However, the dispositions to utter *or* interpret a specific utterance in a particular situation must be systematically alike. This is because natural language speakers are necessarily hearers, too. The dispositions of applying a word that I have *as a speaker* (relative to my intentions) are to a large extent determined by my dispositions of word interpretation as a hearer (relative to the intentions that I ascribe). Accordingly, if the overall success of human communication is given, then this success is probably due to the fact that speakers' dispositions are 'designed' in such a way as to match the hearers' disposition to interpret accordingly. Simply put, if I want to refer to salt, my disposition to utter "salt" in order to achieve this is determined by (i.e. matches with) those dispositions that, I suppose, I would have as a hearer if I were in exactly that situation my current interlocutor is actually in (what he is able to see from his point of view; what background knowledge he probably shares with me; what the prior conversational context was; and so forth). Therefore, it does not really matter whether the dispositions associated with a given linguistic sign are described in terms of speakers or in terms of hearers.

6.2 Meanings Are Dispositional Analyses

I have shown that it is possible to give a usage-based account of "primary meaning" that does not presuppose that words actually 'have' their literal meaning in all actual conversational contexts. Rather, it seems more plausible to go just the other way around by saying that "primary meaning" must be spelled out in terms of uniform expectations, thereby picking out specific subclasses of utterances (namely those that correspond to literal uses in classical terminology). Also, I have noted that "primary meaning" may be defined in terms of the 'homogeneous majority of uses (if any)'.[17] I should now spell out more precisely what this claim amounts to.

The qualification "homogeneous" in my definition is particularly important. Several utterances of a word qualify as having the same meaning by exemplifying similarities; eventually, these structural similarities justify counting several utterances as instances of one particular type. For example, it has often been noted that some words have such a shallow 'core meaning' that their actual—'literal'—meaning differs effectively with each new linguistic context.[18] The classical example here is "cut", presented by Searle:

> Consider the following sequence of rather ordinary English sentences, all containing the word "cut".
>
> 1. Bill cut the grass.
> 2. The barber cut Tom's hair.
> 3. Sally cut the cake.
>
> [...] It seems to me the following is more or less intuitively obvious about this list. First of all the occurrence of the word "cut" [...] is literal. There is nothing metaphorical or figurative in our understanding of any of those sentences. (1980, 221)

---

[17] The "if any" simply rules out those words that *lack* (what I call) primary meaning. There are some words that are perfectly meaningful, yet lack proper primary meaning, since no homogeneous set of its tokenings may be determined yet: for example, the German term "wulffen" during its first two or three months of application.

[18] In contrast to indexicals, what differs from context to context is not merely semantic value (e.g. the referent) but meaning as such, i.e. the property that determines semantic value.

6 Dispositional Analyses

The most prominent, slightly more recent reconsideration of this topic is in Recanati's work. In discussing a variety of similar examples, he notes the following concerning "red":

> What is it for a car, a bird, a house, a pen, or a pair of shoes to count as red? To answer such questions, we need to appeal to background assumptions and world knowledge. Linguistic competence does not suffice: pragmatic fine-tuning is called for. [...T]o determine a suitable sense for complex expressions, we need to go beyond the meaning of individual words and creatively enrich or otherwise adjust what we are given in virtue purely of linguistic meaning. We must go beyond linguistic meaning, without being linguistically instructed to do so, if we are to make sense of the utterance. (2005, 183–184)

The basic idea is always the same and indeed quite simple: "cut" (and the like) seems to differ enormously in meaning, depending on what it takes as object, so to speak. It goes without saying that something like a 'core' meaning is common to all those variants. There are, though, different things that can be literally cut (grass, hair, etc.) and different ways of doing so. Hence, "cut" instantiations are to a large extent *heterogeneous* in certain respects. Still, one is typically inclined to say that "cut" has primary meaning. Thus, something must be in common between all literally interpreted "cut" utterances: the instantiations must be homogeneous *in some sense*. The trick is to acknowledge that, due to the different varieties of cutting, the homogeneity of "cut" utterances must be paraphrased in *very general* terms,[19] whereas the superficial heterogeneity is attributed to regularities in the use of those words that denote the things cut ("grass", "hair", and so on). Ultimately, *homogeneity* of use is what determines that several

---

[19] Along the lines of: "to cut" is a verb that often expresses a reduction of a certain mass (of grass, hair, etc.), where the object that retains the remaining amount (of grass, hair, etc.) is also its syntactical object (grassland, head, etc.). Note, though, that the underlying problem that Recanati describes remains. A 'liberal' formulation of the relevant meaning is incapable of solving it. The problem persists that the abstract meaning of "cut" as such does not suffice to determine sentential truth conditions in particular contexts. In order to determine (literal) truth conditions, one needs to consider contextual features (e.g. cotext, intentions, common knowledge, etc.) that are not 'allowed' at the 'semantic' level in truth-conditional theories such as Borg's.

6.2 Meanings Are Dispositional Analyses

tokenings of 'words' belong to the same word type. Because we would not want to *individuate word types* solely according to their spelling or other formal features. That would be absurd. Rather, we want word individuation processes to be guided by differences in use: for example, word type 1 of "bank" is used to refer to riverbanks; word type 2 is used to refer to institutions. Thus, if "to cut" actually *is* one word (type), this must be reflected in at least some, albeit very general homogeneity of all its supposed instances.[20]

The "majority" in "the homogeneous majority of uses" highlights the fact that the "primary" in "primary meaning" makes sense only in sharp contrast to some 'derived' or 'pragmatic' meaning. In my terminology, 'pragmatic meaning' is what all (meaningful) utterances have. In this view, 'primary meaning' is the meaning that words have if they are used (what is typically called) 'standardly'; e.g. "dog" in contexts in which it is used to refer to dogs. These two things might look circular at first sight. Firstly, the use of "reference", which might look as if I were smuggling referential relations back into my account. This, I think, would be a misunderstanding. Nowhere in the text do I say, for example, that the meaning of "dog" is (or can be given by saying) that it refers only to dogs. On the other hand, it is an empirical fact that very often people use "dog" in order to refer to dogs. If I now pick out this particular fact in order to characterise the likely primary meaning of dog, then this 'citing of facts' is fairly independent of one's underlying semantic theory, i.e. fairly independent of whether you think that meaning is, for example, reference. Secondly, the way I describe primary meaning might look dangerously circular. If using words with their primary meaning is using them standardly; then what is using them standardly? Supposedly, using them with their primary meaning. Again, I

---

[20] In section 8.3, I link my discussion of the distinction between the 'constitution base' of a word and its appropriate 'semantic description' with the question of what determines that a particular expression token belongs to a specific expression type. In other words, that section describes how, I think, tokens should be 'counted'. In this sense, that section also answers the question what it takes for any given set of expression tokens to be homogeneous: tokenings are homogeneous in the relevant sense iff there is a theoretically fruitful way of describing them as instantiations of a particular type. Of course, such a notion of 'homogeneity' presupposes that words *already have been typed* accordingly. But that seems justified, as it is not the task of a theory of meaning to provide its own (full-blown) account of how expressions are typed.

6 Dispositional Analyses

think this would be a misunderstanding as well. I define "primary meaning" in terms of majorities of use. Strictly speaking, it is perfectly possible (i.e. in principle possible) to look naïvely, without prior theoretic understanding, at the whole set of actual word type instantiations. In sorting all instances according to certain similarities among them, one could find out that most instances share a specific feature. For example, one might find out that most "dog" instances share the feature that people use them in order to refer to dogs. Now, in characterising my own account, I presuppose that competent speakers of English are, in general, aware of such empirical facts. Presupposing such knowledge does not render the account circular.

Words 'have' their primary meaning in a subset of cases relative to *all actual instantiations of the corresponding type*. It is relatively easy to recognise a "dog" utterance as an instance belonging to a specific type, e.g. due to phonetics, spelling, etc.[21] Similarly, it also quite straightforward to determine whether some such instances form a majority, given one's ability to recognise homogeneity. Accordingly, in my terminology associating a primary meaning with a given term means forming expectations about the future application of this word that is based on one's ability to recognise (implicitly) that there is a majority of past instantiations of this word type that shared relevant commonalities. For example, the commonality might be the circumstance that, in the majority of cases, "dog" utterances have been used to refer to dogs.

Before I return to the actual topic—dispositions and relativisations—let me very briefly add a caveat. The 'homogeneous majority' that people consider in order to form their expectations about 'standard usage' happens simultaneously with or after disambiguation. Here is a very illustrative example. "Bank" is a word whose instantiations are by and large distributed equally amongst its two major interpretations ('riverbank' and 'institution'). That is why, strictly speaking, no clear *majority* can be determined here. So if I say that the 'homogeneous majority' of cases determines expectations, I have in mind the majority of cases *within* the set of tokenings of *one* interpretation. This is because it is possible to have distinct non-literal (i.e. minority) uses for both types separately. The same applies to cases in which there are two or more possible interpretations, but one of

---

[21] Müller (1996) offers some nice remarks on type recognition.

6.2 Meanings Are Dispositional Analyses

them is so prominent that, in fact, it supplies the majority, all instances considered (e.g. "great" as 'excellent' vs 'large').

Back to dispositions, then. Dispositions have the significant advantage that they must be relativised in several respects, anyway. They thus provide a natural framework for distinguishing homophones, distinct meanings in particular social groups, different meanings according to contextual factors, and so on. Let me explain. Relativisation to social groups will serve as an example. In German, the word "Mongo" (eng. "mongo") differs slightly in meaning depending on the social group within which it is used.[22] For sake of simplicity, I consider only its *offensive* usage. The ordinary, established variant is to use it, in appropriate circumstances, with racist connotations. In the idiolects of today's youth, "Mongo" means, roughly, 'idiot'—without any racist connotations whatsoever. Thus, we have *one word type* that is associated with slightly different sets of dispositions regarding today's youth and prior generations. These differences in meaning trivially fall off any empirically informed dispositional analysis of "Mongo", as one needs to relativise dispositions to all meaning-relevant factors. Simply put, one can't just say that a particular word type *w* is associated with such-and-such dispositions simpliciter. Rather, dispositions require *objects* to which they can be attributed (like properties) and *circumstances* in which they take effect (in philosophical prose, 'antecedent conditions').

I can imagine that the most likely response to this argument is this: trivially, if "Mongo" falls into two different types in modern German (as secured by the description), then this is just as easy to account for in truth-conditional semantics as it is in use theory. Either "Mongo" is actually two types with two different *intensions* (and thereby extensions (e.g. the set of idiots and something else), or it is just that two different *connotations* are

---

[22] "Mongo" differs with respect to its use in adolescents and adults, though it is arguably only one word type (a fortiori by classical standards). The following is a quote from a recent newspaper article: 'A spokesman of the ministry of defence said in Berlin that, apparently, the colloquial [German] word "Mongo" can most likely be identified with 'Idiot'. It does not in a pejorative manner refer to Asian people', Frankfurter Allgemeine Zeitung, 27/02/2013, my translation. For the record, the original reads: 'Ein Sprecher des Verteidigungsministeriums sagte in Berlin, das Slangwort "Mongo" sei offenbar in der heutigen Jugendsprache am ehesten mit "Idiot" gleichzusetzen, es beziehe sich nicht in herabwertender Weise auf Menschen asiatischer Herkunft.'

6 Dispositional Analyses

associated with it. In the first case, there are two words to which, respectively, two different references can be attached. In 'Tarskian' terminology, the two relevant types get associated with two different base clauses. In the second case, truth-conditional *semantics* could just treat it as a single word and leave connotations to pragmatics.[23]

The reply does not succeed for the following reasons. Treating "Mongo" as *one* word whose different connotations become relevant only at a pragmatic stage is highly implausible, since this would require *that both variants can be treated equally because of a common truth-conditional impact* (rooted in an alleged referential relation). That is absurd, for *truth conditions* are absolutely irrelevant in determining the meaning of "Mongo". Not only do both variants not *share* a common intension (and thereby extension), they both *have* no 'extensional' commonality. To see this, consider the most likely candidate for the offensive reading: the intension that picks out the set of idiots. It makes no sense to say that "x ist ein Mongo" is true iff x is an idiot, or anything reasonably similar. The reason is that this intension is not even accurate for offensive use of the term: people typically do not refer to *anyone* in these cases. Yet, the word *is* meaningful unless you *define* meaning in terms of extension. The meaning of "Mongo" can be explicated, e.g., in terms of its *conversational function*: it is successfully applied if the addressee feels discredited, etc.[24]

Given that "Mongo" has two distinguishable meanings in modern German, this might be captured in truth-conditional semantics by simply *postulating* two types. One might even assume—if only for the sake of argument—that this could be done be postulating two different intensions.[25] I

---

[23] For example, by following Borg in claiming that pragmatics is only relevant for communication; which, again, is not to be dealt with by a theory of meaning, since the objects of study in semantics have their meaning independent of the communication-related ends they serve.

[24] I suggest that, in general, some classes of words are best described by recurring to the conversational functions that they fulfil. These classes are particularly hard to integrate into truth-conditional semantics, as they lack content that affects truth-evaluability. The most relevant examples in this regard include words that contribute absolutely no such content, but which at the same time have a very precise, easily specifiable meaning: e.g. "hello", "come on", "ouch", etc.

[25] The argument would run as follows: if you insist that there are two distinguishable uses in younger and elderly people, then this necessarily implies that these assumed differ-

6.2 Meanings Are Dispositional Analyses

will not argue against this possibility. Note, however, that the *only* possible reason for postulating two word types is due to differences in use. In this regard, there is no difference at all between use theorists and rival theories. A proponent of truth-conditional semantics is thus forced to claim that there is a fundamental difference between finding out what a word means (the epistemology of semantics, if you like) and finding out what meanings essentially are (semantic metaphysics). But this way out is blocked, as there is nothing more to meaning over and above what is suggested by empirical evidence, i.e. use.

Both ways, type differences of words boil down to differences in the dispositions associated with them, i.e. the properties that constitute their overall employment. Relativising dispositions to social groups is probably the most effective way of attributing differences in use to these groups (e.g. youth vs elderly people). Further relativisations work absolutely similarly. For instance, one could relativise the dispositions of using "cool" to different situational contexts[26] in order to distinguish two types: e.g. 'cold' and 'awesome'. Or, one might relativise dispositions to time or region: think of "tall person" in Asia vs in North America; or in 2014 vs in 311 BC. There are probably many such differentiations, contrary to what is suggested by the typical, in fact obligatory relativisation to language communities. Which relativisations are necessary to make is, of course, an empirical question. My point is that dispositions are a particularly adequate means to meet this need, as they have, so to say, an in-built demand for such relativisations.

Ad (ii): A recurring theme in the literature on the semantics of words and concepts is public access to meaning. Here, I briefly summarise the relevant parts of the discussion. Theories that emphasise the importance of the internal structure of speakers in the context of meaning determination (of words, of concepts) face the problem that for many different words the speaker's disposition to apply those is identical (cf. the narrow/wide

---

ences manifest themselves in attributing "being a mongo" to different sets of objects. Subject to correction for misapplications, these attributions hint at different intensions of the two involved types.

[26] Here, I mean contexts that differ in regard to whether *this* "cool" variant is applicable. Say, "$cool_1$" is applicable in linguistic contexts that suggest that temperature is at stake; "$cool_2$" otherwise. (This is simplified and for illustration purposes only.)

6 Dispositional Analyses

content debate, for instance)[27]; and that individual dispositions can't determine meaning anyway, for this would render successful communication implausible (cf. also the debates on inferentialism or holism)[28]. The worry is that the dispositions that presumably constitute speakers' overall language use are, with nomological necessity, not directly accessible to their interlocutors (i.e. they can only infer them). That is a serious problem, because two equally legitimate aims collide. I propose to go something like a middle way by claiming that both sides are right: meaning is determined by individual speaker dispositions *and*, at the same time, meaning is publicly accessible. Concerning the first point, meaning simply must be determined by speaker dispositions, because if meaning is use, then there is no way of finding out about meaning other than scrutinising speakers' dispositions to apply language. Accordingly, I would suggest that dispositional analyses are the most efficient way of capturing use. The second point is slightly more complicated, which is why it is worth going into a bit more detail.

For the following argument, I take the tentative results of preceding sections for granted. The meaning of a word is determined by the totality of actual past instantiations of this type. Barring some exceptions, this implies that nobody can have perfect knowledge of meaning, for nobody is familiar with all past instantiations of a given word type. Concerning dispositions, it is important to note that the individual dispositions to apply (or understand) a given term are determined by acquaintance with only a limited set of past instantiations.[29] Yet, there is an 'ideal' set of dispositions, namely the set one would associate with a given word if one had heard or otherwise experienced all its past instantiations.[30]

---

[27] Fodor (1987), Loar (1988).

[28] For overview articles, consult Cohen (1999) and Pagin (2006). Devitt (1993) is a critical discussion of meaning holism.

[29] In linguistics, this is known as the 'bottleneck problem'. The 'bottleneck' refers to the circumstance that, roughly put, every speaker hears a different set of word instantiations during their lifetime; still, every speaker (of a given language) ends up with the 'same' semantic knowledge. For each generation, the semantics of a given language (e.g. the semantics of "snow") goes through this bottleneck, whereby, interestingly enough, it retains its relevant properties (cf., again, Kirby 2002).

[30] I come back to this in 8.3.

6.2 Meanings Are Dispositional Analyses

Regarding public access to meaning, there are two separable problems, I think. Firstly, the meaning of words is a property of whole language communities, while the relevant dispositions to apply words belong to individual speakers. I call this the 'community problem'. Secondly, every speaker has a slightly different set of dispositions to apply a given term, while different people are nevertheless able to talk about the same thing. I call this the 'communication problem'. Now, the trick is to utilise the notion of an 'ideal set of dispositions'. To begin with, note that this is only a terminological definition. Of course, the 'ideal' set is not ideal in the folk sense of the term. Rather, it is ideal in that it is that particular disposition one would arrive at if one's overall application of a term were based on the experience of the totality of all word instantiations of this type. My argument will be that the theoretical notion of an ideal disposition can explain away both problems at hand.

I begin with the communication problem. Successful communication requires, or so people sometimes claim, that two or more people are able to talk about *the same thing*, e.g., snow, Johnnie Walker, the Seventh Sun, etc. If meanings were dispositions, then nobody would *ever* be able to talk about the same things, since, in fact, no two speakers ever share the *exactly* identical set of dispositions (concerning language use). I think that the flaw in arguments of this type is that they presuppose identical dispositions for communication success. Before turning to the key issues, let me begin with a short remark on the terminology employed in this objection. Apparently, the vocabulary that is used here is tendentious. Speakers' ability to 'talk *about* the same thing' is sold as the relevant hallmark for communication success. This is clearly inspired by referentialism, i.e. the prevailing idea that a theory of meaning is first and foremost a theory of reference. Doing away with this terminology will help to make clear what is actually at stake.

Communication success is, roughly put, a relation between a speaker's intentions and the results of his communication efforts. No matter what philosophers believe that communication needs in order to be successful, a communicative act such as "Could you please pass the salt?" is successful if, and only if, the addressee passes the salt to the speaker (given that was his intention).[31] In particular, the *success* can be determined independently

---
[31] See Pencil (1976) for a comprehensive review of the relevant literature.

6 Dispositional Analyses

from whether "salt" successfully refers to salt.[32] Thus, the 'bridge principle' that is required to reconcile necessarily diverging dispositions with successful communication is this: people are able to talk 'about the same things' if the semantic properties of their respective idiolects are *sufficiently similar*. Consider Wittgenstein's prominent example. We all have different concepts of chairs—and, hence, associate slightly different meanings with "chair". Our respective dispositions to apply "chair" to any given object are (supposedly) never 100 % identical. Remarkably enough, communication is still successful with respect to chairs. In other words, communication success is based on similarities of our dispositions to apply terms (or interpret others' utterances), not in their identity.

In technical terms, this point can be captured thus: the dispositions of two speakers, S_1 and S_2, concerning the applicability of a word w are similar iff there is a significant overlap between the situations that specify w's applicability for S_1 and S_2, respectively. The more overlap between these sets of situations, the more similar S_1's and S_2's use of w. The basic idea here is this: success means success in specific situations. Significant overlaps of situations in which two speakers would apply given terms ensure that their expectations regarding the use of these terms are compatible. Again, compatible expectations lead to communication successes. Please note that the descriptions of the respective sets of situations can be quite specific (depending on one's analysis interests). "Chair", for example, is a word whose applicability is somewhat vague. Interestingly, communication about chairs is still often successful. I am usually not surprised about what people get me when I asked them to bring a chair. The obvious explanation for this is that the set of situations in which a word is applicable is determined, among other things, by the relevance of a potential tokening. Roughly put, in the research on vagueness we can distinguish three different cases (ignoring higher-order vagueness): 'applicable', 'not applicable', and 'unclear whether applicable'. Philosophically interesting questions like reference-fixing (and, thereby, truth conditions) are determined—one may reasonably suppose—by one's *overall inclination* to apply a term. However, in situations in which success is relevant, people's dispositions are probably guided by only the clear cases, where the clear cases are those

---

[32] Whereby I do not mean that reference relations are never involved in explaining success.

of which they think that their interlocutor's dispositions are the same as their own. This explains why even in cases that involve instances of such words like "chair", communication success might in principle be exceptionless. It is because people are capable of recognising those situations relative to which their understanding of the applicability of a word is compatible with the understanding of others. Accordingly, they are able to 'confine' themselves to these overlapping situations whenever the applicability of a word is relevant for their communication success. In most cases, the range of possible overlap is so huge that one is easily led to the impression that communication is always successful, i.e. that we are always in a position to 'talk about the same things'.

Furthermore, our respective dispositions are, to a large extent, *impressively similar*—especially concerning connectives, termini technici, proper names, etc. This is because they converge to the ideal set of dispositions. The individual sets of dispositions (of speakers) diverge, because particular speakers are confronted with only a limited set of word type instantiations (plus differences regarding their belief sets and their remaining semantic knowledge). Note, however, that the individual instantiations themselves with which language learners get confronted are also very, very similar: for example, "snow" is very often used to talk about snow. Thus, it is highly plausible to assume that the similarity of actual "snow" utterances is passed on to the individual sets of dispositions that language learners derive from a particular subset of those utterances. It seems indeed plausible to assume that this effect is fairly independent of the fact that the *particular* set of instantiations with which individual speakers are confronted differs from the corresponding sets of their interlocutors. Thus, ideal dispositions solve both problems at once. Concerning the communication problem, it is important to acknowledge that communicational success can only be 'measured' in terms of fulfilment of intentions, for which similarity—as opposed to identity—seems to be sufficient. Concerning the community problem, I have shown that it is possible to attribute meanings to the words of whole language communities by abstracting from individual dispositions, which is unproblematic because the latter are remarkably similar, anyway.

One last note on similarity. I assume that communication success is rooted in similarities of individual sets of dispositions, which again is presupposed to be rooted in similarities of individual tokenings. Granted this,

6 Dispositional Analyses

it is easy to see that the strong, widespread conviction in philosophy of language that the semantic knowledge between any two competent speakers of a language such as English is identical stems from a biased choice of example cases. The by far most obvious example that illustrates this is logical connectives. One of the most popular examples especially in the philosophically minded literature on theories of meaning is the connector "and". Superficially, choosing comparatively simple examples serves the purpose of explaining in simpler terms mechanisms that work similarly in more complicated cases. The meaning of "and" is supposedly simply its contribution to the truth value of a sentence as a function of the truth values of its conjuncts (⌜p and q⌝ is true iff both p and q are true, false otherwise). The following argument does not just concern truth-*functional* connectives, which are somehow special in that they only 'relate' truth values. The important point is theoreticians' tendency to discuss word meanings that are easily specifiable due to their (relative) univocal use (e.g. the alleged fact that "snow" refers to snow). Up to a certain point, it seems that exemplifying complicated issues (e.g. meaning) by using relatively simple examples (e.g. "and" or "snow") is a perfectly legitimate strategy. However, it gets problematic as soon as the simplicity of the chosen examples obscures what is actually happening. The assumption that communication success is essentially rooted in the alleged identity of dispositions associated with individual words seems to be due to the fact that, *as far as the chosen examples are concerned*, the similarity of individual dispositions is indeed *overwhelmingly obvious*. When I say that example cases are chosen based on biases, I do not intend to imply that the complexity of the chosen examples does not go beyond the complexity of "and" or "snow". It is only that people—for good reasons, by the way—tend to choose examples that have *clear, unambiguous* semantics. Anyway, it would be odd if that were different. But a side effect of this strategy is that people often also tend to think that the relevant dispositions to apply a certain term are more or less distributed equally among competent speakers. And *that* certainly holds only for the examples typically chosen, if at all.

Ad (iii): Obviously, some people understand some words better than others. I have defined elsewhere (3.2), following Horwich (1998, 16–18), that to understand is to have implicit knowledge of the use of a given term. Even opponents must admit that knowledge of meaning comes in degrees, and

6.2 Meanings Are Dispositional Analyses

that these degrees of understanding manifest themselves in how the term is used. The most natural way to explain these differences in use is by referring to the differences in the sets of implicit knowledge every language user associates with a given term. Even more importantly, not only is this strategy unavailable to the opponent of usage-based approaches, but there is no obvious alternative that may be offered.

Within a usage-based framework, it is—barring complete descriptions—relatively easy to 'model' degrees of understanding. If meaning is total use and use is described in terms of dispositions, then full understanding may be equated with full, implicit knowledge of this use.[33] Accordingly, degrees of understanding can be understood in terms of divergence from this set of knowledge. Apparently, to really *model* these divergences might be very difficult or indeed impossible. But this does not undermine the present framework, for the following two reasons.[34] Firstly, it *is* an answer to the question what degrees of understanding are (i.e. an in-principle answer), whereas, as I said before, other theories do not provide such an answer. Secondly, the underlying problem is not that modelling degrees *as such* was especially difficult, but finding the right dispositions in the first place.

There is an important area in which *privileged* semantic knowledge is possible, namely self-knowledge. A person's knowledge regarding the semantics of his own idiolect is special in that introspection is available as a possible source of evidence. I said that understanding implies implicit knowledge of use. I have a particular, though not perfectly reliable, epistemic access to my dispositions that I do not share with anyone else. The least I can do is go through different imagined scenarios and ask myself whether I would be disposed to apply a given term in such a situation.

---

[33] This directly follows from how "understanding" has been defined plus the dispositional analysis of what meaning is. By the way, note that, except for some rare cases (coinage, omniscience, termini technici, proper names), full knowledge of this kind is impossible, which is highly plausible.

[34] A similar problem with modelling appropriate distances arises in the area of truthlikeness (Oddie 2014). Issues concerning only the modelling leave unaffected the intuitive grasp of which propositions are 'closer' to the truth than others. For instance, if the actual amount of rain was 50 cl, a theory that predicted 50.3 cl was closer to the truth than the one that predicted 17 cl. Analogously, the difficulties in modelling divergence from the ideal set of dispositions leave unaffected the intuitive grasp that some people's understanding of a given term seems 'better' (closer to the ideal) than others' understanding.

6 Dispositional Analyses

This ability explains both why one has the impression that self-knowledge is possible (because my own dispositions are 'transparent', so to speak) and why self-knowledge is a relatively reliable source of evidence. It is because we continuously use language, hence we invariably check the applicability of words according to our own standards.[35] It would, however, be a mistake to transfer this conviction that individual semantic knowledge is relatively reliable in respect to the idiolects of others or to the semantics of whole languages (i.e. the idiolects of a language community taken together). For here, one's implicit assumptions about others' use of a word is always an approximation whose scope is limited by severe epistemic restrictions. The restrictions result from the fact that every speaker of a language community is familiar with only a limited set of actual tokenings (cf. 'poverty of the stimulus' arguments), which indicates possible future use. By the same token, this line of reasoning shows why perfect semantic knowledge *is* possible in some cases. For example, it is possible to completely understand proper names. The reason is simply that a limited evidence basis *will* result in the same assumptions regarding future use as familiarity with all available evidence would result in.[36]

Ad (iv): Diachronic developments are very important in semantics, grammar theory, and general linguistics. Words, morphemes, and syntactic constructions might today have a different meaning than they had some time ago. There is broad consensus that semantics develops on different timescales. In artificial settings, meaning shifts occur quite frequently; very often they are even continuous (cf., for instance, the work of Simon Kirby). There are some classes of words that are hardly ever affected by meaning shifts, the most prominent examples of which probably include logical connectives, as indicated above. Presumably, everything else lies in between

---

[35] This is not to say that this proves that our assumptions concerning our own dispositions or others' dispositions need to be 'correct' in the Kripksteinian sense. Still, we 'continuously check the applicability' of a term in the—relatively weak—sense that we have certain assumptions about which expressions might be useful for which purposes. For example, I usually suppose that "Kill this dog!" is, ceteris paribus, a good means of convincing someone else to kill this dog. In this sense, the applicability of, e.g., "dog" can be 'checked' regularly, for one can simply observe whether the application of "dog" is successful relative to one's prior assumptions.

[36] This is an immediate consequence of the definition of "ideal disposition".

these extremes, i.e. significant changes take a number of generations to occur.[37] In a usage-based understanding, diachronic meaning shifts can be conceived of as a special case of relativisation (cf. first point). Meaning statements must be relativised to particular times (independently of disambiguation of indexical expressions). I contend that they normally are thus relativised (i.e. implicitly), and that this fact is obscured by choosing example sentences that involve only terms which are unlikely to undergo any significant meaning shifts within reasonable periods of time.

Consider "snow is white". Apparently, the 'constituents' of this sentence did not mean anything else three hundred years ago than they mean nowadays. Especially the 'x is y' construction is relatively stable in regard to its semantics. Also, "white", denoting a colour, is unlikely to shift its meaning all too much within short periods of time (say, within a few generations). If anything, "snow" might undergo significant semantic shifts, for as we know from Inuit languages, it might be quite important to differentiate between sorts of snow, depending on how much one needs to interact with it. Overall, however, "snow". "white", and "x is y" have such a stable semantics that one easily gets the impression that it has always meant the same thing and always will mean the same thing, i.e. that snow is white.

A quite impressive meaning shift on historic scales concerns "weil" ('because'). Originally, "weil" simply functioned as a 'subordinating conjunction', i.e. as a conjunction that stands in initial position of a subordinate clause (Uhmann 1998). This is one extreme end of its semantic scale. At the other extreme, "weil" is used solely as a discourse marker, viz. as a means of negotiating metalevel aspects of conversations such as turn taking. Several shades of grey lie in between these extremes. From a philosophical perspective, two features of the meaning shift of "weil" are particularly interesting. Firstly, the shift happened—and still happens—astonishingly fast (a few speaker generations). Secondly, the semantically relevant aspects of "weil" in its discourse marker variety is hard to characterise as well as

---

[37] Cf. today's use of the German term "weil" as a discourse marker, parallel to its established use as subjunction and conjunction; which is a possibility that, in this form, did not exist fifty years ago (see below). In English, a parallel development can be observed with regard to "because" (or "cuz") that may also be used as a discourse marker in today's English (Schiffrin 1987).

6 Dispositional Analyses

it is hard to locate particular "weil" instantiations on the continuum from subjunction to discourse marker. The first observation does not speak in favour or against any particular theory. It is only remarkable to the extent that common philosophy of language very often presupposes that natural language sentences express, plus-minus a bit, eternal contents (e.g. <snow is white>), which requires that, if meaning change occurs, there must be discrete steps in the shift from 'one' meaning to 'another'. However, in cases such as the meaning shift that affects "weil" such discrete steps are hardly identifiable.

The second observation is even more interesting in this regard. "Weil" as subjunction and conjunction is more or less easily identifiable:

> While syntactic integration (finite verb at the end of the sentence) indicates a close link between two clauses and is primarily used to express factual causal relations ("des is besser, weil's schneller is"[38]), syntactic disintegration (verb following subject; V2) indicates a loose link between two clauses and contextualises a "weil" sentence as an independent assertion. Accordingly, "weil" in V2-position is typically associated with epistemic ("der hat sicher wieder gsoffen. weil sie läuft total deprimiert durch die Gegend"[39]) or speech-act-related causal relations ("warum kauft Ihr denn keine größeren Müslipäckchen. weil DIE reichen doch nirgends hin"[40]) (Gohl & Günthner 1999, 40, my translation, notation simplified)

As regards the use of "weil" as a discourse marker, though, its status within that class can only be specified rather vaguely. Moreover, the semantics of its discourse marker function is hard to specify. Most such uses seem to 'inherit'—at least partly—the original semantics, i.e. they indicate *reasons*. However, this only holds in a metaphorical sense: the explanations regarding "weil" may provide reasons for mentioning specific information (as opposed to giving reasons for why a particular state of affairs obtains). Other uses, again, lack even this 'core' semantics; they merely indicate that a

---

[38] 'This is better, because it is faster.'

[39] 'He must have been drinking again, because she looks so depressed.'

[40] 'Why don't you buy bigger packs of muesli? Because these will never be enough.'

speaker wants to postpone turn taking. Thus, the semantics itself is hardly specifiable. Even worse, often different functions of "weil" *within* the discourse marker class seem to overlap. Gohl & Günthner (1999) conclude that

> The boundaries between [...] different discourse marker function associated with "weil" are sometimes uncertain. There are clear cases as well as a lot of overlaps, which is due to the fact that [...] "weil" can operate at different levels of discourse organisation. (54–55, my translation)

Abstracting from the particular difficulties of accounting for "weil", the philosophically interesting aspect here is that as soon as one turns to real-life examples, it is hard to ignore that many terms simply *lack* a clearly identifiable semantics. Rather, the semantics of many terms is—more or less—continuously evolving (on timescales of, say, decades). Describing the semantics of genuine natural language terms is necessarily an approximation. The development of "weil" shows, moreover, that *referential relations*—e.g. relating a main clause describing a state of affairs with another clause describing the reasons for why that state of affairs obtains—are particularly irrelevant in some cases. Rather, the meaning of a term like "weil" can be best described in terms of the conversational function that it fulfils—an element that is foreign to formal or truth-conditional semantics.

My primary intention is not to convince you of the ubiquity of semantic shifts. Rather, my point is that meaning shifts, prevalent as they are, have to be accommodated within a comprehensive theory of meaning. Usage-based approaches that cash out their main thesis in terms of dispositions are particularly likely to provide the easiest way of modelling meaning shifts. Simply put, the flexibility, mentioned above, to relativise dispositions to social groups is equally applicable to different times. Words mean and meant different things at different times due to the fact that people at different times had different overall dispositions to apply them.

6.2.2 More On Dispositions

I now want to describe in some more detail what I think a good dispositional analysis for word semantics might look like. To this end, I should say

6 Dispositional Analyses

clearly that I think that Horwich's insights are brilliant and that the mechanisms he employs are excellent means for this specific purpose. The main worry that I have concerns the scope of his theory, i.e. my worry is that by saying that dispositional analyses in semantics must eventually recur to acceptance properties—i.e. the properties with which use properties get identified in Horwich's view—he is committed to a rather restricted theory of meaning that leaves the semantics of wide areas unspecified.

Dispositional analyses consist of two parts: they state certain antecedent conditions and they define what, given that the antecedent conditions hold, a manifestation of a disposition is.[41] Horwich's analysis depicts particular such antecedent conditions and manifestations, namely 'the properties that explain [a term's] overall use and thereby provide it with the meaning it has' (Horwich 1998, 170). The problem here is that Horwich assigns a special role to declarative sentences in that the semantics of any given expression is identified with the role it plays in declaratives. Plausibly, the semantics of questions, for example, can be 'traced back' to acceptance properties. For example, the semantic contribution of "red" to "Is there a red elephant behind the door?" can plausibly be traced back to one's basic inclination to accept "This is red" when looking at something clearly red. But even if it is possible to employ this 'tracing back' strategy for *some* areas in linguistics, there are probably large areas in which this strategy fails. Examples include classes of words like "hello", "thing", "mongo", "go-gogo", and so on.[42] I come back to this in due course.

This is one reason for widening the scope of a Horwichian theory of meaning. Another one is this: reducing use properties to acceptance properties is—although it works in some areas—a strategy that is detached from what *motivates* language use in the first place. Therefore, a promising strategy to account for language use would be to ask first what language is used *for*, and then construe a dispositional analysis according to these insights. The idea is to scrutinise first which vocabulary gets employed in describing communication success (where the background assumption is that language use is primarily motivated by what leads to communicative

---

[41] Sugar is soluble (disposition): if sugar is put into water (antecedent condition), then it dissolves (manifestation).

[42] Probably, the strategy fails for a variety of different reasons in each case.

6.2 Meanings Are Dispositional Analyses

successes). Arguably, this tells us, without further ado, which concepts are relevant for meaning statements. In a nutshell, the most important variables to which dispositional analyses arguably must be sensitive are situational circumstances, intentions, and language users. Let me now briefly justify my decision to take *intentions* into account.

As people have no direct access to the intentions of other people, do they therefore, in a broadly 'intention-based' theoretic framework, only know the meaning of their own words? No. Firstly, the intentions involved here do not concern meanings themselves (as in the Humpty Dumpty cases discussed by Davidson; see below for a discussion). The relevant intentions concern *states* (e.g. the state in which the salt gets passed). Intentions can't be observed directly, but they can be inferred from observable behaviour. That is to say, one may (i) reasonably hypothesise whether a given speaker's intention was to get some salt, and (ii) one may also observe whether an assumed aim was reached, i.e. whether some salt was passed (in which case the hypothesised intention was fulfilled). Incorporating intentions into one's semantic analysis is therefore not a constraint on people's possibilities to find out what others mean.

Secondly, the regular expectations that I, or others, have regarding the use of a word are governed by successful applications of the word in the past. These past successes are observable by anyone (given they successfully guessed my prior intentions before; otherwise it would be hard for them to distinguish successes from failures). The connection between observable behaviour and regularities in expectations is even stronger: the observability of successes pushes expectations into a particular direction (entrenchment). In other words: both from the hearer's as well as from the speaker's perspective, intentions are important in guiding future applications of linguistic expressions. Roughly put, to determine the likelihood of achieving one's aims by producing particular utterances, one needs to take into account the past success of similar utterances relative to the hypothesised intentions (hearer's perspective) or known intentions (speaker's perspective), respectively.[43] I return to this further below.

---

[43] Although I do not want to pursue this any further at this point, it may be worth considering whether this little argument can be extended to a more general argument in favour of the relevance of intentions for semantics (as opposed to pragmatics). Horwich (1998) says about the normative power of the factual: '[...] the explanation [of the fact that

255

6 Dispositional Analyses

Thirdly, expectations and intentions are, in effect, two sides of the same coin. Hence, 'Humpty Dumpty'-like cases can be excluded, because it is impossible to freely *intend* to mean something without taking into account what one would *expect* how a given utterance might be interpreted. Here is why. People want their intentions to be satisfied.[44] Hence, *deviant* use, combined with the intention to be interpreted in a specific manner, only makes sense if this intention is made *transparent*.[45] Otherwise, one would *need to expect* that one's utterances probably will be interpreted according to the usual practice, by which the alleged prior intentions were dissatisfied.[46]

From an ontological perspective, intentions are peculiar. Especially so if they figure in theories of meaning. For instance, it might be questioned whether a specifically intention-based theory of meaning is naturalisable. An integral part of naturalism is the constraint that every theoretical statement must be open to scrutiny by everyone. Applied to my project, this

---

one ought to mean DOG by "dog"] is plainly pragmatic: it is good for [someone] to give words their English meanings because that is what member's of [one's] community do [...]' (1998, 186). I take it that a certain actual use *per se* can't enforce a particular future use. The reason is the following. My observation that people, including myself, in the past successfully 'referred' to dogs by uttering "dogs" is *only* interesting for me—i.e. a factor that could possibly guide my future use of "dog"—to the extent that I (implicitly) presuppose that this explains my past success in achieving dog-related aims and others' success in reaching theirs. In other words, the past success in using "dog" lies not in established reference (from "dog" to dogs) but in the achievement of dog-related aims (killing a dog by uttering "Kill that dog!"; conveying the information that this dog is brown by uttering "This dog is brown"; and so forth).

[44] This is an analytic truth.

[45] The 'later' Davidson (1986, 258) is quite explicit about this:

> [Humpty Dumpty, who intends to use "glory" with the meaning 'a nice knockdown argument,] cannot mean what he says he means because he knows that 'There's glory for you' cannot be interpreted by Alice as meaning 'There's a nice knockdown argument for you'. We know he knows this because Alice says 'I don't know what you mean by "glory" ', and Humpty Dumpty retorts, 'Of course you don't—til I tell you'.

[46] This is probably one major motivation that leads people to consider whether, e.g., text types could be treated as constructions. For text types (and the like) *systematically determine certain, possibly 'deviant', interpretations.* See note 5 for references.

6.2 Meanings Are Dispositional Analyses

means: a meaning statement involving intentions is useless if, in principle, language users are unable to check others' intentions. But there is no reason to assume this in the first place. Consider an example already cited above; the intentions underlying utterances of "Could you pass the salt, please?" Here, the intentions themselves are not the direct objects of investigation. However, it is possible to observe *everything else*. And everything else surely is enough for having a reasonably broad basis of evidence, from which intentions can be derived. In fact, describing particular kinds of situations (for instance, those involving the above question) in terms of intentions *just is* a specific way of description. The only way to deny ascriptions of intentions in action explanations is via an intention-involving alternative description.[47]

To conclude, a theory of meaning should be open to involve explanations that recur to intentions and intention ascriptions, as this provides the opportunity to take into account the *point* of using language in the first place. The point of having language is, following Tomasello here, that it is a means that helps achieving common goals.[48] Accordingly, appropriate dispositional analyses of individual terms are highly likely to recur to intentions and mindreading abilities. My point here is not that appropriate descriptions should generally involve intentions. Rather, this should be one possibility among many. For instance, I have repeatedly emphasised that the semantics of many terms can't be stated in terms of acceptance (and a fortiori not in terms of reference), but have to be described with regard to their *conversational function*. The meaning of an utterance like "How are

---

[47] Imagine that a person observes again and again that an utterance of "Could you pass the salt, please?" is followed by salt passing from the addressee to the speaker. These are observable behavioural patterns (utterances and reactions), hence uncritical from a naturalistic point of view. Observance of these regular patterns—and the correlation between the two actions—suffices in ascribing intentions to a given utterer of the question. (He probably intends to get salt.) From a naturalistic point of view, ascribing intentions is an observance-based strategy to explain kinds of behaviour. In slightly more philosophical prose, one does not necessarily need to be realist about intentions in order to employ them fruitfully in otherwise naturalistically uncritical explanations, i.e. explanations that recur to observables only.

[48] For constructionist frameworks of language acquisition, see Diessel (2007). For the relevance of cooperation, see Birch (2014) and Reich (2011). For mindreading in the Tomasellian paradigm, consult Moore, Liebal & Tomasello (2013).

6 Dispositional Analyses

you?" is to establish or cultivate a certain (temporal) social relationship.[49] Correspondingly, a speaker understands "How are you?" if, in appropriate circumstances, she is typically disposed to utter that phrase *in order to* establish or maintain such a relationship. Hence, at least for certain classes of terms (phrases, etc.) it seems essential to allow that their corresponding meaning statements involve intention-based vocabulary.

---

[49] This is not to deny that "How are you?" also has a 'literal' reading, on which it can be interpreted as a request. The point is simply that a semantics that, due to omission of intentions, is restricted to describing this 'literal' meaning would fail to capture that aspect of meaning that is most relevant.

Part III

Method

7 Semantic-Methodological Concerns

The first two parts of the book dealt with an overview of established mainstream theories in philosophy and with my own thoughts about it. The third part is a bit more 'programmatic'. Here, I lay down the methodological background that complements my arguments in the first two parts of the book. The present chapter is divided into two sections: In the first section (7.1), I present a variety of important background assumptions that play a role in several places throughout the book; in 7.2, I summarise what I think my methodological commitments are.

7.1 Background Assumptions

I would like to highlight three specific background assumptions. The first assumption is that, as a philosopher, it makes sense to take a liberal stance in semantics. By this I mean that, to put it in Fodor and Lepore's terms, 'the semanticists do the work and the philosophers do the worrying' (Fodor & Lepore 1991, 328) and that, therefore, philosophy should first and foremost simply *observe* the work the semanticists (and linguists more generally) are doing. For example, when 'the philosophers do the worrying' of finding an accurate definition of "meaning", they should primarily be concerned with taking into account the relevant notions of the term that are employed in flourishing theories in linguistics (cf. the decline of the semantics/pragmatics divide in CxG). The second assumption is that semantics in philosophy of language and 'semantics' in the field of mental representations are two *more or less* independent research endeavours, which are defined according to their explanatory goals. Since these goals, again, might differ, there is reason to suppose that the study of the semantics of natural language expressions should be pursued independently

7 Semantic-Methodological Concerns

from the study of concepts. Finally, my third background assumption concerns the (in-)compatibility of semantics and acquisition theory, which is a recurring theme throughout the book. I repeatedly remark that, in particular, the Tomasellian paradigm in language development lends support to a usage-based account of meaning in philosophy. In this section, I give a detailed justification for this claim.

7.1.1 A Liberal Stance On Contrary Explanations

Some general remarks that situate my discussion in the discourse of theory choice are in order. What makes a theory of meaning a good theory? And, more to the point at hand, which adequacy constraints do apply to theories of meaning? In the previous chapters, I have implicitly assumed a very liberal stance towards meaning in the sense that an appropriate definition of "meaning" should be broad enough to cover a wide variety of different established theories. This is particularly true of chapter 2, in which I gave a very general review of some mainstream theories in semantics. I specified the notion of "meaning" that is especially relevant for philosophy in chapter 6. Still, the view on meaning presented there is also pretty liberal. In the present chapter, I will therefore look in some more detail at the reasons for such a particularly liberal approach to meaning.

Some semantic theories (in philosophy and linguistics alike) are better than others. There are many criteria by which one may decide between two competing theories: generality, scope, simplicity, parsimony, elegance, overall coherence, compatibility with related theories, etc. In light of these criteria, it would seem odd to dismiss a particular theory merely because of one's definition of "meaning": to dismiss, for example, possible world semantics just because possible worlds do not fit one's pre-theoretic conception of meaning. Of course, if meaning *were*, for example, use—if meaning, to use Kripke's phrase, 'turned out' to be use—then a theory incompatible with this could be dismissed just by being incompatible with a usage-based conception of meaning. However, from a methodological perspective, one's general approach should be as liberal as possible, because thus far no semantic theory has been proven to be ultimately superior.

On the other hand: meaning can't be just anything. To be sure, we are free in *defining* "meaning" as we like. Some, for example, distinguish natural from non-natural meaning; others define the meaning of sentences relative to worlds and models; again others claim that the reference of a proper name exhausts its meaning, and so on. That is, there are a huge variety of different definitions of "meaning" established in the literature. Again, though, meaning can't be anything. The meaning of "meaning" varies enormously from theory to theory. So much that some think the notions employed in different paradigms or schools are hardly compatible with each other (e.g. Partee 1982). Be that as it may, the outermost boundary—if that much metaphor is allowed—of using "meaning" is determined by common sense. For whatever purposes one construes semantic theories (explaining cognitive abilities; explaining language competence; explaining inference patterns; explaining language acquisition; explaining diachronic and dialectal varieties; explaining word order; etc.), it seems reasonable to use "meaning" in a way that is at least remotely similar to common-sense use. And this is exactly what my characterisation of "meaning" employed in chapter 2 demands: the paraphrase that is supposed to be a meaning statement must be illuminating to the (otherwise) competent speaker. Or, in simpler terms, one must *learn* something about the meaning of a term by hearing or reading an adequate semantic description.

I assume that meaning statements are first and foremost reactions to 'meaning questions'. Typically, one says that '"x" means y' in cases when someone else inquires the meaning of "x" beforehand. In these cases, people are usually not satisfied with an answer if the meaning statement given in response does not help them understanding what "x" means. People are *right* in being not satisfied in such cases, for the question "What does 'x' mean?" serves just one single purpose: inquiring of the interlocutor about the meaning of "x". In line with this reasoning, it seems reasonable to say that not only *do* people typically learn something from a given meaning statement, it is also necessary that meaning statements are such that they convey potentially new information. In other words, meaning statements that are uninformative relative to *any* background assumptions—like "'Pegasus exists' means that Pegasus exists"—are not proper meaning statements in this account.

In truth-conditional semantics, no information that goes beyond the information included in the general principles of the theory is given in in-

7 Semantic-Methodological Concerns

dividual meaning statements.[1] This makes it particularly difficult, though not impossible, to see why these statements are informative. Eventually, the explanation will probably recur to compositionality again, since the 'informative' aspect of meaning statements like "'Paris' refers to Paris" is that it is supposed to explain competent speakers' ability to comprehend utterances containing "Paris" (all else equal). Actually, the situation is slightly more complicated as it is not entirely clear what TCS's meaning statements *are* in the first place. Presumably, one could argue that, strictly speaking, the individual base clauses belong to a complete, spelled-out theory of meaning for English. In a more narrow sense, Tarskian reference postulates are not part of the actual Davidsonian theory. His claims are more programmatic. In this sense, claims along the lines of "Singular terms get associated with individual objects via Tarskian reference postulates" belong to TCS, but statements like "'Paris' refers to Paris" do not. In the end, my methodological concerns remain the same in either case though.

This, then, is the first reason why I defend a decisive liberal stance towards meaning. As long as there is no independently justified reason for favouring one semantic theory over another, the definition of "meaning" should be broad enough as to cover all established theories. Common sense ensures that we do not get too liberal; e.g. common sense would prevent us from thinking that "'Pegasus flies' means that Pegasus flies" is a proper meaning statement.

A second methodological reason for taking the stance that I defend in this book is what I dub 'Primacy of Phenomena'. A good piece of advice when construing a theory is to begin things naïvely, i.e. by not assuming anything that is not immediately validated by the relevant phenomena themselves. For example, it seems undeniable that people communicate (for whatever purposes). On the other hand, the assumption that terms refer is not obviously validated by the given phenomena.[2] The adequacy

---

[1] By "general principles" I mean rules such as that singular terms always refer to their respective referents (where these relations are known before), and by "individual statements" I mean the axioms such as that "'Paris' refers to Paris'.

[2] Although one might want to argue that reference relations have indirect phenomena status due to their role in 'speaking about the world'. This terminology, I think, presupposes what is at stake here. Describing acts of communication in terms of our ability to talk 'about the world' is interpreting the available data in a specific manner. If you just

7.1 Background Assumptions

of given theories should be measured relative to their success in accounting for the phenomena they are designed to explain. The reason is that the phenomena to be explained are the only reason for introducing a new theory in the first place. Concerning the case at hand, this means that without human communication there would be no need at all for semantic theories. There is no semantics without language use. Accordingly, semantic theories should be guided by what is required by the phenomenon, i.e. by human language use. Referential facts, for instance, only enter into the picture *insofar as they are required to explain the phenomena that originally required explanation*.[3] Approaches that acknowledge this accord with the Primacy of Phenomena, as I shall put it.

This theoretical principle was applied in my discussion of Novelty and compositionality (cf. 4.1.2 and following). There, Novelty is the phenomenon to be explained. Interestingly, many people arguing for a specific view on compositionality start by considering the Novelty issue first. Here is the opening paragraph of *Truth and Meaning*:

> It is conceded by most philosophers of language, and recently by some linguists, that a satisfactory theory of meaning must give an account of how the meanings of sentences depend upon the meanings of words. Unless such an account could be supplied for a particular language, it is argued, there would be no explaining the fact that we can learn the language: no explaining *the fact that*, on mastering a finite vocabulary and

---

look at the 'data', without any theoretical background whatsoever in mind, you can only determine that people act in certain ways and that their acts, including their uttering noise, have certain specifiable effects on others. Pre-theoretically, it is simply not a phenomenon that people talk about the world. (Describing the available phenomena that way might be one possible way of making sense of the data. But that's another story.)

[3] The part in italics is especially relevant here, for otherwise one would immediately face the objection (i) that semantics is an area worth investigating independently of communication (Borg 2004*b*), or (ii) that people who do semantics by applying pragmatic conceptions seem to confuse the former with the latter. In a nutshell, I claim that pursuing semantics in the narrow sense (e.g. minimalism) might be justified if that were suggested by the phenomena. However, given that the raw phenomena are necessarily communication-related, you need independent justification for all semantic properties that you might want to posit and which are not immediately warranted by the properties of utterances.

7 Semantic-Methodological Concerns

> a finitely stated set of rules, *we are prepared to produce and to understand any of a potential infinitude of sentences.* (Davidson 1967, 304, emphasis added)

The important point is that Davidson makes several, arguably independent, claims here. The passage in italics suggests that he implicitly accepts my assumption that the phenomenon that needs explanation is humans' ability to comprehend novel sentences (relative to the relevant provisos). This suggestion, then, is mixed with further claims. The first is that the only solution to the Novelty problem is via a compositional theory of meaning. Davidson attributes this view to others in the cited paragraph, but it is essentially his. The second is that humans do 'master a finite vocabulary and a finitely stated set of rules', which is, at least, not immediately obvious in light of observable behaviour alone. The third is not even a proper assumption but clearly a mere suggestion: namely that our mastery of (only) a finite vocabulary is somehow related to our ability of sentence comprehension, if only to the effect that limited vocabularies and rules restrict the range of possible solutions to the Novelty problem.[4]

The three assumptions just highlighted are widely accepted in the literature. Their truth, however, is not warranted by the phenomenon that, as Davidson says, needs explanation. In particular, it is not clear that only compositional theories can account for Novelty. Taking the Primacy of Phenomena seriously, one should refrain from taking the link between compositionality and Novelty for granted. In particular, one should bear in mind that the link between these two problems (for which TCS is a unified solution) is merely *assumed*. The compositionality of natural languages is not among the phenomena. Which, by the way, is not to say that natural languages are not compositional. The Primacy of Phenomena, then, is my second methodological principle besides the liberalism toward meaning statements.

This principle indirectly suggests that we should handle contrary explanations liberally. Prima facie, all explanations (or whole theories) that

---

[4] The motivation for this rhetoric is that, from within a truth-conditional semantics perspective, an infinite number of rules would allow us to get away without compositionality. The obvious alternative then would be that people who understand sentences do so because they know the relevant truth conditions individually (i.e. 'one rule per sentence').

accord with the available data are equally good, so long as no *independent* reasons suggest favouring one explanation (theory) over another. Applied to semantic theories, this argument provides good reasons for the following strategy: begin theorising by first looking—naïvely, as it were—at the established theories that are available on the market. In particular, a philosophical theory of meaning should begin by evaluating the currently most successful theories in relevant disciplines. In this view, establishing an ordering of theories according to how well they can handle the data is a different task altogether.

7.1.2 Meaning & Concept

It is common among philosophers of language to neglect or downplay the differences between concepts and (their corresponding) words. The most common way of expressing such a stance on concepts is by saying that, as far as a specific argument is concerned, talk of concepts and of words is allegedly *interchangeable* (cf. especially Fodor). Others, who stop short of equating both concepts, claim that, *ultimately*, words correspond one-to-one to the concepts they express (e.g. Horwich 1998). I assume that the connection is less tight, and I shall lay down my reasons for this in the following few paragraphs.

To begin with, there is a lot of evidence favouring an explanatory role for concepts in the area of semantics. Most importantly, concepts are needed in philosophy anyway. So, postulating them does not expand one's metaphysics. According to the traditional understanding in the philosophy of mind, concepts are just the 'building blocks' of thought (Weiskopf 2013). That is, whenever there is evidence in favour of cognition operating on distinguishable 'blocks', this evidence likewise lends support to the idea of concepts. A very simple example of such evidence would be systematicity: everyone who is able to think JOHN LOVES MARY is—ceteris paribus—likewise able to think MARY LOVES JOHN. Here is why: the thought JOHN LOVES MARY is *structured* and *built up from atomic units*. These are: JOHN, LOVES, and MARY. Everyone who thinks JOHN LOVES MARY is able to *recognise* the atomic units of her thoughts (the 'building blocks') and to *rearrange* them in accordance with the structure imposed on the thought by verb semantics. (I simplify.)

7 Semantic-Methodological Concerns

Apparently, concepts *correspond* to the words that express them. It would be absurd to deny that there is some sort of correspondence relation. For example, the concept DOG corresponds—some way or other—to the word "dog". The usual way to express this connection is by saying that "dog" *expresses* the concept DOG. Likewise, sentences are typically said to express propositions. Arguments involving, for example, systematicity are spelled out in terms of concepts and, afterwards, are applied to words too, or the other way around (Fodor & Lepore 2002). This depends on which type of entity is taken to be basic. Now, the interesting bit is how exactly words correspond to concepts (or sentences to propositions).

Concepts and words are similar in important respects. For instance, my "dog" and my DOG have *the same meaning* as your "dog" and DOG. My individual "dog" utterances instantiate the same single word type ("dog") as yours: there is a big enough overlap between both uses (big enough, that is, to ensure successful communication about dogs). Similarly, my DOG thoughts belong to the same type of thoughts as your DOG thoughts, because there is a big enough overlap between our two behavioural patterns in order to classify both as instantiating (the type) DOG thoughts. So this is one way of saying that you and I *share* one concept and one word for dogs (i.e. by instantiating types). This is an important step in the argument in favour of one-to-one correspondence between words and concepts, as such a correspondence requires that a theory of meaning for words and concepts applies equally to your words and concepts as to mine.

But here the analogy ends. The ultimate problem for theories that posit too close a correspondence between words and concepts is that the respective theories serve completely different purposes. That is to say, the explanatory aims of both theories differ. I shall now argue that insofar as this is true, there is no reason to suppose that a semantic theory for words must, at any point, involve concepts.

Mental representations are required in philosophy of mind[5] to account for particular kinds of behaviour. To be slightly more precise, representations must be assumed to account for exactly those behavioural patterns

---

[5] I explicate the argument using philosophy as an example. Of course, the argument equally applies to empirical disciplines as well, provided similar identifications of concepts with words were applied in these areas.

7.1 Background Assumptions

that would otherwise remain inexplicable (Newen & Bartels 2007). In particular, mental representations are posited to explain or predict flexible behaviour in humans. Crucially, there is absolutely no way to get away without representations as that would, again, require tight links between certain sets of inputs to a system (describable in terms of something like nerve signals) and the corresponding sets of outputs of that system (behaviour). That, essentially, is the idea of behaviourism—an idea that is virtually dead these days. As a matter of fact, certain behavioural patterns are linked with certain inputs (e.g. being hurt is typically linked with crying), but there are no *strict* connections, in that the presence of certain antecedent conditions would necessarily lead to certain kinds of behaviour (one can be hurt without crying, and vice versa).

Concepts are the units from which full propositional content is built. The arguments that suggest that a comprehensive theory of the mind would be incomplete without the notion of concepts runs parallel to the argument above. There are behavioural patterns that can only be explained under the assumption of concepts. For example, systematicity. In general, it seems immediately obvious that when we attribute thoughts to someone, we do so only in cases in which we would likewise be willing to attribute different thoughts containing the same constituents to the same person (in relevant circumstances). Here is an example: say, we attribute the thought NORTH AND SOUTH ARE TWO DISTINCT CARDINAL DIRECTIONS to Harry. It seems unlikely that we would do so *unless* we also attribute him thoughts such as I THINK NORTH IS THAT WAY (given appropriate circumstances, i.e. circumstances that suggest that Harry thinks that North is that way, etc.). And similarly for endless other thoughts and other constituents involved.

I am concerned here with language, so I will give only a rough sketch for an argument for the last point. Attributing thoughts to people is essentially guided by the observable behaviour that they show (including verbal and non-verbal aspects). Attributing NORTH AND SOUTH ARE TWO DISTINCT CARDINAL DIRECTIONS to a given person necessarily requires—in order for the attribution to be justified—that the person in question shows a particular kind of behaviour. In order for this specific attribution to make any sense at all, attributors must assume that Harry has some idea of what North and South are. That is to say, attributors must assume that he possesses these concepts. Similarly, one must also assume that Harry knows

7 Semantic-Methodological Concerns

what cardinal directions are. Note that in the present context it does not matter whether Harry has words for these concepts, or whether he is able to articulate his thoughts. Still, the main point remains: assuming concept possession is essential for attributing beliefs. Proof by counterexample: imagine someone of whom you are *sure* that he does not know what North is and try to consistently attribute to that person the thought that North and South are two distinct cardinal directions. End of proof. The difficulties here arise because all evidence in favour of your assumption that a given person lacks the concept NORTH (i.e. observable behavioural evidence) would likewise count as evidence against the latter attribution.

As already said, philosophy of mind is not my primary concern here. There is no need to develop the above arguments in any more detail. The gist is just that these considerations apply across the board in the philosophy of mind. One is not confined to particular theories by accepting these assumptions. Even more importantly, these very broad and general considerations serve as an excellent backdrop against which I can contrast and illustrate the purposes of a semantic theory.

The idea many theorists start from is that a semantic theory is, in the end, equally applicable to concepts and propositions as to words and sentences. Indeed, there seem to be some remarkable similarities between both 'systems', such as systematicity, compositionality, reference, truth-conditional content[6], inference rules, and so on. Be that as it may, due to the significant differences with respect to what, on the one hand, a theory of mental representation and, on the other hand, a theory of meaning is supposed to account for, the arguments stemming from philosophy of mind can't be applied to philosophy of language without further ado, and vice versa.

For instance, ascription of concept possession is mainly motivated by the need to explain flexible behaviour. That is to say, certain behavioural

---

[6] In the area of truth theories, people usually assume that one kind of entity (proposition, sentence, belief, utterance, judgement, etc.) is a so-called primary truth bearer, i.e. the type of entity to which, properly speaking, truth must actually be attributed, and from which the remaining entities derive their respective truth values (/truth conditions). In either account, the truth values (or, in general, propositional content) of two *corresponding* entities will always be identical. For example, irrespective of one's theory of truth (including commitments to primary bearers of truth), the truth-conditional content of <snow is white> corresponds to the (derived) truth-conditional content of SNOW IS WHITE and "snow is white". This, at least, is what most people presuppose.

patterns seem to 'make sense' only under the assumption that a given subject exemplifying this pattern possesses a specific concept. Knowledge of words, in contrast, is posited for completely different reasons. For instance, it is typically verbal behaviour that leads to the supposition of linguistic knowledge. Accordingly, a tight link between concepts and words, for example, can only be established on the basis of further arguments. One might want to argue that systematicity is a feature of languages that they inherit from the realm of thoughts. In this view, language is systematic by virtue of the systematicity of its underlying thoughts for whose expression language is employed in the first place. By analogy, arguments designed for being applicable to words do not likewise apply to concepts. Consider reference relations, for instance. These are arguably primarily—though certainly not exclusively—investigated in the philosophy of language. Take Kripke's causal-historical account of reference. No matter whether his argument is sound, *if* it were sound, then it would apply only to words, not to concepts (at least not without further premises). Note two things in this regard. Firstly, the causal-historical account presupposes that reference is passed from generation to generation. But whereas I can reasonably pass referential relations of words onto the next generation, there is no reason to assume that I can do so likewise for concepts (at least not without further premises). Secondly, the plausibility of the causal-historical story is at least partly fostered by the circumstance that the continuity of reference is ensured by language communities. Whereas members of language communities continuously and implicitly correct their interlocutors concerning their language use (especially during acquisition), there is no similar possibility for correction when it comes to concepts (at least not without further premises).

In sum, it seems reasonable to acknowledge that language and thought share some remarkable similarities, but there is also ample reason to assume that the correspondence is not as strict as many scholars in semantics presuppose. From a methodological point of view, it is therefore important to treat both areas separately and not to aim for a semantic theory that is designed to apply equally to both areas of research.

7 Semantic-Methodological Concerns

7.1.3 Compatibility of Acquisition Theories and Theories of Meaning

In chapter 2.2.1, I defended the claim that a theory of meaning must be compatible with any theory of language acquisition, ideally with the currently most widely accepted theory. In a nutshell, the argument is that the latter theories deal with the languages we actually speak and that if a theory of meaning is supposed to account for *our* languages (English, Italian, etc.), not any other (e.g. artificial languages), it better be compatible with its corresponding acquisition theories.

In this section, I shall now lay down the overall picture of how such a compatibility can be verified. First, though, I need to illustrate why this is a problem at all. Generally speaking, the way to prove *in*compatibility is by deriving contradictory sentences from each theory. For example, the type identity theory in philosophy of mind is incompatible with certain theological theories that assume souls. The identity theory implies, let us assume, that there can't be souls; so the contradiction between the two theories lies precisely in the affirmation and denial, respectively, of the sentence "There are souls". The reason it is so easy to derive contradictions in this case is because both theories deal with the *same* subject matter.[7] Their 'object of study'—I simplify, of course—is mental properties. One theory provides an explanation of these properties by identifying them with brain states, while the other theory explains them in terms of abilities of a non-material entity that somehow affects and is affected by the body.

The identity thesis does not itself contain the denial of the sentence in question among its theorems. Rather, some background assumptions are needed in order to arrive there. In this case, one needs to assume that the identity thesis is a comprehensive thesis that accounts for all mental phenomena that there are. No further entities, which were not already postulated by the theory itself, are needed for the explanation of the mental. In this sense, the identity thesis implies that there are no souls. This is

---

[7] If this particular example does not move you (because you think that either their respective objects of study are not identical, or because both theories do not contradict themselves), then you may replace it accordingly. I am here interested in showing how inter-theoretic contradiction works in general, no matter whether identity theory, as in my example, is a particularly good example to demonstrate this.

exactly the kind of reasoning also involved in the historic case of incompatibility between oxygen theory and phlogiston theory. There is, as it is often put, simply no place within either theory for the entities postulated by the respective rival theory.

In the context of theories of meaning and acquisition, the problem is that both kinds of theory do not apply to the (exactly) same subject matter. Both deal with natural languages. But the aspects they are focussing on are completely different. I have described in some detail what theories of meaning are dealing with. These theories are not particularly interested in how languages are acquired. Rather, they take the status quo for granted and as their starting point. On the other hand, issues of acquisition are handled relatively independently from what meaning is. This is particularly true if "theories of meaning" is meant to refer to philosophical theories. Whether such an approach is justified does not matter in the present context. What is important is that this is how both kinds of theories de facto currently proceed.

All this makes it hard to check their compatibility. One could at this point reasonably ask why questioning their compatibility is relevant at all if, as admitted, their respective subject matters differ anyway. I have shown that in order to check for incompatibility one would need to derive contradictions. In turn, the *compatibility* of one theory with another is not shown that easily. When comparing two theories, one can't, as in formal logic, *prove* that no contradictions are derivable. At least, this is not as easy as in the opposite case (i.e. proving incompatibility). This is partly due to the structure of philosophical theories. To name only two virtually insurmountable problems, consider the following. Firstly, in contrast to many empirical theories, philosophical theories often draw on plausibility considerations, which, in turn, means that very often there is no fact of the matter that could decide between two rival theories. Secondly, philosophers seldom produce genuine *theories*—which, by the way, is nicely illustrated by the fact that in philosophy many people call their respective theories 'framework', 'theory sketch', 'account', 'approach', and so on. For instance, what is called 'Davidsonian semantics' or 'truth-conditional semantics' is typically associated with Davidson's *Truth and Meaning*. But most people would probably *deny* that Davidson's theory is simply what he says in this article. On the other hand, most people would probably *agree* that the claims made in *Truth in Meaning* are the theoretical core of Davidsonian semantics. The most important claim being, arguably, his conviction that a Tarskian theory of truth can be transformed into a theory of meaning. But, again, this claim is not 'the' theory.

Generally, compatibility between theories is hard to prove, as it is very often not entirely clear what the relevant theorems are in the first place. Also, there is probably no help to be expected from the field of theory reduction. One might very easily have this impression, because if one theory were reducible to another, then these theories are (in this sense) compatible (e.g. chemistry might be 'proven' to be compatible with physics by showing the reducibility of chemistry to physics). But this is of no help here because the phenomena that both theories account for—language use and language acquisition—are almost completely different, so that for this reason alone they are hardly reducible to each other. Their alleged compatibility concerns only the notion of "meaning" employed in both theories. Hence, in order to show that a particular theory of meaning fits well with a given acquisition theory, the most promising strategy seems to be to demonstrate that their respective notions of 'meaning' match. For the present context, inter-theoretic compatibility is the most interesting case. I have already demonstrated why compatibility between theories of meaning and of acquisition is a virtue. However, one immediate problem is that one would first need to find areas within the respective theories that qualify for comparison. The only reasonable candidate is meaning itself, or, rather, the definition of "meaning" employed by the relevant theories. Two complementary observations justify this claim.

Firstly, acquisition theories typically rely on the assumption that words (or other basic units) have particular meanings. They do so because natural language is first and foremost a communicative means. Meaningless expressions can be seen as artefacts of highly developed languages that are irrelevant for acquisition processes. Utterances of 'meaningless' expressions—"Das Nichts nichtet"—arguably appear relatively late in ontogeny. It may be that this is because they serve no clearly identifiable communication purpose.[8]

---

[8] Whether there really is *no* communication purpose at all involved and, hence, no meaning is probably debatable. For example, it might be that such sentences are meaningful in the sense in which poems are meaningful.

7.1 Background Assumptions

"Mama", for example, typically one of the first utterances made by toddlers, clearly serves some such purposes; in many cases it is probably used to attract attention. The explanation for this communication action is parasitic on "Mama" having the meaning it has—for example, that it refers[9] to a particular person (normally the mother). Importantly, though, the communication success does not depend on the referential 'success'. What is relevant, rather, is that speakers achieve their goals. Still, the semantic aspects enter the picture indirectly. The semantic fact about "Mama" that it refers to Mama—provided this is a fact—can explain why, very often, toddlers are very often successful in attracting their mothers' attention by uttering "Mama".[10] The baby's utterance would *not* have had the desired effect *if*, according to the linguistic practice of the community in which the baby participates, "Mama" actually refers to dentists. This holds if certain background conditions hold, which I am tacitly assuming here. Most of them, I think, go without saying. In this particular case, I assume, for example: (i) the mother knows the convention that "Mama" refers to dentists; (ii) there is no 'private' convention established between the baby and her mother that "Mama" refers to mothers (in the baby's idiolect). In other words, language acquisition and language use are intertwined. Describing scenarios of language acquisition implies recurring to how language is actually applied. This lends support to my conviction that the notion of 'meaning' employed in theories of acquisition should correspond to the notion of 'meaning' that is applied in theories of meaning.

Secondly, the theories of meaning that are most interesting from the current perspective are so-called 'foundational theories' (Speaks 2011) or

---

[9] In 8.2 and 8.3, I say a bit more about the distinction between semantic description and constitution base. Bearing this distinction in mind makes it easier to see why I see absolutely no problem in using "refers to" in a supposedly usage-based semantic description.

[10] Note that there is no relevant epistemological problem here in the sense that their 'mother' maybe is not their mother. This is irrelevant to the case at hand. For if that were a different person but the baby intends to attract the attention of the person in front of her, we would certainly not wish to call her linguistic activity 'unsuccessful' just because she did not attract the attention of the person to whom her words 'actually' referred. This person maybe absent. But, anyway, this is not the person whose attention the baby wanted to attract. So her linguistic behaviour is successful if she gets what she wants. In this sense, it is, strictly speaking, wrong to say that in such a case toddlers' "Mama" refers to Mama.

7 Semantic-Methodological Concerns

'reductionistic theories'. Theories of this kind explain the semantic properties of linguistic entities in terms of their underlying non-semantic properties. They acknowledge that (certain) expressions have meaning: they do not 'explain away' the phenomena but explicate constitution relations that seem to exist between non-semantic properties such as use and semantic properties such as reference. Put simply, at least some linguistic entities seem to be meaningful. Somehow they *became* meaningful, since strings of letters *as such* are meaningless. Acquisition theories provide explanations for this process and naturally *complement* theories of meaning in this regard.

These two observations are two sides of a coin. In effect, they demand that theories from both fields share *a common notion of meaning*. This is the litmus test for both. However, as I have already shown above, there is a certain asymmetry between the two (see especially 5.2). However, there is a methodologically highly important asymmetry between philosophical and empirical theories. Either of these theories can be falsified empirically. Acquisition theories from psychology or anthropology as well as grammar theories in linguistics are empirically informed anyway, whereas the relevant philosophical theories of meaning are based—mainly—on armchair methods. This means that theories of meaning have to comply with the 'demands' set by acquisition theories, grammar theories, and the like. The latter are, so to speak, free to postulate meanings according to their respective explanatory needs. If, to cite just one prominent example, the theory entails that the meaning of

>   X let alone Y

is

>   'stronger proposition, a fortiori weaker proposition' (Fillmore,
>   Kay & O'Connor 1988, 528, emphasis omitted)

you better make sure that an accompanying philosophical theory of meaning fits this requirement. In this sense, the definitions of "meaning" employed in philosophy are constrained in a way by empirical enterprise (e.g. by grammar theory). The underlying assumption here is that a philosophical theory of meaning generally aims at being empirically adequate. Empirical theories, qua being empirical theories, have a greater overall likelihood of being empirically adequate. Evidence that could possibly falsify 'empirical' theories typically comes from the very same disciplines that produce these theories in the first place. Hence, empirical theories constrain the empirical adequacy of philosophical theories, which, in turn, amounts to saying that philosophical notions of 'meaning' should at least cover the definitional variants applied in empirical disciplines (as in "X let alone Y").

7.2 Methodological Commitments

The purpose of this section is twofold. In 7.2.1, I provide a detailed argument for why it is a virtue of my theory that I am committed to the view that a theory of meaning is essentially a theory of *communication*. Correspondingly, in 7.2.2, I complement this line of reasoning by laying down my reasons for the assumption that *utterances*, or, generally, *instantiations* of types of meaningful expressions, are the basic semantic unit (rather than the corresponding types).

7.2.1 Unity of Science

One particular advantage of my semantic framework is that it gives a unified account of communication. I shall say first what the unity consists in; then I say a few words about why I think it is an advantage at all.

Mainstream philosophical theories of meaning usually confine themselves to written texts and to oral speech based on written texts. By the latter, I mean that, firstly, they are often restricted to declarative sentences (cf. also chapter 4.2), and, secondly, they are concerned with the alleged properties attributed to sentences and words, independent of the corresponding occasions upon which they are uttered. Both directions are wrongheaded (Tomasello 2003b). In regard to theories based on declarative sentences, I have already argued that they are unable to successfully account for other sentence types (cf. also Horwich 2008b). This seems to be the case even though especially neo-Davidsonians have spent quite some effort on broadening their theories in this respect. It is remarkable how much effort people spend on adjusting a theory in such a way that it gets applicable to

7 Semantic-Methodological Concerns

all kinds of sentences, although it was actually designed to handle only the semantics of declaratives.

The present proposal, on the other hand, applies (or is applicable) across the board. This is true in two related respects. In regard to utterances, no type of sentence is theoretically more relevant than any other. For instance, it might be that the 'unifying feature' of communication (i.e. of utterances) is that it fosters cooperation. In contrast, it might be that the semantics of certain types of sentences can be explained *in terms of the semantics of other sentence types* (e.g. questions in terms of declaratives). In this sense, utterances are theoretically on a par in a way that types of sentences are not. In another respect, the proposal is even more general. It is a sketch of a semantic theory that concerns not only categories that traditionally have been assumed to belong to the realm of semantics—written and spoken sentences—moreover, it is also an approach that is concerned with all aspects of communication. Communication is viewed here as a means that is embedded in other human activities. Accordingly, one idea underlying the methodology of this book is first to look more closely at the structure of *these* activities in order to find out about meaning.

Regarding this second point—flexibility in emphasising different aspects of a communication situation—the advantages of my own framework are rooted in the liberal notion of 'meaning' in use here. If meaning were just any description that is informative (relative to a given theory framework), then many different things might count as more or less important in particular scenarios. In this context, it is highly relevant that, for example, the dispositions that individual speaker-hearers associate with a given term are defined schematically on my account. The dispositions actually acquired are those that correspond to what an otherwise competent speaker would take into account as relevant relative to her evidence. Another important point in my theory sketch is the emphasis on tokens or tokenings. This allows me to say that *in individuating the things that ultimately can be said to be meaningful* one can't just focus on certain formal properties such as sequentially ordered letters ("s"-"n"-"o"-"w"). Rather, individuating meaningful units necessarily involves stating the conditions under which sender (speaker) and receiver (hearer) act in a given communication situation. Amongst other things, the factors that influence meaning are intonation, gesture, facial expression, body movement, spatial context, visual field (of sender and recipient), text genre, world knowledge, etc.—things that are typically 'not allowed' in a formal theory (cf. e.g. Borg 2004b).

Both in terms of the phenomena that are covered as well as in terms of the resources that are needed to account for these phenomena, the notion of 'meaning' in the present framework is very broad. What are the advantages of such a strategy? The following will be rather programmatic. I shall argue for each point only very briefly. In any case, I believe that—from a methodological perspective—an approach that is as universal as possible is marked by these merits:

(1) A universal theory covers areas that are left out by its more minimal rivals, which, however, need to be dealt with somewhere in philosophy anyway (e.g. communication, language evolution, diachrony, cooperation, etc.).

(2) The phenomena a theory of meaning is designed to explain suggest a unified approach.

(3) Influential strands of current empirical research are based on a usage-based understanding of language.

(4) A universal understanding of 'meaning' is implicitly assumed in a variety of established theories in philosophy.

(5) A range of different modalities that contribute to utterance meaning can be accounted for within one theory of meaning (e.g. verbal, gestural, contextual, and so on).

Ad (1): The framework developed here is more like a 'theory of communication' than a 'theory of meaning' or a 'semantic theory' in the sense of classical 20th century philosophy of language. Its scope is significantly widened as to include phenomena that thus far have been considered to either belong to pragmatics (e.g. metaphor) or which have been widely neglected by philosophers of language altogether (e.g. posture). One of the most important points that, I believe, justifies such a procedure is that those aspects that have been neglected by traditional semantic theories still need to be accounted for; for instance by an 'accompanying' theory of communication. Gesture, posture, facial expression, etc. on the one hand and

7 Semantic-Methodological Concerns

metaphor, malapropisms, irony, etc. on the other hand simply *are* important aspects of communication, though. Whereas I concede that semantics in the classical sense is important in some areas (e.g. irony), I think that it is fair enough to say that semantics is an area of research that can't be pursued independently of communication.[11] But if that much is agreed on, it seems quite natural to pursue a comprehensive theory of communication rather than two independently developed theories. In any case, one needs a theory that takes care of the mentioned phenomena.

The last claim is probably pretty uncontroversial. Everyone who agrees with it could, of course, stress that this is just the point of having a theory of pragmatics and a theory of communication, whose job is to complement semantics. So, the problematic aspect of my claims is the other half of the argument. If we only knew that certain aspects must be covered by any theory, then it would suffice to just have two appropriate approaches for both areas (semantics and pragmatics/communication). First, build a more or less minimalistic *semantic* theory. Then, in a second step, build *accompanying* theories that, in conjunction with minimalistic semantics, account for all 'remaining' aspects of communication.

However, a recurring theme in the foregoing chapters is that the given phenomena demand rather a one-step strategy. One crucial aspect is that all well-formed utterances *necessarily* mean something in some pragmatic sense, whereas this meaning can only *sometimes* be traced back to meaning in the semantic sense. Irony and related systematic effects are typical example cases in which tracing back actually *is* successful. That there are other areas in which such tracing back does not work means that, strictly speaking, a semantic theory completely leaves out a rather wide field of utterances. Namely all those utterances that clearly have meaning, in which case, however, this meaning does not systematically depend on the alleged meanings of its constituents (see sections 5.1.2 and 5.2.4 for examples and discussion). So, the first step of a two-step strategy would be massively and systematically incomplete in these cases, which is a rather unwelcome result.

Ad (2): Moreover, in order to account for the pragmatic meaning of utterances that *can* be traced back to some form of 'primary meaning', it

---

[11] For example, because semantic meaning is parasitic on utterance meaning.

is not necessary—and therefore not demanded by the phenomena—to assume primary meaning in the sense that was relevant in the 20th century philosophy of language (in particular, primary meaning defined in terms of reference, satisfaction, and truth conditions). Rather, only a very minimal notion of 'primary meaning' is required here (cf., again, section 5.1.2). From this point of view, primary meaning can be explained *in terms of pragmatic meaning*, rather than the other way around. At the same time, it is still possible to explain why, for example, "hot", if used ironically, means 'cold'. Simply put, this is because "hot" normally means 'hot'. Due to its normal meaning, "hot" has a relatively high chance of meaning 'cold' in specific situations.[12] Therefore, one major motivation for a two-step strategy (first semantics, then pragmatics) is dropped.

A related argument that is relevant in this context concerns the prevailing emphasis on literal meaning in the philosophy of language. The historical origin probably lies in the fact that philosophy was for a long time concerned exclusively with written texts.[13,14] Most communication, however, takes place in the form of conversation. Written texts lack a lot of the characteristic properties of conversations. In particular, texts lack contextual cues that normally help interpreters to determine the reading of an utterance that they think is the most probable one, given what they are able to figure out about the speaker's intentions. Traditionally, a further emphasis was on declaratives, which, again, form only a subset of actual spoken communication. The example sentences that were most influential are exemplary for this tendency: cf. "Snow is white", "Socrates is white",

---

[12] All things considered, the likelihood is higher than in the case of, say, "rectangular".

[13] A good starting point for getting an overview here is by consulting the relevant 'literal/non-literal' literature. Israel (2005) is an easy-to-read review article. Ravid & Tolchinsky (2002) discuss the distinction from a developmental perspective. Ariel (2002a) is a rather critical discussion; cf. also her introduction to a special issue of the *Journal of Pragmatics* on this topic (Ariel 2002b), plus the other articles therein. Historically, Cresswell (1982) might be interesting as well.

[14] One of the readers of this book rightly remarked that the prevailing emphasis on written text was probably fostered by the fact that the study of language very often served purposes other than studying it for its own sake. Rather, since ancient times people tended to study texts in order to gain insights in areas that they thought were intimately related to language such as ontology, epistemology, philosophy of mind, etc. Studying language for its own sake is a rather modern phenomenon in philosophy.

7 Semantic-Methodological Concerns

"It's raining", "The cat lies on the mat", "The Earth is round", "That man over there is drinking a Martini", "Nine is the number of the planets", and so on and so forth.

So, a theory of meaning should, firstly, recognise that most communication takes place orally, and, secondly, that declarative sentences are just a subset of all actually uttered sentences. However, looking at history of analytic philosophy of language this way helps us to see more clearly where its potential deficits come from. Traditionally minded theories of meaning have never *ignored* the research areas I am taking into account here. For instance, much research into truth-conditional semantics is inspired by the question how to incorporate questions into TCS (references in footnote 46 on page 155), to name just one prominent example. Ignorance is not the issue. Rather, the problem with all these attempts that are supposed to fix established theories is the following. They are all based on the unfounded assumption that written declarative sentences are somehow basic, and that the semantics of all other types of sentences is derivable from the semantics of declaratives, or can at least be modelled in analogy to them.

One hardly ever sees serious arguments for giving priority to written texts (as opposed to conversation) or to declaratives (as opposed to other types of sentences). When it comes to such methodological concerns, pragmatic considerations are typically brought in. The reasons for starting one's theory of meaning with simple declarative sentences are, I think, partly justified, and partly unjustified. It makes sense to study the semantics of *simple* sentences first, leaving complex issues out, and then expand these findings to more difficult areas. For example, one often sees that indexicals, adjectives, quantifiers, colour terms, etc. are initially postponed, because taking them into account from the beginning would unnecessarily complicate things (cf. Portner 2005). Subject to the possibility of expanding one's simple theory to more difficult areas, such a strategy seems reasonable. Simplifying, however, can't justify the recurring restriction to declaratives and written texts in many theories. Especially bearing in mind that declaratives or written texts per se are not 'easier' to study than, say, commands or transcripts of conversations.

It is *impossible* to make context-free, meaningful statements. Meaningful statements always involve context, i.e. descriptions of meaningful statements necessarily involve contextual descriptions. Semantics, to be sure,

7.2 Methodological Commitments

is concerned not with statements but with sentences. Sentences, however, are abstractions of contextually determined content. They are not out there in the world (except as tokenings), and hence can't be the data of our object of study.[15] The relevant data are written and spoken *instantiations of sentences*. Which is to say that if one focuses on the available data alone, one's object of study necessarily involves context. To view semantics as that area which is concerned with the part of human communication that can be studied independently from context can mean two things (at least). It might mean that semantics should not be concerned with statements but rather with sentences (i.e. sentence types); or it might mean that semantics should be concerned with statements, but instead of dealing with particular statements it should be concerned with the general properties of statements of a given type. I shall discuss both options in turn, arguing that both are inadequate to make the point.

Semantics is an empirical project.[16] As such, the ultimate source for judgements about meaning must be tokenings (e.g. of sentences). Abstract

---

[15] It is quite telling in this regard to consider again Borg's example that is intended to demonstrate that she is able to comprehend sentential content irrespective of context. She says (2004b, 89–90) that without any contextual cues she is, in a situation in which "There is an alligator in the corridor" was uttered, able to understand that this sentence means that there is an alligator in the corridor (see section 6.2.1). But this is absurd. In a situation in which contextual factors that could possibly trigger a specific interpretation are completely lacking, *this is the relevant context*.

[16] This is pretty much common sense in philosophy as well as, obviously, in linguistics. In linguistics, there are basically two strands of research. One is intuition-based, which means that the main source for determining, e.g., the grammaticality of sentences is the scholar's (i.e. trained linguist's) intuition. This strand of research assumes that, broadly speaking, the fact that all linguistic judgements (with respect to grammaticality, sentence meaning, etc.) are based on intuitions anyway, and that this circumstance licenses an approach that is based only on one's own intuition. The opposite to this is corpus-driven, i.e. usage-based research (cf. section 3.3.2). The mark of corpus-based approaches is that grammaticality judgements (and the like) are validated by looking at—usually quite big—corpora. From a philosophical point of view, calling intuitions-based research 'empirical' may sound a bit odd. But viewed from within linguistics, everyone agrees that linguistics should be conceived empirically; the dispute between corpus- and intuition-based researchers just concerns the proper methodology. In philosophy, the situation is a bit more complicated. I shall be going more into the details in the main text. Note, however, that even Davidson construes truth-conditional semantics as an empirical endeavour (1967, 311).

7 Semantic-Methodological Concerns

entities such as sentence types can't be studied directly. That is, even if semantics is confined to the study of sentences, it ultimately needs to be tested against the available evidence, which is utterances (or, concerning written texts, tokenings). This, again, amounts to saying that semantics as the study of sentence types can't be pursued independently of contexts, i.e. independently of utterances that instantiate the relevant types. The means to validate meaning judgements are essentially context-bound.

The second option does not fare any better. The proposal would be to focus not on *particular* utterances, which in fact are always embedded in contexts, but on their general, non-token-specific properties. The problem here is this: insofar as that means studying commonalities of utterances, it amounts to the very same strategy defended in this book. For example, the primary meaning of the word "snow" might be that it is, say, usually used to refer to snow. Far from being a statement about the properties that "snow" has independently from specific contexts, this only means that—within the class of all actual "snow" tokenings—a homogeneous subset can be determined, the most prominent property of which is that many of its elements are utterances that have been used to refer to snow. That is a generalisation (or abstraction[17], if you like) concerning the utterances of "snow" that is essentially bound to contexts, namely in that the generalisation is true by virtue of the contextual properties of individual "snow" tokenings.

In sum, the phenomena require that semantics takes into account contexts. In this respect, an approach that focuses solely on written texts, in particular on declarative sentences, is inadequate, as it is based on an inaccurate picture of how sentence/word types (abstractions of sentence/word tokenings) get their semantics. Generally, focusing only on declaratives is inadequate, given that one's aim is a universally applicable theory of meaning (Fotion 2013).

Ad (3): Empirical research and philosophical, apriori research develop widely independently in the area of semantics. That is, both 'strands' share a common subject of study, but the respective research agendas and methodologies diverge significantly. Allow me to take for granted that one major keystone of philosophical thinking is its empirical foundation, or less

---

[17] In Tomasello's (2003*a*) way of using this term.

poetically: philosophical theories of meaning must respect the developments taken by research in linguistics, psychology, anthropology, cognitive science, etc. and must themselves develop accordingly. Given this, a third argument in support of a unified theory of communication is that current developments in empirical disciplines suggest such a theory.[18]

The most important developments in this regard are: the increasing importance of construction grammar in grammar theory (Goldberg 2003, Ziem & Lasch 2013); the theoretical framework of shared intentionality inspired by Tomasello in language acquisition (Tomasello 2014); the Tomasellian paradigm in language evolution (2008, 2009); research on the semantics of gestures and, in general, multimodality (Müller et al. 2013). To be sure, the list is not comprehensive. But it concerns core areas of semantics that just can't be neglected. And although CxG, for example, is certainly not entirely undisputed *within* linguistics, its importance has increased so rapidly in recent years that philosophy of language needs to acknowledge this.[19]

The philosophically important aspect of these developments—which is also their common feature—is that they do not leave the semantics/pragmatics divide unaffected. Relative to the underlying definition of "semantics", the cited research agendas either abandon the distinction altogether (many areas within CxG) or, at least, shift the edge massively towards pragmatics (Tomasello's work). The latter means that elements which traditionally belonged to pragmatics are now considered part of semantics (for example, world knowledge). This gives indirect support to a unified approach to semantics, since frameworks that take declarative sentences as basic crucially depend on a clear-cut distinction between semantics and pragmatics. Strands of research that tendentiously neglect the semantics/pragmatics divide or include context-sensitive elements into their semantics thus lend indirect support to a unified theory.

---

[18] To be fair, this is controversial:

> The notion of communication has little demonstrated use in the development of a synchronic theory of meaning. (Horisk 2004, 197)

[19] Cf. also Hoffmann & Trousdale (2013) and Michaelis (2006, 2012, 2013).

7 Semantic-Methodological Concerns

Ad (4): Established, philosophical theories of meaning *pretend* to individuate meaningful entities in terms of their formal structure. They thus assume that the sequence "s"-"n"-"o"-"w" is relevant for identifying the word type "snow", which, again, is said to have a particular meaning. In other words, the relevant unit of entities to which meanings can be attributed are word types, which, from this perspective, can be individuated strictly formally. The identity criterion of a given entity concerning whether it belongs to a certain word type is, according to this view, a specific sequence of letters, for instance. Structurally, the same is true for identity conditions of sentence types. Presumably, they can also be individuated formally.

The point is: in this view, sentences seem to be individuated without taking any contextual factors into account.[20] The latter are only mentioned when extraordinary situations are discussed, or when pragmatics comes into play. This underestimates the importance of context for determining meaning. In contrast, in the view defended here, context is *always* relevant for determining meaning. Even more importantly, the cited formal strategy underestimates the importance of contexts in cases in which no context is explicitly given. So, the gist of the present argument is: not mentioning contexts is the only viable way to state context-free meaning.

If someone says that "snow is white" means <snow is white>, then, I take it, there are essentially the following two options. One option is that she is just plain *wrong*, for the sequence "s"-"n"-"o"-"w"-SPACE-"i"-"s"-SPACE--"w"-"h"-"i"-"t"-"e" *as such* does not mean anything. Surely, the sequence is often used in such a way as to express <snow is white>. But that is not what people usually mean when they say that "snow is white" means <snow is white>. (It would not help, anyway.) Another option is that they are *right*, but only relative to certain contexts. Without diving into the deep waters of defining "standard contexts", it seems quite plausible to suppose that in standard contexts "snow is white" means 'snow is white' (or expresses <snow is white>). I think that this is what is meant when philosophers write about "snow is white" having this and that meaning. The context in which *they* make their statements also ensures that their words get interpreted in a particular way. The observation is blatantly trivial but still

---
[20] Save for contextual features necessary for word disambiguation.

7.2 Methodological Commitments

worth being mentioned here. One simply *never* makes context-free statements. If I say that "snow is white" means 'snow is white' *and* if that statement is part of a book entitled 'Philosophical Semantics 101' *and* if I do not mention any particular contexts of utterance *and* if in the paragraphs preceding this statement nothing can be read off that would signal a certain reading, then all this *is* the relevant context. This context determines, as it de facto very often does, that my statement about the meaning of "snow is white" is meant relative to standard contexts (in which case it would be true in the actual world).

Imagine someone replies as follows. Agreed, "snow is white" means 'snow is white' in standard contexts. But this is not what I am pointing at when I say—without saying anything else—that "snow is white" means 'snow is white'. Rather, I indicate the *conventional meaning* that "snow is white" has independently of conversational contexts. Standard contexts leave the conventional meaning unaffected, so to speak. This is why utterances of "snow is white" in such contexts might mean 'snow is white'. In other contexts, it might mean something else: but only due to the fact that its conventional meaning, irrespective of particular contexts, is 'snow is white'.

This is putting the cart before the horse. Conventions are regularities in behavioural patterns. That a word has conventional meaning means that people use it somewhat regularly, namely in accordance with some convention they associate with it. The conventions for "snow", for example, require that it is used to refer to snow (or so I assume for the sake of argument). So the just-cited counterargument amounts to saying that because "snow" has this conventional meaning, it can be used to refer to snow in standard contexts, referring to something else otherwise. But note that in order to say what is *conventional* about "snow", you need to recur to standard contexts. If the context does not indicate anything different, "snow" means 'snow'. Or, in the jargon of my proposal: within all actual "snow" instantiations, a subclass can be extracted the elements of which are more or less homogeneous in that they are similar in one important respect. Namely, they are all used in order to refer to snow. So, even if meaning statements were interpreted as expressing something about the conventional meaning of a given word (if such a thing exists), this is a statement that is essentially based on the assumed circumstance that this word has specific meaning in specific contexts. In other words, both epistemologically and metaphysically, context-bound tokenings are primary relative to the types they instantiate. Hence, a faithful description of superficially 'context-free' meaning statements like "'snow is white' means that snow is white" would acknowledge that the relevant conversational contexts are implicitly mentioned.

Ad (5): See 2.2.4. The basic idea here is that the desideratum of a comprehensive theory of meaning to being able to integrate multimodal compositionality is a more a less direct consequence of my assumption that the basic unit in semantics is utterances. If full-blown utterance meaning is at least partly determined in a non-trivial way by gestures, then one ought to ensure that one's theory is capable of accommodating this fact. I emphasise "non-trivial", because, as I have shown above, some gestures—in particular pointing gestures—already have been taken into account by philosophical theories. However, gestures have typically been integrated in relatively trivial cases, e.g. with respect to reference-fixing. Here, gestures *merely* serve the purpose of, for example, increasing salience. The problem, though, is that a great deal of gestures are significantly more complex than basic pointing gestures. Therefore, a theory should be able to integrate them as well, in order to then explain how gestures can serve as proper 'constituents', as it were, in the determination of utterance meaning.

A universal approach to communication, as I suggest it here, is particularly well-equipped to meet this requirement. The most important reason is that both constitutive basis of meaning (use) as well as meaning itself (semantic description) are described schematically. That is, basically all empirically adequate descriptions are 'permissible' in my view. With respect to use, this is straightforward. The use of a gesture is just the way a certain gesture type gets instantiated (relative to one's classifications of gesture types). The semantic description is probably best given in terms of dispositional analyses. Importantly, I propose no constraint whatsoever on semantic descriptions—i.e. ways of stating meaning—other than their empirical adequacy. All descriptions of the semantics of gestures that are available on the market are essentially usage-based. So, although I am not able to present a full-blown account of multimodality at this point, I think that the available evidence in gesture research suggests that gestural semantics should be described in usage-based vocabulary and be based, first

7.2 Methodological Commitments

and foremost, on a theory of communication. In the following few paragraphs, I shall justify the claim underlying my argument—namely that utterances are the basic objects of study in semantics.

7.2.2 Basic Meaningful Entities

What are the basic meaningful units? In philosophy, the most widely discussed proposals are sentences and words.[21] Words have the significant advantage that they fit so well to compositionality arguments and systematicity/productivity. Sentences, on the other hand, are seldom considered to be the basic semantic unit. The classical arguments in favour of words are not convincing, because they do not make sense with respect to the logic of language acquisition.

If language faculty is not (fully) innate, then the material language learners are confronted with must somehow determine their success in the acquisition of language skills. This is true for all relevant aspects; it certainly holds for learning meaning. Children, for example, are confronted with instantiations of sentences. They hardly ever learn the semantics of words from hearing isolated words. Accordingly, children's ability to learn the meaning of individual words *must* derive from their ability to understand (context-relativised) full sentences first (Tomasello 2003a). A nice side effect of theories which posit that sentences are the basic semantic units is that this goes hand in hand with a plausible account of *syntax* acquisition. The currently successful and influential accounts of language acquisition such as Tomasello's do not make a fundamental distinction between the acquisition of syntax and the acquisition of the lexicon. In general, the distinction between semantic knowledge and syntactic knowledge is significantly blurred in CxG, since both 'kinds' of information are jointly represented by constructions (cf. subsection 2.2.1). The *linguistic* reason for this is that in construction grammar all form–meaning pairings

---

[21] In linguistics, another important unit in semantics is morphemes. In CxG, though, the status of morphemes is controversial (Ziem & Lasch 2013, 12). From a philosophical point of view, the relevant divide is between, if you like, 'atomistic' approaches (morphemes, words, etc.) and approaches that consider sentences as basic units. Philosophically speaking, it is not particularly important whether one makes a fuss about the priority of words, morphemes, suffixes, syntactic structures, and the like.

7 Semantic-Methodological Concerns

(constructions) belong to the so-called constructicon, which is an assembly of constructions covering semantic, syntactic, pragmatic, and sometimes discourse-functional information. In the same way that learning words is basically learning to recognise patterns across multiple instantiations of words, so learning syntax is basically also just an abstraction process. However, someone who thinks that *words* are basic—and hence must be learnt individually—is forced to believe that syntax is also acquired piecemeal, not by abstraction. There is no plausible acquisition theory for learning word meaning individually.

Insofar as current acquisition theories suggest that sentences are basic, an accompanying philosophical theory of meaning should do likewise. However, one needs to be more specific with the terminology here. Thus far I have taken for granted, as is common practice in philosophy, that it is self-evident how to individuate sentences. Outside of philosophy, the status of sentences is less clear. It is actually quite hard to give a satisfying definition of "sentence". Sentences are certainly not merely what stands between two full stops. Judging from the available evidence in linguistics, the unit 'sentence' is not applicable to all areas of research anyway (e.g. spoken-language research). More importantly, talk of sentences in acquisition theories typically refers to utterances, i.e. sentence *tokenings*. When children are confronted with sentences, they are of course confronted with instances, not with types. So, from all this one may reasonably conclude that the basic meaningful unit in a philosophical theory of meaning that respects the empirical evidence should actually be utterances. Utterances have all the advantages one would like them to have, in particular:

(i) Utterances are easily *recognisable*;[22]

---

[22] Typically, people assume that especially sentence types (as opposed to utterances) are easily identifiable, i.e. by virtue of formal properties such as sequences of letters. However, one immediate problem here, which, e.g., Borg (2004b) acknowledges, is that word disambiguation takes place on the basis of contextual information beyond the reach of formal semantics (e.g. world knowledge). To solve this problem, Borg suggests that pragmatic processes might play a role in disambiguation prior to semantic processing. In contrast, recognising utterances including utterance meaning is pretty straightforward from the outset: in describing utterances (and their meaning) one is allowed to use just *any* contextual information that might be relevant.

(ii) Utterances are *real* in that language learners actually experience them;[23]

(iii) Due to their context relativity, utterances have *determinate meaning*;[24]

(iv) Utterances fit nicely with an overall *usage-based* methodology.[25]

I do not assume that this cursory list is read as a concluding argument 'against' (word/sentence) types in semantic theories. However, I do think that the evidence collected in this section—together with the considerations in previous chapters—indicates that a token-based approach to semantics has some significant virtues, without neglecting the type-level properties of expressions. For type properties can be explained in terms of token properties.

---

[23] Utterances are real in a sense in which sentences are not. Sentences understood as sentence types are real in that their tokenings instantiate the relevant type. But the type itself is just an abstraction. In this respect, language learners can't be directly acquainted with sentences themselves but only with their instances. This, however, effectively amounts to saying that what people experience is utterances.

[24] As I have shown in chapter 5, it makes sense to attribute meaning to all utterances and to attribute primary meaning only to a subclass of these. In this view, word types and sentence types derive their 'primary meaning' from *regular expectations of language users concerning usage*. Accordingly, sentences *in contexts* can be viewed as the primary object of study in semantics.

[25] Cf. section 6.2. At any rate, this holds if the slogan 'meaning is use' is not taken at face value but specified somewhat more precisely. One variant (i.e. Horwich's) is to cash out the motto in terms of use properties (acceptance properties). Use properties, however, even if they concern *types* of meaning—as they must do—are nevertheless crucially *determined by the tokenings associated with a given word type*. Therefore, a serious *usage-based* theory of meaning should rather build its central thesis on the concept of word/sentence tokens, rather than on their corresponding types.

8 On Phenomena and Tokenings

The aim of this chapter is to step back and take a look at the big picture that emerged in the foregoing chapters. To this end, I take the main results of these chapters for granted. This chapter may be read as a brief summary. Though I think it is slightly more accurate to conceive of it as an outlook for potential future research, since, admittedly, the framework that I present here is really a *framework*. There are a range of topics worth to investigating in greater detail. Most importantly, the fundamental claim that meaning is *total* use, i.e. the sum of all actual word type instantiations, needs to be specified more precisely than I have been able to do here.

The chapter starts off with a short remark on what I think are the most important 'results' established in the book (8.1). After this, I will be discussing the relevance of tokenings in usage-based approaches, arguing that usage-based theories of meaning are forced to adopt a token-focused view on language (8.2). In 8.3, then, I explicate my view on the relationship between, on the one hand, semantic descriptions (i.e. usage-based analyses) and, on the other, the constitutive basis of meaning (i.e. use).

8.1 The Big Picture

In this section, I briefly call to mind the four most important results of the book (from my perspective). Expect no arguments here. They all can be found in the relevant chapters.

The constitutive basis of meaning is use. In philosophy of language as well as in linguistics, semantic theories divide into two main strands. The above chapters showed that usage-based theories of meaning are more advantageous in a variety of respects, especially in comparison to truth-conditional semantics and its relatives. One main reason is TCS's ongoing tendency to deal solely with declaratives. This problem turned out to be especially pressing in regard to utterances that serve a specific conversational function. Another reason was the following: in individuating word types, truth-conditional semanticists feel free to recur to use; whereas in specifying the semantics they take into account only referential and truth-functional relations. I showed that such an ad hoc divide between the epistemology of semantics and semantic metaphysics is unwarranted. A third 'philosophical' reason against truth-conditional semantics is that a thorough review of the relevant literature reveals that a crucial argument *against use theories* is unsupported by the evidence; all serious usage-based theories on the market are compatible with compositionality and acknowledge its importance.

Use theories are empirically validated. To be sure, that continues to be controversial. But many influential developments in empirical disciplines base *their* respective theories on usage-based considerations, among them most notably Michael Tomasello's work on common ground, joint attention, and language development;[1] most varieties of construction grammar (especially the 'cognitive' variants (cf. Ziem & Lasch 2013), i.e. Croft (2001), Goldberg (1995), and Langacker (2008)); and some influential linguistic subdisciplines concerned with perspectives (Evans 2012). It would be silly to deny that other areas of empirical research work with different assumptions. But it seems relatively safe to say that (i) the mentioned areas gained some weight in the last two decades, which gives 'philosophical' usage-based theories some indirect support, and (ii) to the extent that empirical researchers are justified in basing their theories on usage-based assumptions, it is the philosopher's duty to provide them with an adequate basis.

No established usage-based theory works perfectly. This is a major premise that I take to be justified by the above discussion. I have shown that Paul Horwich's theory is today the by far most plausible account of such a theory of meaning. Therefore, if it turns out that this theory only insufficiently accounts for meaning (as I think is the case), this complaint applies a fortiori to other usage-based theories as well.[2] I think it is fair to say that

---

[1] Tomasello's habit of starting six out of nine chapters of *Constructing a Language* with a quote from the later Wittgenstein is quite telling in this regard.

[2] Horwich gives the following overview of related theoretical frameworks:

> What I shall be calling "the use theory of meaning" is intended to answer the question: in virtue of which of its underlying properties does a word come to possess the particular meaning it has? The theory I am going to articulate

8.1 The Big Picture

Horwich's theory is considered 'state of the art' in today's usage-based philosophy of language. So the controversial aspect of my own framework is not so much what I say about other theories, but my misgivings concerning Horwich's ideas. The major problems that I have discussed above (in chapter 6) can only be summarised very briefly here. Although strictly departing from the truth-conditional mainstream (cf. also Horwich 2008b), Horwich keeps focussing on declarative sentences. This leads him to propose acceptance properties as a general solution to the problem of how to cash out use properties. Both the idea to spell out the general disposition to apply 'referential' words (words like "dog", "red", etc.) in terms of acceptance and the accompanying idea to have a unified framework in which all word types get the same *kind* of underlying property associated (i.e. acceptance) is brilliant. Yet, I think that the constraint on acceptance is only due to the focus on declaratives—a factor that severely limits the theory's scope.

Compositionality is conceptually tightly linked with language use. This counter-intuitive result is justified by combining several consequences established in the prior chapters. Basically, it all boils down to the question: what are the demarcation lines for semantics? In particular, the relevant question is where to separate semantics from pragmatics, and where to separate semantics from issues of communication. In line with the principle of the Primacy of the Phenomena (defined in 7.1.1), I propose acknowledging the explanatory priority of communication over semantics. Simply put, communication (not semantics) is a proper phenomenon, hence the adequacy of linguistic theories in this area is determined by what is required to explain communication (not semantics). This affects one's understanding of what constitutes an *utterance*. If non-verbal aspects can be potential constituents of utterance meaning, then these non-verbal aspects—e.g. gestures—must be assigned appropriate meanings. These meanings, again, must be formulated (or must in principle be re-formulatable) in a semantic

---

bears certain affinities to ideas in the works of Wittgenstein [(2009)], Sellars [(1954, 1963, 1969)], Field [(1977)], Harman [(1982, 1987)], Block [(1986)], Peacocke [(1992)], Brandom [(1994)], Cozzo [(1994)], and other philosophers whose views could reasonably be labelled *use* theories of meaning. (1998, 43)

framework that would make them *compatible* with verbal constituents. In general, multimodal compositionality seems to favour usage-based meaning descriptions.

These intermediate results suggest that the relevant empirical disciplines are particularly likely to combine with some variant or other of usage-based semantics, i.e. they suggest that we need *some* use theory; but these considerations do not unequivocally determine the exact structure of such a theory. It is to this issue that I now turn. The answer depends crucially on one's conception of "meaning" itself. Or, in other words, being clear about one's favoured notion of "meaning" means committing oneself to a specific theory. The following sections aim at bringing together some puzzle pieces scattered over previous sections of the present book.

8.2 Use, Token, Constitution

Let me begin with the notion of 'use' employed in this book. A central distinction in philosophy in general, and in philosophy of language in particular, concerns the type/token difference. In slogan form, a use theory says simply that meaning is use. Is use best spelled out in terms of word types or in terms of tokens? I think the only reasonable answer here is: tokens. When people claim that meaning is use (and the like), then they surely mean *actual* use—in fact, this is the only viable option. But types are abstract descriptions. They can't be used. They can only be 'used' insofar as a type can be instantiated. But instantiations of a word type are tokens, again.

This is pretty much in line with what William Croft, one of the most prominent defenders of Construction Grammar, says when, in describing language change, he points out that

> An utterance is a particular, actual occurrence of the product of human behavior in communicative interaction (i.e. a string of sounds), as it is pronounced, grammatically, structured, and semantically and pragmatically interpreted in its context. [...] An utterance as defined here is a spatiotemporally bounded individual. Thus, unlike sentences, only actually occurring tokens count as utterances in our sense. It is critical to the the-

8.2 Use, Token, Constitution

ory of language change that utterances be actually occurring language; recall that selection operates only over actual, not possible, alternatives. Since an utterance is an actually existing entity, all levels of its structure are included, in particular its specific pronounciation and meaning in context as intended by the speaker and interpreted by the hearer [...]. (2000, 26)

Theories of meaning that are bound to the usage-based tradition apparently do not simply claim that meaning is use. But they do insist, in some form or other, that the meaning of words is *determined* by the way they are *used*. That is to say, meaning—from this point of view—is determined by instantiations/tokens. What is called a word type is, analogously, determined by tokenings. For example, the alleged 'fact' that "bank" is separable into two distinct word types ('institution' vs 'riverbank') is determined by "bank" tokenings, and the distinction is justified by structural dissimilarities within the set of all formally individuated tokens. Hence, it is relatively easy to see that usage-based theories of meaning are forced to accept the view that what constitutes meaning is tokenings. The types that are instantiated by these tokens are theoretical constructs to systematise linguistic data. To be sure, *which* type a given token is a token of is an essential aspect of linguistic theory. For example, an ironic interpretation of "cool" might mean 'warm' or 'boring', depending on the type of "cool" instantiated. But typing is an post hoc issue; it is determined by the available evidence (i.e. mere tokenings), not the other way around.

Given that for these reasons usage-based theorists are committed to relativise their theory to word tokens, some immediate problems arise. The basic issue here concerns meaning holism. Meaning holism can take many different forms (Horwich 1998, 59–65). It often arises in the context of inferentialism à la Brandom (1994). Inferentialism, or conceptual role semantics, is the idea that the meaning of a word is determined by the specific contribution it makes toward the 'commitments' one enters into by using that word in declarative sentences (see especially pp. 157–166 of *Making it Explicit*). For instance, by saying "This object is a cat" I am committed to also claiming that "This object is an animal". This is due to the conceptual role of "cat". I do not intend to go too much into the details here. But let me stress one particular difficulty that conceptual role semantics shares with token-based use theories.

Conceptual roles are necessarily defined holistically: if the meaning of a given word is defined in relation to the meaning of related words (cf., in particular, Brandom 1994, 180–198), then each (word) meaning changes *with every change of the conceptual roles of related terms.* This problem is particularly pressing if one takes into account the varying idiolects of individual speakers, e.g. that every speaker is competent with respect to a different set of words. The 'commitments' associated with individual words can be related either directly to idiolects, or to whole language communities. In both cases, holism is a problem for word semantics spelt out in terms of conceptual roles. In the former case, meaning would be constituted by idiolects. This would imply different word meanings for every dialect—a result that is hard to swallow. In the latter case, meaning would be constituted by the sum of idiolects of, for instance, all competent speakers of English. Here, meaning would not vary in between two persons. But, still, holism would turn out problematic here, since meaning would change continuously. That is because the individual idiolects that constitute meaning on this view change continuously as well. Either way, the holism implied by inferentialism is problematic.

A token-based use theory faces a very similar difficulty. This time meaning *variance* enters not due to holistic concerns (indeed, I think my approach is immune to holism issues in general), but rather due to its focus on tokens. The immediate—in fact, obvious—response to the proposal that the meaning of a given term is the sum of all its actual instantiations is the following: this can't be right, for this would imply that meaning changes with every new utterance of a term. True. The 'variance' in meaning in conceptual role semantics would look absolutely harmless in comparison. But then, it would seem, we face a paradox here: by their very nature, use theories must be token-based; but explaining meaning in terms of tokenings implies wild meaning variance. The solution that I proposed in the foregoing chapters avoids these problems, yet at the same time it is really simple.

The paradox, I should emphasise, is a paradox indeed, i.e. it is no dilemma. In particular, it is absolutely implausible to assume that a possible way out would be to go for one of the two 'horns'. Firstly, it is not an op-

8.2 Use, Token, Constitution

tion to deny that use theories are forced to take tokens as the basis of their explanation, i.e. as the eventual formulation of their slogan that meaning is use. To see this, consider all *actual* theories on the market, in particular Wittgensteinian, Horwichian, Brandomian, or Sellarsian approaches. They all essentially recur to word type tokenings.

> Here, then, is a way of thinking about implicitly normative social practices [e.g. linguistic/discoursive practices]. Social practices are games in which each participant exhibits various deontic statuses—that is, commitments and entitlements—and each practically significant performance alters those statuses in some way. The significance of the performance is how it alters the deontic statuses of the practitioners. (Brandom 1994, 166)

> Let us now turn our attention to rule obeying behavior. We have already noted that it involves a distinction between game and metagame, the former, or "object game" being played according to certain rules which themselves are positions in the metagame. Furthermore, we have emphasized that in an object game played as rule obeying behavior, not only *do the moves exemplify positions specified by the rules* (for this is also true of mere pattern governed behavior where even though a rule exists the playing organism has not learned to play it) but also the rules themselves are engaged in the genesis of the moves. (Sellars 1954, 214, my emphasis)

> Think of all the facts regarding a person's linguistic behaviour—the sum of everything he will say, and in what circumstances. The thesis [of the use theory] is that this constellation of data may be unified and explained in terms of a relatively small and simple body of factors and principles including, for each word, a basic use regularity. (Horwich 1998, 45)

> Suppose that the tools A uses in building bear certain marks. *When A shows his assistant such a mark, the assistant brings the tool that has that mark on it.* In this, and in more or less similar ways, a name signifies a thing, and is given to a thing.—When

8 On Phenomena and Tokenings

> philosophizing, it will often prove useful to say to ourselves: naming something is rather like attaching a name tag to a thing. (Wittgenstein 2009, 10e, my emphasis)

In linguistics, the related notion of 'usage-based semantics' does not mean quite the same as 'usage-based theories' in philosophy. Still, there are more similarities between the two research directions than differences. In linguistics, it is even clearer that "usage-based" always means 'token-based', because what usage-based linguists do, at the end of the day, is analysing corpora. Corpora analysis is a paradigm example of a token-focussed approach to meaning. Thus, both in empirical and in theoretical research, a closer look at existing, established theories is enough to show that there is no way around tokenings when it comes to usage-based theories of meaning.

The second horn of the pseudo-paradox is acknowledging that there is huge, in fact continuous, variance in word meaning, but to claim that this is in fact unproblematic. This would be blatantly absurd, for language is, in the long run, relatively stable. At least, it is as stable as to be not affected by single tokenings. It takes some time until meaning changes occur. So even if—as seems plausible—meaning shifts are caused by tokenings, one tokening surely does not suffice. Hence, the overall stability of natural language meaning suggests that single tokens leave meaning unaffected.

Accepting that the paradox is a proper paradox indeed, one must reconcile the two aims. As I already said above, it all hinges on one's definition of "meaning". As I see things, it is possible to work with a definition of "meaning" that is broad enough as to cover all 'usages' of "meaning" in relevant sub-disciplines. I have already argued for a liberal stance towards competing conceptions of "meaning" in different semantic theories. It is time now to refine the rather naïve notion introduced in section 2.1. Replacing it with a more sophisticated version, I still want to stick to the basic idea that it makes sense to have a *unified* definition that puts different theoretic frameworks under one umbrella.

The solution I want to propose here is to distinguish between the *constitution basis* for meaning and an appropriate *description* thereof. This distinction is relatively widespread in the relevant literature. In contrast, the way this divide helps to solve serious problems in linguistics is seldom discussed in detail. In line with the way "meaning" is commonly employed in everyday life and in empirical research, it might turn out fruitful to associate semantic descriptions with meaning as such, or, simply put, with *meaning*. I take it that this proposal is in fact quite 'conservative', since to a large extent it is simply an elegant way of systematising what is common practice anyway (inside and outside academia). As distinguishing between 'constitution basis' and 'semantic description' is motivated mainly by the paradox presented above, I shall jump into the details by discussing both aspects of that paradox in turn.

To begin with, the metaphysical claim underlying all varieties of so-called use theories is—in slogan form—that meaning is use. The problematic step for each theory is to cash out this slogan appropriately. I have already shown that the most natural way would be to spell out 'use' in terms of instantiations/tokenings of a given word type. However, this strategy would immediately face two problems already discussed above. Firstly, this strategy would lead to the epistemological problem that, in such an account, meaning would turn out to be de facto unknowable (save exceptions like word coining). Secondly, continuous meaning shifts would occur with every new tokening. Furthermore, it seems really problematic to equate *meaning* directly with the sum of all actual word type instantiations.

The natural solution to this is to equate the *sum of all actual past instantiations of a given word type* not with meaning but with *the constitution basis for the meaning of that word type*, i.e. with that *fact that constitutes the meaning of the word in question*. I concede that this really sounds counterintuitive at first, but this impression vanishes as soon as this account is linked to an appropriate conception of meaning (itself). In this view, the meaning of a word is identical with the *most efficient, most general way of summarising the use of a word type as exemplified by the sum of all actual past instantiations*. I shall now discuss, step-by-step, possible problems and objections, some of which have already been mentioned above. My aim is to show that, in conjunction, both theses overcome these objections very elegantly.

8 On Phenomena and Tokenings

8.2.1 Meaning Shifts

First of all, let me note that the threat of extreme meaning shifts—i.e. shifts accompanying each tokening—are avoided in this account. Meanings are—as I will put it in what follows—efficient descriptions of use. But in contrast to the constitution basis of meaning, meaning is not affected by individual tokenings (save for some minor exceptions). Assuming that we are dealing with 'established', normal, words of English like "dog", "red", "snow", "hello", "Aristotle", and so forth, it seems extraordinarily unlikely that the *efficiency* of the currently best description of their respective uses could possibly be affected by individual word type instantiations. For example, assuming that "'Aristotle' is used to refer to Aristotle" is currently the most efficient summary of competent English speakers' use of "Aristotle", the appropriateness would remain the same if, for example, I now say this: I quite like Aristotles. Crucially, "I quite like Aristotles" involves an "Aristotle" token whose interpretation, taken individually, can't be explained solely by referring to the above description.[3] But that does not matter for the appropriateness of the description. The description that is singled out as the meaning of a word is, in my account, defined in relation to the sum of all instantiations. And relative to *this*, the summarising description "'Aristotle' is used to refer to Aristotle" is still most efficient; and it would continue to be the most efficient variant unless a significant number of people would decide to use "Aristotle" for structurally different purposes than for referring to Aristotle.

At the same time, the framework can account for meaning shifts quite easily. Moreover, it answers the use theorists' intuition that meaning shifts are intimately bound to tokenings. The reason is simply that, since meaning is constituted by all word type instantiations, a certain amount of tokenings may alter the meaning of a given term. To be sure, the amount varies according to a huge variety of factors. The two most important ones are probably these: (i) how established is the word and (ii) how central is it relative to our 'web of beliefs' (Quine 1951)? The latter is particularly important, as there are whole *classes* of words that are hardly ever affected by

---

[3] Note that by "interpretation" I mean 'semantic interpretation', as the point is that meaning shifts, caused by individual tokenings, might lead to a situation in which a 'literal' interpretation of "I quite like Aristotles" is indeed possible and plausible.

meaning shifts: proper names, logical constants, connectors, indexicals, to name but a few. Philosophically speaking, it is indeed quite uninteresting to determine an actual threshold here. For the *general, abstract* threshold for meaning change is simply: the amount of tokenings it takes to make a different description of the overall use more efficient.

8.2.2 Appropriate Descriptions

My framework specifies that *the* meaning of a term is the description that describes its use most efficiently. It seems obvious that, if, for a given term, there were contradictory descriptions, all of which purportedly summarise its use, then it is simply an empirical question which description is *most* efficient. Thus, my framework ensures that there is always an order forced upon rivalling meaning statements. But this might lead to a further possible objection: "most efficient" suggests that there is no *perfect* description, i.e. that all existing proposals that summarise the meaning of a given term are always mere approximations. This collides with the deep conviction of most philosophers (and laymen) that every word type can be associated with only one specific meaning. Referential relations are a good example here, as the reference relation allegedly can be specified almost schematically for many terms: names refer to their bearers; indexicals refer to what is specifiable via their corresponding Kaplanian characters; natural kind terms, let's suppose, refer to the set of things exemplifying a particular essence (DNA, molecular constellation, etc.); predicates, in general, refer to sets of objects (e.g. "green" refers to the set of green objects); and so forth. But we also find this intuition in 'usage-based' approaches to semantics; cf., for example, Horwich's often-repeated example that one's overall tendency to apply the term "red" is governed by the basic acceptance property to accept "This is red" in the presence of red objects. In general, many scholars tend to think that words have *one* specific meaning. In this view, individual theories of meaning are just different characterisations of one and the same thing.

Before I turn to the actual counterargument to this objection, let me very briefly point out that I think that at least the *impression* that ordinary meaning statements are not merely approximations but deal with the alleged definite meaning of a given term is reasonable. This tendency stems, I think, from the range of examples that are typically chosen in philosophy. Focussing on specific examples—commonly those with quite entrenched meanings—fosters an understanding, according to which speaking of correct meaning statements in terms of *most appropriate approximations* looks absurd. Therefore, my aim in the following few paragraphs is to show that even statements concerning the most entrenched meanings are nothing more than (probably quite accurate) approximations.

The main thesis defended in this chapter is that distinguishing between the constitutive factors for meaning (i.e. use) and an appropriate description thereof (i.e. meaning) is the most plausible way to make sense of usage-based approaches to semantics. Use, according to that account, is the totality of actual past instantiations of a word type. With the exception of recently coined terms, this conceptually implies that the constitutive basis of word meaning is necessarily unknown to human beings. Accordingly, it can be shown for in fact *any* word that its corresponding meaning statements only approximates this constitutive basis. In light of this, it makes sense to exemplify this by discussing a word with a very stable meaning.

Now to the counterargument against the assumptions that terms really have *one* meaning, i.e. one 'correct' semantic description. The word "and" will again serve as an example. "And" is a logical connective; simply by belonging to that class, its semantics is more stable than words belonging to other classes, which is why it is particularly appropriate for making the point at hand. If we assume that the constitutive basis of meaning is use, the main task of a semantic theory for "and" is to state, in the most general and efficient terms, how "and" is used in the language community of English. The most general, but at the same time least efficient way, would be to *list* all actual "and" tokenings. A list would be inefficient in two respects: firstly, a list would ignore the apparent fact that most "and" tokenings bear striking similarities (i.e. continuing with the list would be pointless after a certain time). Secondly, a list would therefore fail to generalise accordingly (i.e. it would lack the powers to account for the role "and" plays in inferential reasoning).[4] Presumably, a good candidate description would be along the following lines: "and" is used in English in a way that corresponds to

---

[4] Still, this list plays a relevant role in determining the 'ideal disposition'; cf. below, section 8.3.

the use of introduction and elimination rules for "and" in algebraic logic, i.e. that people who have a tendency to accept, in Horwich's terminology, "p" and "q" would have an equal tendency to also accept "p and q", and vice versa. Due to its central role in inferential processes, this description is probably indeed quite accurate. Still, it only approximately describes the use of "and", as there are tokenings that do not accord with this rule.[5] But if this already holds for logical connectives, i.e. for terms the meaning of which can be relatively easy agreed upon, it holds a fortiori for other terms as well.

This argument hints at something more fundamental. At several places throughout the book, I have emphasised that *phenomena* figure prominently in my account in the following sense. One needs to carefully distinguish between, on the one hand, the phenomena that give rise to the need for specific theories (e.g. semantics), and, on the other hand, artefacts that result from our theorising about these phenomena (e.g. compositionality). Impressions to the contrary notwithstanding, there is striking disagreement among professionals as to what meaning actually is. The range of existing rival theories in this area speaks for itself.

Another quite illustrative example is this: one of the most uncontroversially accepted examples of a semantic relation is reference. In particular, reference relations are of central importance in formal approaches to semantics (as in those theories, the meaning of singular terms gets equated with their referents). Emma Borg's 'minimalism', which is a variant of a formal-semantic approach, delegates questions of reference to areas outside of semantics (Borg 2004*b*, ch. 3.3). For example, in regard to the actual referent of an indexical expression, the semantics is confined to specifying the relevant token-reflexive rule that is capable of resolving reference relation only in conjunction with further information (i.e. information from outside a Fodorian semantics module). In her view, only the 'conditionalised' rules associated with indexicals are genuinely semantic (i.e. only those rules are *meanings* of indexical expressions), whereas the actual referents are determined by, and hence part of, pragmatics (i.e. the *semantic values* of indexicals belong to pragmatics). This shows the enormous vari-

---

[5] For example, people sometimes tend to read causal or temporal relations into "and" conjunctions; cf. "John married Mary, and Mary got pregnant".

ety of views in semantics, as the view *that the referent of a given term (its semantic value) is an integral part of a semantic theory* is probably the view most philosophers of language would subscribe to or agree with. Thus, giving the debate a fresh start by looking at the phenomena first looks like a strategy that could possibly provide a solution to a discussion that often seems to continuously go around in circles. Often, the 'data' with respect to particular example cases (e.g. which proposition is expressed by utterances of the type "It is raining") is, to a large extent, uncontroversial between the involved parties, i.e. they agree, for example, on the range of plausible interpretations. Therefore, there seems to be no fact of the matter that could decide the discussion in favour of either side. I contend that focussing on the phenomena first might be a practicable solution.

Anticipating a response that is likely to be raised at this point, let me stress that *all* instances of a given word enter into its constitution base, i.e. not just those in which the term is applied 'correctly'. First of all, the distinction of correct vs incorrect applications is only fully comprehensible in light of the fact—repeatedly emphasised in the previous chapters—that language is a means to achieve extra-linguistic ends. It is not false per se to apply, say, "dog" to things other than dogs. It is only false in the sense that, given our current language, it is rational in most cases to apply "dog" only to dogs, because that helps achieving one's aims. In simple terms, the only reason to apply "dog" to dogs (i.e. correctly) is because that is what people usually do. Including correct and incorrect applications into every word's constitution base gives just the right results for their semantics, e.g. with respect to meaning shifts.

8.2.3 Specifying Context, Tokening, and Meaning Constitution

For the semantic framework I put forward in this book, the notion of context is specifically important. The underlying reason is that I propose to think of usage-based theories of meaning first and foremost in terms of *tokenings* or *instantiations* of a given word type. Focussing on tokenings—in particular, focussing on the sum of all actual tokenings—involves specifying how tokenings are 'counted', if you like. That is, I need to specify (i) the way tokens are identified as instantiations of a particular word type and (ii) what details of the context are relevant for counting actual instantiations.

In different theoretical frameworks, "context" might mean very different things. A very common locution is that of a 'context of utterance', where contexts are conceived simply as possible worlds that are specified with respect to time, place, and speaker. That is, if you like, one end of the continuum of possible variations of the meaning of "context". Here, contexts consist solely of three formally specifiable variables. At the other end, contexts may involve any number of additional features. For example, contexts might involve whatever turns out to be relevant for determining the communicated content of an utterance, as in relevance theory (Sperber & Wilson 1986). The theoretically most important divide between different conceptions of 'context' concerns the question whether a particular theory allows contexts to include (ascriptions of) the intentions of speakers and hearers (Borg 2004*b*).

When it comes to my own proposal and the 'contextually relevant' features, it will help to consider the above-mentioned distinction of constitution base versus semantic description first (cf. also next section). The constitution base of the meaning of a term is 'fixed', so to speak. It is simply use. One can't get it wrong, as it were. Contextual factors *only* come into play when semantic descriptions are taken into account, i.e. descriptions that try to approximately summarise this use. My hunch would be that a particularly *philosophical* theory of meaning should describe contextual relevance as *schematically* as possible. Simply put, the relevant features are those circumstances of a conversational context that a competent language user would recognise as being relevant for a given word to have a particular meaning relative to the context in question. I go a bit more into the details in the following section.

8.3 Constitution Base

Conceiving of meaning in terms of actual word type instantiations only makes sense within the broader context of the specific theory that I propose here. The distinction between constitution base and semantic description, which I already mentioned briefly in section 8.2, is crucial in this regard.

8 On Phenomena and Tokenings

It will be worth the effort to now look in more detail at which contextual factors are relevant in 'counting' tokenings. More precisely, the relevant question is: which factors of conversational contexts are relevant in determining what a given word actually means?

Traditionally, there has been a well-established tendency in the philosophy of language (of whatever variant) to think of *context* only in terms of the just mentioned three formally specifiable features: time, place, and speaker. Although these three features are indeed particularly relevant in semantics, their applicability is somewhat constrained, to say the least. Apparently, the focus on time, place, and speaker is inspired by the idea that one of the central aims of semantics is to account for reference fixing. This idea is so obviously taken for granted that it is hard to cite *explicit* evidence in its favour. Anyway, this tendency, I take it, is the reason behind the enormous popularity of indexicals in the semantics literature. The actual referents of indexical expressions, however, seem to be particularly hard to determine.[6]

The (values of the) variables of time, place, and speaker of a given utterance seem to fit the bill. It goes without saying that semantic knowledge concerning token-reflexive rules that are attached to indexicals help people in determining referents in contexts. For example, people tend to think that a tokening of "here" refers to the place of the utterance.[7] From today's perspective, the discussions from the early 1970s seem far too optimistic as regards the convictions that (i) all referential 'facts' are clear as soon as the reference of indexicals is resolved and that (ii) the referents of indexicals are determined by specifying the relevant input to their characters. Be that as it may; since then the classical way to think of contexts has been in terms of the three mentioned factors.

There are alternatives to this, one of which is to leave contexts unspecified. Often, people talk as if the only features of the context that are relevant for a particular task (e.g. reference fixing) are those that are (de facto) contextually relevant.

---

[6] This, to be sure, is only true under the assumption that the actual referents of non-indexical expressions such as "dog" are particularly easy to determine.

[7] Ignoring the fact that this oversimplifies things, since 'place of the utterance' is notoriously underdetermined.

8.3 Constitution Base

If I say that meaning is constituted by actual tokenings, I certainly want to include 'more context' into my analysis than just time, place, and speaker. Also, I want to be more precise than just saying that contexts include everything that is relevant (which is tantamount to saying that context is always relevant, except when it is not). However, the reason for going beyond time, place, and speaker is not so much that these three key features do not uniquely determine referents. This, by itself, is a problem, but only insofar as (actual) reference is relevant to how a given term is used. In fact, reference fixing as such is absolutely *unimportant* from the current perspective. I need to include more context, though, since more features *of* the context are relevant for determining how a given word is used *in* a specific context than time, place, and speaker.

The fundamental distinction with which I began was between constitution basis and semantic description. Of the latter, I said that it is necessarily always only an approximation of an accurate description of use. If I now try to account for the constitution basis, this, again, is also just a *description*, albeit a different one. Figure 8.1 illustrates the relations that hold between linguistic descriptions and the constitution bases that justify certain descriptions. The idea here is that there are two things that can be described accurately at a metalevel. Firstly, the relation between constitution base and meaning: particular meanings (i.e. linguistic descriptions) approximate the use associated with a given term. The use of a term, in turn, constitutes its meaning, which is to say that it justifies exactly the most faithful (i.e. general and efficient) descriptions. Secondly, the *kinds* of entities involved can also be described very precisely. Although it is conceptually impossible to know the particular (complete) constitution basis of a term like "table", it *is* possible to describe precisely the general nature of constitution bases, e.g. in terms of full sums of actual type instantiations.

In 8.1, what is below the dotted line represents actual practice in linguistics. The *individual* semantic descriptions produced by linguistic theories are always inaccurate to a certain extent. These descriptions—i.e. what is commonly called 'the' meaning of a term—are mere approximations of uses associated with particular terms. In this sense, it seems fair to say that although specific semantic descriptions lack accuracy, the corresponding metalevel description of the kinds of entities involved and how they relate to each other might still be quite precise.

8 On Phenomena and Tokenings

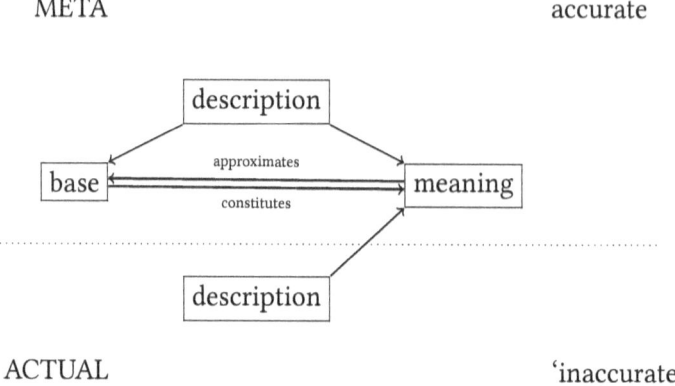

Figure 8.1: Relations between constitution base and linguistic description

I think that whereas what I call 'semantic descriptions' are always inaccurate to a certain extent, the philosophical account of the basis that constitutes meaning can be formulated very precisely. To this end, I now turn to some very general considerations. It is a recurring theme in (usage-based) semantics that use plays a double role. Besides determining meaning, it 'determines', if you like, use itself. Clearly, how I actually use "apple"—and thereby partly determine how "apple" is actually used (by my linguistic society)—is influenced by how "apple" is actually used (by my linguistic society). The fact that, for example, "apple" means what it does (is used in the way it is de facto used) is kind of a self-preserving mechanism. The de-facto usage of a given term is a valid reason for everyone for aligning their usage accordingly. This, to be sure, is nothing new. But it helps showing what is relevant when it comes to tokenings and their respective contexts. The following explanations will be hearer-centric as opposed to speaker-centric. The fact that use determines use is rooted in the fact that hearers make certain assumptions about what function a given term previously had in specific situations.

Here, "Could you please pass the salt?" will again serve as an example. People would usually assume that sentences of this type are typically used to express one's wish to get the salt passed. Moreover, people would also assume that "salt" is used to refer to salt. It seems reasonable to suppose that our tendency to apply "salt" to salt is rooted in the successes that people, who want to get the salt passed, have when they try to get the salt passed by tokening "Could you please pass the salt?" These *successes*— and similar successes in other contexts that involve "salt" tokenings—are relevant reasons for people to assume that "salt" will be used in a specific manner on future occasions (cf. also section 6.2.2). Analogously, observing these successes will be reason for *them* to use "salt" in a way that accords with just those factors, of which they think they have been relevant to the successes. In other words, observing "salt" utterances plus their accompanying situations helps in interpreting future "salt" utterances and in producing "salt" utterances that are likely to be interpreted accordingly (all else equal). The likelihood depends on how well the hearer is able to determine which factors were 'responsible' for the relative success of a given word type tokening to serve the communication intentions at hand. For example, whether she knew in advance that the "Could you please pass the x?" construction is typically used by people in need of x and that the speaker was, in fact, in need of salt—if, at least, that was her assumption—then the behaviour (salt passing) relative to which the success of the utterance gets evaluated will be traced back to a particular property of "salt", namely its 'ability' to refer to salt. In other words, what people assume about the meaning (use) of words directly hinges on what they expect with respect to communication intentions (and their success or failure) in situations in which these words are applied.

Note that the relevant communication intentions need not be as specific as in the 'salt' example. For instance, the communication intention that motivates the use of "please" is relatively unspecific. Yet, people are still able to determine reliably how "please" is used in English. Note also that the intentions I am talking about here need not be real at all (in the realist's sense). The only claim I want to make is that the uniformity in use in natural language must stem from the intentions people *ascribe* to their interlocutors combined with what they can infer about (alleged) communication successes. For "salt" to mean what it does, it is not necessary that people have specific intentions; but what is required is that they *think* others have those intentions (e.g. to get the salt passed) and that they *can* observe that these (alleged) intentions get fulfilled (e.g. that salt gets passed). So neither do I assume that intentions directly affect the meaning of words, nor that intentions are real, besides the need to ascribe intentions in order to make sense of the (non-)verbal behaviour of others.

I said earlier that one of the most promising ways to summarise use is by way of dispositional analysis. With the explanations above in mind, it is now possible to describe in more detail what I mean by 'ideal dispositions'. What I just said about communication intentions and successes can easily be rephrased in terms of dispositions. For a particular hearer, the best dispositional description that summarises their specific usage of a given term is just this: the disposition (to apply the term in question) that emerges from that hearer's prior experience with instantiations of that term and corresponding assumptions about which communication functions have been fulfilled by using it.

For every *particular* hearer and every *particular* situation in which a word was tokenened and with which that hearer is familiar, the disposition that is 'derivable' from this varies enormously. But that does not undermine my claim that the general remarks about constitutive bases might be true simpliciter. For the constitutive basis of the meaning of a given term is independent of the contingent set of tokenings particular language users are acquainted with. By the same token, the 'correct' dispositional analysis is also independent of particular analyses that apply to *particular* language users. For the 'ideal disposition' is fixed (relative to a given constitutive basis); namely it is just that disposition an otherwise competent hearer would arrive at if he were familiar with all actual tokenings of a particular word type.[8] Accordingly, the 'correct' dispositional analysis is whichever analysis approximates this ideal. For instance, the analysis that people who understand "dog" have the overall tendency to apply that term to dogs and dog-like appearances might turn out to be the best analysis, because it best approximates the disposition that a speaker/hearer would have who knew all instances of "dog".

---

[8] Note the proviso "otherwise competent" in this regard. The dispositions *particular* speakers acquire not only depend on their respective evidence basis but also on their cognitive resources. For instance, in order for 'abstraction' (Tomasello 2003a) to get off the ground, one needs to be able to recognise what is similar between different communication scenarios. This might be easier or harder, depending on individual resources.

9 Conclusion

The main idea defended in this book is that the rise of construction grammar in linguistics indicates the coming decline of truth-conditional semantics in philosophy. My main argument is that there is converging evidence in areas of empirical research that suggests that semantics should be pursued with a usage-based underpinning. CxG comprises research areas as diverse as language acquisition, language evolution, semantics, conversational analysis, pragmatics, psycholinguistics, artificial language learning, and more. In philosophy, though, CxG has thus far attracted not much attention. This is remarkable insofar as the basic theoretical commitments of CxG concern core areas of philosophical theorising. Most notably, the increasing importance of constructionist approaches undermines philosophical commonplaces such as the fact that there is a strict boundary between semantics and pragmatics; that there is a strict boundary between semantics and syntax; that there is a clear distinction between 'literal' and 'non-literal' meaning; and that the universal applicability of the compositionality principle is relatively undisputed.

In this book, I have shown that these commonplaces are brought into question by CxG. I showed that the plausibility of formal and truth-conditional approaches to semantics is severely undermined. Furthermore, I showed that there are currently no adequate usage-based approaches available that could serve a philosophically informed basis of CxG. Lastly, I shaped the outline of such an alternative.

Crucially, the proposed outline is nothing more, really, than an *outline*. Allow me to use the allotted space of this conclusion to highlight the aspects of the theory that I consider most relevant and that merit being laid down in more detail than I have been able to do in this book. There are three points that I would like to mention here, all of which are closely linked.

Phenomena-based philosophising: A recurring theme in this book is that in many areas there does not seem to be a 'fact of the matter' that could

9 Conclusion

decide certain debates in favour of either side. For instance, after decades of research there is no consensus as to what are appropriate definitions of "what is said". People keep rehashing the same examples and thought experiments again and again without any significant progress. The most important point in these debates seems to be that there is no datum that could possibly convince the respective other side. Therefore, I suggest in the text that a viable 'way out' would be to first agree on what the relevant phenomena are. Because it is the phenomena—nothing else—that give rise to the need for *theories* in the first place. If there were no relevant phenomena, there would be no theories either. This is why the phenomena should guide one's search for adequate theories.

Metaphysical and 'descriptive' semantics: One of the major topics that I discuss repeatedly is that the—certainly not new—distinction between the reductive programme in semantics and adequate semantic analyses gets neglected far too often. The metaphysical project in philosophical semantics is to account for semantic properties in terms of 'underlying' non-semantic properties. In this sense, use can be identified with the constitutive basis of meaning. The important point in this context is that possible counterarguments to such an identification, such as holism or rapid meaning change, refer to semantic descriptions, not to their underlying metaphysical basis. In this sense, I argue that although the metaphysical basis of meaning develops, in fact, continuously, there need be no corresponding shift in the relevant semantic description whatsoever. This is because the *adequacy* of semantic descriptions might be completely unaffected even by rapid 'changes' in its metaphysical basis.

Token-focused approach: Taken together, these two methodological considerations suggest that theories of meaning in philosophy should be construed on the basis of tokens. With respect to the metaphysical programme, usage-based theories are best conceived as dealing with instantiations of word and sentence types. This is the most integral part of my proposal and, likewise, the one that is definitely worth being pursued further. In semantics, instantiations are relevant first and foremost as instantiations of particular types. In the main text, I indicate how this requirement might be achieved. The basic idea is that 'solutions' to such puzzles must be designed *schematically*. Given that what an expression means is determined by how it is used—which is, in its entirety, unknown—philosophical theories of meaning must focus on explaining the development of astonishingly similar semantic knowledge in language users. Dispositional analyses are probably most suitable for this task, as they do not require that subjects with similar semantic knowledge acquire this knowledge on the basis of the same piece of evidence.

Bibliography

Akmajian, A., Demers, R. A., Farmer, A. K. & Harnish, R. M. (1995), *Linguistics: An Instroduction to Language and Communication*, MIT Press, Cambridge, MA.

Ariel, M. (2002a), 'The demise of a unique concept of literal meaning', *Journal of Pragmatics* **34**, 361–402.

——— (2002b), 'Introduction', *Journal of Pragmatics* **34**, 345–348.

Bach, K. (1994), Semantic slack: What is said and more, *in* S. L. Tsohatzidis, ed., 'Foundations of Speech Act Theory', Routledge, London, pp. 267–291.

——— (2001), 'You don't say?', *Synthese* **128**, 15–44.

——— & Harnish, R. M. (1979), *Linguistic Communication and Speech Acts*, MIT Press, Cambridge, MA.

Bar-Hillel, Y. (1953), On recursive definitions in empirical science, *in* 'Proceedings of the 11th International Congress of Philosophy', North-Holland Publishing Company, Brussels, pp. 160–165.

Bar-On, D., Horisk, C. & Lycan, W. G. (2000), 'Deflationism, meaning and truth-conditions', *Philosophical Studies* **101**, 1–28.

Bartels, C. (1999), *The Intonation of English Statements and Questions: A Compositional Interpretation*, Garland, New York.

Belnap, N. D. (1982), Questions and answers in Montague grammar, *in* S. Peters & E. Saarinen, eds., 'Processes, Beliefs, and Questions', Reidel, Dordrecht, pp. 165–198.

Bibliography

Biletzki, A. & Matar, A. (2014), Ludwig Wittgenstein, *in* E. N. Zalta, ed., 'The Stanford Encyclopedia of Philosophy', spring 2014 edn.

Birch, J. (2014), 'How cooperation became the norm. Book review of 'Cooperation and Its Evolution' by Kim Sterelny, Richard Joyce, Brett Calcott, and Ben Fraser', *Biology & Philosophy* **29**, 433–444.

Block, N. (1986), 'Advertisement for a semantics for psychology', *Midwest Studies in Philosophy* **10**, 615–678.

Bloom, P. (2000), *How Children Learn the Meanings of Words*, MIT Press, Cambridge, MA.

Boas, H. C. (2013), Cognitive construction grammar, *in* T. Hoffmann & G. Trousdale, eds., 'The Oxford Handbook of Construction Grammar', Oxford University Press, Oxford, pp. 233–252.

Bonini, N., Osherson, D., Viale, R. & Williamson, T. (1999), 'On the psychology of vague predicates', *Mind & Language* **14**, 377–393.

Borg, E. (2004*a*), 'Formal semantics and intentional states', *Analysis* **64**, 215–223.

―――― (2004*b*), *Minimal Semantics*, Oxford University Press, Oxford.

―――― (2012*a*), *Pursuing Meaning*, Oxford University Press, Oxford.

―――― (2012*b*), Semantics without pragmatics?, *in* K. Allan & K. Jaszczolt, eds., 'Cambridge Handbook of Pragmatics', Cambridge University Press, Cambridge, pp. 513–528.

Brandom, R. (1994), *Making it Explicit*, Harvard University Press, Cambridge, MA.

―――― (2001), *Articulating Reasons*, Harvard University Press, Cambridge, MA.

Brent, M. (1994), Surface cues and robust inference as a basis for the early acquisition of subcategorization frames, *in* L. Gleitman & B. Landau, eds., 'The Acquisition of the Lexicon', MIT Press, Cambridge, MA, pp. 433–470.

Brooks, R. & Meltzoff, A. N. (2005), 'The development of gaze following and its relation to language', *Developmental Science* **8**, 535–543.

Burge, T. (1979), 'Individualism and the mental', *Midwest Studies in Philosophy* **4**, 73–122.

Butterfill, S. (2012), 'Joint action and development', *The Philosophical Quarterly* **62**, 23–47.

Cappelen, H. & Lepore, E. (2004), *Insensitive Semantics. A Defense of Semantic Minimalism and Speech Act Pluralism*, Blackwell, Oxford.

Carnap, R. (1956), *Meaning and Necessity*, University of Chicago Press, Chicago.

Catford, J. C. (1965), *A Linguistic Theory of Translation*, Oxford University Press, London.

Chalmers, D. (2006), Two-dimensional semantics, *in* E. Lepore & B. Smith, eds., 'The Oxford Handbook of the Philosophy of Language', Oxford University Press, pp. 574–606.

Chomsky, N. (1965), *Aspects of the Theory of Syntax*, MIT Press, Cambridge, MA.

——— (1986), *Knowledge of Language: Its Nature, Origin and Use*, Praeger, New York.

Cienki, A. & Müller, C., eds. (2008), *Metaphor and Gesture*, John Benjamins, Amsterdam.

Clark, B. (2006), Recursion, *in* 'Encyclopedia of Language and Linguistics', Elsevier, Oxford, pp. 414–415.

Cohen, J. (1999), 'Holism: Some reasons for buyer's remorse', *Analysis* **59**, 63–71.

Cozzo, C. (1994), *Meaning and Argument*, Almqvist & Wiksell International, Stockholm.

Bibliography

Cresswell, M. J. (1982), The autonomy of semantics, *in* S. Peters & E. Saarinen, eds., 'Processes, Beliefs, and Questions', Reidel, Dordrecht, pp. 69–86.

Croft, W. (2000), *Explaining Language Change: An Evolutionary Approach*, Longman, Harlow.

———— (2001), *Radical Construction Grammar*, Oxford University Press, Oxford.

Davidson, D. (1965), Theories of meaning and learnable languages, *in* Y. Bar-Hillel, ed., 'Proceedings of the International Congress for Logic, Methodology, and Philosophy of Science', North-Holland Publishing Company, Amsterdam, pp. 383–394. Reprinted in Davidson 1985, pp. 3–16.

———— (1967), 'Truth and meaning', *Synthese* **17**, 304–323. Reprinted in Davidson 1985, pp. 17–36.

———— (1985), *Inquiries into Truth and Interpretation*, Oxford University Press, Oxford.

———— (1986), A nice derangement of epitapths, *in* E. Lepore, ed., 'Truth and Interpretation: Perspectives on the Philosophy of Donald Davidson', Blackwell, Oxford, pp. 433–446. Reprinted in Davidson 2005, pp. 89–108.

———— (1990), 'The structure and content of truth', *The Journal of Philosophy* **87**, 279–328.

———— (1994), The social aspect of language, *in* B. McGuinness & G. Oliveri, eds., 'The Philosophy of Michael Dummett', Kluwer, Dordrecht, pp. 1–16. Reprinted in Davidson 2005, pp. 109–126.

———— (2005), *Truth, Language, and History*, Oxford University Press, Oxford.

Devitt, M. (1993), 'A critique of the case for semantic holism', *Philosophical Perspectives* **7**, 281–306.

Diessel, H. (2007), Komplexe Konstruktionen im Erstspracherwerb, *in* K. Fischer & A. Stefanowitsch, eds., 'Konstruktionsgrammatik: Von der Anwendung zur Theorie', Stauffenburg, Tübingen, pp. 39–54.

―――― (2013), Construction grammar and first language acquisition, *in* T. Hoffmann & G. Trousdale, eds., 'The Oxford Handbook of Construction Grammar', Oxford University Press, Oxford, pp. 347–364.

Dietrich, E. (2001), 'Concepts: Fodor's little semantic BBs of thought: A critical look at Fodor's theory of concepts', *Journal of Experimental & Theoretical Artificial Intelligence* **13**, 89–94.

Dretske, F. (1986), Misrepresentation, *in* R. Bogdan, ed., 'Belief: Form, Content, and Function', Oxford University Press, Oxford, pp. 17–36.

Emmorey, K., Borinstein, H. B. & Thompson, R. (2005), Bimodal bilingualism: Code-blending between spoken English and American Sign Language, *in* K. R. James Cohen, Kara T. McAlister & J. MacSwan, eds., 'Proceedings of the 4th International Symposium on Bilingualism', Cascadilla Press, Somerville, MA, pp. 663–673.

Evans, V. (2012), 'Cognitive linguistics', *Wiley Interdisciplinary Reviews: Cognitive Science* **3**, 129–141.

Ferguson, B., Graf, E. & Waxman, S. R. (2014), 'Infants use known verbs to learn novel nouns: Evidence from 15- and 19-month-olds', *Cognition* **131**, 139–146.

Field, H. (1977), 'Logic, meaning and conceptual role', *Journal of Philosophy* **74**, 379–409.

Fillmore, C. (1988), The mechanisms of "construction grammar", *in* 'Proceedings of the Fourteenth Annual Meeting of the Berkeley Linguistics Society', Vol. 14, pp. 35–55.

―――― (2013), Berkeley construction grammar, *in* T. Hoffmann & G. Trousdale, eds., 'The Oxford Handbook of Construction Grammar', Oxford University Press, Oxford, pp. 111–132.

―――― & Kay, P. (1993), Construction grammar. Manuscript, University of California, Berkeley.

――――, ―――― & O'Connor, C. (1988), 'Regularity and idiomaticity in grammatical constructions: The case of *Let Alone*', *Language* **64**, 501–538.

Fischer, K. (2013), Beyond the sentence: Constructions, frames and spoken interaction, *in* M. Fried & K. Nikiforidou, eds., 'Advances in Frame Semantics', John Benjamins, Amsterdam, pp. 183–206.

―――― & Stefanowitsch, A., eds. (2007), *Konstruktionsgrammatik*, Stauffenburg, Tübingen.

Fodor, J. (1975), *The Language of Thought*, Harvard University Press, Cambridge, MA.

―――― (1984), 'Semantics, Wisconsin style', *Synthese* **59**, 231–250.

―――― (1987), *Psychosemantics*, MIT Press, Cambridge, MA.

―――― (1990), A theory of content, ii: The theory, *in* 'A Theory of Content and Other Essays', MIT Press, Cambridge, MA, pp. 89–136.

―――― (1994), *The Elm and the Expert: Mentalese and Its Semantics*, MIT Press, Cambridge, MA.

―――― (1998), *Concepts*, Oxford University Press, New York.

―――― & Lepore, E. (1991), 'Why meaning (probably) isn't conceptual role', *Mind & Language* **6**, 328–343. Reprinted in Fodor & Lepore 2002, pp. 9–27.

―――― & ―――― (1996), 'The the pet fish and the red herring: why concepts still can't be prototypes', *Cognition* **58**, 253–270. Reprinted in Fodor & Lepore 2002, pp. 27–42.

―――― & ―――― (2002), *The Compositionality Papers*, Oxford University Press, Oxford.

Fotion, N. (2013), '"Pursuing Meaning' by Emma Borg', *Analysis* **73**, 580–582.

Fried, M. & Östman, J.-O. (2004), Construction grammar: A thumbnail sketch, *in* M. Fried & J.-O. Östman, eds., 'Construction Grammar in a Cross-Language Perspective', John Benjamins, Amsterdam, pp. 11–86.

Fulop, S. A. & Keenan, E. L. (2002), Compositionality: A global perspective, *in* F. Hamm & T. E. Zimmermann, eds., 'Semantics', Buske, Hamburg, pp. 129–136.

Gendler Szabó, Z. (2006), The distinction between semantics and pragmatics, *in* E. LePore & B. Smith, eds., 'The Oxford Handbook of Philosophy of Language', Oxford University Press, Oxford, pp. 361–390.

――― (2012*a*), The case for compositionality, *in* M. Werning, W. Hinzen & E. Machery, eds., 'The Oxford Handbook on Compositionality', Oxford University Press, Oxford, pp. 64–80.

――― (2012*b*), Compositionality, *in* E. N. Zalta, ed., 'The Stanford Encyclopedia of Philosophy', winter 2012 edn.

Geurts, B. (2002), 'Donkey business', *Linguistics & Philosophy* **25**, 129–156.

Gibbard, A. (2012), *Meaning and Normativity*, Oxford University Press, Oxford.

Gibbs, R. W. (2002), 'A new look at literal meaning in understanding what is said and implicated', *Journal of Pragmatics* **34**, 457–486.

――― (2005), Literal and nonliteral meanings are corrupt ideas: A view from psycholinguistics, *in* 'The Literal and Nonliteral in Language and Thought', Peter Lang, Frankfurt am Main, pp. 221–238.

――― & Perlman, M. (2010), 'Language understanding is grounded in experiential simulations: a response to Weiskopf', *Studies in History and Philosophy of Science* **41**, 305–308.

——— & Tendahl, M. (2006), 'Cognitive effort and effects in metaphor comprehension: Relevance theory and psycholinguistics', *Mind & Language* **21**, 379–403.

Glanzberg, M. (2013), Truth, *in* E. N. Zalta, ed., 'The Stanford Encyclopedia of Philosophy', spring 2013 edn.

Gleitman, L. (1990), 'The structural sources of verb meanings', *Language Acquisition* **1**, 3–55.

Glüer, K. (2013), Convention and meaning, *in* E. Lepore & K. Ludwig, eds., 'A Companion to Donald Davidson', Blackwell, Malden, pp. 339–360.

Günthner, S. (2009), 'Konstruktionen in der kommunikativen Praxis – zur Notwendigkeit einer interaktionalen Anreicherung konstruktionsgrammatischer Ansätze', *Zeitschrift für Germanistische Linguistik* **37**, 402–426.

——— (2010), Grammatical constructions and communicative genres, *in* H. Dorgeloh & A. Wanner, eds., 'Approaches to Syntactic Variation and Genre', de Gruyter, Berlin, pp. 195–217.

Godfrey-Smith, P. (1989), 'Misinformation', *Canadian Journal of Philosophy* **19**, 533–550.

Gohl, C. & Günthner, S. (1999), 'Grammatikalisierung von *weil* als Diskursmarker in der gesprochen Sprache', *Zeitschrift für Sprachwissenschaft* **18**, 39–75.

Goldberg, A. (1995), *Constructions: A Constructions Grammar Approach to Argument Structure*, University of Chicago Press, Chicago.

——— (2003), 'Constructions: a new theoretical approach to language', *Trends in Cognitive Sciences* **7**, 2019–224.

——— (2006), *Constructions at Work: The Nature of Generalization in Language*, Oxford University Press, Oxford.

Grandy, R. E. (1990), 'Understanding and the principle of compositionality', *Philosophical Perspectives* **4**, 557–572.

Gärdenfors, P. & Warglien, M. (2013), The development of semantic space for pointing and verbal communication, *in* C. Paradis, J. Hudson & U. Magnusson, eds., 'The Construal of Spatial Meaning: Windows Into Conceptual Space', Oxford University Press, Oxford, pp. 29–42.

Greenberg, M. & Harman, G. (2006), Conceptual role semantics, *in* E. Lepore & B. Smith, eds., 'Oxford Handbook of the Philosophy of Language', Oxford University Press, Oxford, pp. 295–322.

Grice, H. P. (1975), Logic and conversation, *in* P. Cole & J. L. Morgan, eds., 'Speech Acts', Vol. 3 of *Syntax and Semantics*, Academic Press, New York, pp. 41–58.

——— (1989), *Studies in the Way of Words*, Harvard University Press, Cambridge, MA.

Groenendijk, J. & Stokhof, M. (2005), Why compositionality?, *in* G. Carlson & J. Pelletier, eds., 'Reference and Quantification: The Partee Effect', CSLI, Stanford, pp. 83–106.

Gutzmann, D. (2015), *Use-Conditional Meaning: Studies in Multidimensional Semantics*, Oxford University Press, Oxford.

Hacker, P. M. S. (2013), *Wittgenstein: Comparisons & Context*, Oxford University Press, Oxford.

Harman, G. (1982), 'Conceptual role semantics', *Notre Dame Journal of Formal Logic* **23**, 242–256.

——— (1987), (Nonsolipsistic) conceptual role semantics, *in* E. Lepore, ed., 'New Directions in Semantics', Academic Press, London, pp. 55–82.

Hauser, M. D., Chomsky, N. & Fitch, W. T. (2002), 'The faculty of language: What is it, who has it, and how did it evolve?', *Science's Compass* **298**, 1569–1579.

Heck, R. G. (2007), Meaning and truth-conditions, *in* D. Greimann & G. Siegwart, eds., 'Truth and Speech Acts', Routledge, London, pp. 349–376.

Heil, J. (2005), 'Dispositions', *Synthese* **144**, 343–356.

Heusinger, K. v. & Turner, K. (2006), (By way of an) Introduction: A first dialogue on the semantics-pragmatics interface, *in* K. v. Heusinger & K. Turner, eds., 'Where Semantics Meets Pragmatics', Elsevier, Amsterdam, pp. 1–20.

Higginbotham, J. (1994), 'Priorities in the philosophy of thought', *Proceedings of the Aristotelian Society, Supplementary Volumes* **68**, 85–106.

——— (1996), The semantics of questions, *in* S. Lappin, ed., 'The Handbook of Contemporary Semantic Theory', Blackwell, Oxford, pp. 361–384.

——— (2007), Remarks on compositionality, *in* 'The Oxford Handbook of Linguistic Interfaces', Oxford University Press, Oxford, pp. 425–444.

Hoeltje, M. (2012), *Wahrheit, Bedeutung und Form*, Mentis, Münster.

Hoffmann, T. & Trousdale, G., eds. (2013), *The Oxford Handbook of Construction Grammar*, Oxford University Press, Oxford.

Horisk, C. (2004), 'Meaning theory and communication', *Mind & Language* **19**, 177–198.

Horton, W. S. (2005), 'Conversational common ground and memory processes in language production', *Discourse Processes* **40**, 1–35.

Horwich, P. (1997*a*), 'The composition of meanings', *The Philosophical Review* **106**, 503–532.

——— (1997*b*), 'The nature of vagueness', *Philosophy and Phenomenological Research* **57**, 929–935.

——— (1998), *Meaning*, Clarendon, Oxford.

——— (2004), 'A use theory of meaning', *Philosophy and Phenomenological Research* **68**, 351–372.

——— (2005), *Reflections on Meaning*, Clarendon, Oxford.

―――― (2008a), 'A new framework for semantics', *Philosophical Perspectives* **22**, 233–240.

―――― (2008b), 'What's truth got do with it?', *Linguistics & Philosophy* **31**, 309–322. Reprinted as 'Semantics: What's truth got do with it?' in Horwich 2010, pp. 143–166.

―――― (2010), *Truth – Meaning – Reality*, Clarendon, Oxford.

―――― (2012), *Wittgenstein's Metaphilosophy*, Clarendon, Oxford.

Ibbotson, P., Theakston, A. L., Lieven, E. V. M. & Tomasello, M. (2012), 'Semantics of the transitive construction: Prototype effects and developmental comparisons', *Cognitive Science* **36**, 1268–1288.

Imo, W. (2010), "Mein Problem ist/mein Thema ist" – how syntactic patterns and genres interact, *in* H. Dorgeloh & A. Wanner, eds., 'Syntactic Variation and Genre', de Gruyter, Berlin, pp. 141–166.

Indefrey, P. & Gullberg, M., eds. (2010), *The Earliest Stages of Language Learning*, Wiley-Blackwell, West Sussex.

Israel, M. (2005), Common sense and 'literal meaning', *in* S. Coulson & B. Lewandowska-Tomaszczyk, eds., 'The Literal and Nonliteral in Language and Thought', Peter Lang, Frankfurt am Main, pp. 147–177.

Janssen, T. (2006), Montague semantics, *in* K. Brown, ed., 'Encyclopedia of Language and Linguistics', Vol. 8, Elsevier, Oxford, pp. 244–255.

Jaszczolt, K. (2005), *Default Semantics*, Oxford University Press, Oxford.

―――― (2011), Default meanings, salient meanings, and automatic processing, *in* K. Jaszczolt & K. Allan, eds., 'Salience and Defaults in Utterance Processing', de Gruyter, Berlin, pp. 11–34.

―――― (2012), The semantics–pragmatics interface, *in* C. Maienborn, K. von Heusinger & P. Portner, eds., 'Semantics', de Gruyter, Berlin, pp. 2333–2360.

Johnson, K. (2006), 'On the nature of reverse compositionality', *Erkenntnis* **64**, 37–60.

Jung, E.-M. & Newen, A. (2010), 'Knowledge and abilities: The need for a new understanding of knowing-how', *Phenomenology and the Cognitive Sciences* **9**, 113–131.

Kamp, H. & Reyle, U. (1993), *From Discourse to Logic*, Kluwer.

Kaplan, D. (1989), Demonstratives, *in* 'Themes from Kaplan', Oxford University Press, New York, pp. 481–564.

Katz, J. J. (1966), *The Philosophy of Language*, Harper & Row, New York.

———— & Fodor, J. (1963), 'The structure of a semantic theory', *Language* **39**, 170–210.

Kay, P. & Michaelis, L. A. (2012), Constructional meaning and compositionality, *in* C. Maienborn, K. von Heusinger & P. Portner, eds., 'Semantics', Vol. 3, de Gruyter, Berlin, pp. 2271–2296.

Kayser, D. (2003), 'Abstraction and natural language semantics', *Philosophical Transactions of the Royal Society B* **358**, 1261–1268.

King, J. C., Soames, S. & Speaks, J. (2014), *New Thinking About Propositions*, Oxford University Press, Oxford.

Kirby, S. (2002), Learning, bottlenecks and the evolution of recursive syntax, *in* T. Briscoe, ed., 'Linguistic Evolution Through Language Acquisition', Cambridge University Press, Cambridge, pp. 173–203.

Kölbel, M. (2001), 'Two dogmas of Davidsonian semantics', *The Journal of Philosophy* **98**, 613–635.

Krifka, M. (2007), 'The semantics of questions and the focusation of answers', *Studies in Linguistics and Philosophy* **82**, 139–150.

———— (2012), Questions, *in* C. Maienborn, K. von Heusinger & P. Portner, eds., 'Semantics: An International Handbook of Natural Language Meaning', de Gruyter, Berlin, pp. 1742–1785.

Kripke, S. (1980), *Naming and Necessity*, Blackwell, Oxford.

——— (1982), *Wittgenstein on rules and private language*, Blackwell, Oxford.

Lakoff, G. (1987), *Women, Fire, and Dangerous Things*, University Press of Chicago, Chicago.

Langacker, R. (1987), *Foundations of Cognitive Grammar. Vol. I: Theoretical Prerequisites*, Stanford University Press, Stanford.

——— (2008), *Cognitive Grammar: A Basic Introduction*, Oxford University Press, Oxford.

Lasch, A. & Ziem, A., eds. (2011), *Konstruktionsgrammatik III*, Stauffenburg, Tübingen.

——— & ———, eds. (2014), *Grammatik als Netzwerk von Konstruktionen: Sprachwissen im Fokus der Konstruktionsgrammatik*, de Gruyter, Berlin.

Lepore, E. (2006), Truth conditional semantics and meaning, *in* K. Brown, ed., 'Encyclopedia of Language & Linguistics', Elsevier, Oxford, pp. 120–124.

——— & Ludwig, K. (2005), *Donald Davidson: Meaning, Truth, Language, and Reality*, Oxford University Press, Oxford.

——— & ——— (2006), *Donald Davidson's Truth-Theoretic Semantics*, Oxford University Press, Oxford.

Levine, J. (2010), 'Demonstrative thought', *Mind & Language* **25**, 169–195.

Lewis, D. (1969), *Convention*, Blackwell, Malden.

——— (1970), 'General semantics', *Synthese* **22**, 18–67.

——— (1975), Languages and language, *in* K. Gunderso, ed., 'Minnesota Studies in the Philosophy of Science', Vol. VII, University of Minnesota Press, Minneapolis, pp. 3–35.

——— (1980), Index, context, and content, *in* S. Kanger & S. Öhman, eds., 'Philosophy and Grammar', Reidel, Dordrecht, pp. 79–100.

Bibliography

Liebal, K. (2009), *Infants' and young children's understanding of common ground and markedness in communication*. PhD thesis, University of Leipzig.

Linell, P. (2005), *The Written Language Bias in Linguistics*, Routledge, London.

Liszkowski, U., Schäfer, M., Carpenter, M. & Tomasello, M. (2009), 'Prelinguistic infants, but not chimpanzees, communicate about absent entities', *Psychological Science* **20**, 654–660.

Loar, B. (1988), Two kinds of content, *in* R. H. Grimm & D. D. Merrill, eds., 'Contents of Thought', University of Arizona Press, Tucson, pp. 121–139.

Lycan, W. G. (2010), 'Direct arguments for the truth-condition theory of meaning', *Topoi* **29**, 99–108.

Michaelis, L. A. (2006), Construction grammar, *in* K. Brown, ed., 'The Encyclopedia of Language and Linguistics', Vol. 3, Elsevier, Oxford, pp. 73–84.

——— (2012), Making the case for construction grammar, *in* H. Boas & I. Sag, eds., 'Sign-Based Construction Grammar', CSLI, Stanford, pp. 31–69.

——— (2013), Sign-based construction grammar, *in* T. Hoffmann & G. Trousdale, eds., 'The Oxford Handbook of Construction Grammar', Oxford University Press, Oxford, pp. 133–152.

Mill, J. S. (1916), *A System of Logic, Ratiocinative and Inductive*, Longmans, London.

Millikan, R. G. (1989), 'Biosemantics', *Journal of Philosophy* **86**, 281–297.

——— (2008), 'A difference of some consequence between conventions and rules', *Topoi* **27**, 87–99.

Mittelberg, I. & Waugh, L. R. (2009), Metonymy first, metaphor second: A cognitive-semiotic approach to multimodal figures of thought in co-speech gesture, *in* C. Forceville & E. Urios-Aparisi, eds., 'Multimodal Metaphor', de Gruyter, Berlin, pp. 329–358.

Müller, C. (2013a), Gestures as a medium of expression: The linguistic potential of gestures, *in* C. Müller, A. Cienki, E. Fricke, S. H. Ladewig, D. McNeill & S. Teßendorf, eds., 'Body – Language – Communication: An International Handbook on Multimodality in Human Interaction', de Gruyter, Berlin, pp. 202–217.

———, Cienki, A., Fricke, E., Ladewig, S., McNeill, D. & Teßendorf, S., eds. (2013), *Body – Language – Communication: An International Handbook on Multimodality in Human Interaction*, de Gruyter, Berlin.

Müller, O. (1996), 'Zitierte Zeichenreihen: Eine Theorie des harmlos nichtextensionalen Gebrauchs von Anführungszeichen', *Erkenntnis* **44**, 279–304.

Müller, S. (2013b), *Grammatiktheorie*, Vol. 2, Stauffenburg, Tübingen.

——— (2013c), *Head-Driven Phrase Structure Grammar. Eine Einführung*, Vol. 3, Stauffenburg, Tübingen.

Montague, R. (1974), *Formal Philosophy*, Yale University Press, New Haven.

Moore, R., Liebal, K. & Tomasello, M. (2013), 'Three-year-olds understand communicative intentions without language, gestures, or gaze', *Interaction Studies* **14**, 62–80.

Newen, A. (1996), *Kontext, Referenz und Bedeutung: Eine Bedeutungstheorie singulärer Terme*, Ferdinand Schöningh, Paderborn.

——— & Bartels, A. (2007), 'Animal minds and the possession of concepts', *Philosophical Psychology* **20**, 283–308.

——— & Schrenk, M. (2008), *Einführung in die Sprachphilosophie*, Wissenschaftliche Buchgesellschaft, Darmstadt.

Nicolle, S. & Clark, B. (1999), 'Experimental pragmatics and what is said: a response to Gibbs and Moise', *Cognition* **69**, 337–354.

Noveck, I. A. & Reboul, A. (2008), 'Experimental Pragmatics: A Gricean turn in the study of language', *Trends in Cognitive Sciences* **12**, 425–431.

——— & Sperber, D. (2007), The why and how of experimental pragmatics: The case of 'scalar inferences', *in* N. Burton-Roberts, ed., 'Pragmatics', Palgrave, Hampshire, pp. 184–212.

Oddie, G. (2014), Truthlikeness, *in* E. N. Zalta, ed., 'The Stanford Encyclopedia of Philosophy', summer 2014 edn.

Pacherie, E. (2011), 'Framing joint action', *Review of Philosophy and Psychology* **2**, 173–192.

Pagin, P. (2006), Meaning holism, *in* E. Lepore & B. Smith, eds., 'The Oxford Handbook of Philosophy of Language', Oxford University Press, Oxford, pp. 213–232.

——— & Westerståhl, D. (2010*a*), 'Compositionality I: definitions and variants', *Philosophy Compass* **5**, 250–264.

——— & ——— (2010*b*), 'Compositionality II: arguments and problems', *Philosophy Compass* **5**, 265–282.

Partee, B. H. (1976), *Montague Grammar*, Academic Press, New York.

——— (1977), 'Possible world semantics and linguistic theory', *The Monist* **60**, 303–326.

——— (1982), Belief-sentences and the limits of semantics, *in* S. Peters & E. Saarinen, eds., 'Processes, Beliefs, and Questions', Reidel, Dordrecht, pp. 87–106.

Patterson, D. (2005), 'Learnability and compositionality', *Mind & Language* **20**, 326–352.

——— (2012), *Alfred Tarski: Philosophy of Language and Logic*, Palgrave, Hampshire.

Peacocke, C. (1992), *A Study of Concepts*, MIT Press, Cambrdige, MA.

Pelletier, F. J. (1994), 'The principle of semantic compositionality', *Topoi* **13**, 11–24.

———— (2003), 'Context dependence and compositionality', *Mind & Language* **18**, 148–161.

Pencil, M. (1976), 'Salt passage research: The state of the art', *Journal of Communication* **26**, 31–36.

Perry, J. (1986), 'Thought without representation', *Proceedings of the Aristotelian Society* **137**, 137–152.

Pietroski, P. (2000), 'The undeflated domain of semantics', *Sats: The Nordic Journal of Philosophy* **1**, 161–176.

Pinker, S. (1994), How could a child use verb syntax to learn verb semantics?, *in* L. Gleitman & B. Landau, eds., 'The Acquisition of the Lexicon', Elsevier, Amsterdam, pp. 377–410.

Pollard, C. & Sag, I. A. (1994), *Head-Driven Phrase Structure Grammar*, University of Chicago Press, Chicago.

Portner, P. H. (2005), *What is Meaning? Fundamentals of Formal Semantics*, Blackwell, Malden.

Priest, G. (2006), *In Contradiction*, Oxford University Press, Oxford.

Putnam, H. (1975), 'The meaning of 'meaning'', *Minnesota Studies in the Philosophy of Science* **7**, 131–193.

———— (1985), 'A comparison of something with something else', *New Literary History* **17**, 61–79.

Quine, W. V. O. (1951), 'Two dogmas of empiricism', *The Philosophical Review* **60**, 20–43.

———— (1960), *Word and Object*, Wiley, New York.

Ravid, D. & Tolchinsky, L. (2002), 'Developing linguistic literacy: a comprehensive model', *Journal of Child Language* **29**, 417–447.

Recanati, F. (1989), 'The pragmatics of what is said', *Mind & Language* **4**, 295–329.

────── (2004), *Literal Meaning*, Cambridge University Press, Cambridge.

────── (2005), Literalism and contextualism: Some varieties, *in* G. Preyer & G. Peter, eds., 'Contextualism in Philosophy: Knowledge, Meaning, and Truth', Oxford University Press, Oxford, pp. 171–196.

────── (2007), *Truth-Conditional Pragmatics*, Oxford University Press, Oxford.

Reich, W. (2011), 'The cooperative nature of communicative acts', *Journal of Pragmatics* **43**, 1349–1365.

Robbins, P. (2001), 'What compositionality still can do', *The Philosophical Quarterly* **51**, 328–336.

────── (2005), 'The myth of reverse compositionality', *Philosophical Studies* **125**, 251–275.

Röska-Hardy, L. (2005), 'Reframing the philosophical issues: On Donald Davidson's sea-change in philosophical thinking', *Protosociology* **21**, 186–203.

Sag, I. A. & Wasow, T. (1999), *Syntactic Theory*, CSLI, Stanford, CA.

Saka, P. (2007), 'The argument from ignorance against truth-conditional semantics', *American Philosophical Quarterly* **44**, 157–169.

Schiffer, S. (2015), 'Meaning and formal semantics in generative grammar', *Erkenntnis* **80**, Issue 1 Supplement, 61–87.

Schiffrin, D. (1987), *Discourse Markers*, Cambridge University Press, Cambridge.

Searle, J. (1980), The background of meaning, *in* J. Searle, F. Kiefer & M. Bierwisch, eds., 'Speech Act Theory and Pragmatics', Reidel, Dordrecht, pp. 221-232.

Sellars, W. (1954), 'Some reflections on language games', *Philosophy of Science* **21**, 204-208.

——— (1963), Empiricism and abstract entities, *in* P. A. Schilpp, ed., 'The Philosophy of Rudolf Carnap', Open Court, La Salle, pp. 431-468.

——— (1969), 'Language as thought and as communication', *Philosophy and Phenomenological Research* **29**, 506-527.

Sosa, E. (1995), 'Fregean reference defended', *Philosophical Issues* **6**, 91-99.

Speaks, J. (2011), Theories of meaning, *in* E. N. Zalta, ed., 'The Stanford Encyclopedia of Philosophy', summer 2011 edn.

Sperber, D. & Wilson, D. (1986), *Relevance*, Blackwell, Oxford.

Stalnaker, R. (1970), 'Pragmatics', *Synthese* **22**, 272-289.

——— (1984), *Inquiry*, MIT Press, Cambridge, MA.

——— (1999), *Context and Content*, Oxford University Press, Oxford.

Stanley, J. & Williamson, T. (2001), 'Knowing how', *The Journal of Philosophy* **98**, 411-444.

Steels, L. (2011), *Design Patterns in Fluid Construction Grammar*, John Benjamins, Amsterdam.

——— & Kaplan, F. (2002), Bootstrapping grounded word semantics, *in* T. Briscoe, ed., 'Linguistic Evolution through Language Acquisition', Cambridge University Press, Cambridge, pp. 53-74.

Stefanowitsch, A. & Fischer, K., eds. (2008), *Konstruktionsgrammatik II*, Stauffenburg, Tübingen.

Stern, D. (2011), Private language, *in* O. Kuusela & M. McGinn, eds., 'The Oxford Handbook of Wittgenstein', Oxford University Press, Oxford, pp. 333-350.

Bibliography

Östman, J.-O. (2005), Construction discourse: A prolegomenon, *in* J.-O. Östman & M. Fried, eds., 'Construction Grammars: Cognitive Grounding and Theoretical Extensions', John Benjamins, Amsterdam, pp. 121–144.

——— & Fried, M. (2005), The cognitive grounding of construction grammar, *in* J.-O. Östman & M. Fried, eds., 'Construction grammars: cognitive grounding and theoretical extensions', John Benjamins, Amsterdam, pp. 1–16.

Streeck, J. (2009), *Gesturecraft*, John Benjamins, Amsterdam.

Tarski, A. (1935), 'Der Wahrheitsbegriff in den formalisierten Sprachen', *Studia Philosophica* **1**, 261–405.

——— (1944), 'The semantic conception of truth and the foundations of semantics', *Philosophy and Phenomenological Research* **4**, 341–376.

Tomasello, M. (2003a), *Constructing a Language. A usage based theory of language acquisition*, Harvard University Press, Cambridge, MA.

——— (2003b), Introduction: Some surprises for psychologists, *in* M. Tomasello, ed., 'The New Psychology of Language: Cognitive and Functional Approaches to Language Structure', Erlbaum, Mahwah, pp. vii–xxiii.

——— (2008), *Origins of Human Communication*, MIT Press, Cambridge, MA.

——— (2009), *Why We Cooperate*, MIT Press, Cambridge, MA.

——— (2014), *A Natural History of Human Thinking*, Harvard University Press, Cambridge, MA.

Travis, C. (2008), *Occasion-Sensitivity: Selected Essays*, Oxford University Press, Oxford.

Uhmann, S. (1998), 'Verbstellungsvariation von *weil*-sätzen: Lexikalische Differenzierung mit grammatischen Folgen', *Zeitschrift für Sprachwissenschaft* **17**, 92–139.

Weiskopf, D. (2013), Concepts, *in* B. Kaldis, ed., 'The Encyclopedia of Philosophy and the Social Sciences', Sage, Thousand Oaks, pp. 138-144.

Werning, M. (2005), Right and wrong reasons for compositionality, *in* M. Werning, ed., 'The Compositionality of Meaning and Content. Volume 1: Foundational Issues', Ontos, Frankfurt, pp. 285-309.

——, Hinzen, W. & Machery, E., eds. (2012), *The Oxford Handbook of Compositionality*, Oxford University Press, Oxford.

Wide, C. (2009), Interactional construction grammar: Constructional features of determination in dialectal Swedish, *in* A. Bergs & G. Diewald, eds., 'Contexts and Constructions', John Benjamins, Amsterdam, pp. 111-144.

Wittgenstein, L. (1967), *Remarks on the Foundations of Mathematics*, Blackwell, Oxford. Edited by G. H. von Wright, and R. Rhees, and G. E. M. Anscombe. Translated by G. E. M. Anscombe.

—— (2009), *Philosophische Untersuchungen*, Wiley-Blackwell, Chichester. Edited by P. M. S. Hacker and Joachim Schulte. Translated by G. E. M. Anscombe.

Ziem, A. & Lasch, A. (2013), *Konstruktionsgrammatik: Konzepte und Grundlagen gebrauchsbasierter Ansätze*, de Gruyter, Berlin.

—— & Staffeldt, S. (2011), Compositional and embodied meanings of somatisms: A corpus-based approach to phraseologisms, *in* D. Schönefeld, ed., 'Converging Evidence: Methodological and Theoretical Issues for Linguistic Research', John Benjamins, Amsterdam, pp. 195-220.

www.ingramcontent.com/pod-product-compliance
Lightning Source LLC
Chambersburg PA
CBHW032221010526
44113CB00032B/186